THERE

to

HERE

THERE
to
HERE

Ideas of
Political Society

JOHN LOCKE
AND HIS INFLUENCE ON
300 YEARS OF
POLITICAL THEORY

CRAIG THOMAS

HarperPerennial

A Division of HarperCollins*Publishers*

to

probably the last great Liberal Prime Minister
The Rt. Hon. Margaret Thatcher, OM, FRS, MP—

some radical insights and confirmations

FIRST EDITION

Designed by Karen Savary

LIBRARY OF CONGRESS CATALOG CARD NUMBER 90-56211
ISBN 0-06-096607-6

91 92 93 94 95 CC/MB 10 9 8 7 6 5 4 3 2 1

CONTENTS

ACKNOWLEDGMENTS

IN THE TASK OF WRITING this book and preparing it for publication, I wish to thank my wife for her patience and support, my publisher, Eddie Bell, for his enthusiasm, my editor, Ed Breslin, for his dynamism and care . . . but especial thanks must go to Dr. Raymond M. Lorantas of the Department of History and Politics at Drexel University, Philadelphia, whose comments, support, and constructive suggestions resulted in the book achieving its present form and structure.

None of the above, however, bear any responsibility for the attitudes, beliefs, and opinions that inform the pages of the book.

. . . it is utterly impossible
to deduce the science of
government from the principles
of human nature.

—T. B. MACAULAY
IN THE *EDINBURGH REVIEW*, 1829

PREFACE

THIS COLLECTION OF ESSAYS began its existence in a desire to celebrate the three-hundredth anniversary of the publication of that farsighted and deeply influential work of political theory, John Locke's *Two Treatises of Government*, composed largely while Locke was in self-imposed exile after the accession of James II and first published in London in 1690. There seemed sufficient material and enthusiasm for a single essay. To understand Locke's influence, especially upon the Founding Fathers of the American Revolution, is no difficult task. To comprehend Locke's *failure* to be of immediate influence upon his contemporaries, or to remain influential in a Europe that once cheered him (especially France in the eighteenth century), is much more difficult.

Hence the other essays in the volume. To understand Locke's bequest to his inheritors and its disappearance required some description of French and German philosophical systems and influences, of the French and Russian revolutions, and—above all else—of the attractions and origins of determinism and collectivism. The history of our century may be described as the catastrophe of collectivist theories of nation, state, race, human nature, and political system in collision with one another. Collectivism, indeed, has prevailed throughout our own century and for half of the previous one.

But how and why did such systems, such interpretations of human nature and political society, arise? How did they maintain their hold upon the imaginations of theorists, historians, demagogues, and politicians of genuine principle, especially since most of them (Marx's theories are the evident exception) were metaphysical or 'idealist' in purpose and scope, concerned with theories of epistemology and ontology rather than with the sublunary sphere of political 'science'? Further, how did political theory become absorbed into what we understand as social science, into a pendant to theories of society and history?

The task became the understanding of the intellectual contexts of political theory from the seventeenth century to—at least—the early writings of Marx and the foundations of modern sociology. I was intrigued to discover how we arrive at Marx and his 'tradition', beginning from the English Revolution and John Locke's democratic ideology. How did Europe (and much else of the world) decide—wrongly—between the great individualist and the greatest of collectivists, so that our world has been shaped by the opposition of those two influential philosophies of politics?

These essays are as much about metaphors as they are concerned with political actualities—metaphors of the state, of history, of human nature and human society. Above all, they concern one theorist who saw in human nature no analogous condition or circumstance—merely the empirical fact of that human nature—and a great many other thinkers who could, and did, conceive of human beings primarily in terms of scientific, physical, biological, and historical analogy.

Locke's time and ideas were postponed by oligarchic government and landed interests in eighteenth-century England until, like a capped volcano, his theory of government emerged from this crust in all its force three thousand miles away from the battlefields and debates of the Civil War. By that time, English liberalism had been captured by the utilitarianism that derived from Bentham and was only slowly discovering the strength of purpose and influence to effect the reforms of 1832 and the remainder of the last century. Political theory in Europe (and in

England) had meanwhile been kidnapped and utterly changed by Marx and his successors. It would, however, be premature on the eve of the last decade of our century to claim that Locke's time has gone. I intended no prophetic irony—rather a more local and pious hope—when I gave the essay on Locke its title. I can only hope prophecy is not, therefore, excluded.

Craig Thomas
Lichfield, September 1990

INTRODUCTION:
NO ONE AT THE PARTY?

1990 MARKED THE TERCENTENARY of the first appearance in print of the *Two Treatises of Government,* the work of the English empirical philosopher John Locke—though at the time of writing and indeed until his death he wished his authorship to remain anonymous. The *Treatises* appeared two years after the Glorious Revolution of 1688, which occasion has been taken by historians to signify the real completion of that struggle between Parliament and absolute monarchy which resulted in the Civil War.

This special anniversary of publication should have been an occasion for celebration. It should also have been a spur to a major consideration of what respect we pay and weight we give to political theory in this country. Yet what can a book written largely in voluntary exile during the years following the death of Charles II, whose reign followed the upheavals of the English Revolution and the absolutism of the Protectorate, have to say to the last decade of the twentieth century?

Locke must have something to say to us, despite the disregard in which his political theories are held and despite the obsequies which were held in 1918 for that strand of English thought he is commonly regarded as having founded—liberalism. When not ignored or regarded as passé, Locke is most commonly regarded as unradical, middle class, a defender of the status quo. True, he is credited with having produced a seminal political work in English which inspired the Founding Fathers of the United States in their revolution against the Crown and in their Declaration of Independence and Bill of Rights. His was also the inspiration behind the Declaration of the Rights of Man of 1789, another radical event in modern history—indeed, perhaps the single event or series of events that created modern Europe. Locke deeply influenced the Enlightenment of the eighteenth century in Scotland and throughout Europe, and the *Second Treatise* is arguably the most important political document in our language. The values of democratic government and the relationship between the individual and the state have never been more cogently reasoned and presented. And yet . . . Locke's significance has slipped into some crack in history's pavement and become lost.

To understand Locke's continuing importance and the present deep unfashionability of his theories is the purpose of these essays. What chasm divides us from him? The death of English liberalism and its tradition in the holocaust of the Great War should not have caused Locke to be lost along with that dreary, cautious, ultimately pessimistic version of liberalism expounded by Mill and his contemporaries and derived from the utilitarianism of Bentham. Locke had been lost for a century before 1914, disappearing in another holocaust, that presaged by events in France in 1789.

The reader may here object that all ideas are bounded by their historical contexts and that the passage of time renders them of smaller and smaller significance to succeeding generations; they become something to be studied rather than practiced. Locke's principal contribution to empirical philosophy, the *Essay Concerning Human Understanding,* great and influential though it has been, reads now for huge passages like a parody of early psychology. Must not, therefore, the increase in human knowledge, the changes in human society, and the demands of changed societies upon their members have rendered his political ideas invalid and arcane? After all, it may be reasoned, Locke lived and wrote before the Industrial Revolution, before capitalism, before socialism, before Marx. Surely such facts of history will have made him outdated? Further, Locke was a Puritan gentleman whose arguments either proceeded from or at least required the presence of his Christian faith, and we live in the most secular of historical periods. Therefore, he cannot be as relevant to us as Marx, or even the founders of modern social thought, Max Weber and Émile Durkheim. Our society is far more recognizably akin to the societies examined by those three thinkers, the trinity who established the discipline we know as sociology, than it is akin to Locke's society.

If the above strictures are true, then we should indeed leave historians and students of philosophy to quietly continue to ignore the tercentenary and John Locke. That we should not do so is the principal argument of these essays.

II

There are two broad traditions of political theory, of almost equal antiquity, one deriving from metaphysics and the other from what has historically been termed natural law theory. The former is best represented by Plato, especially in the *Republic*. The latter derives from the Stoic school of Greek philosophy, was reinvigorated by Cicero and the Scipionic circle and the theory of Roman law, and was incorporated by the early fathers of the Church into the Christian tradition. Locke may be best seen as the last great representative of this latter tradition, while Marx is the most influential inheritor of the 'metaphysical' tradition of political thought. The American Declaration of Independence and the Tennis Court Oath and the Declaration of the Rights of Man in France are the most important political utterances of the tradition of natural law theory since Roman times. The political demonstrations of the metaphysical tradition most significant in modern history may be Robespierre's Terror and the Soviet state established by Lenin.

It is not my purpose to examine the tradition which culminated in Marx's theories in its transmission from Plato, only to consider the more immediate influence of Hegel and the French Revolution upon Marx's thought. Natural law theory, however, being more unfamiliar, requires more detailed explication. But these essays contend that it is the metaphysical tradition (or, more precisely, the consideration of the sublunary sphere of ethics and politics and human society by philosophers who were essentially metaphysical in their approach) which has predominated in European thought since Hegel and that the decline of the empirical tradition of natural law theory may be dated from the first decades of the nineteenth century.

To refer to a metaphysical tradition is simply to refer to a tradition espoused by metaphysical philosophy since the time of Plato. Metaphysics seeks the *essence* of reality, of nature and human nature, an understanding of the universe—to describe reality as a whole and to describe what really exists, what the essential (and probably unifying) underlying truth of reality is. For metaphysicians (and only Spinoza and Kant may be regarded as honorable exceptions), the rudely empirical sphere of political society becomes a part or an exemplification of the underlying reality; society and government become (or should become) analogous to that reality, should conform with it or be altered so as to demonstrate the harmony and universality of the truths discovered by the metaphysician. Society must be constructed (or must be made to demonstrate the same 'reality') in such a manner that it becomes an expression of the 'form' or 'essence' that exists beyond and behind sense-apprehensible reality (the concern of empiricism). Society and its form of government and law become an equivalent *model* of the system uncovered by metaphysical inquiry. Also, the method of argument and proof is that of metaphysical inquiry, relying upon deductive argument from first principles rather than upon inductive reasoning, which arrives at first principles from observation of particulars ('evidence' in the material world). Further, the method of metaphysical inquiry is that of *a priori* propositions, those which can be known without reference to experience and are not contingent upon facts, unlike *a posteriori* knowledge.

To all practical intent, the political theories of metaphysicians are often hierarchical in their models of social organization and government, they are not infrequently illiberal and impositional, and they are what may be termed 'static', because they are regarded as 'ideal.' They are also collectivist, creating in the model of society or the state the preeminence of the collectivity rather than of its individual members. This is as true of Plato as it is of Marx and Hegel. Reality or 'essence' resides in the organization, the collectivity itself, and not in the individuals it contains. And, again for all practical purposes, it is this that differentiates the two traditions of Plato and the Stoic school. It is crucial to differentiate the two traditions, at the outset, along the lines indicated above, especially since it is the metaphysical tradition with its conformist, regulated 'models' of society and government that has predominated since Hegel, via Marx and his successors.

Our century has inherited a tradition derived from metaphysics and, furthermore, has assumed that the science of society is a satisfactory and entire replacement for the tradition of political thinking. Sociology, in our century, has appropriated the function of political theory. As will be seen, sociology at its emergence as a science of society in the work of Marx, Durkheim, and Weber (not to mention Saint-Simon and Comte and other Positivists in France before and succeeding the Revolution) is essentially concerned with ideal societies and with what has become fashionably known as social engineering. It also becomes concerned with the 'idea' of society itself (which, in the sense of the 'idea' as equivalent to the term *eidos* or 'form', represents something behind or beyond material reality to metaphysicians since Plato). Therefore, sociology began as neither a pragmatic nor an empirical discipline but as a sphere of inquiry concerned with discovering the essential form or system of a society *and* the re-creation of societies—the shaping of the 'good' society—by means of intellectual effort,

planning, and determination. There is an attempt, from the outset, to determine society rather than simply to understand it,
especially in Marx and Durkheim. Mere comprehension, as in the
case of Max Weber, reduces sociology to a pessimistic catalog of
the ills of the present and a deterministic assessment of any
expectable future.

Even a cursory examination of the ideas of Weber and Durkheim in particular makes it difficult to credit the persistence of
any discipline based upon some of their theories. However, it may
be said that they, together with Marx, set the agenda of political
theory for a century; thus these three founding fathers of the
science of society must be considered in any attempt to understand how our century arrived at its ideas of political society. Karl
Marx, most influentially since Plato himself, has upheld the metaphysical tradition in political theory, just as Locke was the most
influential upholder of what may be termed the empirical tradition of natural law theory. In part, to explain the nature and
degree of adherence to their traditions by Marx and Locke is one
of the purposes of these essays.

The industrial and capitalist societies of Europe differed one
from another when Marx wrote, and they differed from Marx's
conception of them when Durkheim and Weber theorized. Yet
their theories, based upon individual societies, have been 'univer-
salized' in their twentieth-century application. Their concentration upon that pervasive and 'modern' economic system labeled
capitalism has, perhaps, ensured the universal recognition of their
ideas. But it is important to reflect that the process of making
their ideas universally applicable begins with the thinkers themselves. They were prepared to extrapolate from first principles
arrived at in what far more closely imitates *a priori* judgment than
it does the empirical process of inductive reasoning. Weber on
the "Protestant ethic" ignores the emergence of similar religious
and social factors in Scotland, for example, which did not lead to
that Puritan–Dutch model of the emergent capitalist society,
while Durkheim had his sense of the 'spiritual' or religious potential of society itself—rendering neither of them good or trust-

worthy empiricists. They were seduced by the metaphysical potential of their apparently *echt-* empirical discipline. The mechanisms of metaphysical inquiry remain too firmly in place for their credence and modernity to be anything more than an 'appearance' rather than a reality. There is an ideological, even religious, holism about the foundations of sociology which is markedly unscientific.

Metaphysicians (and political theorists of all shades following the metaphysical method) have often sought the analogous in the natural sciences of their time. The imitation of Darwinian method to produce the same kind of holistic, 'single-principle-underlying-reality' image of human nature and human society reinforces the metaphysical tendency of sociology. Philosophers have not often been good scientists (Hobbes misunderstood optics, Darwin has been misunderstood by almost every social thinker!), but it is the search for scientific validity that attracts; the attempt to elevate political and social theorizing to the imagined absolutism and universality has always seduced, usually, though not always, without the strict and painstaking methodology of empirical observation, whether *a priori* or *a posteriori,* that alone grants validity to scientific theory.

III

The pursuit of essentialism by metaphysicians disguised as social and political theorists creates a sense of the imposition of a view of the world (a Weltanschauung) by the 'discoverers' upon the rest of society. This is embodied most clearly and decisively in Plato's philosopher-kings or guardians in his ideal republic. A parallel may be found in lunatic and murderous Jacobin ideals enacted by the Committee of Public Safety and by Marx's own "dictatorship of the Proletariat." Metaphysics, with its emphasis upon the *real,* the underlying, has a tendency toward hierarchy and domination, toward an intellectual elitism. The emphasis upon *knowledge* itself, whether that term is understood in an epistemological or ontological sense, carries the implication that the 'knower' is superior, since it is only he or she who sees the 'real' for what it is and mere 'appearance' likewise. Who should govern, who should shape and direct society then becomes a question easily answered—the philosophers. Hegel finds here complete agreement across the centuries with Plato (as Karl Popper, in that most brilliant of analyses, *The Open Society and Its Enemies*, has observed).

Since metaphysics seeks the simplest, most profound, and universal principles underlying reality, this has the effect in the metaphysical tradition of political theory of producing a single, holistic pattern not only for social organization but for human nature itself. Reduced to a handful of basic elements or passions or capacities, human nature may be consummately defined—which itself leads to the significance of education in the metaphysical tradition, from Plato onward. Human nature is described by degrees of 'self-awareness' as to its value as well as its fact, with a corresponding emphasis placed upon the 'civic' education espoused equally by Plato and Hegel (and the growth of the right kind of self-awareness that Marx required of the proletariat). Education will produce a universal awareness, a consensus in the collectivity. Education is for the purpose of awareness of the 'good' in the sense that the prescribing metaphysician conceives the good; it is not designed to produce the autonomous individual who might remain, nevertheless, incapable of appreciating and accepting the 'good'. It is in this, as in so much else, that the metaphysical tradition, paradoxically, is the conservative tradition of political theory, and that gouty old ancient—natural law theory—may conversely be regarded as the radical tradition, since there is an absence of models, systems, patterns, and a single, universal sense of the 'good'. There is little or no hierarchy, and little or no sense of the collectivity. There is simply the consenting, free individual accepting the limitations upon that freedom concomitant with the unavoidability of a social existence. There is, above all, no single, overriding conception of human nature itself. In place of metaphysics, another branch of philosophy makes its claim to be regarded—ethics. The decisive ground of empirical political theory, and natural law theory in particular, is the necessity to decide upon and legislate to enforce the ethical behavior of individuals toward one another in society—to preserve both the notion of free individuality and the harmonious fabric of the society itself.

Ethical theory is based upon the assumption that human beings are different, individual. If they were not, there would be no need for any kind of ethical theory or inquiry. Metaphysics, in its search for essential reality, inclines to regard human nature as basically indivisible, identical. People may be distinguished, therefore, only in *understanding*, in their grasp of reality, by intellect and their capacity to philosophize. Therefore, the philosophers may be regarded as those most capable of instructing, illuminating, and, unfortunately, ruling. Ethics, in granting of necessity a moral dimension to each rational individual, admits an equivalence among individuals which the metaphysical tradition either avoids or is incapable of recognizing. The equivalence of potential for rational insight and behavior that ethics posits in every individual also posits the accommodation of individuals within society. It preserves notions of individuality and democracy. By this one does not mean that metaphysicians are immoral or unethical, though they are prescriptive of behavior and 'worth' in a very restrictive and impositional sense. Ethics at its simplest requires consensus of behavior rather than a conception of the 'essence' of human nature beyond a capacity to distinguish right from wrong and, in any society pretending to an ethical code, a legal code designed to prevent the unethical from occurring. The association of human beings is free and voluntary—society exists by virtue of the consent of its members—but ethics requires the protection of each of those individuals by means of an agreed and legislatively enforceable set of rules.

IV

Natural law theory remained both enshrined and disguised within the Christian 'ethic' for a millennium and a half, to re-emerge in the empirical political theories of Locke and subsequently in the violent secularism of the French Enlightenment. This would imply its existence as a force for conservatism—which, however, it was not. Even within Christianity, the invaluable Stoic and Roman recognition of the equivalence of individual human beings was preserved in the doctrine of the pricelessness of every individual soul. While society adopted forms that analogously copied the 'model' of the hierarchical Church in various shades of feudalism and other pyramidal shapes, doctrine and espousal of that doctrine promulgated the individuality and worth of each human soul as well as its moral accountability at death. Of even greater significance for the preservation, almost intact, of the corpus of natural law theory was the Judeo-Christian tradition in regard to human reason. Man's perilous gift of reason, by which Adam fell, was the property of *all* men. Thus, all men possessed a capacity for ethical behavior, and all men were both alike and unique in this. The preservation of these two essential ingredients of Stoicism by their incorporation into Christian theology, it may be argued, essentially produced a metaphysical image or 'model' of human nature that mirrored the divine, just as human society was represented ideally as an image of the celestial polity. Nevertheless, despite natural law theory's ineffectuality in the temporal sphere, its conception of human nature and human rational (and therefore ethical) capacity was preserved within the theology, just as the equivalence of human souls in the eye of the Divine preserved that equality of all men inherent in Stoicism.

Stoicism may be regarded, at its inception, as a 'universalism' in direct reaction to the decline—but more importantly the particularism—of the Attic city-states, the model for Plato's ideal republic: hierarchical, disciplined, and insufficiently enfranchised.

But it was a universalism that elevated each individual to an equivalence of status and capacity. Platonic man (and even Marxist man) may be regarded as a creature of education rather than a creature of given or inherent rationality. Human nature is malleable—indeed, in all our metaphysicians and their political theories there is an estimation of 'brute' human nature that one can only call Hobbesian—the creature of passion, selfishness, unrestrained ego. Therefore, human nature must be molded toward and educated up to the ideal, out of its egoistic morass of will and desire. Human rationality is, therefore, inculcated rather than innate, in opposition to the Stoics and the tradition of natural law theory.

One should not, of course, regard the Stoic schools as promulgating popular democracy or any such "Leveling" doctrines. They believed in the superiority of the "wise." However, the Stoics did not assume that wisdom, achieved through the exercise of human reason, must inevitably remain the preserve of the few—rather, the assumption of their teaching was that this innate capacity of human reason might be cultivated in all. Thus the exercise of reason is an *individual* as well as a universal phenomenon. In Stoicism, it was the degree of self-understanding that distinguished men from each other, and, even though this was 'idealized' into a kind of asceticism and denial of the temporal, it nevertheless denied any sense of oppressive, impositional, or hierarchical political society.

To a degree, the empirical reassertion of natural law theory, particularly by John Locke, is a process of demythologizing the theory of its Christian (i.e., metaphysical) accretions. Christianity allowed hierarchical 'images' of the celestial arrangement, even promulgated, supported, and finally shored them up. The mirror of society was the Church rather than the Gospels until the Reformation. What this empirical reassertion of the theory during the Enlightenment promulgated was that other essential element of Stoicism, the concept of 'self' that is the basis of individuality. Platonic thought promotes the primacy of identification with the *polis*, the community, while Stoicism recognizes *iden-*

tity. The metaphysical tradition adheres to this detrimental strand of Platonic political thought—the primacy of the collectivity, the identity of the self or 'person' deriving from the fact of membership in a collectivity—rather than from the self-awareness and the self-regulation of action that is the essence of the Stoic view of human nature. For Stoicism and natural law theory, man is 'explained' by reference to himself, not by reference to some more universal or essential 'reality'. It is this conception of identity rather than *identification,* of course, that is the basis of all democratic theories of political society; the basis of all true radicalism, also.

V

Natural law theory itself is generally recognized as having emerged in the period that succeeded the decline of the Greek city-states; that is, that period in the history of ideas that succeeded the era of Plato and Aristotle. The governing perception of the individual as citizen, as member of the Greek *polis,* loses its authority, to be replaced by a concept of man as a "citizen of the world," in the imagery of the Stoic school. Natural law was derived from the law of nature, and it is the primary object of human existence to live consistent with nature (and therefore with our own essential nature, characterized as reason). Reason becomes the goal of human existence and the sole manner in which man emulates, or partakes of, the divine. Natural law theory and its values, therefore, were in origin part of a theistic view of reality, and remained so until the eighteenth century. The cosmopolis, or 'world-state', to which all rational creatures necessarily belong, demands values that can be equally shared and participated in by *all* rational creatures. Thus the origin of what history has called liberal values. As well as the Stoics, the Cynic school, epitomized by Diogenes, accepted the universality of human nature, combining it with a vigorous individualism, what we might now call 'radical' individualism. The Stoics, however, assumed that the truly rational, or wise, man was an exception, and it was Panaetius in the second century B.C. who propounded the theory that reason was a law for all and thus human nature demanded an equality of rights, treatment and justice. It is this crucial and abiding concept that Cicero codified and reiterated and which was the basis of the Roman legal concept of the *ius gentium*, the law common to all peoples, which was intended to embody the principles of the *ius naturale*, natural law. In one great passage in the *Republic*, Cicero encapsulates the whole theory of natural law when he says:

> There is in fact a true law—namely, right reason—which is in accordance with nature, applies to all men, and is unchangeable and eternal . . . The man who will not obey it will abandon his better self, and, in denying the true nature of a man, will suffer the severest of penalties, though he has escaped all the other consequences which men call punishments.   BK. III

This eternal law makes all men equal—not in learning or necessarily in property but in the possession of reason. It is also evident that Cicero regards this natural law of right reason to be derived from God.

It is Cicero's clarification and codification of Stoic natural law theory (and the elements of the Cynic outlook which easily cohabited with Stoicism) that influenced the early and medieval Christian thinkers, who preserved natural law theory and made it irrefutably dependent upon the Christian deity. It is a history of continuity that attends natural law theory rather than one of change or adaptation. We might encapsulate this continuity simply by comparing the original Stoic concept of the cosmopolis with that of the "kingdom of ends" Kant expounds in his essay *Perpetual Peace*—the similarities are remarkable. Natural law theory enshrined and preserved the ideas of equality of reason, justice, rights, and liberties. By doing so, it also preserved the conception of the unique value of each individual as a rational being and thus entitled to equality. Equally, the theistic origin or guarantee of natural law is also preserved. There is no profound change within, or decline of, natural law theory until the materialism of the French Enlightenment, when reason becomes divorced from all theistic conceptions of the universe for, perhaps, the first time.

There is continuity, too, in the Stoic conception of the passions as malfunctions of reason, as requiring government by the rational faculty in human nature, together with the sense of transcending mere 'nature' through the employment of reason in the pursuit of knowledge. It is a tradition that reawakens in Descartes and Spinoza, however applied or altered, in their emphasis upon reason as the essence of human nature and existence, particularly in Spinoza's ideals of liberty and justice and in his theory of the necessity of reason to subdue and order the 'passions'. Natural law theory, in other words, illuminates the theories of the great rationalists, just as it forces upon us a recognition of the tradition to which Kant belonged and upon which Locke drew.

In Stoic and Roman thought, therefore, natural law theory is nothing less than a theory of human *identity*, since it avoids all classifications of human beings into groups or classes or within any exclusive idea of citizenship or even of the status of the "wise" in human society. It allows and promulgates a common identity to *all* human beings as opposed to any more partial means of identification, just as it establishes the spirit of any legal system or positive law, which must imitate and embody natural law. Natural law becomes the paradigm of positive law (the legal system), just as it thereby becomes the paradigm of identity, since its ideals represent what it is to be human in terms of rights, liberties, and responsibilities. It is an epistemology, a psychology, and an ethic, and in all its aspects it promulgates the unique value of each individual human being, 'blessed' with reason and thus a participant in the universal rights and liberties that are the just deserts of every rational being. What become in Locke "inalienable rights" are those very principles which admit the equivalence of identity (and therefore significance) between ourselves and others—you are as *individual* as I am. In Locke, especially, where the divine encouragement, as it were, of natural law theory is minimal, natural law theory may be seen as pre-psychology in the sense that the modern world understands that science of the human personality. Natural law theory, and its cohering individualism, is the essence of human identity from the Stoics to Kant, so that perhaps the greatest philosopher since Plato may speak unequivocally of "ends-in-themselves" and of the unique value of all rational human beings. For both Kant and Locke, the loss of rights enshrined in natural law is the loss of what Locke would call *personhood,* the reduction of man from the status of "person" (self) to that of mere man. The loss of primacy of reason in ideas of human nature is equivalent to the loss of self, since it is reason, over a period of almost two thousand years, from the Stoics to Kant, that alone perceives the significance of natural law and the equality of human beings. Natural law theory and the importance of reason are synonymous throughout those two millennia, in Greek, Roman, and Christian thought.

Inherent in natural law theory, too, almost from its origins, is the idea of *compact* or *consent,* the precedence of the individual over the group, the sense of voluntary and free engagement in human society. Natural law, in its primacy over positive law, is thereby asserting that rights and justice for all individuals are the basis of social organization and interaction. Thus, the theory of consent (always ahistorical, as we shall see, rather than the statement of an actual place and time in ancient history when the original society was formed) is a further guarantee of identity and individuality.

During the two millennia when natural law formed the basic ethic of society and its legislation and the fundamental concept of human identity, there was no call similar to that of the Greek *polis* upon human beings to perceive their identity in terms defined by some larger grouping (except as members of the universal Catholic church). The identity of men lay not in what the social grouping might grant or allow but in what it *must* allow to the consenting or contracting individual who accepts membership in such a group. Rights—natural rights—establish in reason and law his guarantee to individual identity. Catholic dogma may supplant, to a degree, the insistence of natural law that men govern their animal nature by means of reason by its insistence upon the *sins* of desire and the passions, but it does not supplant entirely the means of achieving this self-government; therefore, it does not disturb the primacy of reason, nor, in its concept of man's immortal soul, does it supplant the bases of human identity as professed by the Stoics, the rationalists, and the empirical Locke. It remains to empiricism in the eighteenth century, and to the materialism of the Enlightenment, to accomplish that task. Before this crux in the history of ideas, whether he is achieving the salvation of his immortal soul or his personhood, individual man must recognize and obey the dictates of reason and its noblest apprehension, natural law.

VI

Further tasks must be to examine the effect of ideas upon history and of history upon political theory and, perhaps most importantly, to examine philosophic interpretations of the *idea* of history itself. It is during the period embraced by the theories of political society discussed here that the notion of purposive history emerges and indeed becomes preeminent, just as this is also the period when that initially German academic discipline, historical studies, becomes not only a recognized branch of study but a branch of philosophic speculation. History and the study of history in the sense that the modern world understands those terms become instruments of philosophy.

The cyclical view of history contains both the ancient world and Christian theology, where the lives of the great and the lives of societies obey a pattern of rise and fall (or a revolution of the wheel of fortune, as its most popular and abiding image has it) returning to an initial point. There was no evolutionary theory of history, since there was no evolutionary theory of life, and the 'purpose' of history was to morally instruct. History, in the medieval period, was a moral implement; the lesson of history was that of individual lives and fates or, by an increase only of scale, the moral rise and fall of whole societies.

The transformation from this to purposive history is dealt with in detail elsewhere, but it must be remarked here that the purpose of history remains instructional, though the lesson to be learned from history becomes its pattern, its progress or 'evolution'. The 'progress' that history exhibits is, broadly speaking, positive (though in the instance of Marx, regressive in its effect of alienation upon human beings with the emergence of the capitalist system) and is illustrated most vividly by the almost unqualified optimism of the French materialists of the Enlightenment—the *philosophes*—and in the derived Positivism of Comte and others. Philosophers deal with epochs or eras of human history, exchanging primitive forms of hierarchical society for more sophisticated examples. Often the model of emerging or predicted societies is Plato's ideal republic, under the governance of the wise or the 'elect' (the "priesthood of sociologists," for example, envisaged by Saint-Simon). Whatever the specific form of hierarchical society postulated, the assumption of a continuing and identifiable pattern in the whole of Western history persists, though it is the pattern of social organizations rather than that of 'great men' or even great empires.

History has assumed, then, by the beginning of the nineteenth century, a 'scientific' capacity. It becomes analogous with the natural sciences (and predicts the biological sciences quite remarkably), assuming that laws and patterns, even a single, inclusive system, can be deduced from the multifarious facts of the past. It becomes, quite expectedly, the implement of the metaphysical tradition of political theory rather than assisting a resurgence of empiricism. There is a concentrated search for first principles via deductive argument, for a holistic view of the whole of human history—at least the history of man in society. Continuity is what lies behind this search and is its assumed and often unconscious goal. Discontinuity is demonstrated, for almost every nineteenth-century thinker other than Marx (and his view was severely qualified by the imposition of his views of political economy upon recalcitrant history), by the act of revolution, the disruption of *process*. And the most cataclysmic disruption occurred in France in 1789.

However, it is not 1789 and the Tennis Court Oath and the Declaration of the Rights of Man, or the attempt at constitutional monarchy that briefly ensued, but the shadow of Dr. Guillotin's invention that most profoundly influences political theory in the nineteenth century. Robespierre must be regarded as one of history's villains, since, for so much influential political thought after 1800, the Terror he inspired proved the contiguity between democracy and anarchy, suffrage and the mob and blood. This is the starkest fact that emerges from even a cursory study of Hegel, Marx from a very different standpoint, Burke in his *Reflections* (the foundation of modern conservatism in political thought and perhaps the last great exhalation of Whiggish hierarchical attitudinizing), and Lenin, that most apt and studious of Robespierre's pupils.

While French materialism and the Enlightenment's secularism and cult of human reason, together with the theories of Rousseau, may be regarded as influential forerunners of the Revolution, the nineteenth century's tradition of political theory ought rightly to be regarded as lagging in the footsteps of events, as an attempt to 'recover from' the horrors of the Revolution and the perpetrations of the nation-in-arms that succeeded the Directory and made itself an empire, briefly and bloodily. The history of France, and therefore of Europe, from 1789 to 1815 provided various models of an instructive nature to philosophers of history, but perhaps most influentially it provided a *pattern*, a whole governed by inevitability, so that there was a need to explain Robespierre and Napoleon in terms of 1789—the assumption that the storming of the Bastille and the Declaration of the Rights of Man inevitably and inexorably led to the Terror and the empire and, finally, to the assumption that democracy was inevitably aggressive, the 'suffrage' of a nation-in-arms. Democracy was nothing but the monster mask of the loss of all liberty, so that even J. S. Mill could fear, decades later in England, the tyranny of the majority.

The effects of the revolt of the British colonies in North America upon subsequent events in France is too well documented to require rehearsal here. Suffice it to remark that that 'revolution' was never regarded by nineteenth-century political theorists as a viable alternative to the 'pattern' of events in France. The revolution inspired by Locke, as much as by any thinker, was eclipsed by that inspired by his illegitimate offspring, the materialists of the French Enlightenment. The last (and one of the very few) revolutions to have been inspired by natural law theory provided no instruction to philosophic historians.

The French Revolution, both as event and object of reflection, displays both our traditions of political thought, the empirical and the metaphysical, and it is a simple enough task to regard the period 1789–92 as a genuinely democratic revolt against the social conditions of France. The Terror and the strange gods it threw up (Hébert's Cult of Reason of 1793, replaced by Robespierre's Festival of the Supreme Being of 1794) serve to illustrate the metaphysical, holistic tradition, the attempt to remake rather than to liberate society. The metaphysical nonsense noted above in parentheses, the complete illiberality of the Terror, the 'ideal' of citizenship (from which so many might so easily dissent unless executed) are extreme forms of impositional government, of the "wise" at their most dictatorial.

The Revolution, for the most influential thinkers who reflected upon it from a metaphysical position, damaged beyond recovery the concept of the primacy of reason—equated with the Terror, with pitiless blood lust, et cetera and ad nauseam—and destroyed, too, that other essence of natural law theory, the concept of the autonomous, 'equivalent' human individual. Robespierre was the father of the collective identity of man as he was of so much else. The conclusion was inescapable for Hegel and equally, though for different reasons, for Marx—the ideas of individuality, social disharmony, and historical discontinuity were inextricably bound together. The Jacobin extremists, professional revolutionaries as we would now regard them, despite the manner in which their aspirations and ideals continuously changed, regarded human beings collectively, whatever their promulgation of the rights and liberties of the individual (the idea of 'all men' is not necessarily that of 'all *individual* men' or all 'persons'). Thus they were the intellectual forerunners of Marx and Hegel, Durkheim and Weber, the first practical 'sociologists'. (It is another irony of the Revolution that the continuity of Comtian philosophy embraces the period of the Revolution and the Terror, emerging from it unscathed, it might be said. There are grounds for considering that upon the French strand of the science of society the Revolution had little or no effect—the restoration and the appalling Second Empire were to influence Durkheim more deeply. Comte was able to ignore the Terror as utterly as Hegel was unable to do so.) The image of man which emerges from the Revolution, and which was profoundly influential, is that of man collectivized, his human nature an 'aspect' of the larger, more 'real' social organization (or organism, as later thinkers were to regard it).

The further influence of history upon ideas must lie in the emergence of the nation-state during the period under consideration. However, what history had 'taught' the historians and philosophers of history of the late eighteenth and nineteenth centuries was not that simple and obvious 'fact'. Rather, the examples of Louis XIV and Napoleon instilled the lesson of history that the nation-state was embodied in its aggressiveness toward its neighbors, in its militarism, and its rigidly centralized form of government. This lesson was digested and yearned after especially in Germany, where the lessons of a patrician democracy in the Netherlands and of that offshore island Britain were disregarded, along with so much else. From Hegel to Weber, the equation of the nation-state with militarism, with *nationalism*, the curse of our century, is certain and unquestioned. The 'sense of nation' *is* militaristic, expansionist, and aggressive, for German idealism and for German sociology. Hegel's apologia for the Prussian state and Weber's support of his government's approach to the Great

War are more than sufficient evidence of the power of history on ideas, rather than the reverse.

The grip of ideas rather than history upon successive generations of thinkers is nowhere more evident than in their approach to the problem of capitalism. Comte was optimistic regarding this 'new' form of economic determination of the social organization, while Marx was entirely pessimistic. However, when one comes to examine the attitudes of thinkers belonging to later generations, one finds the persistence of attitudes rather than facts. Though Durkheim and Weber, for example, developed their principal theories at the end of the last century and the beginning of this one, their ideas exist in a historical vacuum to a large extent. They are determined by Marx and their other predecessors rather than by the empirically observable society around them. And, if Weber ever threw off the influence of Marx (and he spent his life refuting the greater German), he did not discard the persistent influence of Hegel and what one might call 'Prussianism'. Ideas of political society in the nineteenth century did, to one degree or another, operate under the umbrella of the metaphysical tradition, revivified with a vengeance by Hegel. They became 'philosophical' and, like the other branches of speculation, derived much of their energy, antithesis, and conclusions from reaction or response to other ideas.

One is left to conclude, perhaps, that the ideals which first inspired the French Revolution were those, however altered by the elevation of a secularist conception of human reason to 'essence' or model, that had inspired both the English and the American revolutions that preceded it. However, contemporary reflection upon the aftermath of the initial changes of the revolutionary period served only to throw political and social thought gratefully into the arms of collectivist theorists, another generation of metaphysicians. It is necessary, therefore, to regard the triumph of the Revolution not as the triumph of the individual and the values of what historians term liberalism but rather the reverse. Confirmed by history, it was the triumph of a peculiarly French form of idealism which masqueraded as materialism, a close relative of Lockian empiricism. Reason itself had become something 'ideal', something essential, *a priori* and self-evident—and something to be elevated to the status of the divine. Added to this is the fact that the tradition of French philosophy, from Descartes to Rousseau, was metaphysical. Materialism, at its best, is an accommodation of Locke's empiricism with the prevailing current.

For the moment, all that need be additionally remarked is that nineteenth-century political (or 'sociological') theory is dogged by other minor legacies of the new science of history and from those who professed to interpret its mysteries for the benefit of the uninitiated, and these are derived from the sense of pattern attempting to accommodate itself with the 'fact' of the contemporary or spring from the recognition of pattern itself in history. We are dealing with determinism on the one hand and pessimism on the other. Determinism is the vigorous offspring of pattern and system, bereft of Comte's optimism and douched by the chill water of the Terror. Not only is history beyond the control of the individual (even the individual society or government or state), but its pattern, given the continuing vigor of the capitalist system, despite Marx's optimistic prognostications, implies lack of change, the "iron cage" that Max Weber eloquently spoke of. Conditioned by Marx's analysis of capitalism, no nineteenth-century social or political thinker accommodated his ideas to the changes that *people* had wrought upon the capitalist system.

As to pessimism, it has the same root in the unquestioning fidelity to philosophical tradition and practice that nineteenth-century political theory seems to have obeyed. Empiricism seems to have been kidnapped and conditioned to an obedience to metaphysics unrivaled since Plato. (Or perhaps empiricism was a brief, shining escape from the tradition that had always, before the Stoics and during the long appropriation of natural law theory by the Church, predominated, rendering political theory no more than a branch of metaphysics, Kant's "queen of the sciences.") Pessimism, whatever the precise cause, if there was one, is the result of the acceptance of the primacy of the collectivity and the inevitability of history, given that the social organization of Western Europe persisted under the identifying label of capitalism. Darwin appeared to confirm all the worst fears. The social 'organism' was a predetermined and evolving entity—but it could not be changed by the efforts of men, by *man,* let alone the discredited individual.

That such assumptions persisted, despite empirical evidence to the contrary, is one of the deeper mysteries of political and social theory in the last century. That they did so persist is the subject of these essays—that, and the alternative tradition that remained ignored, perhaps locked in that same east wing of the history of ideas after the release of mad nationalism.

THE STATE OF POLITICAL SOCIETY: A PREAMBLE TO LOCKE, HOBBES, AND MARX

THERE IS AN ENCOUNTER during the seventeenth century in England other than that of Parliament and the king, or the army and Parliament, or even the country and the Protectorate, which has more significance for the history of political theory than any of those matters of state, and that is the philosophical encounter between the theories of Thomas Hobbes espoused in his *Leviathan* and the ideas of John Locke expressed in the *Two Treatises of Government*. While both dissertations owe a great deal, even derive almost exclusively from, the political circumstances surrounding their genesis, they do, more profoundly, exhibit what may be concluded to be the two main strands of political theory—the 'ancient' and the 'modern'—so that it is possible to characterize Locke as the last great proponent of natural law theory while at the same time designating Hobbes as the ancestor of collectivism. Neither description is lightly earned or lightly worn, but they may at least enable us to discover some essential differences between the two political theorists who held sway—indeed, struggled with each other—until *Capital*.

It is both extremely easy and improbably difficult to characterize the essential differences between Hobbes and Locke and, perhaps even more importantly, between the 'schools' they attempted to reinvigorate, those of empiricism and materialism. It is possible for a commentator to choose authority and democracy, monarchy or parliament, their divergent views of human nature, bourgeois capitalism and . . . (but this is where Marxist critics find them in deadly combination, to the ridiculous degree that both are characterized as joint forefathers, in perpetuity, of the tradition of bourgeois liberalism that gave rise to the French Revolution and which held sway during the period of laissez-faire capitalism in England and much of Europe) atheism and Christianity, Shaftesbury and Charles II, James II and William of Orange—the possibilities of divergence are endless; indeed, apart from the peculiarity of that anti-Marxist conspiracy to which they apparently both belonged, there seems to be a consensus of opinion that diametrically opposes the one to the other and a suspicion that while Locke easily outpointed his opponent during the earlier rounds, Hobbes retained sufficient vigor to win the contest. Thus, in the broadest sense, Locke's was the eighteenth century while Hobbes was required to hover in the wings until the nineteenth.

It seems to this critic that one may group the distinctions that exist between Hobbes and Locke (and that they are both profound in nature and of continuing significance there is no doubt) under a smaller number of generic headings. There is in Hobbes, for example, a promulgation of the state (that *degree* of government beyond "political society" and which is necessitated by human nature itself), whereas in Locke there is perhaps the first (and last?) great attempt to prevent the state's emergence; there is the essential difference between two branches of philosophy and methodologies, those of empiricism and materialism, and there is that view of human nature upon which most theories of the state ultimately depend. Further, and subordinately, there are the views of substance taken by the two philosophers, their views of the *state of nature*, and there is history and 'ahistory'. One might also consider their different views of what has been termed the "original position" with regard to theories of society, the origins of social man, together with their divergent views of recent English history. Whatever one selects, it seems, proves both more intractable and of greater importance than the popular distinctions between Locke and Hobbes. To this writer, at least, it seems that one should begin with some understanding of materialism—before coming to Hobbes's variant upon that tradition—and of empiricism and the separate views both of *essence* and *substance* they espouse, and of human nature itself coming into that congregation that is regarded as society. Above all, perhaps, we should consider the ideas of *civil society* and *political society*.

II

Locke's epistemology or theory of knowledge is unable to define what one may call the essential nature of *substance*. In Kant's terms, Locke distinguishes between the noumenon and the phenomenon. Since, according to Locke, we derive our experience and understanding of the world from our senses, and the mind remains a "blank paper" until written upon by our experiences, then we can never truly apprehend the noumenon; we are, in a very different sense from the greatest German metaphysician, trapped in a world of apprehensions, the appearance of reality rather than its essential nature. Locke concludes that there can never be any certainty that we have apprehended the underlying or hidden reality of things. Except for what we can deduce from our sensuous experience, we are marooned in this world of appearances, though he has no fears on this score. Materialism, however, apprehends the world as matter alone. And, since we partake of the matter of the world, we are constructed of similar, or even identical, material; materialism assumes that human nature is entirely apprehensible through human activity in the world and the matrix of circumstances in which any individual human nature exists. Nothing *other* than our material apprehension of ourselves and others is permissible. What we *do* and appear to be is alone what is real about us. There is a gap, therefore, between empiricism and materialism which empiricism fills with 'likelihood' or intuitionism—what might be reasonably supposed—and which materialism denies exists.

Materialism is equatable with its opposite, therefore, which is metaphysics. By denying the existence of any *essence* in reality other than what can be apprehended, it produces an essentialism akin to that of metaphysics—except that in materialism, that essence is described in pronouncements regarding human nature and the physical world. A single (and 'simple') essential nature can be ascribed to human beings upon which basic theories of behavior, society, and government can be erected which either correct, restrain, or fulfill human nature. Thus, materialism is an ontology rather than an epistemology, a theory of being rather than knowledge of being. The materialist ontology is that of *activity*—behavior, response, influence, engagement in social activity define the human being entirely (not forgetting, too, that human nature obeys *laws* not dissimilar to those discoverable and observable in the physical universe). The *physics* of man, that apprehensible and observable *body* that occupies space and time, precedes *any* metaphysic of man, whether of thought, emotion, or spirit, either in individual behavior or in society.

Materialism, therefore, is capable of reducing the world to a few (even a single) basic principles (as Hobbes does in terms of *motion*), and in that sense, too, it is akin to metaphysics or to the kind of scholasticism that Locke set out to oppose in his *Essay*. Empiricism is intent, at least in Locke, on creating doubt and plurality, in refuting the excesses of metaphysics, which become the same excesses in materialism. That plurality extends, most importantly, to human nature, whose essence we cannot know, at least in the case of *others* (the multiplicity of persons engaged in the activity that Locke terms political society). Thus, political society is a situation in which human beings find themselves without any sense of the noumenon of human nature, only with the plurality of phenomena exhibited by the members of that society.

In the simplest terms, where metaphysics may propose something like the atomism of Democritus, in which reality is composed of indivisible particles which differ in form and relation to one another in their composition of that reality, materialism proposes what may be called a molecular theory of reality, society, and, especially, human nature, molecular in the sense that a molecule is the smallest particle of something that still retains the *properties* of that substance. In other words, materialism supposes that human nature can and must be regarded as the smallest realization or *example* of some other, and larger, substance and may only be understood in terms of its existence as this molecular form. In the case of Hobbes, the single principle which is exhibited by human beings and of which the whole of reality essentially partakes is that of motion. His hypothesis is based upon the barely understood physical sciences of his age, and then upon his own partial understanding of contemporary science. In Marx, such molecules as human beings are partake of, or demonstrate, the universal 'substance' of labor, activity in the world. Similarly, thought, feeling, ideas are all reducible to *matter* and to the influence upon the molecular human beings of phenomenal and pertaining causes (the nature or essence of the substance or principle that composes the universe, especially the 'human' universe). Human nature and activity thus become the effects of discernible causes, or a discernible principle. Such a reductive explanation is regarded by materialists as both complete and entire; materialism proposes to describe the only and sole essence that may be ascribed to human nature.

Because the above are basic and essential assumptions of any materialist view of the world, an essentialist view of human nature is unavoidable and results in a sociological view of human beings, where they are the product of their social circumstances, essentially that and no more. In so assuming, materialist philosophies require the invention of a new category of society, beyond that of community or conglomeration—what becomes in Hobbes and later in Hegel (as well as in Marx) *civil society,* an intermediate rather than a median stage. This is the view that man-in-society is defined in his nature by the very fact of his being within and part of that conglomeration or community, together with the notion that human nature can be reduced, at least in theory, to a principle of activity. This is opposed to Locke's view that all societies, at the moment of their inception, become, and *need* to become, *political societies* (i.e., the conglomerations require, as a first principle, *law*).

This notion of civil society is a means of describing human agglomerations as they exhibit essential human nature rather than any form of government, structure, polity, or law. Civil society is the display of human nature in community, which will *then* require a system of government imposed upon it (since materialist views of human nature are inevitably pessimistic and concerned with the pessimistic activity of human beings toward one another—as in Marx's conception of capitalist society). There is, and must be, for materialist philosophers, a 'thing' or reality which is *civil society* that is the expression of 'mere' human nature, since human nature can only be expressed and demonstrated in a social context, society playing the role of substance to the individual's molecule. The molecule does not exist outside its activity as expression of its society. (If this is seen as confusing the chicken and the egg, then that is perhaps the deliberate and intended confusion of materialists. Civil society is human nature "red in tooth and claw," merely human, actively demonstrating a human nature that is pessimistically described by philosophers who would doubtless point to the vast armies of unjust, villainous, oppressive, exploitative societies of history as the final proof of their thesis, all of them having been the expression of a human nature itself corrupt and villainous, and confirmed in those capacities by the existence of civil society in any of its various corrupt forms.)

To extend the earlier metaphor, the truth about human beings is their molecular relations with each other, in one sense producing their society out of their behavior toward each other; but more importantly (since societies in the past have a familiar and repetitious injustice about them, an exploitative, aggressive 'essence'), they behave as society instructs or influences them to behave. This is *civil society*. There is no atomic theory of human nature in materialism, such as distinguishes, even metaphorically, the atomic or autonomous individual, only a molecular conception of human nature as particular illustration of a principle of activity or behavior. And the principle is not only active but distinguishes society as the mode of expression of the principle. The choice as to the exact roles fulfilled by the chicken and the egg are thus twofold. The form and reality of civil society either demonstrates the expression of essential human nature (Hobbes) or is responsible for what has become of human beings in their essential natures (Marx). Hence, materialism arrives at the condition of a sociology. And in civil society, there can be no evolution or growth toward the condition Locke describes as political society. Such a *form* of social organization must either be imposed (Hobbes) from without or above, or all such forms must be abandoned (Marx) since they are crystallizations of the predominant elements of human nature displayed in civil society. Both are routes toward a conception of the state, whether the optimistic necessity of an authority imposed that Hobbes discusses or the exploitative unavoidability of all forms of the state, as in Marx, where the only genuine *community* exists without the state (a community strangely peopled with self-sufficient, all but autonomous, individuals).

Political society, within the tradition of Stoic and Roman natural law theory, is a society of self-invented or discovered government and law. Its *form* (ideal or real) is governed by the necessity to consider and to accommodate a *plurality* of human natures rather than a mere multiplicity. The form of government or commonwealth is predicated by this recognition of the continuing individuality of human natures in congregation. Therefore, society must evolve a system of *law*—protective, minimally constraining, maximally guaranteeing, and concerned with the rights, liberties, and duties of citizenship. This is *political society*, an attempt at human combination which protects the essentially unknowable noumenal individual human nature but concerns itself with the *phenomenal behavior* of such natures in their congregated state.

It is necessary, at this point, to consider the modern notion of the state, and its provenance, and to remark that a state may be regarded in some senses as no more than an organization but in another sense as an *organism*, a collectivity in a manner that is not the case with the traditional understanding of a political society. In time of war or national crisis, of course, all political societies will adopt at least some of the characteristics of a state—the limitation of personal freedoms, the increased mobilization of the society and its economy by the government—where, in fact, what hopefully remains latent in a political society becomes actual, to some degree or another. The organs of government become more visible, effective, even arbitrary, emergency powers are granted to the executive (as even Locke was prepared to countenance), and the state becomes, albeit temporarily, actual.

However, a state may be said to exist in other times than those of national political crisis where, as in Hobbes, all notion of *sovereignty* has been surrendered to the organs and institutions of government (for whatever purpose and with whatever outcome) by the people, the Greek *demos*. In exchange for such a surrender, confiscation, or denial, arises the notion and 'status' of the *citizen*, the member of the political community. In other words, the condition of a state is that in which sovereignty is invested in a person, an administration, in the organs of legislation and execution, rather than in what may be termed the communal individualism of the political society. The idea of the citizen replaces (or is adopted for the first time) the idea of the consenting member or individual. As in the Greek *polis*, the 'body' of the city-state, the idea of citizenship is both exclusive and embracing. It is the condition of identification with and identity within the political or national (or even racial) organization or *organism* which may then be termed a state.

We owe the modern sense of a state to Machiavelli, who may be regarded as wishing for a nation-state when lamenting the decadence of the Italian city-states as degenerated imitations of the Greek city-state; and in Machiavelli the concept of the state is indivisible from the concept or idea of power, a *power-authority* (a means of control and national or regional expression rather than a political circumstance of guarantees and limited government). The state exists, or should come to exist, for Machiavelli, for the purpose of the exercise of power (which is also the case with Hobbes). Therefore, we may conclude that a state in any meaningful modern sense must be regarded as a *concentration* rather than dissemination of power and authority, whether in the person of a "Prince," as is the case with Machiavelli and Hobbes, or in some other form of legislature and executive. It is not a means of governance but a government for purposes that are other than the welfare, rights, liberties, and equality of the members of the community. It may, or may not, be a just or 'good' state, but that is not its purpose. Its purpose is the focus and expression of authority over its own citizens or other political communities outside itself. Thus, Machiavelli's view of liberty may be regarded as being that of the *liberty to be powerful* (as in Athens against Sparta or Florence against other Italian city-states or, even in the Marxist–Leninist state, the authority and power to export the vision of collectivism enshrined in the state).

The condition of a state requires a strong central authority; therefore, its purpose is self-evidently that of expressing its power successfully. It has come to exist as an organism (usually aggressive, especially in its nation-state manifestation) rather than as a means of fulfilling the legislative aspirations of its members. It is therefore an imitation of other groupings or tendencies to centralism or exclusivity or both, such as classes, estates, nationality, and wealth—a fact demonstrated by Machiavelli's belief in the preservation of liberty by means of the representation of separate and distinct classes or groups in the organs of government, a situation not too far from the arguments of people like Ireton and Cromwell when confronted by the demands for universal suffrage of the Levelers.

Finally, a state comes into existence, or has existence, when the form and organs of its government require an identification by the community with the personification of itself, whether they are the inhabitants of a distinct, national geographic region, the voters in a democracy, the sectional interests of oligarchy. The state or proto-state, the "Prince" or the parliament assumes the personhood of the whole or expresses that whole by assuming itself as *an archetype rather than as a representation.* Indeed, on such grounds, we may well be able to conclude at the close of a subsequent essay that it is Hobbes, far more than the ever-execrated Machiavelli, who is the originator or codifier of the concept of the modern state, however much he may be regarded as an apologist for anachronisms in his defense of the divine right of kings theory. It is Hobbes, far more than the much later Hegel or his eventual successor Weber who distinguishes the nature of the modern state, its essential condition of *personation* of the community in the figure or form of a person or institution. It is this assumption of embodiment rather than of representation that makes a state of a political society.

However, to return to the problem of a materialist outlook upon human society, in light of the above, it becomes necessary to remark that, as in Marx and therefore perhaps at its most optimistic regarding human nature, materialism assumes that a moral judgment upon essential human nature predicates the form of political society that must be regarded as 'ideal'. Thus, the task of reforming or fulfilling human nature becomes the task of the government, of what begins to be the state. The phenomenal conditions of society are not the object of materialist theories of government; they intend the re-creation or improvement (or in Hobbes, the repression) of the essence, human nature. This is precisely because civil society is either an expression of human nature rather than an artificial construct of laws or is essentially the product of social forces. At either point of conclusion lies the beginning of the state, that elevation of political society based

upon a system of law to a moral force, an executive and legislature
in combination which assumes to itself the moral leadership of the
community, a form of political society which ascribes to itself a
greater importance than the individuals congregated in the society and which demands a recognition of such primacy from the
members of the state. The *form* of the state is decided by the
state, by the organs of authority and law; *by* has replaced *for.*

III

Civil society, as a concept employed by materialist philosophers
to describe human beings in community, embodies a view of
human nature as nonethical rather than simply *unethical.* This
intermediate condition of a political community expresses *only*
essential, 'simple' human nature, usually without rational capacity
and certainly lacking moral principle. Civil societies may be either
good or bad, just or unjust, but only because they demonstrate the
moral qualities of human nature or have a moral influence upon
human beings. Plenty of ethics there, one may conclude—but *not*
an ethical view of society, only of human nature. And the view
that requires this intermediate stage of civil society is one which
recognizes, then elevates to a principle of behavior, an essentially
nonethical 'character' to human nature. Left to themselves, so the
argument runs, people will behave egoistically, selfishly, aggres-
sively, without moral or rational principle—unenlightened self-
interest, as it were. This is the condition of civil society, one which
requires an educative, instructive, 'improving' form of political
society to direct and order it. Political society, conversely, is concerned essentially and consistently with the *ethical society,* with
that form of society and system of law which will best recognize
and preserve the equivalence of the members of the community
while protecting society's members from any 'flaws' and 'villainies' of which human nature may be capable. Rights and liberties,
yes—more significantly, the admission of equality and the em-

ployment of a model of what has been called the "original position" (not a historical fact, simply a universal measurement that
is ahistorical), an origin theory of society that assumes consent
and the ambition of mutual benefit as the bases of society. Ideas
of political society (as opposed to theories of the state) *do* assume
the moral nature of the individual and the capacity of the individual to exist within the community in a nonexploitative manner—
enlightened self-interest, at worst, some form of altruistic principle at work in most individuals at most times, at best. Being so,
the form of political society is predicated as the means of best
preserving individuality, rights, and liberties, the 'freedom' of
pluralistic, *different* human personalities. No judgment has been
made on a general principle regarding human beings except that
they are all—and each—existants, equally 'real'. The ethic of a
genuine political society which is not, nor will become, a state is
no more than this, and it is by this ethic that all political societies
must be judged.

The distinction between materialism's view of civil society and
empiricism's assumption that all societies are political societies
and are—or must become—just societies can be remarked most
clearly in any comparison of Hobbes and Locke. In *Leviathan* and
the *Two Treatises*, a vision of the state confronts an ideal of
political society as surely as materialism confronts empiricism;
history confronts ahistory, too, for it is the contradiction of both
Locke's empiricism and natural law theory that while each posits
an original of society (and Locke even employs examples of primitive and 'pre-' societies from the Americas of his own day), they
do not contain, or need to contain, a Genesis theory of society.
The ethically just society that it supposes is ahistorical. Materialism, in Hobbes at least, does suppose, and requires the support
of, an origin theory of society's evolution from primitive beginnings at some point in history (even as Hobbes claims that social
man has always existed and cannot be conceived as an individual
human nature outside or preceding society. It is these contradictions within the theories of both Locke and Hobbes that require

elucidation, depending as they do on what both philosophers determine as "the state of Nature."

The state of nature, or "man in the naturall state" (as Hobbes often phrases it), is indissolubly a part of natural law theory as promulgated by the Stoics and Cicero and therefore as inherited by Locke. It imagines rather than describes a human situation that is not social but individual, but it does so not in order to describe some period of prehistory, even less to consider society in its primeval beginnings (expressly in order to examine its later development or evolution), but rather to provide the theory with an antithesis and a model. In other words, to Locke, the state of nature, man unconfined by and lacking membership in a society, is both *present* and continuing, just as is his political society. The state of nature is a convenient fiction (or wilderness parallel, in Locke's American references) which allows consideration of man with and without government, with and without a system of law that allows the *justice* and liberties of isolated existence, the rights of the individual, to continue to exist within society. Locke's use of the state of nature model is at its most evident in his conscientious attempt to refute the Genesis theory of paternalism and inherited authority, to which he opposes continuing *consent.* The state of nature is an ideal condition, not a historical circumstance. For Hobbes, in contrast, the natural state in which human nature finds itself is that brutish, uncivilized, *anti*social existence we might suppose it to be—a condition that the individual prolongs and promulgates by his behavior in *civil* society. Whereas Locke's model or ideal is *non*social, Hobbes's "naturall state" is that of the "unrestrained ego" of Marx and Hegel, without, in Hobbes's case, the restraints, impositions, and suppressions of absolute authority. It is the "warre of all against all" which Hobbes evokes so frequently and with the most profound vivacity and power in *Leviathan.* The "state of Nature" in Locke is one of complete, though not "perfect," freedom, because it is an isolated personhood that the individual outside a social conglomeration experiences. Nevertheless, the primary predication of any society is that it preserve, as far as is possible, that personhood and its liberties.

For Hobbes, too, of course, the state of nature is contemporary, rather than merely historical, though there is a crucially important sense in which Hobbes employs the idea to represent some period *before* rather than a condition *without* society. Hobbes envisages both a historical and a morally judged *antecedent* to society, in which there is a continuity of unrestrained egos from the stage of pre-society into that invented category, *civil* society—a mere multiplicity of egos. Both conditions are, as regards human beings, not so much premoral as immoral, and therefore a third stage or period of evolution within society is required to achieve anything recognizable as a just or valid *political* society, the stage that takes us to the "commonwealth," in Hobbes's term, and to "Leviathan"—and that stage is the imposition of restraint upon the unrestrained egos that constitute civil society. Some authoritative (and authoritarian) suppression is regarded by Hobbes as the only effective and *material* (a superior force acting upon other forces or bodies) moral or ethical 'government' of the behavior of individual, exploitative egos.

Locke, however, does assume a similar continuity in one sense between 'non-society' and "political society," as concerns human nature. Nevertheless, he assumes *society* to be a new and different entity, a new condition which requires government, not *of* human nature but *for* human beings. That is, he assumes the requirement for an ideal original or model of society where, unless *all* historical societies and all contemporary societies are or were always exploitative at best or slave societies at worst (which plainly they were and are not) some *agreement* was and is achieved whereby individual human beings are recognized, and, together with that recognition, there is a continuation of their convenient and efficient association. For Locke, it is at this point that society becomes ethical, or *just*. Society must recognize *equality* or equivalence of its members, otherwise its members would refuse to join or to remain. (The idea of departing from existing society to found or belong to a new society is an often-evoked symbol in the *Two Treatises*—easily comprehended if we recollect the Puritan exodus even before the Civil War and the nature of the founding of that "City on a Shining Hill" that became New England.)

Indeed, Locke's view is founded upon an ethical necessity in human association, the alternative to which is anarchy, while Hobbes's view is based upon an immoral reality (which *is* anarchic) and which requires the imposed restraints of authority which alone serve as 'morality'.

Locke's purpose, and therefore method, in the *Two Treatises* is to make contemporary natural law theory—the idea of a just and equal society of members who belong by *consent* or *contract*—the basis of any discussion of social man and his institutions, while Hobbes's method and apprehension begin from nothing more or less than human desire. Not that this is the antecedent of utilitarianism, as is sometimes claimed. Hobbes does not assume that people desire the *good*—in fact, he assumes no spark of altruism in human nature. Any good that is desired is not only selfish but self-aggrandizing, self-fulfilling. The "good of the greatest number" never enters the calculations of his human beings, except in a single and overwhelming desire for *peace.* In that goal, that good of the whole, Hobbes is a utilitarian, though not necessarily one that Bentham would have acknowledged. Peace (order) becomes a reluctant admission, a cease-fire in that endless "warre of all against all" that is the condition of human society. Hobbes's thesis is nothing less than the abrogation of human desire rather than its mitigation for the utilitarian good of the whole. It is a matter of protection from *like* egoistic and aggressive natures which have no recognition of any ethical principle of the 'right' or the 'good' that is extra-personal. Every act is based upon a calculation of self-advantage, and peace becomes the restraint of a sovereign power upon individual human wills and their desires.

In that sense, as far as Hobbes is concerned, one may conclude that there is no such extrasocial ethical sense in human beings, no "state of Nature" as Locke envisages. The "naturall state" is utterly and entirely nonethical. Thus, human beings are unable, in Hobbes, to achieve a sense of the necessarily ethical society either from the standpoint of the "original" or from apprehension of contemporary political society. They can only desire "peace" as the sole good because of, literally, the insecurity and even terror of their social condition. There is no model for them, only a forceful contradiction of the reality they experience. A system of law in any way equivalent to the ideals of natural law theory can only be imposed. Law is the product of rule, not the necessary outcome of cohabitation or community.

It may be objected, of course, that Locke uses the state of nature as a metaphor of human moral agency but makes it occupy the position of a theory of the origins of society. Yet to do so is to automatically pose an opposite, that is, if the state of nature (man's nonsocial existence) is nothing more than a metaphor to represent an ethical measurement of society, then why are not *all* societies in a permanent and aggressive anarchy? If the model of the "original" is that of Hobbes's civil society, then such a condition would surely be valid throughout history and the world. Civil society may be regarded as far more a metaphor than the image of a society originating in consent and contract. Locke's model and his adherence to natural law theory seems, on balance, both a more realistic explanation of the possible "original" of society and a description of how society actually functions, however imperfectly, than does Hobbes's incessant, internecine warfare.

Hobbes's, however, has always been the more persuasive and even seductive argument. It may be regarded as 'scientific', and it is essentialist and complete. It has a further appeal to self-esteem and indeed a symmetry of appeal to that emotion in providing both an excuse for and explanation of amoral, immoral, 'antisocial' behavior. It is overridingly secular, even antitheological (or may easily be taken to be so), and it is therefore more favorably placed than natural law theory to survive in a secular age, since the Stoic tradition, as has been remarked, became almost entirely absorbed into Christian conceptions of society. Finally, Hobbes's theory recognizes, always and everywhere, forces greater than the individual, thereby disqualifying those difficulties all individual egos experience in admitting the rights and equivalence of other individuals. They are satisfactorily explained by Hobbes as more aggressive egos than we are.

Hobbes, unlike Locke and Kant, elevates the state as the moral archetype, beyond the individual, who is not regarded as a moral agent. Rationality, detachment, an ethical sense, lie outside the individual, embodied in Hobbes's "sovereign Power," in kingship of an autocratic stamp.

> "Upon the King! Let us our lives, our souls,
> Our debts, our careful wives,
> Our children and our sins, lay on the King!"
> HENRY V, ACT 4, SCENE 1

Shakespeare's fiction may indeed be lamenting his position as autocratic focus of his society, but Hobbes believes it both inevitable and *just*. The position of the autocratic "single Person" (and without "a parliament," as even Cromwell recognized was his lot as Protector) as the embodiment of law, authority, justice, and *all* moral sense and sensibility in human society is the extent of Hobbes's essentialist materialism. All moral responsibility and culpability is removed from the citizen, or "subject." They can only act upon desire, to satisfy their egos, and the state (as moral capacity, the 'reason' of this 'body') will provide the necessary constraints to ensure peace. This is, indeed, the continuing appeal of Hobbes to autocrats and to autocratic or *sovereign* parliaments, and the consequent weakness and archaism of John Locke—this transplanting of moral responsibility and agency from the individual to the state, which becomes both moral arbiter and moral progenitor. It is this distinction, the most profound, between Hobbes and Locke that requires any political society to understand them both.

IV

If the basis of any intelligible view of society beyond those of history, anthropology, sociology, et cetera, is, or must become, an ethical view (and even Locke and Hobbes would agree here), then one is still left with the great dichotomy of traditional ethics, the concept of the *good* society and the idea of the *just* society. The gravitational pull of the former has consistently been greater than that of the latter, especially since the eighteenth century. Also, within any conception of the good without, or in place of, the just there arises the idea of the *good of society* itself, the rendering of some kind of quasi sentience to the collectivity rather than to its divisible membership. Utilitarian and authoritarian views often seem to meet at this point. The good of the abstraction-made-real becomes primary, over the consequential good to be perceived in the actions of the society's government or system of law. There is an ethical sleight of hand which presumes that the abstraction-made-real, the society itself, can be spoken of as both the ethical subject and ethical object, cleverly pocketing the notion of divisible membership as unwanted or as equatable with the whole discussed as an entity. Thus, while Marx and Hegel are both collectivists who obey the above, they also assume the "greatest happiness principle" of classical utilitarianism or assume that they are positing such a position.

Hegel, it is true, accepts a neo-Hobbesian view of civil society, while Marx may be regarded as utopian in his idea of human perfectibility, though in the determinism with which he interprets political economy he owes a great deal to the Hobbesian tradition. Hobbes's view of the unrestrained and aggressive ego, the exploitative individual, becomes explicable in terms of the economic system pertaining to modern society rather than to an essential view of human *nature*. However, the exploitative 'fact' of human nature, whatever forces are responsible beyond the essential quality of that human nature, is as significant for Marx as it is for Hobbes.

As with Hobbes, too, in Marx and Hegel (as with Durkheim and Weber) it is easy to perceive the elevation of an imposed principle or authority which will supply a *good* in social terms. In Hegel, it is the concept of the rational state, in Marx the disappearance of the state itself and, more importantly, the disappearance of alienation as a fact of the human condition. Human society must be elevated beyond the condition of civil society. There is no conception of society's existence of itself demanding government and, above all, law. Those necessities of a functioning, let alone a good or just, society must be elucidated and then imposed, or evolve in history.

Civil society, therefore, can be neither *just* nor *good*. A different society must evolve or be imposed to replace it, to make it ethical. This is, perhaps, Hobbes's most profound legacy to social and political theory, and by light of which Hobbes may be regarded as the greatest and most influential Platonist since Plato. His, after all, is the perception of society, and of human behavior within society, that has remained predominant in European theory for the last two centuries. It is with the invention of the nonethical intermediate stage of civil society that Hobbes develops a means of regarding the function of the state as a moral function—indeed, the sole moral agent in human society. Impositional or sovereign ethics is an essential assumption of modern social and political thought, and it is to Hobbes that we must look for its most powerful and influential statement. Ethical decisions and activity of which individuals are incapable must be reached for the 'good' of civil society. And they must be imposed upon a society of recalcitrant egos, thereby presupposing the necessity for sovereign, monarchical, autocratic authority. A 'fiction' (certainly an inconclusive proof) finds its way to the essence of social theory—the fiction of civil society as an indisputable 'fact' and principle.

BACK TO THE FUTURE: JOHN LOCKE'S *TWO TREATISES OF GOVERNMENT*

IN ALMOST EVERY DISCUSSION of authority, as in similar disputations concerning individuality and collectivism, one consideration would seem to be absent, and that is the vexed problem that John Locke designated (as did Hobbes) as *sovereignty.* The current and currently received wisdoms regarding that often-pejorative term are "national sovereignty" and the "sovereignty of parliament." To Locke, one is led to suggest, both phrases would possess sinister undertones or a conjunction of opposites that he might regard as erroneous. For both Hobbes and Locke, the question of sovereignty focused upon, in one sense, monarchy and absolutism of varying degrees and, in another sense, upon the 'fiction' of the sovereignty of the members of a community or political society, a fiction which even Hobbes found himself having to accommodate in his idea of *covenant,* the once-for-all transfer by agreement of sovereignty from the people to their "sovereign power."

Locke's solution to the crisis of sovereignty both in the political storms of the 1680s and in the theory of his time is the notion of *consent,* which is certainly not original but which he employs and develops with a peculiarly radical emphasis. The idea permeates the *Second Treatise,* and, in short, to understand its employment is largely to understand Locke. It is one of the turns of time and the tricks of fame that Locke has been absorbed into the defensive genetics of the Whig oligarchy that ruled England from the Glorious Revolution almost without interruption for a century. Locke has become, especially since the popularization of Marx's theories, characterized as the great proponent of the status quo and the defender of the rights of private property. (The orthodox Marxist view may be discovered, almost laughably, in George Novack's *Empiricism and Its Evolution,* one of the most woeful documents masquerading as a history of political theory to have been produced since the war.) Whatever spirited or even halfhearted defenses have been made for him, Locke has become perceived as the father of a tradition of rule by oligarchical means, as a defender of the power, authority, and even sovereignty that is derived from private property, just as Hobbes, almost as lamentably, has become perceived as the proponent of bourgeois capitalism in its seventeenth century, generic form, an equally preposterous characterization. It is, therefore, necessary to rescue Locke and to perceive him, as his opponents would have done with remarkable clarity, as a radical and original political theorist *as well as* England's, and perhaps Europe's, last great proponent of natural law *(rights)* theory.

To be radical and traditional implies no small legerdemain of mind—to be merely radical implies a novelty, an originality of mind that breaks with tradition. Locke did, indeed, break with most tradition, and if there is to be a traditional element to his thought, it is not discovered solely in his defense of natural law theory (one perhaps should employ the term 'use' here, for it is his reinvigoration of and rendering once again 'useful' that tradition that distinguishes Locke). Rather, he has an immediate as well as a historical tradition which he quite consciously inherits and expresses, and that immediate tradition is derived from the

1640s and 1650s and from the Levelers, that most radical wing (with the small, esoteric exception of Winstanley and the Diggers, or "True Levelers," those arcadian communists doomed even more surely than the Levelers under the Commonwealth and the ensuing Protectorate) of the Puritan opposition to Charles I and, even more intriguingly and importantly, to Parliament. There is a perspective of perhaps a millennium and a half in which to see Locke clearly, but there is a finer focus, that of the forty years since the heyday of the Leveler cause at the Army Debates of Putney and Whitehall; both of these may be employed as quizzing-glasses of more true perspective and greater magnification than the period which succeeded Locke and the Revolution of 1688.

It is the Leveler cause with which we must first deal in this essay, without a lengthy consideration of the factions of the Puritan cause, the origins of the "Great Rebellion," or the tawdry triumph of Charles Stuart's Restoration of 1660, for it is in the writings and speeches of Lilburne, Wildman, Overton, Rainborough, et cetera, that distinctions between church and state, privacy and 'sovereignty' of conscience, equality of representation, and the enlargement of suffrage (albeit only male, though Leveler support among women was remarkably strong and unique in seventeenth-century politics) are most vigorously voiced and perhaps originally codified and made into more than mere theory, into a program of political development—a *settlement* of the crisis of the nation after the struggle for sovereignty that constituted the Civil War between Charles Stuart and his ungrateful and obstreperous Parliament. It is, indeed, from the Levelers, as well as from his conscious opposition to Hobbes and his extended refutation of Filmer's *Patriarcha*, rather than from Hooker or even the Republican Harrington—or, for that matter, from the Presbyterian or Independent factions of the Puritan 'party'—that Locke derives his basic constitutional position. It is the Levelers, in terms of a direct political program for a settlement of the constitution rather than in some allegorical presentation of republicanism or democracy, who most directly and fundamentally challenge the whole basis of royal authority—of sovereignty, whether of persons or institutions. The humanist utopianism that descends from Erasmus and More directly to Harrington's *Commonwealth of Oceania* (1656) was couched almost exclusively in allegory, if it opposed the status quo or questioned royal authority, a testimony to censorship and the dangers of such treasonable activity. Harrington was arrested on a trumped-up charge of treason and died, mad, in prison, after the Restoration of the vindictive Charles II. The problem with allegory is that it is deliberately indirect and literary, and it *remains* allegory. The circumstance that required *direct* and radical political statement was, of course, the Civil War (though censorship and arrest on the basis of opinion did not disappear during the war and certainly regained its rude vigor after the execution of Charles I—John Lilburne, the Leveler leader, being arrested and imprisoned for his opinions on numerous occasions). Radicalism no longer required the anonymity (which even Locke sought) or the envelope of allegory. The masks were, bravely and briefly, removed. The Levelers began to deal in certainties, in political facts—and the principal fact which they promulgated was the division between authority and sovereignty, itself a concept all but unique *outside* the realms of dissenting allegory or utopianism.

The concept of what may be termed *derivative sovereignty,* or authority without a transfer or resignation of sovereignty by the people to their representatives in authority over them, was the single great *radical* idea of the seventeenth century. Even Republicans such as Harrington and Milton assumed, after the establishment of a republican constitution, the separateness or 'otherness' of authority (i.e., they continued to identify sovereignty with the authority and its institutions), consequent upon which is some kind of analogous model of the status quo, a devolving or *granting* of rights and liberties by the sovereign power, whoever or whatever it may be. This is opposed by the Levelers and is the basis of Locke's theory of government, that rights *originate* with the individual-in-community and that the function of authority (by representation) which has been consented to as having authority

to make and enforce law and perform other functions of government is simply and entirely to protect the rights and liberties—
the *sovereignty*—of the members of the political society who have
elected the legislature.

The Levelers may never have elevated this central and original
idea to the philosophical level, since their principal intent was the
individuality of the religious conscience, and the fundamental
liberty that must be protected was liberty of conscience (and
worship). Locke, however, with his minimalist Christian outlook
as regards the nature of political society—regarding it as an almost
entirely *secular* artifact or construct—left such freedom entirely
in the private province and expanded the principle it implied to
the public sphere. Thus, during the turmoil of the 1640s, the
Levelers assumed that any settlement after the conflict would
require a fundamental reassignment of sovereignty, a redefinition
and reassignment that Cromwell flouted, metaphorically and actually preparing the route via which Charles would return in 1660.
What they opposed was not merely the divine right of kings but
the whole basis of the conception that rights are authority-granted
or -derived, together with the notion of monarchical sovereignty
itself. Their dissenting, religious radicalism called into question
any such sovereignty beyond that of God himself, unless it lay in
that vessel of communion with the Almighty, the individual conscience or soul. Such a vessel of grace and 'election' was, subordinate to the sovereignty of God, sovereign itself. From this narrow
base, Locke expands the *secular* implications of such a sovereignty
of the individual. What for Hooker, who may be regarded as
much more radical than traditional, was an "ecclesiastical polity"
became for Locke a secular polity, a political society. Such a
secularization of the state or "commonwealth" does not,
strangely, occur in Hobbes, since it is at least an element of his
task to mythologize the nature of authority and to defend the
divinity of kingly power. The concept of a secular polity, of
course, is radical by its very nature, since it demythologizes the
institutions and persons of the polity, extending the notion of
dissenting, radical Puritanism to the entire political sphere in the

concepts of equivalence and, especially, *consent*. The recognition of only one supreme or divine authority, God, which was so central to all Puritan opposition to Charles I, becomes in Locke the retention of sovereignty by the consenting members of the community when they appoint their representatives and grant them their authority. The radicalism of Locke's ideas cannot be in doubt when one recalls the terrors of republicanism and democracy among the propertied interests in the months before the settlement of 1688—not only among Tories, though they did their best to blame "Whiggery" for encouraging such ideas. James II might have to go, but a new *sovereign* must appear at once (or, in this single case, two monarchical sovereigns, William and Mary, James's daughter). It is not surprising, and certainly excusable, that Locke chose anonymity for the authorship of the *Two Treatises* in 1690.

Hobbes employed the traditional notion of *contract,* making of it a quasi-religious *covenant* in *Leviathan,* whereby the people transfer, completely and forever, their sovereignty to the single person. Contract, as between king and subjects and for which Locke substitutes the idea of *consent* quite deliberately, is of the essence a tradition of agreement *by* the monarch with his subjects, rather than the *appointment* of an authority. The arguments of 1688–89 attempted to define, and thereby limit, the sovereignty of William and Mary, but the weight of traditional monarchical authority hampered any radical approach. The power of tradition is the power that, as we shall see, invests Hobbes's cunning employment of the human model as analogy for the state, the monarch or "soveraign Power" representing what, again traditionally, had been represented as 'sovereign' reason, governing the emotions and desires. Even a Puritan would have difficulty in refuting the argument other than as a false analogy.

As to Locke's tradition, while inheriting that of Hooker, whom he praises, and Harrington, he expands Hooker's "ecclesiastical polity" into a secular polity that is radical in its institutions and bases, demythologizing the entire political sphere; there is no agreement between the parties of subject and monarch that *allows* rather than protects liberties and rights, nor is there any sense of *granting down* such rights. For Locke, there is the authority of the law rather than of persons or institutions. The sovereignty of such institutions as are required—legislature and executive—is granted by the subjects, but only as authority which may, in extremis, be challenged and removed. The purpose of this granted authority is the functioning and order of political society *without* the loss of sovereignty by the members of the community.

The granting of authority to persons, assemblies, and institutions is therefore no more than a necessity of political society and is consented to for that reason alone. Representation implies the personation of authority but not any transfer of it to those who rule. Locke may, or may not, have been a Puritan (his theological minimalism was summed up when he claimed that all that was required for salvation was a belief in Christ as the Messiah—which may be taken as a laissez-faire Anglicanism bordering on indifference or may be regarded as a Puritan statement, the essence of anticlericalism), but he certainly regarded Puritan–Leveler political principles as essential; that much at least may be said of his 'faith'.

Further evidence of his radical intent and bias may be seen in the minimal way in which he argues the nature of the executive power in the *Second Treatise*. There is the merest reference to "Princes" and to monarchy, and the abstract rather than particular level at which he argues may explain this slight; or, we may prefer to regard Locke's abstract theorizing as an effort to establish the *original pattern* and to avoid the contemporary and even the traditional, to begin anew with a vigorous definition in the most abstract terms, avoiding practical example and contemporary circumstance, of the secular and legislative nature of political society, to the deliberate exclusion of tradition (which would indicate, as in Hobbes, the primacy and even inevitability of monarchical government). The whole of the *Second Treatise* may, therefore, be regarded as a definition and description of the *elemental pattern,* significantly one in which the monarchical executive power plays little or no part, especially not in terms of inheritance!—which leads one to wonder whether Locke's concern with the adoption of the "native constitution" by someone wishing to inherit (Chapter 8, "Of the Beginning of Political Societies") and coming from another country in order to do so, is not merely a tacit warning to William of Orange but also an indication that Locke would wish to imply a constitution which exists even in the absence of monarchy, after the flight of James II to France in 1688.

Hence, too, one suspects, the lack of particular detail regarding suffrage in Locke's theory. Suffrage allows us, in a democratic state where parliament is *sovereign,* to do little more than alter the composition of our sovereign institutions and not to affect them essentially, or especially to "dissolve" them.

In Locke there are no ancient or hierarchical institutions in the elemental pattern or original position, especially any which might be regarded as having derived from the *tribe,* as is the case with both Hobbes and Hegel. Rather, Locke's image of the settler or pioneer, available to him vividly in the seventeenth century, is one which antedates any conception of tribe or society. Hence, in large part, his emphasis in an early chapter of the *Second Treatise* upon the number of people in the world in some prehistoric time, which allowed a period of noncommunal existence to be supposed (though anthropological ideas of the communal life of primates might be suggested to 'predate' Locke's idea). As such, there is no inevitable and ever-extant notion of primitive society which has either developed, can be dignified or hallowed, or must of necessity be the best or even the only solution to community. His purest Puritanism appears in this concept of the pioneer, because it is intimately linked to the idea of men being able to turn their backs upon society if it is not to their taste (as the Puritan settlers of New England indeed did). Locke regards the possibility of removing oneself from a society from which one dissents as real, but he also regards it as an abstract principle which opposes any *inevitable form of political society.* Withdrawal or cancellation of membership is the obverse of consenting to belong, which consent retains the power to shape, and to accept or dissent from, political society. Otherwise, without such retention of sovereignty, men either would not join or would vote with their feet and leave. Locke's state of nature, whatever recent scholarship may argue, may not signify an atomistic notion of human beings. Such an idea more correctly is to be discovered in Hobbes, but it *does* presume a noncommunal condition that antedates society, in which situation rational men, in consenting to belong to society, perceive and agree that society requires *law* in order to function justly and successfully. His "state of Nature" may conveniently be regarded, at the outset, as an *aspiration,* a condition of which man in community should, and must, have some clear notion, rather than as a historical phenomenon.

Locke's theory is far more closely concerned with consent than it is with the exact nature of the rights and liberties to be protected and upheld by a political society and its legislature. Rights, for Locke, may not be granted or imposed from above, thereby becoming the *duties* of citizenship as envisaged by a sovereign power. Citizenship, that right of membership so basic to the Roman, Ciceronian version of natural law theory, is not the central thrust of Locke's theory, as it is of the arguments of many modern liberal thinkers. The greatest weight and force is reserved to the idea of consent, from which basis *alone* political society must develop.

Because of his connection with Shaftesbury and the lukewarm and opportunistic adoption of his theories by Whigs rather than by the more monarchical Tories in the early eighteenth century, Locke has been deprived of his radical laurels. Indeed, he has been characterized (together with his great antagonist, Hobbes) as the archetypal bourgeois-capitalist apologist, which fact should convince any reader of Locke how conventional and misguided conventional wisdom really is—or perhaps may convince them that successive political historians, especially those of this century, have regarded only one or other of the forms of collectivism as truly radical. As such, any claim to such a title is impossible on behalf of Locke, since he is the greatest proponent of equivalence and the equal sovereignty of individual persons since the Stoics and Cicero and before Kant.

II

Unless we regard Locke as that unique and implausible creature, the self-creator and originator of *all* his ideas and notions, then we ought to seek to understand what he might have inherited and what he valued (and built upon) of that inheritance. Rather than a doctrine or a coherent theory of political society, there is a single, powerless, suppressed, and discredited body of opinion, ideas, and principles that qualifies as a 'tradition' which Locke inherited, within the overarching tradition of natural law theory itself (which had become but half-rescued from the sphere of theology by the humanists of the sixteenth and seventeenth centuries)—and that contains the various expressions of moral and political principle espoused by the Levelers during the turbulent 1640s. Apart, as has been mentioned, from the much smaller and less significant movement that termed itself the "True Levelers"—Winstanley's pacific, helpless, proto-communists—the Levelers formed the radical wing of the Puritan cause immediately prior to, and during, the rebellion against the personal government of Charles Stuart. The Diggers, and Winstanley, were cast aside from the political debate. Indeed, they hardly deigned to enter into the debate at all, preferring to express their principles by cultivating enclosed common land, which they regarded as belonging to the people, and rejecting much, if not all, of the theory that banged about their ears, as the opposition to their subversive attack on private property was to bring the military about those same ears before very long. But the Levelers only slowly became suppressed and disregarded; eventually, John Lilburne, their great moving spirit, became a Quaker. After Cromwell's assumption of the title of Lord Protector (that great "single

Person and Parliament" shift rightward from the 1640s that paved the way for the return of Charles II with some sort of palm fronds), the imprisonment of the leaders (Rainborough's death is still suspicious even after the intervening centuries), most notably Lilburne, who continually escaped unrighteous punishment at his various trials by the eloquence of his appeals to radical popular sentiment, and the stifling of each and every Leveler hope and expectation, the decline of the movement's popularity and power was inevitable. If Locke did revive Leveler radicalism in his *Second Treatise* (and it is my firm belief that he did in his opposition to Hobbes), then he was virtually alone among the welter of opinions and shades of political color in 1688–90. The continuity of the sovereign-in-parliament was the concern equally of Whigs and Tories during the Exclusion Crisis and the Glorious Revolution. The Protectorate and the Restoration had effectively quashed both republican sentiment and radical democracy. Historians who recognize that that Glorious Revolution was, to a marked degree, a compromise with the Restoration are but half right when they acknowledge that the chance for reform offered in 1688 did not come again until 1832 and that Britain remained paralyzed by the Restoration Settlement for almost two hundred years. It was the Protectorate which initiated the return to a monarchical executive, to the principle of hereditary executive power and the manifest subordination of democracy to existing and traditional institutions of authority. Cromwell stifled radicalism in Britain, to the extent that the Convention of 1689 merely imitated his respect for oligarchical power, until the case was such that our political society required the severe instruction of thirteen colonies in revolt three thousand miles away and a declaration of independence to rediscover its radical possibilities.

The essence of Leveler principles is the sovereignty of the individual person as moral agent (i.e., a question of identity rather than of identification, whether political, monarchical, national, or racial). The Levelers professed no loyalty to nor identification with the institutions of church or state, as expressed in the *person* of the king. Indeed, they are diametrically opposed to the 'personation' of the state and the hierarchical structure and spiritual beneficence of the established church. Hobbes's ideas of authorship and personation are descriptions of identity, as is Hegel's description of the rational State. *Real* identity arises from identification with the state, an identity that is superior to (or more ethical and meaningful than) that of *personal* identity. For the Levelers, however, there was no basis of support for the institutions of either church or state, and therefore no sense of identification with them or derivation of identity from them. There was, in short (and this is their essential radicalism), no *respect for their authority*, and therefore no attempt to compromise with them or to ameliorate them. Instead, there must be a new beginning, new *forms* of the commonwealth, and a complete freedom of conscience and worship. The question of identity is presupposed, residing in the Puritan view of the personal relationship of the individual with his God, even in that sense of *election* and elective grace that Puritanism also assumed. There is also behind the Levelers an adherence to that quasi-pessimistic view of the sublunary sphere as inevitably imperfect, probably corrupt, and certainly fallen, which does not lead, in the Levelers, to a rejection of the world at large, nor does it lead to Weberian ideas of the "Protestant ethic" of gathering up this world's riches and engaging in the new capitalism, but instead seeks to reduce the authority of secular institutions and to establish a minimal state in which there exists maximum personal freedom (as is concomitant with the protection of fallen man from his fallen fellows—but more, protection from his *fallen institutions*). The Levelers presuppose a just political society which is both necessary and as far as possible imitative of the condition of grace in which a personal relationship with God places the individual. Since political society is not concerned with questions of identity, or identification, the condition of the state derives from its members, not from its institutions; therefore, those institutions must *reflect* the freedoms and liberties of its members and be designed for the purposes of protecting and guaranteeing them, not *granting* them. This is the assumption that lies behind the Glorious Revolution (i.e., that we must have a monarch but he must guarantee certain rights and liberties). It is the 'must have' as regards the monarchy that is the measure of the decline into traditionalism between the 1640s and 1688—or, perhaps, the measure of the power of conservatism and the triumph of that strain of theory in the 1650s.

While the Presbyterians (powerful in the city of London) and the Independents (from which faction—the most powerful among the Puritan groupings—sprang Cromwell) during the 1640s favored the sovereignty of Parliament (sometimes the army) as opposed to that of the king, albeit in a rudimentary form, the Levelers opposed the sovereignty of both king and Parliament. On the other hand, they did not identify themselves with the kind of theocracy instituted by Calvin in Geneva. Theirs, as they envisaged it, was a secular state and a minimal one such as Locke describes in the *Second Treatise*. Separating church and state, they also separated identity and politics, assuming that political society was not a state in the Hobbesian sense (or even the Presbyterian, Independent, or parliamentary sense) but instead was a matter of *just law*, of a legislature which provided against the *instances of the unethical* that might arise in the relations of fallen individuals with one another in a social context—and to prevent the *intrusion of institutions* into the private sphere (which was paramount, the individual's relationship in terms of faith and moral activity with his God).

However archaic some of the preceding may seem, it is that challenge to the sovereignty of Parliament that is as radical as any other element of the Levelers' program. (If there is a political Heaven, then Lilburne, Rainborough, Overton, Wildman, and the others will be seated on the right hand of its god.) And just such a challenge is implicit in Locke's notions of the dissolution of the commonwealth, in extreme circumstances. Without the possibility of dissent, there is only the state; with that possibility, there cannot be a transfer of sovereignty. During the 1640s, and especially during the Army Debates at Putney and Whitehall and in various appearances before the House of Commons, the Levelers, for perhaps the first occasion in the history of this country,

presented from a position of *voice* if not authority the notion of
the sovereignty of the people and the doctrine of equivalence
between high, middle, and low, which ground no parochial axe.
The Levelers were, perhaps, just like Locke, attempting to reclaim
the irrenounceable, to subvert the constitution in any and every
sense that it had been and was currently understood. For that
alone, they should not be subjected to their unending obscurity—
nor should Locke be characterized as a propagandist for bourgeois
capitalism.

Locke's "state of Nature" and the Levelers' confidence in the
moral agency of the individual may both be regarded as attempts
to shrug off and replace the *tradition of society,* which of itself had
no moral or ethical connotations but which, *de facto,* bore the
most unbearably weighty freight of hierarchy and the suppositions of *rule* and *imposition.*

It is, of course, easy and pleasant to dramatize moments of
history—and the most sober historians are inclined to do so—but
it may well be legitimate to suggest that, for political society in
Britain, the 1640s presented a unique opportunity, a fulcrum
between democracy underived and unevolved and authority in
the latest of its various manifestations. It was also a moment
where the concept of the sovereignty of the individual and the
equivalence of individuals achieved articulate and determined
expression at an abstract level above the squabbling and prejudices of the moment. Further, and most importantly, it was the
last native opportunity for political theory to shrug off the weight
of *tradition* before a theory or theories of *history* became of
moment in all political thought, so that Burke could murmur of
tradition while Hegel philosophized upon history, and the British
lumbered slowly toward the reforms that were promulgated by the
Levelers and made into political philosophy by Locke. It is this,
above all, that unites Locke with the Levelers and which makes
them his inspiration, this attempt to break with tradition itself in
all its forms and to assume that political society can be born anew,
made afresh, by the light of ethical principle (as the Founding
Fathers in that rebellion across the Atlantic assumed and, with

more terrible consequences, as did the participants in the Tennis Court Oath a century after our Glorious Revolution).

All the above being so—and taken at the writer's word for the moment—what, precisely, did the Levelers have to say for themselves and their principles at the Army Debates and in the countless pamphlets and other publications that so littered the period? Because, while the republican John Milton was subsuming his political ideas in what might be termed the *matter of man*, the Levelers were concerned with the *matter of Britain*, without a single reference to characters either Biblical or mythological. Therefore, it might be best to begin with one of Lilburne's more controversial titles, *The Freeman's Freedom Vindicated* of 1646, where, after acknowledging "God, the absolute sovereign Lord and King of all things in heaven and earth," he speaks of "individual man and woman" as always having been and remaining "equal and alike in power, dignity, authority and majesty, none of them by nature having any authority, dominion, or magisterial power one over or above another; neither have they, or can they exercise any, but merely by institution or donation, that is to say, by mutual agreement or consent and agreement, for the good benefit or comfort of each other . . ." The naked power of such an assertion has long since departed, and the novelty has long since been suppressed by cliché. However, it is certainly instructive to recapture the sense and time in which such a notion was uttered—1646. In the midst of the civil strife that may be variously termed a revolution, a rebellion, or a war, John Lilburne, one of the nation's greatest unsung heroes, was able to speak authoritatively and calmly concerning political principle. And this quotation aptly begins any examination of their cause—their cry in the wilderness, even in 1646, before their defeat by Ireton and Cromwell in the debates at Putney and Whitehall (which to remark in Cromwell's favor were perhaps the only two moments in history when an army putsch has paused to debate the nature of the ensuing constitution).

In Lilburne's observation, "nature" is assumed to be a state of equality (which Locke also assumes it to be); that is, the natural state of man is not necessarily a noncommunal condition but is instead, and more importantly, a condition in which no individual is advantaged by property, position, inheritance, wealth, or title. Lilburne's men and women, the individual human beings in any political society, stripped of anything that does not necessarily adhere to their human condition, are all equal. Lilburne continues that it is ". . . unnatural, irrational, sinful, wicked, unjust, devilish and tyrannical . . . for any man to appropriate and assume unto himself a power, authority and jurisdiction, to rule, govern or reign over any sort of men in the world *without their free consent* . . ." (my italics). One ought, perhaps, to conclude the discussion at this point, since Lilburne's own statement seems an adequate proof of the Levelers' concern to establish and ensure a *new* constitution in England. However, one pamphlet never made a summer, though it may make a generous beginning to the season, short as it was for the Levelers.

Therefore, from what was termed the *Large Petition of the Levelers to Parliament,* which was presented to the sole sitting house in 1647, one may begin the supplementary evidence with the claim that ". . . we still find the nation oppressed with grievances of the same destructive nature as formerly . . . and which are so much the more grievous unto us because they are inflicted in the very time of this present Parliament, under God the hope of the oppressed." Thus begins the *Large Petition,* an extreme (as it was regarded at the time) document presented before the institution representing the opposition to Charles I. And it condemned the Levelers to the role of subversives, simply because they were *petitioners* before a legislature which they envisaged as authorized to guarantee their rights and liberties, and no more. The Levelers found themselves confronted with that 'modern' and 'traditional' phenomenon, the *sovereignty* of Parliament. As the Levelers point out: "And though it is not now to be made a crime to mention a Parliament, yet it is little less to mention the supreme power of this honourable House." Conditions in March 1647 were such that the Levelers were still capable of promulgating, indeed pleading for, a new sovereignty, that of

Parliament, as opposed to that of the king and the court. However, there is a profound irony in the statement, since the sources of complaint—tithes, summary imprisonment, torture and corporal punishment, the exactions and impositions of the Merchant Adventurers, et cetera—still exist, as they claim, "in the very time of this present Parliament." In other words, Lilburne and the other Leveler leaders were already having to come to terms with a shift to sectional-interest sovereignty rather than a radical reform of the constitution and the circumstances of ordinary men and women. The Levelers are remarking that Parliament possesses sovereignty (either the struggle was about that or it availed nothing, or in default of Charles's authority they must be the surviving branch of the sovereign tree), yet does not exercise it for the *reforms* for which the struggle was waged. The status quo of sectionally oppressive powers appears *strengthened* by the absence of the monarch. Thus, ". . . in all these respects this nation remains in a very sad and disconsolate condition, and the more because it is thus with us after so long a session of so powerful and so free a Parliament . . ." The most telling accusation comes at the conclusion of the same paragraph in the *Large Petition,* as: ". . . the end of your trust was freedom and deliverance from all kind of grievances and oppressions." In other words, the Levelers are claiming that a "trust" was granted to Parliament, not a rigid and irrevocable sovereignty. Indeed, in their attitude, changing as it was, toward Parliament (the House of Commons, to be exact) may be seen the expression of challenge to the idea of sovereignty residing in Parliament. Though the *Petition* claims that Parliament possesses such, it is evidently a secondary and questionable sovereignty, requiring the granting to it of the "trust" of the people.

In a ringing conclusion to the first of their detailed demands of Parliament, the Levelers state that the object of the House they are addressing may be summarized as securing a "settled peace and true freedom, which is the end of the primitive institution of all government." We shall find that phrase almost exactly echoed, time and again, in Locke. Its significance lies in judgment of the conscious object and limitations of all government by means of the "original position"; lies, too, in the fact that the document is couched as a petition to Parliament (a court of law, and thus subject to petition). There is a sense of constitutional disillusion which assumed that the representatives of the people had broken or delayed their trust, granted by the people, and that to forcibly remind them of their laxity and indifference was the method of proceeding concomitant with a political society.

The whole tone of the *Large Petition* expresses that confluence of law and freedom which may be denoted as justice. The detailed wrongs against which the Levelers are petitioning concern wrongful or arbitrary imprisonment, freedom of conscience and worship, reform of the law as regarded compulsion in religious matters, the "insolence of office and the law's delay," arbitrary employment of capital punishment, tithes, imprisonment for debt, concern for the poor, et cetera. As such, the petition amounts to the expression of a program—that it was not is the clearest indication of the minority in which the Levelers discovered themselves. However, the petition does establish what can only be termed a Lockian view of the nature and business of government, as well as Lockian limitations upon its prerogative and, most importantly, its sovereignty. It is hardly necessary to remark the radical nature of much that is contained in the *Petition*—rather, it is more important to recognize the qualifications it places upon the power of Parliament, which seemed to the Levelers to have slipped into the king's chair while it was still warm.

Richard Overton's *Appeal from the Commons to the Free People*, also of 1647, elevates the principles implicit in the *Large Petition* to a level of abstraction where it is more recognizably consistent with Locke's own signature, when he claims that *"reason hath no precedent; for reason is the fountain of all just precedents."* It is here that the Levelers coincide, in the instance of their most philosophic voice, with the tradition of natural law theory, perhaps that other principal reason why Locke was attracted to their history and principles. Overton continues, sounding remarkably (and probably intentionally) like Cicero and the Stoics: ". . . neither morality nor divinity amongst men can or may transgress the limits of right reason. For whatsoever is unreasonable cannot be justly termed moral or divine, and right reason is only commensurable and discernible by the rule of merciful justice and just mercy."

Overton proceeds by examining the equivalence of human nature, regarding all differences as questions of *degree* rather than *kind* (i.e., superficial rather than fundamental), so that, in a telling analogy, "a dwarf is as much a man as a giant though not so big a man." Further, Overton promulgates the enshrining of his principles of rational justice in all "magistracy" and "government." Though this may be regarded as a theocratic foundation for government, because of Overton's appeal to the supremacy of the divine in all matters, it is, in fact, entirely secular in its functions and *operation.* There is no reference to the Bible, to any Biblical law or text in Overton's argument, simply the assumption that earthly government must be obedient to the *facts* of a divine creation (i.e., that all men are *created* equal, et cetera, and that the Almighty has a supreme investment in justice). The law, and its legislature, must therefore be "a sure and safe refuge to fly to, in all straits and extremities whatsoever." The law's function is "preservation, safety, removal of oppressions, et cetera." Overton deliberately conflates divine rule and the rule of secular law (and its making in a legislature), which is something Locke takes further, by employing the secularized identity of the law with little reference to its divine example. Overton proceeds to argue that— even if one may disregard the divine example—one may appeal to the "firm law and radical principle in nature" for evidence that the laws of political society must function in the manner he has described. Men are empowered by nature to deliver themselves from "all oppression, violence and cruelty," which is perhaps the primary sense in which natural law theory had come to be understood in the seventeenth century and one which Hobbes seizes upon to regard such principles as mere self-preservation. The very fact that natural law theory is couched in such a way implies that it is expressive of the 'nature' and the sense of justice of those who may be, or are in a position to be, oppressed and offered violence and cruelty. "To deny it is to overturn the law of nature," Overton claims.

He later suggests that "all betrusted powers, if forfeit, fall into the hands of the betrusters," and nowhere more clearly in the Levelers' preserved writings and speeches is the claim for the retained and immutable *sovereignty of the people* so clearly expressed. Once government has "degenerated from safety to tyranny," then "their authority ceaseth, and is only to be found in the fundamental original rise and situation thereof, which is the people." It will become unnecessary to emphasize the parallels once the reader encounters Chapter 19 of the *Second Treatise*— it is as if Locke were transcribing rather than creating his argument. Overton continues in this vein, expanding his argument for the retained sovereignty of the people and the trust that, once betrayed by arbitrariness and the absence of the rule of just law, returns to the people so that they may make a new contract with other representatives. He continues, in fact, with the most uncanny echoes of Locke, to claim that "by natural birth all men are equal, and alike born to like propriety and freedom," to talk, too, of "joint and common consent," and finally to describe his own *Appeal from the Commons* in the following manner: ". . . an appeal from them to the people is not anti-parliamentary, anti-magisterial; not *from* that sovereign power but *to* that sovereign power."

It is here, of course, that the various radical strands in what might be described as the Leveler 'program' become at one with the tradition of natural law theory, demythologizing it, and with those feared *democratic* tendencies in the radical elements of the Puritan cause during the 1640s. It is also where the tradition of natural law theory is revived and is handed on to Locke. Overton goes on to delineate the limits of parliamentary authority, expanding what has already been remarked, until he can consummate the argument with the pithy: "Even so may the commonalty of England reply to their Parliament-members, that they are made for the people, not the people for them." He further claims that all "degrees, orders or titles amongst men . . . are all subservient to popular safety," which is the overriding principle why men enter "human society." Again, as we shall see, this has an uncanny second life in Locke. Indeed, the whole tenor and the progress of Overton's *Appeal* parallels the *Second Treatise*'s method. Though it would be foolish to suggest that Overton's text is the sole and exact model for the *Second Treatise*, it is not beyond the bounds of possibility that the matter and arrangement of Overton's argument resonated in Locke's head as he expressed his own ideas. Overton proceeds to describe human community in Lockian terms before approaching the subject of "magistracy" in more detail. Here, of course, he is consistent in his arguments, opposing compulsion and any kind or form of injustice—indeed, anything which disqualifies any man or woman from being able "freely to enjoy his liberty, peace and tranquility, civil and human."

The remainder of the *Appeal* is addressed to Fairfax, and reiterates those matters essential to the *Large Petition*. However, it is unnecessary to remark them here; Overton has succeeded in removing the discussion to a level of abstraction equivalent to that employed by Locke himself in the 1680s, and expressed the argument in terms contiguous with the tradition of natural law theory, the principal tradition of democratic or rights-and-liberties political theory. Further, Overton raises the profound question of the source of sovereignty, asserting indeed that it lies elsewhere than in the two contending forces claiming it as each one's sole preserve and responsibility during the 1640s. It might even be suggested that it is Overton and the other Levelers who first raise this question, one which was largely obscured during the second half of the seventeenth century, especially during the reign of Charles II and the life of the Cavalier Parliament. It was questions of *legitimacy* and *authority* that were then pursued and which dominated the convention that decided the limits of royal sovereignty which was to be exercised by William III and which also dominated the Exclusion Crisis and the Bill of Rights which followed William's accession. The polar questions were the strength of legitimacy in the exercise of power and the sharing or limitation of authority—none of which addressed sovereignty except in terms of the established institutions of government. Legitimacy, authority, and sovereignty were not considered to lie *elsewhere or other* than in the monarch-in-parliament, in legislature and executive. They were debated as existing elsewhere, in the community and its members themselves, only by the radical political tradition of the Levelers and John Locke. And, except for Locke, the principles espoused by the Levelers became lost between the 1640s and 1688–90; the mainstream of Puritan or dissenting opinion continued within the institution where it had first become vocal, Parliament, without questioning the sovereignty of that place or limits to its authority. The Levelers could not succeed, since the weight of Puritan opinion, as well as Restoration monarchy, was against them, and that weight was also the weight of landed and commercial interests as demonstrated by the Presbyterians and the Independents, the Puritan factions that survived 1660 to influence 1690.

1647 was a significant literary year for the Leveler cause, as it was in terms of the Putney Debates of the General Council of the Army in late October. The General Council itself—despite its increasing domination by Cromwell and his son-in-law, Ireton, so that the Whitehall Debates of the Council of Officers (note the change, the common soldier being excluded) of 1649 display the army, its authority, future, and leverage upon the state as entirely in Independent hands and Leveler protests being brushed aside— may in 1647 be regarded in a very genuine sense as a democratic forum. And the principal Leveler spokesman at Putney was Colonel Thomas Rainborough, abetted by John Wildman. If for nothing else, the Putney Debates are remarkable for the clash between two views of democracy, that of the Levelers, in which every man in the army (and country on the parliamentary side) has an equal stake or interest in the outcome of the struggle and the nature of the constitution that would ensue, while Ireton on the other hand speaks for the Independent and Presbyterian factions and of a "fixed interest in the country" (i.e., landed property) which alone will qualify a man to have a voice in the state. The apotheosis of Rainborough's view is expressed when he claims:

> For really I think that the poorest he that is in England hath
> a life to live, as the greatest he; and therefore truly, sir, I think
> it's clear, that every man that is to live under a government
> ought first by his own consent to put himself under that
> government; and I do think that the poorest man in England
> is not at all bound in a strict sense to that government he
> hath not had a voice to put himself under.

The whole notion of consent and the retention of sovereignty by the people could hardly be more clearly expressed than it is above. A little later, in the same lengthy address, Rainborough claims that "in the Law of Nature" he finds no evidence that "a lord may choose twenty burgesses, and a gentleman but two, or a poor man shall choose none . . . the foundation of all law lies in the people." Further, he adds: ". . . every man born in England cannot, ought not, neither by the Law of God nor the Law of Nature, to be exempted from the choice of those who are to make laws for him to live under." Universal manhood suffrage, almost shocking in its novelty, subversive and outrageous to Cromwell and his son-in-law, is here presented as the grossest of common sense and the core of Leveler principles.

The Putney Debates mark the high water of the Levelers as a political force, with the forces of conservatism and landed interest exercising their eloquence and power, even as the Levelers feel no restraint and assume that their prescription is in no way other than of the mainstream. Cromwell must have prowled, largely silent, those debates much as another significant figure remained largely silent during the convention that attempted to establish a new and democratic constitution for certain colonies engaged upon a critical war—though Washington's silence had, perhaps, other and more democratic motives.

Ireton's reply to Rainborough is a comprehensive, even contemptuous, dismissal of the "Law of Nature" which, in his view, entitles nobody to anything. If the law of nature applies, Ireton questions, "where then remains property?" (Locke is persistent, as his 'radical' critics have pointed out so interminably, on this very subject. His resolution of the property qualification is to redefine the very notion of property, its essential meaning, so that it no longer signifies acres and money—though Ireton would probably have discounted money as property, preferring the votes that lie in, and on, the land.)

After Putney, there is a more pleading and strident tone in their utterances. Meanwhile, Rainborough can say, later in the debate concerning the rights devolving from property: "But I would fain know what the soldier hath fought for all this while? He hath fought to enslave himself, to give power to men of riches, men of estates, . . ." an observation that Ireton dismisses as a "flourish," which is exactly what both Whig and Tory landed interests managed to do until well into the nineteenth century.

It is, of course, quite possible to remind oneself of the theocracy of Calvinism in Geneva and to consider the Levelers' principles as just so much disguised or feigned democracy and which is in reality a democracy of the elect awaiting the opportunity to impose Calvinist authority upon secular government the moment it was opportune to do so. But this fails to recognize that the Levelers, at least, distinguished the tasks and functions of church and state and that their concern with freedom of conscience and worship is an attempt to *prevent* the state from interfering and requiring, by threat of punishment, religious conformity. They had no conformity of their own that they wished to see imposed *upon government.* At best, they desired the institutions of fallen man to approximate in dignity, liberty, and compassion those divine institutions of which they seemed so certain. But in their ideas of the derivation of human authority from God, and therefore instilled in, or at least implicit in, every one of God's creations, renders them, willy-nilly, in the democratic camp. They were obliged, with the utmost consistency, to assume that the equivalence that God grants to human, individual souls be figured, too, in man's secular engagements with the world of men.

If men are equal before the sight of God, then they *must* be equal in political society.

After the Putney Debates, there comes the *Petition to the House of Commons* of September 1648, which is, in large part, a reiteration of the *Large Petition*, though the tone is, as suggested, more insistent from growing powerlessness, with a greater and greater emphasis upon the "common liberties of the nation" and such grandiloquent notions as no longer become discussed in any detail, but achieve a more ringing character, sharing perhaps more and more with the extreme Diggers than was noticeable earlier—"restoring the commanlty thereof to their just rights," et cetera—though the Levelers never advocated the abolition of property, rather its *protection in every case*, which meant a great deal more to the country at the time, in the sense that it was directed against the agglomeration of *power through land*, as in Ireton's argument, and thereby toward the growth of a genuine, uninfluenced democracy through suffrage and the retention of sovereignty. The *Second Agreement of the People* of 1649 is a list of complaints against the arbitrary and undemocratic nature of a Parliament slowly becoming controlled by the Independents and, with more significance, a protest against the power of the sword, the employment of that idealized army that Rainborough referred to at Putney as a political weapon, one of the deepest fears of the English constitution and all shades of its upholders before, during, and long after the seventeenth century. What Lilburne had to say of Parliament in 1649 is summarized when he observes that "I am confidently persuaded their enmity is such at the people's liberties that they would sooner run the hazard of letting the Prince in, to reign in his father's stead, than further really a just agreement . . ." The *Second Agreement*, at least as abstracted in Lilburne's *Foundations of Freedom* of 1648, concerns itself, too, and as one might expect, with the nature of representation, election, and suffrage—all of which has already been sufficiently outlined in the general principles it seems all the Leveler leaders and leading thinkers agreed upon.

What, finally, is being insisted upon by the Levelers is the continuing and untransferable sovereignty of the people, the necessitous protection of individual rights and liberties, the requirement that political society be founded upon consent and *justly* and equally so, and the significance of suffrage to undermine entrenched and especially landed interests. Wildman's may therefore be the final word from them when he remarks that "a just subjection ought to be founded upon an assent of the people to their governors' power . . . how governors shall derive a just power from the people but by an assent of the people, I understand not." They are the inheritors, whether entirely consciously in all cases, of the tradition of natural law theory, together with (most importantly in the instance of those who may so easily be characterized as radical only in religion, and religious in all their opinions of the sublunary sphere of government) humanism's divorce of the secular from the theological—the rescue of natural law theory from its theological constraints, which allowed the perpetration of feudalism, of hierarchy and enslavement on the one hand and the aggrandizement of property on the other simply because *only our souls were equal.*

Finally, the Levelers were the future of the British political system and its constitutional theory—but the future was a great deal of time arriving after the rise and fall of Cromwell and the interests he represented. Which is why Locke *is* a radical voice—and one crying in the wilderness of vested interests that composed the landscape of 1688–90.

III

It is as well to deal with Anthony Ashley Cooper, first earl of Shaftesbury, before we begin to examine the *Two Treatises* in detail. Locke's intimate association with Shaftesbury has led to his being presented as the voice of the *subsequent* Whig oligarchy and that uninterrupted management of power that Walpole so perfectly exemplifies, rather than as the spokesman for Shaftesbury's most radical and unconstitutional designs, which culminated in his fleeing England as a sick and defeated man and dying in Holland, to which Locke also fled after Shaftesbury's fall and death, to remain there until the aftermath of the Glorious Revolution. Shaftesbury may be regarded as many things—direst of radicals, the creator of the party system by his unification of 'whig' factions, someone gladly enrolled into the peerage, undemocratic, bitter, arrogant, spontaneous, and idealistic—but not, in the general catalog of political theory, as a radical who may have inspired Locke, *nor* as a proto-oligarch. And the Whigs may have learned as much from the Tory ministries *before* the oligarchy as they did from the events of 1688–90 and the preceding Exclusion Crisis. Locke did not set out Shaftesbury's theories, nor would he, one strongly suspects, have approved of something like the Rye House Plot, which Shaftesbury *would* have approved, just as he did Monmouth's Rebellion, so elegantly misrepresented— but not entirely—by that greatest conservative apologia in verse, "Absalom and Achitophel," where Shaftesbury is all rebellion and cunning, and a corrupter of fair youth into the bargain. Locke himself is no longer regarded as radical because, one imagines, political historians have averted their gaze from the west and from the genuine revolution of principles which the American colonies undertook and have gazed eastward instead. In short, the historical outcome for Locke has been to become Whiggish—which, in the first half of the century succeeding the Revolution, meant the ally and even propagandist of certain landed interests intent upon the exclusive control of power. Shaftesbury himself may well have envisaged the dangers of proto-absolutism, to which the Stuarts were always given and for which they had an abiding affection, and the rigors of the Exclusion Crisis (where the Protestant Succession required immediate and effective protection, as James II subsequently proved beyond doubt), Charles's failure to summon Parliament and his pursuit of those who had incurred his enmity or flouted his ambitions, all may have seemed to the first earl to have required desperate remedies. However implicated in such desperate remedies (and to generations of literary-minded radicals, Dryden's conservative hymn has held a great deal of sway), Shaftesbury appears to have given Monmouth his blessing on two separate occasions, which disqualifies him from being the "onlie true begetter" of Locke's thoughts regarding political theory. In other words, Shaftesbury may remain that enigmatic character who inspires biographies and puzzles historians, because we are dealing with a complex and single personality, but in the tradition of political theory, one need not concern oneself with the character of politicians, except where they are themselves accredited theorists or where they have employed or overriden theory by harnessing the flow of events and chaining them to their individual will. Locke's influence was more pervasive and less personal, and little or none of the ideas contained in the treatises owe much to Shaftesbury's *activities*, though perhaps something to his ideals. Locke's view of the centrality of *consent by all* both to the mode and *conduct* of government never envisages the idea of the *demagogue*, which function it is possible to regard Shaftesbury as fulfilling during the Exclusion Crisis, though whether as instigator or rider of the storm may be debatable. There is a place only for *representatives of the people at large* in Locke, not for oligarchical, unconstitutional, or *extra-*institutional action, unless that may be construed as a "withdrawal of their consent" by the people at large.

As regards Shaftesbury, it is possible, and by no means entirely mistaken, to regard him as a true inheritor of the upheavals of the 1640s, just so long as one recalls the circumstances of the 1650s, too. One may, cleverly and quite erroneously, regard the 'revolution' of the Civil War as having actually produced a new kind of absolutism, one which required no extension of the franchise and no allocation of sovereignty in the people, merely a challenging and voiding of monarchy as an institution. The Civil War did much, too much, to inculcate in Tories and Whigs alike the idea of the sovereignty of Parliament *which would strive to be as absolutist as the monarchy,* the single person being replaced by the landed interest. Perhaps this was Shaftesbury's ambition, not to set himself up in Charles's stead but to invest Parliament—as had been tried and failed—with the sovereignty Charles seemed intent on recapturing whole and even extending beyond the bounds his father set. From all this implicit talk of, and actual struggle for, the sovereignty of Parliament, Locke turned away, as we shall see. And, if it was *not* the question, why were the parties united in 1689 in their determination to control the monarch through the granting of supply—money? They were concerned on the radical wing to limit the monarchical principle itself, while on the conservative wing they were concerned to ensure the continuity of the institution of monarchy, *but*—with recent history as a guide—to make personal rule financially impossible.

The period 1680–1714 saw each of these two wings, who assumed *themselves and no others* to be represented in the *best* of parliaments, striving to ensure that such a body gathered in the Commons. The Whigs ensured, and supported, the Hanoverian succession, and that entitled them, apparently, to two reigns' worth of power and the Tories to two reigns in opposition, after their high-water mark under Anne. However, it is possible to suggest that Shaftesbury, no more or less than Cromwell or any other political figure of the century, ensured that the progress of democracy was required to wait until the nineteenth century, when it may be regarded as being all but overwhelmed by the floodwaters of laissez-faire capitalism in its vigorous early years. There is a *continuity* as regards the struggle for sovereignty between institutions already in existence, with little or no regard, except where support and popular unrest might become useful as a lever, to the establishment of a wider, more embracing democracy, of new institutions, of an enlarged suffrage. It was a struggle for the *jointure* of executive and legislature, since the Commons could hardly deem itself the former after the Restoration, though it was *perforce* that in the 1640s. There was no wish to divide sovereignty, or to reallocate it—an attitude Shaftesbury shared as a political child of his age. For Locke, attempting already to establish in the *Essay* a new empirical basis for an epistemology which was entirely secular and derived from experience, there could be no such acquiescence with his contemporaries; there could only be the novel or the untried, otherwise what would reoccur would be a 'new' sovereign power, not titled king but wielding much the same absolute powers, whether a "single Person" or an institution. It is for this reason that Locke spends so much time—and quotes "the judicious Hooker" so often—discussing the roles of the executive and the legislature in order for the first time in any real sense, to *divide* them and make the one independent of the other. It is *not* because he was a boring old reactionary that he was so legalistic in his political theorizing; rather, it was because he was a genuine radical.

At all events, Shaftesbury seems to have lacked what Locke possessed, a conviction that the 1640s had offered an alternative form of sovereignty, an alternative constitution. The Exclusion Crisis seemed to offer Shaftesbury only the absence of a constitution, that vacuum nature is said to abhor, if a Catholic king ascended the throne, a defeat for the recent past, as if it had not already been defeated by Charles, the supposed secret Catholic. Shaftesbury was thus fighting, even resurrecting, an old war, having himself been a member of the renowned "Cabal" under Charles. What he was *not* doing was enacting or seeking to bring to reality what were the *radical* issues of the 1640s, only the parliamentary ones.

While Locke was in Holland and France, traveling and writing, what might have been his position regarding James? He may well have, being the author of *An Essay on Toleration,* applauded James's attempts to widen the toleration that existed in Britain to include Catholics (though not Dissenters until he had need of them against the Tories), but he would certainly not have approved of James's attempts to pack Parliament. Locke was to refute Tory patriarchalism as strongly as he refuted the kind of sectional action that resulted in the Rye House Plot and the Popish Plot, which helped to bring Shaftesbury down. Locke may be said to have idealized certain elements of the Civil War, especially that sense in which the "nation" rose against a tyrannous monarch, much as those rebellions that had belonged to previous centuries had always claimed. However, if he did so, then it was in order to regard the events of the 1640s not as the justification of the Long Parliament but as the break with the past that would allow the introduction of the *new*. The absence of parliaments after 1681 would have appalled him and only proven that a 'newness' must occur, for the function of the Commons remained much as it had been during the 1630s, grumbling and objecting and keeping tight fingers on the purse but doing *nothing* to reconcile political realities with new political ideals. Myth clung about kings still; Parliament perhaps desired such garments, but little more except the exercise of power in the interests of those currently elected to it.

There was a stalemate between legislature and executive between 1660 and 1690 which the monarch sought to enhance in his favor and which Parliament resented in its own favor. Locke's *Treatises* were nothing less than an attempt to break that stalemate. Locke's *Second Treatise* in particular, *Concerning the True Original, Extent, and End of Civil Government,* may be regarded as an indictment of the struggle for a sovereignty that has, in Locke's view, never been relinquished by those the Levelers sought to enfranchise, and as an attempt to demythologize the institutions that were each claiming the sole right to such sovereignty. At least Parliament and the de facto ministerial powers of Whig government were attempting to assume sovereignty, while the Tories accepted some continuation of the division of powers between legislature and executive. While England continued, in its political practicalities, to reenact the 1640s, Locke attempted to indicate the future by reference to the past. That the Founding Fathers of another, overseas democracy attended to him with some clarity and lack of bias is one of the ironies of political history, for while they did so with the benefit, perhaps, of that exact science of hindsight and another hundred years of the stasis of English political development, England ignored Locke, both immediately and in successive generations of political leaders and arrangements—subsuming him into a bourgeois or landed interest which assumed that the purpose of government was to represent sectional interests and to fulfill Ireton's foreboding prophecy to Rainborough at Putney, that those who were landless ('unprop-ertied' or lacking in monetary wealth) had no "permanent interest in the kingdom." To which Rainborough's scornful reply may as well as any other remark represent Locke's position—"I am a poor man, therefore I must be oppressed: if I have no interest in the kingdom, I must suffer by all their laws be they right or wrong."

It is therefore the irony of Locke's *Two Treatises* that to break with the past he was required to recall and employ the immediate past and the position of the Levelers, whose radicalism was that of natural law theory, founded upon the individual rather than the collectivity, which even seventeenth-century monarchs and par-liamentarians were apt to deal in, and essentially recognizing the *equivalent worth* of every individual human soul.

It is perhaps necessary here to mention one final accusation that has been leveled against Locke with regard to his being a spokesman for Shaftesbury, and that is the question of the *Funda-mental Constitutions* for the government of the Carolinas which the philosopher did indeed draft in conjunction with the first earl, who was one of the proprietors to whom the colonies had been granted. The *Constitutions* do indeed envisage a highly stratified, hierarchical political society, and they do endorse slavery. They do, however, belong to an earlier period than do the *Two Trea-tises*, to the 1670s at latest and not to the 1680s. They should be regarded as a measure of the progress of Locke's radicalism when seen as 'forerunners' of the theory of politics the later works express. Locke may have come late to radicalism—it is tempting though speculative to imagine an encounter with Leveler princi-ples *between* the *Constitutions* and the *Treatises*—but to it he did come, without doubt.

IV

Locke's *First Treatise*—why? It is now firmly established that this was an earlier work than the *Second Treatise* and that the two were never necessarily intended to be harnessed together. They do have a coherence, but that does not give an equal weight to the first of them, the coherence being in Locke's attack upon an almost archaic defense of divine right which had remained current and influential, together with the fact that Locke's assault upon Sir Robert Filmer's apologia for absolutism and apology for political theory was intended to clear the ground much as he had done in the early chapters of the *Essay*—the pruning, clearing, burning gardener he saw himself as being required this essentially sixteenth-century work as a *focus* for his theories. Further, the Biblical refutation is itself a refutation of the employment of the Bible and Christian theology in debates concerning government. Having refuted Filmer, the *Second Treatise* is, by comparison, a remarkably secular work in its allusions and analogies.

Whatever the provenance of the *First Treatise*, in conjunction with the fact that Filmer's work, *Patriarcha*, was published thirty years after being written (Filmer having died in 1653, the book's genesis belonging to exactly the same period that produced Hobbes's *Leviathan*), it is evident that Locke considered the refutation of a theologically inspired and defended theory of absolutism and patriarchal government required a damning and thorough effort on his behalf. The theories expressed in Filmer's treatise were revived in the person of Cromwell and the pretensions of Charles Stuart after 1660; the conjunction of Puritanism's evident and forceful faith—*without* the Levelers' insistence upon the irrecoverable separation of church and state—with the model of the theocracy of Calvin's Geneva was, one suspects, recognized by Locke as a temptation to which the Puritan cause had already surrendered in the 1650s. Without the Leveler insistence upon the separation of the lay and clerical spheres of theory and action, a theological justification of absolutist forms of government remained a possibility; it remained something that, implicitly, Whigs and Tories, court and country, could essentially agree upon—even as dissenters and the established church might do, with no more than a difference of personation rather than *form*.

Hence, Locke dismisses, in turn, *Paternal and Regal Power* as the former is seen to justify the latter (though Locke, as we shall see, is concerned to dispel *both* kinds of impositional and sovereign authority), and the idea of the divine right of kings, as descending from Adam (the Genesis theory of inheritance, whether of authority in a paternal, hierarchical, or "single Person" sense), whether by donation (God's granting of dominion to Adam), by fatherhood, and by the conveyance of such authority through time and descent—all of which he succinctly concludes, whatever violence is done to the Biblical evidence, is "far enough from that which Subjects owe the Governours of Political Society." Locke divides, consistently and utterly, the Biblical and sublunary spheres, applying only secular standards to the analysis of political society. He then proceeds to challenge Filmer's notions of the descent of monarchy from Adam, while the final chapter of the *First Treatise* poses a question that dominates its successor as well as this treatise—"Who Heir?" In this final chapter, Locke disposes of any remaining tatters of the theological argument, the pillars of the church and doctrine which might be employed to support the arch of monarchy itself, not simply the pretensions of monarchy to a divine inheritance of authority. Locke must break the links entirely, since his task is to develop a theory of *representative* government, one which has legitimacy but not sovereignty. Therefore, it becomes necessary to disprove the idea of the inheritance of authority itself, not simply the *continuity of inheritance* from Adam to Charles II (or Charles I, or the Stuarts in general, in Filmer). In 1688–90, and during the reign of James II, there were varying degrees of legitimacy as regards inheritance, but the principle of inheritance was not itself challenged—indeed, it was embraced by both Whigs and Tories, however it was described. The inheritance of authority suggests, as Locke well understood, the idea that authority exists within, and only within, the ruling person, family, oligarchy, or faction— and it was the place or residence of authority that he sought to redefine. Therefore, he devotes two-thirds of the space in dealing with Filmer that he spends dealing with the whole nature of his own theories of civil government; hereby dealing with Hobbes by way of Filmer. Filmer is the archetypal representative of the divine right theory, and its surviving power in the politics of the late Stuart period justifies a lengthy, vigorous, and successful assault such as Locke mounts in the *First Treatise*. Filmer had more 'appeal' than Hobbes; at least, theorists like Filmer did have. Hobbes was, after all, castigated as an atheist and abhorred. Locke is a secularist—Hobbes would not serve his turn as an object of assault and overthrow; Filmer did. It is in the *Second Treatise* that Locke comes to terms with Hobbes—not by name or in detailed refutation but as a fellow secular theorist and by means of an opposing case, that of democracy, that of the Levelers.

Hobbes is essentially a sixteenth-century political theorist, much as Hooker was, and his, rather than the latter's, may be seen as the last great statement of the medieval position, derived in large part from Aquinas, who subsumed natural law theory into theological discourse as much as any thinker did. That position is the entire retention of sovereignty in the figure and authority of the monarch, while 'Parliament' (and here the discussion can no longer be European but is entirely English because of the traditional existence of that peculiar institution) remains a judicial body—a *court*—rather than a legislature. Hooker, with an emphasis different than Hobbes's, set out to demonstrate that Puritan dissent from the established church—from the "ecclesiastical polity"—undermined and challenged the very foundations of the state and all political obligation, and if one refers instead to a secular polity, one might, in a very real sense, be describing Hobbes's task in *Leviathan*. Hobbes attempts to demonstrate that any diminution of or challenge to the secular god of the state, personated in the monarch, undermines the whole polity.

However, in the 1640s, whatever the basis of the struggle (in reality, for sovereignty), the challenge existed in a very real sense, and the sense of the secular polity established, which polity was, for a brief and perhaps "shining" hour not to be governed as any form of theocracy nor by any mythologized monarch. The traditional estates of government, king, lords, commons, and the courts were displaced by the sovereignty of Parliament. And, from that position, we may regard Locke as proceeding to relocate the basis of sovereignty in the people, to demolish that inherent autocracy in Puritan theories of grace and election which tended to hierarchy or oligarchy and which in part describes the Puritan 'monarchy' (and its support by the landed Puritan interest and the Puritan army's commanders) of Oliver Cromwell.

Following the short introductory chapter of the *Second Treatise,* in which Locke merely connects the subsequent discourse with its predecessor by outlining his dismissal of inherited monarchy and the Adamite argument in favor of paternal authority as exemplified in kings, Locke opens the second chapter, "Of the State of Nature," with the observation:

> To understand Political Power right, and derive it from its
> Original, we must consider what State all men are naturally in,
> and that is, a *State of perfect Freedom* to order their Actions,
> and dispose of their Possessions, and Persons, as they think fit,
> within the bounds of the Law of Nature, without asking leave,
> or depending on the Will of any other Man.

Nothing could be clearer, or more contentious, presupposing as it does a state of nature which is presocial or at least extrasocial, and an "Original" which may be discovered to illuminate that condition of men which is 'natural' to them, as well as the claim that such an original position is a condition of perfect freedom. Locke continues in the second paragraph of the chapter to explain that this state of nature is a *"State* also *of Equality"* and to assert that "Creatures of the same species and rank" are all "born to the same advantages of Nature" and that they are therefore "equal one amongst another without Subordination or Subjection . . ." except insofar as they are all subject to their divine master. What one must initially recognize is that Locke is hardly referring to a social or even extrasocial condition at all, *but to* an ethical-political state of human nature—"naturally" *men are equal* because they are "Creatures of the same species and rank promiscuously born to all the same advantages of Nature." The ethical element in this natural circumstance is referred to explicitly by Locke when he says: "The *State of Nature* has a Law of Nature to govern it." In other words, Locke is presupposing the rationality of human beings as their 'precondition', their reality before they are considered in any *context* such as society or political society, and, furthermore, it is not intended, evidently, to become Hobbes's law of self-preservation, even though Locke stresses that men do not have a "Licence" to destroy themselves or "any Creature in his Possession, but where some nobler use, than its bare Preservation calls for it." We may kill animals, presumably, to feed ourselves, but not gratuitously for pleasure or sport. Having extended the discussion to "any Creature," Locke is demonstrating the radicalism of the *Second Treatise* in the most determined fashion. Human beings must have regard for the equality of animals, except for usage not only to live but as the draft beast, the egg-layer, et cetera. His may be what might be termed a naively creationist view of the universe, even an organic one, but that cannot disqualify him from the radical camp. As to human beings, they are rational creatures who exist rationally in essence, even more than they exist in cohabitation with each other and in any agglomeration called a society, which requires the instruments of a *political* society to guarantee their rights and liberties. Indeed, it is necessary for the scheme of the *Treatise* to establish this sense of human rationality, which Locke calls the "Law of Nature," as a precept to his discussion of political society and government. Further, the establishment of human *equality* overrides all suggestions of rules and laws and the implication of 'self-government' such as exists in the individual.

It is here, in this precept of self-government through a law of nature or some ethical-rational code that Locke is at his weakest against Hobbes's view of human nature. However, when the conditions of political society pertain, that rational or ethical element becomes defined as the sense of equal treatment and the guarantee of equality, which seems a far more reasonable assumption than Hobbes's "warre of all against all," even to the death or destruction of opponents.

Therefore, we may conclude that the "original" is derived from a sense of equal personhood, whether or not in society, which is the condition of the state of nature (i.e., *human* nature). Locke does, of course, assume a rational potentiality, a moral capacity, in his human nature from which deviation produces various unpleasant forms of political society—but then, is he wrong to assume so? Human beings *do* have such capacities and potentials, and the weakness of Hobbes's argument is his assertion that they do *not*, except perforce.

The law of nature is defined by Locke (par. 6) as "Reason, which is that Law" and which "teaches all Mankind, who will but consult it, that all being equal and independent, no one ought to harm another in his Life, Health, Liberty, or Possessions."

It is perhaps pertinent and necessary here to draw attention to the effort and concern that Locke displays, in any and all discussion of natural law theory, to both detach himself from its traditional forms and to render it in entirely secular terms. The theories of Helvétius and Grotius and their peers and successors (i.e., those 'current' or contemporary to the period of Locke's writing) remained firmly intent upon elucidating the *law*, or laws, of nature, and with describing other and perhaps more novel versions of political society as derived from their divine model, Augustine's *City of God*. Natural law theory had not, before Locke's own efforts, rendered political society and its 'values', the rights and liberties of its citizens, in entirely secular terms. Rather, sixteenth- and seventeenth-century natural law theory had continued to understand political society as a construct or derivation of *human nature*, in imitation of a divine or celestial polity. The question continued to be, as it had been for Augustine, Aquinas, and others—What kind of political society can or must stem from human nature as we find it, inspired by divine example? Locke's question has none of this lingering, Christian essentialism about it. His question, put crudely, is—What kind of political society suits *differing* human natures?

Such a secularization of approach to the tradition of natural law theory may, in fact, spring from Locke's Puritanism or from his 'minimalist' Christian position. In either case, Locke is the first—as he was the last—natural law theorist to regard the polity as having no business with the moral behavior of human beings or the condition of their souls. Political society is nothing more—or less—than a means of ensuring that the private relation of human beings to their God, and their public enactment of His strictures on their behavior toward others—their ethical activity—remains their own province *unless* there is an impingement upon the rights and liberties of other human selves.

Such infringements may not be allowed to occur within any political society that wishes to function equitably, efficiently, harmoniously, or *justly*. But there is no sense in which this sense of *harmony* is imitative of any celestial polity or Attic *polis*. There is congregation rather than belonging or citizenship. Seventeenth-century natural law theory, of course, in remaining imitative of ancient or even divine models of the polity, insisted upon hierarchy, upon *government* rather than *jurisprudence*, which is essentially Locke's chief concern. If Locke has any 'model', then it surely must be the Ciceronian one of "right reason," which term he in fact employs in Chapter 2.

It is for this reason, one suspects, that Locke deliberately employs the idea of the "state of Nature" rather than the "law of Nature." He insists not upon uncovering any *laws* of nature (i.e., human nature) but rather upon the capacity of human *reason* to promulgate a code of civil law that is the 'constitution' of a just political society. Government, in other words, is to be examined by a skeptical intelligence cultivated in the attitude of seventeenth-century natural science—by empirical investigation and the rejection of traditionalist theories and concepts. And if natural philosophy uncovered laws of motion and gravity and the nature of the solar system and the circulation of the blood, Locke had no sense that it might ever uncover laws of *human* nature that were universal. Human reason alone was 'universal' among human beings, and by its application would men be able to develop a concept of equivalence linked to necessary justice. A political society. Locke's denial of innate ideas in his epistemological theories is a rejection, politically, of tradition, of 'inheritance', of universalism and essentialism. We have to 'work out' our political society; nothing is given, inherited, or innate. Given that imperative, we must arrive at a political society, a form of government and institutions, that suits *all* of us.

And the purpose of *law* in that ideal polity is simply the prevention of private immorality invading the morality of others. The political society is man-made, an artificial construct, and entirely a secular institution. There are no laws of human nature, merely diverse human faculties; the only one of these that may be regarded as universal is the faculty of reason itself, which is to be the implement employed to imagine and then create the just political society.

Locke therefore continues that rational men are *"bound to preserve"* themselves, but, with such not in question, they are bound *"to preserve the rest of Mankind."* The claim may be regarded as fundamentally Christian (thereby limiting the universality of Locke's argument) or as a very generous assessment of human nature in the face of what any modern inhabitant of the planet may either experience or witness in the media—however, as a basic premise it has little wrong with it. It cannot be empirically disqualified. It is, of course, the statement of an ideal as an instinct basic to human nature which may not actually be much evidenced, but it remains a *potential,* and, further, it defines that original position whereby men must conclude to recognize the personhood of others so that their own personhood may be acknowledged. The world's villainies may not be laid at this door but rather at that which opens onto a universe of inferiors and psychotically 'not-as-real' people who circle the egocentric universe of the self. Out of the *collectivity of others,* where our own self is most *real,* emerge all forms of political society in which some, or many, or even all but one are less real than others, less individual, with fewer rights, liberties, and personhood. Through that broad door lie the ovens, the Golgothas of Asia, the Gulags, and the "niggers" of whatever color who inhabit the world outside the unadmitting, or only self-admitting, self.

The original position, then, is that in which men find themselves, recognizing their own person and, through requiring such recognition from others, being forced to admit the persons of others. Locke's state of nature means no more and no less than this. Since he had ridiculed the Genesis theory or what might also be termed the Adamite position with complete thoroughness in the *First Treatise,* it is *not* an assumption regarding a position that is *presocial.* Locke's arguments regarding both ancient and modern variants upon the presocial—the few numbers of people on the Earth or the colonial example in the contemporary world—are proofs that such an actual condition may exist but *does not need to* in order that we consider man as individual, as a self, *before* we consider man-in-society. Human nature has a more fundamental existence in *personhood,* and, as such, political society must account to such persons.

The individual, therefore, has a right to protect himself and to punish those who infringe his rights and liberties, his "perfect freedom"; but, all individuals being alike and equal through their likeness, "naturally there is no superiority or jurisdiction of one, over another, what any may do in Prosecution of the Law, every one must needs have a Right to do." In exercising our freedom, expressing our persons, we are forced to admit that others may do the same.

It is not idealistic to suggest this, as Locke shows it is merely a *necessity* of being ourselves, and it also proves that Locke does not begin with a presocial human condition, since we are not forced to admit the humanity of others if we are isolated individuals. This may be termed Locke's original position, the point of departure of the *Second Treatise.* The "State of Nature" is that which is governed by a "natural" law or "right Rule of Reason" (i.e., the admission of the equivalence of others). And that, as the

Putney Debates of the Army Council in 1647 would tell us, is a radical assumption. Locke is not out to prove the existence of any law of nature but to *assert it in defiance of the contemporary,* to radically *claim* that it is true by the admission of any individual that his or her requirements of liberty and freedom must be admitted to others, *unless* the form of political society under which they live is unjust. Hence, just as Hobbes felt himself required to establish a model of human nature before discussing the nature of the state, so Locke requires an understanding of *equality of nature* before discussing an egalitarian and just political society. What he is saying is that *if* we were forced to abide *without a distinct and inherited form* of political society, we would be *forced* to choose an egalitarian and democratic one, were we all to begin the race from the same starting line that is our common "species" or "nature." Nothing more or less than that is claimed in Chapter 2 of this treatise—and no further example than Ireton's is required to prove how radical an assumption that of his original position really is.

Locke continues (par. 11) with: ". . . *in the State of Nature, every one has the Executive Power* of the Law of Nature." Objections, he remarks, will be raised on the grounds of partiality, of "Self-love," or "Ill Nature, Passion and Revenge" if all individuals were left with such executive power as they may be supposed to have as *persons.* Locke has already begun to combat this idea with the necessity of recognizing the equal individuality of others, but he is not fool enough to assume that men always accept necessity in the form of principle. Therefore, he edges toward a Hobbesian view of civil society, to prepare to pose and then answer the question—How is such an agglomeration of not entirely principled individuals to be governed? Especially since his view of the state of nature is so radical, he fully recognizes that it is *not* how people behave in the political society that surrounds him. How to get them to behave thus is his problem—at least, how to express a model of democratic society that will *convince* them.

Locke's initial answer to another, but related, form of skepticism (i.e., *"Where are,* or ever were, there any *Men in such a State of Nature?")* is simple, and it is that ". . . 'tis not every Compact that puts an end to the State of Nature between Men, but only this one of agreeing together mutually to enter into one Community, and make one Body Politick." Otherwise, individual men are making compacts or contracts with one another, still as individuals, but those compacts may be overruled or become unjust if "Ill Nature" on the part of one of the contracting parties overcomes his admission of the equality that exists between himself and his contracting partner(s). In such a case, the state of nature (individuality or self) becomes unethical, prey to the beginnings or shadow of Hobbes's "warre of all against all." To avoid this, and in agreement with Hobbes and all other political theorists of the century, Locke assumes that *"Civil Government"* comes into existence, the *"Body Politick."* Thus, he forges a direct link between the idealized state of nature and political society, founded upon *contract* or compact—that between individuals to be analogous to and legalized by some form of authority in political society.

It is evident that Locke is approaching a discussion of the condition of Hobbesian civil society, but it is also clear that he intends to establish a "State of Nature" instead of the condition of "civil society." The distinction between the two views of *society before legitimate authority* is the crucial difference between *Leviathan* and the *Two Treatises.* For Locke, having demolished authority that derives legitimacy either from theology or inheritance in the first *Treatise,* has by the conclusion of the second chapter of the second established a model of civil society that is individualistic but not *materialist.* His empiricism allows a distinction between individuals, though not of "species." The distinct temperaments that constitute human natures in the mass cannot lead to discoverable and scientific *laws* that are predictive and predicative of behavior and attitude, of response to circumstances alike in every case, and conditioning. Therein lies the problem of a democratic ideal, that it must always begin from an original position, such as "all men are created equal" (voiced by men who knew their Locke). One must begin, without theories of an identical nature or temperament but with an identical *beginning*, by assuming that the current or presiding *form* of society does not exist, that no distinctions of inheritance and its accreted disparities disguise equivalence from men.

Locke seeks to inculcate an equivalence based upon a social condition, not upon what might have existed *prior* to society, and the social condition he envisages is that of individuals having to deal with each other without accepted forms of authority and estate and "interest" (property being the principal factor of conditioning here, as the Levelers well understood), and therefore requiring the establishment of some form of authority which would guarantee the honoring of equivalence and the compacts made out of it without the interference of "Ill Nature" and the *bias* of self. Further, he is suggesting that political theory can begin *only* from that original position, otherwise it is, in one or another, a defense of particular interests and inherited forms of authority.

The idea of the "State of Nature," rather than that of civil society shared by Hobbes and Hegel, is employed by Locke because it allows him to consider that condition of society which would exist without authority or so long as authority remained nascent. For Locke to predicate such a condition is to consider the individual as at least a potentially rational and ethical being, not as a product of economic or social forces or as a materialist creature from whom all moral constraint or sense is absent, the individual in the light of "Truth and keeping of Faith [that] belongs to Men, as Men, and not as Members of Society." That being so, Locke avoids both Hobbes's deterministic and amoral individualism which is so like Hegel's demythologized civil society and its individuals, spiritually bereft. Locke's state of nature describes an individual who is a *person* rather than merely a *self*. The allowance for a moral capacity for good or ill derives from Locke's empiricism which, despite his close connections with the Royal Society and the most eminent rationalists and natural philosophers of his day, is not analogous to science as it was developing in the seventeenth century. Locke disbelieves discoverable laws of human nature, and not necessarily because of his religious beliefs but rather by *observation,* while Hobbes believes men are capable of being described scientifically and therefore in the mass as totally and essentially identical. Such persons as Locke envisages are capable of both good and ill, of altruism and justice as well as "Ill Nature" and "Passion and Revenge" if left to their own devices. Preeminently, however, they are *equal,* · providing one removes the onion layers of inheritance, tradition, and property, alike in their essential humanity. As such, they can only *consent* to authority to their *mutual* advantage.

Locke is a democratic theorist and, therefore, in the context not only of his time but of the century and a half that followed, a radical—and perhaps even in the context of our collectivist century, still a radical. Therefore, he begins not so much with the *nature* of persons but, as an empiricist, with the fact of their existence. People *exist* and are individual people, and their temperaments certainly differ, but their very *existence* is an expression of their personhood and the freedom of that personhood and its evident equivalence to other persons; they all *exist* equally, occupying the same space, breathing the same air, having the same physical properties and rational and ethical capacities. And his democratic theory is a plea for the *recognition of the fact* of their equal existence, before proceeding to what is then the only plausible or 'agreeable' form of political society, that of consent and the retained sovereignty by each and all of those factually, equally *existing* human beings. Locke does not begin, therefore, with an ontological description of human nature or its place in the world. Instead, he begins with what might be regarded as the simplistic observation that all existents partake of the same basic nature, that they possess the same capacities, operate by the same physical and biological laws, and that all other distinctions between them derive from the given circumstances in which they find themselves. He does not, however, as Hobbes does, indicate an identicality of personalities, merely an empirical yardstick of 'likeness'.

In Chapter 3, Locke defines the "state of War" as existing

between individuals much as Hobbes had done, though he does not make such a condition generic or inevitable. It is perpetrated and exists on the *individual* level (or national, in the sense of foreign wars, or as a disruption in political society). "He that in the State of Nature, *would take away the Freedom,* that belongs to anyone in that State, must necessarily be supposed to have a design to take away every thing else, that *Freedom* being the Foundation of all the rest," he claims (par. 17). In other words, he assumes the state of war to exist when individual liberties and rights are interrupted or interfered with, since the state of nature is the condition of the individual. In the condition of society, the design to take away the freedom belonging to the commonwealth is the equivalent at the collective level.

He then proceeds, in paragraph 19, to define the error concocted and compounded by "some men" (who can only be Hobbes and those who follow him), whereby the state of nature is regarded as a state of war. For Locke, men living together "according to reason" are *"properly in the State of Nature."* The *"State of War"* is the disruption of that 'normal' condition, a disruptive, violent condition, an abberation. Locke continues: *"Want of a common Judge with Authority, puts all Men in a State of Nature; Force without Right, upon a man's Person, makes a State of War."* The handicap of the state of nature, therefore, is that it has no "common Judge" to whom appeal may be made in a situation or state of war in society, an exact parallel of Hobbes's argument for the necessity of authority, which is just as necessary in Locke's view—the *kind* rather than the degree of authority is what is in question. Without the protection of the common law, to which all men have rendered authority over them, there is little hope to prevent, in the state of nature, that condition of "perfect Freedom" as Locke has termed it, outbreaks of violence, and "a manifest perverting of Justice," a recrudescence of the "State of War." And, to avoid this condition "is one great *reason of Mens putting themselves into Society"* (as says Hobbes).

There is thus no idealization of human nature in Locke's image of the state of nature, nor is there a mechanistic or materialist identicality in human behavior and nature which allows an essentialist simplification of human society into a governance of economic, social, or motivational factors, *without exception.* Instead, there is a full recognition of the diversity of human nature, the implication that social and economic factors will affect behavior, especially the behavior that qualifies as impositional and unlawful regarding others, and their lives, liberties, and property, as Locke is later to say.

Chapter 4, "Of SLAVERY," has caused palpitations among many commentators on the *Second Treatise.* It must, however, be regarded not as some bourgeois-capitalist view of the condition but as part of Locke's concern with rights and liberties. It must be seen, rather as Chapter 3 must be, as part of the preparation for his own description of political society. What Locke is doing in Chapter 4 is describing the impossibility of a man being able "to *enslave himself* to any one, nor put himself under the Absolute, Arbitrary Power of another," since men cannot surrender to another power over their lives. The essential or primary principle of human life is its preservation, and Locke has already accepted this, though he extends it to all human life and the lives of nonhuman sentient creatures unless they are to be regarded as food, draught, animals, producers of clothing material. Therefore, arbitrary power (Hobbes's sovereign authority) possesses the power of life and death over the *subjects* of that authority, which is a moral impossibility. It is in this sense that he uses the term *slavery,* and only in this sense. Other conditions may be similar but not identical, and are termed *"Drudgery"* (i.e., the selling of one's freedom and entering a condition of servitude). *Slavery* as he defines it is the opposite of *Freedom,* it is the condition of war elevated to the domination of political society by an arbitrary authority which removes from individuals, in their state of nature, the power of life and death over themselves. *That,* says Locke, is *slavery.* He thus dismisses, on what were to him the most essential moral grounds, all and any claims to arbitrary and complete 'sovereignty' by the ruler or governor over the 'subject'.

However, it is Chapter 5 that has converted Locke in the

history of political theory from the radical promulgator of Leveler principles and the proponent of the rights and liberties enshrined in natural law theory into the apologist of bourgeois capitalism, such that Marxist thinkers often make little or no distinction between the theories (or at least the *effect* of the theories) of Hobbes and Locke; the chapter is entitled "Of PROPERTY," and it is one of the longest in the treatise and certainly the most contentious—at first sight, at least. The preceding chapter on slavery has as its intent the establishment of the idea of *freedom* as having its essence in the individual and the responsibility of each individual for his own life and the lives of others, except where men have the right to resist an invasion of their rights and liberties, and may even parry or counter an attempt on their lives; the responsibility for one's own life and, by extension, one's rights and liberties, cannot be surrendered to another, and therefore remain with the individual in his individual "State of Nature." The corollary is that no individual has a right or power over the life of another. He cannot have any such arbitrary and complete authority. The chapter on *property* has a similar purpose, and it is this point that has been so misunderstood or misrepresented by commentators. Locke intends, as we shall see, an extension or redefinition of the idea of property—"every Man has a *Property* in his own *Person*"—so that property is not accumulative or impositional, and it certainly does not bring about Ireton's claim of a "fixed interest" in the kingdom or commonwealth. It is a *right*, a possession of each individual which must be protected together with his other freedoms, protected from others who are in a "State of War" against the individual who possesses property (i.e., who is a person).

The right to property is defined as an essential or basic right for the purpose of defining the sovereignty of the individual and the necessity to guarantee his rights and property *against* others, *not* so as to allow him to acquire, to control, to achieve domination through landed property.

VI

As an exact equivalent of the term *property*, Locke occasionally and deliberately uses the more archaic form of *propriety*. We understand this as itself rather old-fashioned and novelistic even when applied to manners, taste, and behavior; for the sixteenth and seventeenth centuries, the term meant *ownership* but also meant character, quality, or property, descriptive of something, pertaining or belonging to something in the sense of attributes. Further, it signified the *particular nature* or *individuality* of something, including a person, and is used by Shakespeare in this sense. To understand Locke's potent notion that "every Man has a *Property* in his own *Person*" requires our understanding of property or propriety in this archaic sense. And it is in this sense of propriety that Locke intends to discuss property as being *part of* the individual (in his idea of men "appropriating" land and possessions to themselves, but *only* from the common or wilderness condition of God's gift of the "World to Men in common," and *not* from others) but with the additional signification that *propriety* describes some essence or quality of the individual person as well as his or her property.

The first paragraphs of Chapter 5 concern Locke's effort to demonstrate that men, having "mix'd their Labour" with the wilderness (and the American analogy that he favors more earnestly at a later point of the chapter is implicit here, since it would be difficult to contradict Locke's argument regarding the ownership of property cultivated from a wilderness), have in some sense appropriated it to themselves, given themselves title to it; hence, it becomes part of their propriety, an attribute or quality of them. Marx's notions of labor, at least in its idealized and unalienated form, are not necessarily opposed to this, since his concern is with the appropriation *by others* of the fruits of the individual's labor, thereby not merely robbing him but alienating him in an essential sense from the expression of himself in his labor. Labor, for Locke, distinguishes the cultivated from the wild, and makes what has been "mix'd" with the individual's labor his by "private right."

From this assertion, Locke proceeds from the "Fruits of the Earth" to "the *Earth it self,*" to the question of property as *land.* Property *in* land is acquired by the same process, so that as much land as a man may cultivate and of the products of which he can use, "so much is his *Property.*" Locke continues: "He by his Labour does, as it were, inclose it from the Common." It is here, despite appearances, that Locke begins to undermine Ireton's position regarding what might be termed the *suffrage of land.* ". . . The Condition of Humane Life, which requires Labour and Materials to work on, necessarily introduces *private Possessions.*" Yet this is not a defense of landed interests nor of bourgeois capital, since we are discussing a limitation upon property expressed in *labor,* and acquiring *title* to, or possession of, land in no other way. "This *measure* did confine every Man's *Possession,* to a very moderate Proportion." We are still discussing the "State of Nature" as it signified in some quasi-historical period, that which Locke later refers to as the time when there were so few people in the world that no one's liberties or entitlements were interfered with. Men spread over a globe that was in the condition of wilderness, cultivating and acquiring it through their labor, is at least as scientifically historical as Marx's arcadianism, and may be accepted as such.

This circumstance no longer applies to Locke's time, he says, because of the *"Invention of Money."* Otherwise, he claims, there is sufficient wilderness for the same laws regarding the acquisition of property through labor still to apply. (Is there not a remarkable pre-echo of Marx in this, too?) This invention of money "and the tacit agreement of Men to put a value on it, introduced (by Consent) larger Possessions, and a Right to them," he claims, which is not the Marxist position. But is it Locke's either?

For the moment, we may conclude that Locke envisages, much as Marx does, an arcadian period of human history during which, because of population levels, there was sufficient land for all and that the acquisition of land occurred solely through labor invested in it. Men took land 'into' themselves, possessing it and making it a "propriety," as it were. But the invention of *capital,* money, totally altered those pertaining circumstances, allowing the acquisition of property, possessions, and *wealth* to a degree utterly unrelated to the labor invested in them, indeed, beyond any direct employment of self-labor.

It is necessary to remark at this point in any examination of Chapter 5 that, together with Chapter 6, it represents the radical essence of the treatise. Locke's task is a subversive one, and, having discussed property, he proceeds in the ensuing chapter to dissect *inheritance.* These two notions may be regarded as the motifs of the whole book, since Locke returns to them in almost every succeeding chapter. One must recall that he has dismissed the Genesis argument regarding inheritance of authority from Adam in the *First Treatise,* but it is the inheritance of property and the authority of a "fixed interest in the kingdom" that springs from both possession and inheritance of property that it is Locke's task to demolish. Hence his already significant claim that property and propriety have something essentially to do with the *person.* The semantic juggling of the term *property* may be seen to have the purpose, therefore, of equating the property a man has *in his person* with *all other forms of property.* At least, that is my contention. Locke is not antiproperty, or even anticapital; rather he is opposed to the *authority* deriving from money and property-as-land and the consequent disenfranchisement of the propertyless, or even of those with less or little property *other* than in their own persons.

Locke's concept of the *person* and the significance he attaches to such a notion is already clear from his analysis of the concept of the "State of Nature"; *every person* is equivalent, unique, perfectly free in the state of nature. Locke discusses the acquisition of property, money, and inheritance *before* he discusses political society in any detail; he is, in fact, discussing the forces operating in civil society, much as Marx or a twentieth-century social theorist or political economist would discuss them—the *basis* of current society (in his sense) deriving from property and wealth. Hitherto, in the state of nature, as he makes clear, property was sustenance and limited by the amount of labor invested in it to cultivate it for the purposes of sustenance *"and the Conveniency of Life";* however, civil society, though distinctly *not* a political society, rather that condition of cohabitation that requires a form of political society to emerge, has developed and agreed to the use of money, which has concentrated wealth beyond labor and "conveniency," has allowed an unequal distribution, a distribution beyond the expression of self in labor and the acquisition, *through effort* by the person, of property. In the state of nature, "it was impossible for any Man, this way, to intrench upon the right of another, or acquire, to himself, a Property, to the Prejudice of his Neighbour." By implication, before Locke proceeds to any actual examination, the invention of money and the unequal acquisition of property by wealth, and inheritance, as will be seen, involve "intrenching" upon the rights of others. I do not see that this is a doctrine much to the taste of either Whig or Tory in 1690—nor, perhaps, today.

Man is confined to "a very moderate Proportion" in "the first Ages of the World," so that this occurred "without Injury to any Body." Apparently, he implies, things have changed for the worse since then—he continues to assert that such a situation would still exist *but* for the invention of money, which he slightingly describes as *"a little piece of yellow Metal,"* the tone of the observation bearing its weight of meaning.

For Locke, the invention of money produces a situation where "the desire of having more than Men needed" has "altered the instrinsick value of things"—and it is that intrinsic value that he is especially concerned with when he comes to discuss the nature and forms of political society such as will not disadvantage the individual.

Men's possessions "inlarged" in due course, but *"without any fixed property in the ground"* until the beginnings of cities and *settled* communities, when the necessity of setting the *"bounds of their distinct Territories"* occurred, a limit between different societies rather than mere individuals, and thus "by Laws within themselves" agreeing also "the *Properties* of those of the same Society." In paragraph 39, however, which follows this assertion, Locke claims that we cannot suppose "any private Dominion, and property in *Adam,* over all the World, exclusive of all other Men, which can no way be proved." In other words, Locke has already begun to challenge the property *and* inheritance qualifications of authority (which is precisely what Marx did in assuming that the economic levers of a society moved its world), because all we can see, he claims, in terms of legitimacy, is that *"labour* could make Men distinct titles to several parcels of it [land], for their private uses." Locke allows, having introduced the subject of money or capital, no legitimate claim upon possession other than that through labor. Indeed, he claims that 99 percent of what "comes to our use" may be "put on the account of labour." " 'Tis *Labour,* then which *puts the greatest part of Value upon Land,"* Locke insists, together with the idea that *"Labour,* in the Beginning, *gave a Right of Property."* The original position has not yet been abandoned, some distance from the introduction of the idea of money, and indeed it is not until paragraph 47 that Locke is prepared to reintroduce the topic, in the following way: "And thus *came in the use of Money."* Money, by *mutual consent,* "Men would take in exchange for the truly useful, but perishable Supports of Life."

To make a small summation at this point, one should remark Locke's insistence, just as significant as in Marx, upon some 'prehistoric' circumstance in which the ideal was real, which later does not weaken Locke's argument as it does that of Marx, since he does not presume that the arcadian element of his survey is anything but a piece of history, rather than a circumstance which may, by a change in the nature of political society, be returned to. Rather, it represents a circumstance that predates *political society* and a consented-to authority; consent to money is *not* consent to its acquisition, to the principle of wealth and that unequally. Instead, Locke envisages a circumstance in which political society was, in some senses, unnecessary, the situation of the wilderness inhabited by a small population where the arbitration of a "common Judge" was not required in terms of the rights and liberties—even property—of any individual. He assumes that a political society is required to deal with current circumstances, as Marx does, those being landed or capital authority—*but*, unlike Marx, he does not assume that control of the means of production and capital is the method to be employed; rather, the retention of sovereignty and the principle of consent to government will produce a political society which cannot be controlled through land and capital alone or even predominantly. Marx's envisaging of an arcadian past is at one with his view of an arcadian future, while Locke remains grappling with his present, with an enfranchisement of all which is to be the *real* control of society. Marx's revolutionary changes may lead—and have led—to the dictatorship of the proletariat, to central control, to a pretense of sovereignty, but it was the abandonment of the concept of the *individual* that condemns Marx. His theory is erected upon the assumption that the notion of the individual is *past* or lost, not merely nascent. Therefore, there is no residence of sovereignty except in control of certain social and economic mechanisms; there is no choice and no possibility of change other than revolution or evolution—which in reality means the collapse through inherent tensions of the capitalist system. For Marx—and Hobbes—there is the underlying assumption that authority must be possessed, that sovereignty belongs to and must be invested in a *section* of the community. Thus, Locke develops his image of civil society as unequal in possessions and wealth, as any good Marxist would, but in order to demonstrate that a *political* society requires a new analysis of the nature of authority *and* of individuality. Locke's prehistoric excursion merely demonstrates that civil society can develop *without or even in spite of* political society, to the extent that Marx's vision of the wealth-owners, the controllers of the means of production and the alienators of labor, control the politics of their society, which is exactly what Locke is here suggesting. Unlike Marx, he does not suggest revolutionary change, nor does he assume that matters cannot be changed without the withering away of all present forms of *wealth.*

Indeed, Locke recognizes the requirement in any society for money as a means of barter, by turning the idyllic image of the state of nature on its head in paragraphs 45 and 46, where over-production is wasteful and where much may remain of only potential usefulness unless it is traded or bartered with others. "And thus *came in the use of Money.*" But such usage was by *consent,* and that is the most subversive element in Locke's argument, because, if men have consented to money, then they must be allowed to consent to the other forms and forces of their political society. This is not to suggest that Locke's debate on property is merely a metaphor, or of secondary importance. Rather, it has enfolded the property-capital argument in the larger question of *consent,* to such an extent that he is able to suggest toward the end of the chapter (par. 50) that ". . . since Gold and Silver, being little useful to the Life of Man in proportion to Food, Rayment and Carriage, has its *value* only from the consent of Men, whereof Labour yet makes, in great part, the *measure,* [nevertheless] it is plain, that Men have agreed to disproportionate and unequal Possession of the Earth." *But*—and it is *the* 'but' of the whole thesis—Locke says: "This partage of things, in an inequality of private possessions, Men have made practicable out of the bounds of Societie, and without compact . . . For in Governments the Laws regulate the right of property, and the possession of land is determined by positive constitutions." To conclude the chapter in a short paragraph (51), he once more provides an arcadian image of that golden age when there were no disputes about property and "Labour" was the sole and predominating means of title to "Property," providing a final parenthesis for the whole discussion and a vantage from which to look back upon the assertions contained in Chapter 5.

The most significant assertion at the chapter's conclusion is that such "inequality of private possessions" occurred and developed without (outside or before) political society and without the sacrosanct *compact* (or enforcible agreement, rather than the more passive consent—at least, passive on this occasion), which conclusion is followed by his view that governments, the organs of a political society, regulate and control such matters via the "law"—which presumably implies no "intrenchment" upon the "right of another," which is what lies at the heart of Marx's analysis of capitalism, rather than the principle of wealth in any neutral or merely existant sense; it is the *employment* or the *derivation of wealth by appropriation* that Marx regards as a violation and even a desecration—and Locke would here agree with him. Locke, however, would disagree that no form of political society could alter these circumstances; indeed, precisely because he regarded his own society as exhibiting such "employment of wealth" and its associated and privileged effects upon *others* less wealthy or landed, he assumed that a *reform of the form* would enfranchise unrestrictedly and thus produce a *political equality*.

Money, of course—and this is its danger, according to Locke— is extendable beyond labor, is disproportionate in its being hoarded beyond the goods that it is used to represent in terms of barter. Further, it was used, especially during the Civil War, to purchase great tracts of land, even though most returned to former ownership, thereby further entrenching the value of land as suffrage. However, with the deepest irony, the equation of money and *consent* with property (consented to, perhaps, but also inherited and accumulated via money), the admixture of all three ideas, prepared Locke's later arguments with regard to political consent. In simple terms, men have 'agreed' to money, therefore they must *agree* to everything of an equivalent importance in their society. And the fact that "every man has a Property in his Person" is the key to what follows this disruptive, contentious, but finally subversive chapter.

Given a knowledge of seventeenth-century history, it is possible to assert that Locke viewed money or capital as less corrosive of the form of political society, or perhaps less likely to dictate the status quo to future generations, than land. The city was more radical than the 'country' during the 1640s and supported Parliament against the personal government of Charles I—though by the 1680s they would hardly have been radical enough for Locke. *Land* rather than capital was what was represented, by Whigs and

Tories alike, in the sovereign Parliament that sought to control the prerogative of the putative monarch, William III. The sectional or vested interest of land was represented long after the idea of parties developed in Parliament (which might well lead one to sympathize with Marx's reading of English history, supplied by Engels in the main) during the 1840s, even though the reforms of 1832 and the first Factory Acts had begun to make up time on the lost opportunities of 1690. Locke, however, saw a means of prevention of the abuses of the century and a half that succeeded the *Two Treatises* which would have prevented much of the abuse of *individuals* during the early stages of laissez-faire capitalism. Had the Levelers' extension of the franchise and the equality dependent upon it have been deep-rooted by the time of the Industrial Revolution, who can say? The opportunity was spurned during the 1640s and again in 1690. For the vast disenfranchised and propertyless inhabitants of Britain, the next significant date is as late as 1832.

Chapter 5 is concerned with no more and no less than establishing the perspective from which we must view the rise of property and capital—the latter being the means, Locke suggests, of the unequal control of, and power derived from, the former in the seventeenth century. Other than his parenthetic invocation of an arcadian image of labor, with which he is evidently wholly in sympathy, he passes little or no judgment upon his analysis. There is no burning, Marxist condemnation, at least not yet—but then, such passion for justice is not Locke's habitual manner. We reach Chapter 6, "Of Paternal Power," therefore, with information and not opinion, with facts rather than values. Yet preceding Chapter 5 with a discussion of the nature of *slavery* is itself predicative. Locke is not a historicist, merely an empiricist who recognizes the 'facts' of society in the seventeenth century but who assumes that political ideas are intended, and have no other use than, to deal with injustices and discrepancies in civil society, in human contiguity and interactivity, in order that a deeper equivalence is admitted and protected within political forms and institutions. The pauper's voice is the equal of that of the billionaire's, and his *justice* before the law is identical. If anything proves we still have much to learn from Locke, it must lie here.

If Locke's intent toward influencing the decisions of 1688–90 is in doubt, one need only remark what he refers to as the advantages of a "Prince" who "shall be so wise and godlike as by established laws of liberty to secure protection and incouragement to the honest industry of Mankind against the oppression of power and the narrowness of Party will quickly be too hard for his neighbours." The reference to a prince is particular rather than archaically general, and William's need of English money and troops against Louis XIV is entirely recognized in the sentence. But with it is the 'trade-off' for the liberties of the people and a detestation of the "oppression of power." More importantly— and where, presumably, Shaftesbury would hardly have agreed with his 'employee'—there is a detestation of the "narrowness of Party." In other words, Locke has undermined the approaches of the Whigs and the idea of an alliance between a prince and a faction in Parliament, an alliance between an executive and an oligarchy.

One other remark of Locke's (par. 44) is relevant here, when he observes that: ". . . though the things of Nature are given in common, yet Man (by being Master of himself, and *Proprietor of his own Person,* and the Actions or *Labour* of it) had still in himself *the great Foundation of Property."* The state of nature has already been clearly identified by Locke as equivalent to the condition of *being* an individual person, and thus the whole structure of Chapter 5 is given value and attitude by that assertion. The *individual person* remains as an extant force and *existant,* whatever the forms or appearances of civil society. On that basis, and that alone, is to be erected political society in a just form.

One may fancifully imagine that chapters 5 and 6 are similar to dealing with the motifs of the ring—power—and the curse— inheritance—in Wagner's great cycle of operas, which may be the only truly significant refutation of Hegel's view of the "rational State" and assertion of the sovereignty of the individual that remains extant from nineteenth-century Germany, whatever Hitler attempted to make of Wagner's radical dreams and myths, for it is with these concepts that Locke has burdened political society if it is to honor the "perfect Freedom" of the "State of Nature" he has already so eulogized.

VII

Locke's challenge to the abiding notion "Of Paternal Power" began in the previous treatise, culminating in the question "Who Heir?" with regard to the theological basis of the office of king. However, in demythologizing kingship and kingly inheritance in refuting Filmer's argument, what remains is a parallel or analogous mythology, that of Ireton's claim during the Putney Debates, which was little more than the reiteration of a conventional attitude shared by the gentry, of whatever parliamentary or royalist convictions during the 1640s, and even the 1680s. Parental authority or power not only bolsters the monarch but preserves, in an analogous fashion, the paternalism, especially on the land, that is more readily associated with the feudal estate. It preserves at least an important part of the substance of traditional forms of authority, which is exactly what Locke wishes to dispense with. We have already seen how he discusses property in the light of consent and the equality derived from labor, together with the independence of cultivating for *need* and "conveniency." There is little that is traditional in Locke's argument, even though it may appear to be arcadian. Similarly, in his analysis of parental authority, it is a radical position that he adopts.

The Levelers, between 1647 and 1649, feared, with any restoration of the king, the restoration of the traditional estates of power, king, lords, and commons in no more than an altered appearance. Locke, confronted with a convention to discuss the prerogative and authority of William and Mary, fears something akin, a persistence of traditional assumptions concerning the nature and 'objects' of authority. His method is to begin with a portrait of his own society and the forms of authority it displays, especially those of property and parenthood. Regarding the latter, he opens his discussion by opposing the term "Parental Power" for reference merely to the father. "Reason or Revelation," he says, will both tell us that the mother "hath an equal Title." Considering the political lot of women in the seventeenth century, the remark cannot be considered as conservative, especially when one considers the property rights denied women except by special arrangement. Fathers and mothers are, he proves, everywhere "joyned together" whenever the obedience of children is remarked or prescribed in the Bible. Had this been clearly understood, he says, then "it might perhaps have kept Men from running into those gross mistakes, they have made, about the Power of parents: which however it might, without any great harshness, bear the name of Absolute Dominion, and Regal Authority," such absolute dominion becoming unacceptable to "Men," since it would be, of its nature, *shared* as "Parental" authority. It is not subtle to observe the metaphoric or analogous employment of parental and "Regal" forms of authority in conjunction here, nor to note that Locke drives home his argument to the very basis of authority and hierarchy, the family, especially, as we shall see, the landed family where "subjection" is ensured on the prospect of inheritance. But it needs to be remarked that he does both things, in paragraph 53, quite deliberately. The following paragraph appears to recapitulate—and qualify—his remarks concerning *"all men by Nature are equal,"* while what in fact he does is to demonstrate that some men may be more intelligent, of greater virtue, et cetera, but their *essential* quality is one of "the *equal Right* that every man hath, *to his Natural Freedom,* without being subjected to the Will or Authority of any other man."

Locke reintroduces his "State of Nature" argument into the center of his examination of paternal authority, in order to demolish any validity clinging to the latter. Such authority is not legitimate; it is subjectional and proprietorial, and this is another sense of Locke's employment of the ideas of *property* and *propriety,* when the notion of ownership and appropriation *by others* is not merely of land or money but of—as Marx would clearly have appreciated—the *labor* and the *selves* of others. Paternal authority or power is clearly intended to be regarded as an appropriation of the freedom of another, in this case the child or children who, as Locke remarks: ". . . are not born in this full state of *Equality*, though they are born to it." Parental authority is no more than "a sort of Rule or Jurisdiction over them when they come into the World, and for some time after, but 'tis but a temporary one," because "Age and Reason, as they grow up, loosen them (The Bonds of this Subjection) till at length they drop quite off . . ." Children, until educated and mature, may not be expected to be "under the Law of Reason"; they are not wholly capable of rational decision and behavior. However, once they are, they are free of any parental subjection, for *"the end of Law* is not to abolish or restrain, but *to preserve and enlarge Freedom."* He adds that *"Law,* in its true Notion, is not so much the Limitation as the direction of a free and intelligent Agent," while liberty is "a *Liberty* to dispose, and order, as he lists, his Person, Actions, Possessions and his whole Property, within the Allowance of those Laws under which he is; and therein not to be Subject to the arbitrary Will of another."

Locke thus continues the discussion of the transition from a state of nature to the condition and consequences of a political society in the midst of defining the limitations upon parental authority, a quite deliberate procedure. The question "For who could be free, when every other Man's Humour might domineer over him?" is pertinent only if Locke is intent upon challenging not only the received wisdom regarding parental authority but the problem of authority per se. Further, he evidently intends that any 'imitation' of conventional theories and *law* of parental authority be not transferred or expanded to the forms of law and authority in political society.

Children achieve an age of reason, therefore, or what Locke terms an "estate" or "State of Maturity" when they may be supposed capable of knowing and understanding the "Law of

Nature." Only those mentally retarded may be regarded as incapable of arriving at this state of rational maturity—otherwise, all adults are regarded as "without any Dominion left in the Father," as free individuals "under the positive Laws of an Establish'd Government." Thus, "we are *born Free,* as we are born Rational," though it is "Age," maturity, that brings "the Exercise" of *both.* For "the *Freedom* then of man and Liberty of acting according to his own Will, is *grounded on* his having *Reason.*" And, just as the age of reason is arrived at by the child, so the individual-in-society matures analogously to the position of recognizing the necessity of an "establish'd Government," a notion which he subtly indicates in his description of children achieving "the infranchisement of the years of discretion" (par. 65).

Locke sums up the limitations of paternal authority in paragraph 69, when he says that "the Father's Authority cannot dispossess the Mother of this right [to be honored by her children after maturity], nor can any Man discharge his Son from *honouring* her that bore him. But both these are very far from a power to make Laws, and inforcing them with Penalties." Children are never to ignore or forget their obligation to honor those who have nurtured them, but, finally, there is no real or analogous lesson for the nature of political authority in the parental example; there is an end to obedience and to the authority exercised by the parent. Indeed, he adds a little later that "these two *Powers, Political and Paternal, are so perfectly distinct* and separate."

It is at this point that he takes up the subject of inheritance, and the power given to any man to leave his estate to whom and how he will. Again, the subject is analogously treated, being concerned to demonstrate that land or wealth, the subject of the inheritance, is left under the settled laws of the political society in which father and child live, since inheritance law is such that a man accepts the "Government of the Country" when he accepts an inheritance. This is not, however, a "Natural Tye" but a "voluntary Submission" by him who would take the inheritance of those terms. "For *every Man's children* being by Nature as *free* as himself . . . may . . . choose what Society they will join themselves to, what Common-wealth they will put themselves under." Again, the observation has an apparent intent, that of parental authority and its bonds regarding inheritance, and a real purpose, which is to begin the great and central discussion of *consent*. Locke fully understands the perpetuation of government and of a particular form of political society or commonwealth by means of inherited wealth. Now, in extension of his analysis of property, he is concerned with the vested authority of inherited property. "By this Power, indeed, Fathers oblige their Children to Obedience to themselves, even when they are past Minority, and most commonly too subject them to this or that Political Power." Only by the promise of reward is such authority exercised, he adds. The assault is opened frontally, then, with the analogous image of a false and greedy obedience being extracted by parents which itself may perpetuate a particular, unfree, political system—unfree because those who participate are not making a free choice or decision. Inheritance perpetuates a traditional system of "Political Power," which, in the immediate context of the *Treatise*, 1688–90, is fraught with direct and deliberate political purpose. It is exactly the *beginning anew* that the deliberations of Parliament regarding William's powers, *not inherited* as king of England and Scotland (and as mere stadtholder in the United Provinces, an intermediate and perhaps indeterminate position Locke would have well understood from his sojourn in Holland), to which Locke addressed this section in Chapter 6.

Locke concludes the chapter by describing a mythical or presocial circumstance in which patriarchal authority was exercised in what one may term a tribal situation, but this effectively and *solely* applies in that period of history when few numbers and the wideness of the world made positive law and a system of settled government unnecessary; even so, such patriarchs existed only "by a tacit and almost natural consent."

The principal matter of the *Second Treatise* thus far has been contained in chapters 5 and 6, though discussed as seemingly preliminary to the discussion of "Political Society" itself. It is self-evident these twin subjects of *Property* and *Paternal Power* occupied Locke considerably, and obvious, too, that his intent in discussing them must have been germane to his argument. That argument has proceeded by analogy, or perhaps by making contiguous the private and political spheres. For his thesis, in these two chapters, is that the form of government in England in 1690 is "inherited" and is based upon the power and franchise of "property," just as the private lives of individuals may be so centered. It is also evident from these chapters that Locke disapproves not of those things and authorities per se, but as they are influential in the political sphere. Parental authority, extended beyond minority, is harmful especially when it affects the freedom of the mature child, most particularly when it *subjects* him by means of inheritance to the paternal authority of the state.

At the close of Chapter 6, Locke is poised upon the brink of the argument that all inherited *and* all paternal political authority is wrong, and thus stares across a widening gulf at the authoritarian theory of Thomas Hobbes.

Locke's antagonism toward what we have termed *the suffrage of wealth* may also be found in the republican political philosopher Harrington who, in *Oceana* (1656), demonstrated the social and economic influences and controls upon political activity and the form of the commonwealth; and Thomas More in another, perhaps the generic utopian satire, *Utopia* (in Latin, 1516), observed:

> [W]hen I do now consider and weigh in my mind all these commonwealths, which nowadays everywhere do flourish . . . I can perceive nothing but a certain conspiracy of rich men procuring their own commodities under the name and title of the commonwealth . . . These devices, when the rich men have decreed to be kept and observed under colour of the commonality, that is to say, also of poor people, then they be made laws.

There is much in More that Marx would have applauded, and it is superfluous to observe of Harrington, as has been done, that he did not parallel Marx because he recognized only the social power of land rather than money and other forms of influential wealth; *land* was preeminently *power* in the seventeenth century, as it had been during and since the Middle Ages. But both More and Harrington were contained within that literary rhetoric previously remarked, and within the conventions of allegory which, by its speculative nature, requires no concrete affirmation of principle and especially practice. Locke the empiricist was not so confined, and therefore is only generally indebted to utopian satires for his anticapitalist and antifeudal attitude to the undue influence of property upon the forms and practices of the commonwealth.

It is only by the notion that a "Man has a Property in his own Person" that any *political equivalence* can be rendered to the propertyless or to those who may be denuded of their property by "inclosing" and accumulating landlords and magnates. It is by recognition of the idea, and moral neutrality, of property that Locke is able to assert the property of rights, the "propriety" that makes property part of the individual as he "mixes his Labour" with the wilderness, and which distinguishes the same generic "propriety" or character and quality in each and every individual. Around him in the 1680s, the equation of wealth with power was inherited by the descendants of the Puritan, parliamentary opposition to Charles I, the Whigs-as-radical-party. There had been no *essential* change produced by the 1640s which the Restoration had not been easily able to smother or which had not declined of its own lack of volition. Now, in 1688–90, the chance had once more, and more peacefully, come—but *who* in the political firmament would assert the Leveler principles? Only a Somersetshire academic, and then only anonymously in print.

It is pertinent for Marxist critics of Locke to observe, as has been observed of someone like Harrington, that he obfuscated or confused the subject of money or *capital,* though his critics of the left do not give credit to the tone of his opinions. For Locke, as has been remarked, *land* was influence in his contemporary experience, as it had been for centuries and as far as political suffrage and power were concerned. To dismiss Locke on more profound grounds of the base-superstructure theory of money versus politics is, of course, to deliberately dismiss the influence of politics itself. Locke could not have become a 'Marxist' without abandoning the one essential principle of his that we must accept—that *politics* profoundly affects the circumstances of our secular lives. Land meant hierarchy, predominance of faction, control of authority and influence, determination of the shape and form of society—what money or capital, control of the means of production, means to a Marxist theorist. However, Locke, as a better student of his Bible than Marx, accepted that *love of* money is the root, et cetera, not money itself. He is unconcerned with the redistribution of wealth, except in the sense that inequalities should not infringe the rights and liberties of others and that *all* may be represented in the forms of authority of the commonwealth; rather, he is concerned with the equivalence, and therefore radical, root-and-branch *redistribution,* of *influence* and *power.* Indeed, it is possible to assume that Locke envisaged money rather than land as a democratizing influence within political society, in that it is less constant, less available to the influences and realities of inheritance, as he would have understood the power of land, and it is subject to *taxation* and therefore to redistribution and to the financing of the legislature and executive in a way that land had never successfully been subjected during the century. Only in the sense that money may be more democratic (more easily acquired by the strenuous individual without precedent advantages) in his view may Locke be regarded, from a modern standpoint, as a conservative thinker. What he opposes is the prevailing orthodoxy of his times, the assertion of landed rather than natural rights.

However, not being an idealist or a materialist but a lowly empiricist, the man clearing the scrub and weeds, as he portrayed himself, from philosophy's garden, he does not assume that the influences that predominate in society require other than political, secular, and empirical change. It is here that one must part company with Locke, if one cannot or does not accept his insistence that political society is remedial by political means—however radical, including the "dissolution of the Common-wealth," as we shall see.

He evidently does not accept the communistic solution of the Diggers, or "True Levelers," since they dismiss the necessity for political society, much as does Marx, once the economic system is changed. Locke does not assume as Winstanley did that human nature itself can be changed by a change of economic system (and as Marx himself so assumed, so that a former purity of heart was regained, absolution through the funeral pyre of capitalism). Therefore, Locke is left to understand and recommend only as regards the form of political society.

To conclude, Locke recognizes the *abuses* to which both land and money (capital) may be put in the shaping and directing of political society but does not conceive that an *equality of property* or a change of economic system will produce—in any consistent, stable, or lasting sense—an *equality* of authority or sovereignty; and this is because he does not assume an essentialist view of human nature, its reduction to simple principles and *therefore* its capacity to be purified and made anew, enhanced in some other manner by either social, political, or philosophic means, as both Hegel and Marx understood to be possible.

Locke may be accused of inheriting the Christian notion of renewal from within, of some deep and spiritual conversion as the sole means of altering or renewing human nature, and then only in an *individual* sense; Hegel and Marx, on the other hand, may be accused of inheriting that confusion and conflation of the Enlightenment and German Romanticism, the *Aufklarung,* with all its admixture of redemption through nationality, poetry, inheritance, identification with the absolute, et cetera.

For Locke, political society is necessitated by the fact that human nature cannot be molded or improved by merely human agencies (nor is that the task of purely secular agencies, even of the law); its vices must be protected against, and its virtues protected, in the form of guarantees regarding individual rights and liberties and a redistribution of *political* power in the form of "infranchisement" and, most particularly, by an equivalence of *consent.*

VIII

Locke begins with the primal or original society, that of marriage, then of the family, including, as would be expected in the seventeenth century, "servants." These various groupings, however, "came short of *Political Society,* as we shall see," he asserts. They represent the civil society of the chapter's title. However, what Locke calls "Conjugal Society" is "made by a voluntary Compact" and it "draws with it mutual Support, and Assistance, and a Communion of Interest too." He is not necessarily remarking the so-called nuclear family as the origin of society, nor even as its applicable microcosm—certainly not its motivation or paradigm. He is representing the family as a union of *contract* or "Compact" which has certain parallels with political society, yet which "came short" of that condition. There is a continuity with Chapter 6 in his concern to discuss the social group of the family, within which he can begin to examine the idea of "voluntary Compact." In such circumstances, there is a retention of "possession" by the wife, and even though the husband may exercise the "last Determination, i.e. the Rule" within the family, Locke in no way denies the right of women to their individuality nor their ability to renounce what was always a voluntary arrangement. One must remark the seventeenth-century context of Locke's quite radical conclusions regarding the situation of the family— marriage, inheritance, "rule," authority of parents, et cetera, before regarding him as a closet conservative in late twentieth-century terms. There are similar contracts between masters and servants which give the master but "a Temporary Power over him, and no greater, than what is contained in the *Contract* between 'em."

Having expanded the numbers of the group, Locke remarks

that though this may resemble a "little Common-wealth" (par. 86), "yet it is very far from it, both in its Constitution, Power and End," and it is at this point that he returns to the state of nature argument of the early chapters, having taken the suspect analogy of the family as far as he may before rejecting it as a model of political society.

"Man being born . . . with a Title to perfect Freedom, and an uncontrolled enjoyment of the Rights and Priviledges of the Law of Nature, equally with any other Man," he reiterates, claiming that man in the state of nature "hath by Nature a Power not only to preserve his Property, that is, his Life, Liberty and Estate, against the Injuries and Attempts of other men; but to judge of, and punish, the breaches of that Law in others . . ." The individual, therefore, must be his own *magistrate,* though he is not the lawgiver, not the legislature, only the judiciary and executive, obedient to the "Law of Nature" and its principles of freedom, rights and liberties, and equality.

Having again established the credentials of the state of nature, Locke turns to political society, observing that "because no *Political Society* can be, nor subsist, without having in it self the Power to preserve the Property" and to punish offenses against what constitutes Locke's definition of "Property," there can only be *"Political Society* where every one of the Members hath quitted this natural Power, resign'd it up into the hands of the Community in all cases that exclude him not from appealing for Protection of the Law established by it." The alteration from civil to political society is not, then, by an expansion of numbers or by the paradigm of the family, but by the transfer of judicial and executive power to the "Community"—a condition which sounds remarkably like that suggested in *Leviathan.* Hobbes's political society is necessitated by the individual, too, but the individual *ego* and its activity of self-preservation and personal security which entailed the domination of others. To establish the principle of *consent,* however, Locke must have recourse to the moral agency of the individual, though this may not be universal nor consistent.

Those individuals who have settled upon a form of common law *"are in Civil Society* one with another," otherwise, merely being together in a social group without such agreement and such established laws is to remain in the state of nature. Locke thus distinguishes *three* stages—the state of nature, civil society, which is the opposite of Hobbes's "warre of all against all," and later, in its precise *form* of government, its means of making and executing the agreed laws, it is accurately described as a *political* society. Only when these conditions of agreed law, and the resignation by each individual of "his Executive Power" to "the publick," can there exist what Locke now calls a *"Political, or Civil Society."* I imagine the deliberate conflation of the two terms, in apparent contradiction of my remarks in the previous paragraph, intends to allow *no distinction of kind,* only of degree, between political and civil societies. In other words, Locke intends us to understand that the essence of both terms—and the societies they describe—is their legalism, their legitimacy through voluntary surrender of executive power, rather than to imply that the final, butterfly form of a *political* society is somehow additional or extraneous to—and imposed upon, in Hobbes's sense—the condition known as civil society. Man, by his surrender of executive power, "authorizes the Society, or which is all one, the Legislative thereof to make Laws for him as the publick good of the Society shall require." The executive and legislative functions of a civil, or political, society are *alike* established by what appears to be a surrender of authority, but Locke is also, somehow ominously, beginning with the law's power to *punish* rather than to *protect.* It is as if he is toying with concepts that abound, and become systematic, in Hobbes and in other absolutist thinkers of the century and is accepting the conventional image of the magistracy as enforcers of laws rather than *arbitrators* in disputes, which seemed to be what he was suggesting earlier in the chapter. However, the confusion is deliberate, because what has been surrendered is no more or less than arbitrary and individual executive power or its possibility. The code of punishment will operate not by any Hobbesian desire or whim or slight of the individual as a species of vengeance or retribution, but under the *"Legislative* and *Executive Power* of Civil Society, which is to judge by standing Laws how far Offences are to be punished, when committed within the Common-wealth." What Locke has achieved by this method of approach is the removal of any kind of personal arbitrariness from the individual exercise of *justice,* and quite deliberately begins with that most affecting quality of arbitrary or retributive justice, punishment. "And this *puts Men* out of a State of Nature *into* that of a *Commonwealth,* by setting up a Judge on Earth, with Authority to determine all the Controversies, and redress the Injuries, that may happen."

It is at this point that Locke deliberately evokes Hobbes, though not by name, in order to challenge his concept of the necessity of absolutism and his designation of absolutism as the sole form of *political* society. *"Absolute Monarchy,* which by some Men is counted the only Government in the World, is indeed, *inconsistent with Civil Society."* Absolute authority, he argues, produces a situation where "no Appeal lies open to anyone, who may fairly, and indifferently, and with Authority decide" because the absolute monarch has "both Legislative and Executive Power in himself alone." Thus, the monarch, not *subject* to the common and accepted law, remains in "the State of Nature" and outside political or civil society, and *above* the law, so that there can be no appeal against him. He becomes a figure to be feared, "being in the unrestrained state of Nature . . . yet corrupted by Flattery and armed with Power." To which Locke adds the sternest of observations, namely, "he that thinks *absolute Power purifies Mens Bloods,* and corrects the Baseness of Human Nature, need read but the History of this, or any other Age to be convinced of the contrary." He then quotes Hooker's *Ecclesiastical Polity* at some length in a reiteration of the "Agreement among themselves" by individuals to ordain "some kind of Government publick." The partiality displayed, inevitably, by individuals in their own favor in executing their rights and liberties against those of others, especially in seeking redress, requires, say Hooker and Locke together, the establishment of an independent and consented-to authority, otherwise (Hooker) "Strifes and Troubles would be endless, except they gave their common Consent, all to be ordered by some, whom they should agree upon, without which Consent there would be no reason that one Man should take upon him to be Lord or Judge over another." By quoting Hooker, Locke displays the consistency of his oblique approach to the ideas he is promulgating. Having thus quoted, he continues his adjuration of absolutism in paragraphs 93 and 94, to conclude the chapter with the admonishment that *"No Man in Civil Society can be exempted from the Laws of it."*

The argument has, by this time and in the exemplum of the abuse of absolute power, shifted ground toward the idea of law as protection of rights and liberties, the theme of punishment having been subsumed into the embracing image of arbitrary punishment which is equivalent to arbitrary authority. Thus, the "perfect Freedom" of the state of nature has been most compromised, thus far in the treatise, by the exercise of arbitrary authority, which is *now* identified with the state of nature, or individual executive power, itself, upon the presumption that power has a corrupting influence, especially because of the partiality of human nature to its own interests. This being so, the state of nature requires to be abandoned for the sake of the equal protection of the rights and "Property" of every individual—the suggestion that society, as opposed to civil society, may yield to the power of the strongest or most selfish, as it does *inevitably* in Hobbes's view, lurks in the wings and casts its shadow. Locke is not an idealist as regards human nature, but neither is he a rigid materialist where one principle of activity or behavior essentially describes human beings. Nevertheless, by employing the image of absolutism for its own sake, only to be discarded, he also uses it analogously to the condition of the state of nature, or individuality, which may be corrupted by its control of executive power unless restrained by "a tacit consent" to agreed and mutually accepted laws. Hobbes's guarantee of liberties is absolutism, Locke's is *consent to law.* Therefore, it has now become clear what Locke actually signifies by the "State of Nature"—not some prehistoric beginning of society in the individual, family, group, then social gathering, and not a political condition, either. Rather, it is the retention of individuality, its sovereignty in the sense that it is unrestrained in its "perfect Freedom" *to enact its own nature on others*—which may be for good, or for ill.

Locke's scant, though significant, references to primitive and tribal societies are important for their relationship with paternal authority discussed in the previous chapter, now that he has returned to a consideration of the development from the state of nature to that of political society. These elementary social organizations represent, for Locke, the elevation of the principle of the state of nature to a form of government, the extension and continuance of arbitrary and absolute authority in a single person or ruler. Such societies may consent *once,* but there is no *law* which provides against the extension into arbitrariness, even tyranny, of such *individual power;* there will be no guarantee of the continuance of the form of political society established by the original and single act of consent. Further, those rights and liberties which have, until now, been regarded as "perfect" in the state of nature can only be *guaranteed for all individuals* by means of law, and the consent to the residence of executive power, the *power* of the law, in appointed, not anointed, hands.

Locke begins Chapter 8, "Of the Beginning of Political Societies," with a reiteration of the claim that "Men being . . . by Nature all free, equal and independent" in order to indicate that "no one can be put out of his Estate, and subjected to the Political Power of another, without his own *Consent,* " intentionally repeating Hooker's remarks quoted in the previous chapter. Similarly, men may only *"put on the bonds of Civil Society"* by "agreeing with other Men to joyn and unite into a Community" for reasons of "Security." When this *initial* consent has been given and *"one Body Politick"* has been established, what has also been established *must be* the principle that "the *Majority* have a Right to act and conclude the rest." Though there is no logical necessity in this conclusion, Locke assumes that the functioning of consent, rather than its absence after the initial contract or agreement, may only be sustained by a continuing process of agreement, which therefore can *only* be expressed as the conclusion or opinion of the majority. The radicalism of this claim is easily proven by reference to the limitations of suffrage and the authority of royal prerogative, et cetera, at the time of composition.

The "Community" can only *act* and function, Locke claims in paragraph 96, "by the will and determination of the *majority.*" This "will and determination" is, however, described as a physical force, drawing upon an analogy that Hobbes might have appreciated, the movement of a "Body" by a greater force, which Locke carefully expresses as the *"consent of the majority,"* for the forces which act upon his "Body Politick" are not those of Hobbes's materialism, or of passion and desire; the *forces of consent* are the volition of his political society. The analogy from the physical sciences or natural philosophy of his age is employed, subtly, to dismiss such analogies, since there can be, in "Nature," no such forces of *consent,* only mere forces. Unless each person agrees to the consent of the majority, then there was no *"original Compact,"* since men are left as free as they were "before in the State of Nature."

Locke is at once, however, determined that we understand that there are limitations upon our surrender of authority to the majority of the body politic, when he remarks that the individuals consenting to join a community "must be understood to give up all the power, necessary to the ends for which they unite into Society," and, therefore, *no more power* than such a condition requires to function by the consent and 'force' of the majority. Only now does Locke regard a *political society* as opposed to a civil society as having been established, by this agreement or "Compact," which is "nothing but the consent of any number of Freemen capable of a majority to unite and incorporate into such a Society" (par. 99).

Locke spends the following four paragraphs dismissing objections on the grounds of opposing historical examples, before reiterating observations from earlier chapters which are now perti-

nent, the question of the "original" of commonwealths as observed in history, that condition he described in Chapter 5 with
regard to property alone, and now relevant to the nature of political society. If, he suggests, we look back "towards the *Original of
Commonwealths,* we shall generally find them under the Government and Administration of one Man," though such authority
has already been demolished by Locke's argument. We are returning to that condition of few people in a wide world of Chapter
5, but if such scattered 'families' "met and consented to continue
together: There, 'tis not to be doubted, but they used their natural
freedom, to set him up, whom they judged the ablest, and most
likely, to Rule well over them." (The colonial example is reiterated at this point.) It may be objected at this juncture that Locke
invents a degree of *consent* unlikely in primitive societies. That
being the case, the alternative is some form of patriarchy, or
subjection, and it is Locke's intent to suggest the *necessity* and
value of consent, not its ancestry. Indeed, it is possible to claim
that Locke well understood that *no* appeal to tradition or history
could produce a pedigree for consent, since he is dealing with a
new 'original' to political society which *overturns* history in favor
of decision. For primitive or original societies to choose a patri-
arch was simply an extension of the authority the choosers were
used to, that of the parent—in other words, a continuation of a
form of authority that maturity disallows and casts off.

Therefore, the entire purpose of Locke's suppositions regarding
original or historically ancient and primitive societies is that they
function by tradition and without rational agreement. This appeal
to history and tradition is the foundation of the defense of monarchical government, and the beginnings of a defense of absolutism. Locke is intentionally and entirely breaking away from both,
to establish the equivalence, and thereupon the necessity for the
consent, of rational beings, in any *just* society that intends to
recognize that rights and liberties extend equally to *all* individuals. Locke's examples—historical, contemporaneously primitive
or tribal, and Biblical—are all reduced to that condition, at best,
of war chieftain or war leader and "captain" (the analogies with

German idealism, nationalism, and National Socialism need not be stressed). The sovereign status of such a leader in wartime, and we may as well cite Churchill here, is itself a refutation of such powers at times *other* than those of danger to the community from outside.

It is at this point (par. 111) that Locke employs his most devastating irony, referring to this as "the *Golden Age,*" which preceded the corruption of power (since power was familial or limited to times of emergency), and it was a time (perhaps Locke's one real excursion into arcadianism, though it is intended ironically) when "there was then *no stretching Prerogative* on the one side to oppress the People; *nor* consequently on the other . . . to lessen or restrain the Power of the Magistrate." Thus, there was "no contest betwixt Rulers and People about Governours or Government."

The pace of the treatise accelerates at this point, as if Locke has already established most if not all of the inherent principles of the ideal government of his political society, for he moves almost at once, in paragraph 113, to answer the objection regarding the fact of *governments in existence* and the consequent fact that people "cannot be at liberty to begin a new one." It is this entwined theme of *beginning and continuity* that forms one of the spinal supports of the *Second Treatise.* In the context of 1688, recent Interregnum precedent and his own principles, Locke seeks to lay the basis of a new form of political society and to ensure its continuation and continuity of consent. This may be regarded as the underlying purpose of the work.

The principle of *consent* is now used, among similarly *"free men,"* to dispose of all "lawful" monarchies, since they must have been established, like the patriarchies of ancient or tribal societies, *without consent of all "free men."* The riposte is abrupt and complete, arguing from Locke's earlier postulates. History abounds, if one wishes to use history, Locke insinuates, in examples of men withdrawing from the political systems into which they were born and *"setting up new Governments* in other places." (This *must* be, now that we have an inkling of Locke's persistent method, an indication that it is only a single step from setting up a new government *in the same place.*)

Locke is therefore able to observe, regarding history and the provenance and authority of tradition, " 'Tis plain Mankind never owned nor considered any such natural *subjection, that they were born in,* to one or the other, that tied them, without their own Consents, to a Subjection to them and their Heirs." The subject of *continuing consent,* which is Locke's next important consideration, is broached in these paragraphs, at first by implication and then through the images from history of the *withdrawal of consent* represented by the *right* to remove oneself from a disagreeable political society and form another according to one's taste or, more accurately, the tastes of the majority of those who withdraw and then congregate to establish a new form of commonwealth.

However, it is at this juncture that Locke returns to the subject of inheritance and the acceptance of the pertaining laws in order to inherit. Property now becomes much more clearly an imprisonment, a restriction upon the freedom of the consenting individual. It robs him (i.e., *land* does) of the capacity to renounce the established political system and make it anew, *unless* the expectant inheritor renounces the *property* that is controlled by the laws of the established system (since laws of inheritance would be resigned to the "magistrate," as all other laws would have been). But when Locke claims that "a Child is born a Subject of no Country of Government," he could hardly make his meaning plainer. Inheritance of landed interest perpetuates traditional forms of government and political society, *but,* because inheritance is characterized as a limitation upon freedom and consent to government, the indubitable conclusion is that the suffrage and authority of *land and tradition* are wrong. They are unjust, confining, imprisoning. The term *subject* is now employed, rather than *member,* and there is no longer *community,* rather *country* (which simply must be an ironic employment of the word as it described those landed interests that opposed the 'court' faction and the ministers of the Crown, in Parliament, themselves as factional as the other).

It is here that Locke adopts an apparently Hobbesian position (and perhaps here is discovered the source of that conservative passion that Marxist and other historians and political theorists are assured he displays) when he regards a *single act of consent* as being immutable, establishing the form of government of the commonwealth which may not then be altered. Locke's words are as follows: ". . . he that has once, by actual Agreement, and any *express* Declaration, given his *Consent* to be of any Commonwealth, is perpetually and indispensibly obliged to be and remain unalterably a Subject to it, and can never again be in the liberty of the state of Nature." There is no equivocation, but neither is there anything other than the roughly half-way point of the treatise arrived at and at stake here (and we should be prepared for this by now, comprehending Locke's method of qualifying assertions by later arguments or by analogy). *Express consent* differs from the *tacit consent* that is required to "enjoy" property or inheritance in a commonwealth where one is not native or to which one has not assented. That is Locke's first significant qualification of the absolute terms in which he has couched what is no more or less than the stability of the *constitution* of the commonwealth, the rules that govern the form, structure, and method of execution of the "Body politick," rather than its laws or *powers*. Locke is to spend the remainder of the treatise defining exactly what, and how great or little, are those powers and of what substance and intent should be those laws. Locke's most virulent critics and jurors of a hostile intent have deliberately or accidentally confused or conflated the legislature (representation and authority) with the executive power of the commonwealth. It is Locke's purpose to distinguish them, and further to make distinct the *nature* or form of the commonwealth, and he begins this process in his habitual manner by introducing it here in preparation for Chapter 9.

Thus, a single act of compact or consent arrives at the constitution of the political society—sovereign, sovereign-in-parliament, sovereign parliament, Lord Protector, junto, Cabal, constitutional monarch, whatever is decided by the *force of the majority* which he earlier distinguished. He has already established suggestions as to the limitations that must be placed upon what was conventionally termed in his time "arbitrary" power but which in reality denotes the power of the monarch as the executive function of the constitution. He *must* circumscribe the executive power. (It was the task of the Long Parliament, the Civil War, the Whigs, and Parliament in general throughout the seventeenth century. One *must* take account of Charles II's secret Treaty of Dover and subsequent agreements with Louis XIV for *subsidies* to prevent his having to become accountable to Parliament for the fruits of taxation—supply—and recognize the inherent tendency of the Stuarts to absolutism. Charles desired to corrupt or ignore the tradition of king-in-parliament in favor of extending the executive power. As it was, he was able to prorogue or dissolve Parliament almost at his will.)

The necessity of curbing the executive power *as it might be exercised* was self-evident to Locke. With Parliament's calling at the behest of the king, and for the purpose of providing him with funds summoned reluctantly (by James II, also), and the attempt to pack both Houses with monarchy's supporters, and the ministerial system being the court faction and not *elected* representatives, it is little wonder that Locke sought both the choice of *all* in the form of the constitution and the stability of the chosen form thereafter, *before* describing the organs of government, their powers, and limitations, in any detail. No *arbitrary* change can be made to Locke's commonwealth—but no *minority* is capable of seizing or controlling power, either. For the moment, Locke is content to allow the impression that he sides with Hobbes in the idea of a single act of consent by all to the form of the constitution, though, in opposition to Hobbes, he does *not* designate this as a resignation or transfer of sovereignty.

He has, of course, begun to distinguish *obedience* from *participation* and to differentiate between the ideas of *membership* and *subjection,* matters he will develop more fully in later chapters.

It is one of his keener ironies that he attaches this distinction, in the first instance, to the idea of property, *the* qualification for participation in seventeenth-century England's organs of government. This is his final rebuttal of Ireton's claim (which now has its own pregnant irony) of a "fix'd interest" in the country which alone qualifies an individual to a 'say' in government. Property, in reality, is as obedient to the law as "Property" (self and liberties and safety). It, too, must become *subject* to the laws which have been agreed by all the community. The exclusive suffrage of property is not to be tolerated in the commonwealth. Indeed, Locke spends what might be considered by a modern reader an inordinate amount of time playing with the metaphor and reality of property—but this is because he so clearly understands that inheritance and/or property *perpetuate* the traditional form of the constitution, which is exactly what he wishes to reform. Membership of the commonwealth is by *express* consent, not by property and/or inheritance; and the decision as to its constitution is to be made by all those able and willing to give express consent, not by any propertied, titled, or monarchical faction.

Thus, by the half-way stage of his argument, Locke has overturned what amounts to the only vigorous tradition of government and authority in England, that of the "fix'd interest," property—*and* he has, in the previous treatise and this, disqualified all forms of *inherited power.* It is having done all this, and nothing less than this, that he now proceeds to define the substance and behavior of the "Commonwealth" that he is intent upon describing as a necessary ideal.

IX

Locke begins the ninth chapter of his treatise with the question as to why "Man in the State of Nature" is ever willing to "part with his Freedom" and accept the limitations upon it concomitant with membership of and submission to a political society.

"Why will he give up this Empire, and subject himself to the Dominion and Controul of any other Power?"

The answer is peculiarly, but by now suspiciously, Hobbesian. "The Enjoyment of" such perfect freedom as is afforded by the state of nature is "very uncertain, and constantly exposed to the Invasion of others." The "greater part" of men are "no strict Observers of Equity and Justice," and it is therefore for the purposes of *security*, what Locke calls "the mutual *Preservation* of their Lives, Liberties and Estates, which I call by the general name, *Property.*" It is therefore the condition or constitution of the political society which is now of the utmost significance. Locke begins his outline of the just and satisfactory form of political society by describing the limitations upon what he claimed were the inherent freedoms and circumstances of liberty in "the State of Nature."

First, he claims that the state of nature admits no *"establish'd, settled, known Law, received and allowed by common consent to be the Standard of Right and Wrong, and the common measure to decide all Controversies."* One must remark here that Locke is engaged in removing the state of nature *condition* to the abstract level of an *idea*. It represents an image of freedom and perfect liberty for the individual, but it effectively provides no basis for the functioning of a settled community. His view of the state of nature—at this point in the treatise—is, as he has prepared us to perceive, the condition of the individual, not of the community in any sense; therefore, the two have no relationship except the state of nature is the *idea* which the institutions of government must embody. Hence the initial emphasis upon the "known Law."

Second, the state of nature lacks *"a known and indifferent Judge"* who has vested in him the authority "to determine all differences according to the established Law." Third, there must be an executive power to carry out the sentences and determinations of the "Judge" in the light of the "Law." Given the establishment of these three conditions, men will freely choose such a settled constitution rather than the "inconveniences, that they are therein exposed to, by the uncertain and irregular exercise of the Power every Man has" of being his own judge and executive. Thus, men "take Sanctuary under the Establish'd Laws of Government."

Society or "community" is, to some degree or other, inevitable, that is clearly Locke's assumption. Therefore, real, free individuality does not exist outside society but *must* exist within it. The "State of Nature" may once have existed in the sense of a non-communal reality, and may do so even in the seventeenth century in the American wilderness settled from England, but in no real sense is it 'common' or likely—inevitably, as Locke has shown, communities agglomerate, grow, become larger and more complex. But, they are composed of individuals who are, in Kant's sense, ends-in-themselves, separate existants. Thus the importance of the metaphorical tradition of the state of nature argument and its employment by Locke as an ideal—or rather, an *idea.* It is not *inevitable* that such a form of political society as Locke envisages will or should be established—rather the reverse, if history tells us anything; but it is *desirable* and just.

Locke now emphasizes what is "surrendered" by the individual in such a political community, namely, submission to the law of his individual sense of *"whatsoever he thought fit for the Preservation of himself,* and the rest of Mankind," also the *"Power of punishing* he wholly gives up." However, Locke emphasizes, "the Power of Society, or *Legislative* constituted by them, *can never be suppos'd to extend farther than the common good,"* which may appear to set Locke's foot to the road that leads to Bentham and utilitarian liberal theory though, as we shall see, Locke does not intend the "greatest good to the greatest number" but an equality of good to all who consent to belong to his political society. "And all this to be directed to no other *end,* but the *Peace, Safety,* and *publick good* of the People." At this point, he concludes Chapter 9.

Of the state of nature, Locke makes one more telling and general observation, that the *"Law of Nature"* (moral rationality, such as Kant and Locke considered all individuals to possess and be capable of employing to express moral response and judgment, just as they are capable of expressing desire or emotion) would continue to govern all men, who are *"one Community,"* which is the great echo of natural law theory and the prescription of the Enlightenment. Mankind belongs to "One Society" which, were it not for the "corruption, and vitiousness of degenerate Men, there would be no need for any other [form of political society]" (indeed, no necessity for political society as Locke has defined it in any form). It is clear from his remarks that Locke does envisage the "Law of Nature" as theoretical or perfect, an ideal, based upon natural law theory's assertion that, in order to have our rights and liberties admitted by other individuals, we must admit *their* rights and liberties to an equal degree. If all individuals always did so, says Locke, then there would be no need of the institutions and limitations of political society; but then such a condition, being perfect, is patently unlikely and nonempirical. Hence, the most complete extension of the "State of Nature" as is possible in a community is what must be aimed at in any theory of the *just* society.

Chapter 10, "Of the Forms of a Common-wealth," is an evident and deliberate parallel of Hobbes's method in Chapter 19 of Part 1 of *Leviathan* and of that most infamous determinist text of authoritarian government, Plato's *Republic,* where democracy is a step away from anarchy, and almost as despicable, in order that Locke may define the type to which his political society approximates. For Locke, the choice between traditional types (or the tradition of types) is more pressing, given the circumstances of 1688. Given his inheritance of natural law theory, he has no need to refute Plato, having made his own choice of tradition clear, though he must, in all conscience, refute the latest of Platonists, and the most subtle, Hobbes. He may also draw upon, if he so wishes, the kind of theocracy that Calvin controlled in Geneva, or upon the republicanism of Harrington and Milton, albeit stigmatized by Cromwell's military dictatorship, or indeed upon various degrees of monarchical government such as had been accommodated in England during the seventeenth century—or even upon the king-in-parliament such as the majority of factions seemed to favor in 1688, since their differences were a matter of religious toleration, and then only in degrees, and the relative weight of authority between the traditional partners of government. Ideologies—and *parties*—abounded which would have justified almost any form of government as a solution to the matter of England in 1688.

Out of this melange, what is it that Locke determines upon as the ideal form of political society? Simply that form that achieves an inevitability from no tradition of government but from the tradition of political theory itself, *and* from the Puritan, especially Leveler, distinction between church and state. England had never seen any danger of a theocracy of Puritan or Anglican, even Laudian, persuasion, not even remotely. However, both in the revival of Anglican authority under Charles, and by Laud under his father, the identification of *authority* with the *established church* was hardly in doubt. And with James II, the perennial fears that linked popery with absolutism gave this peculiar and archaic—thanks in no small part to Locke—tradition its final power over the popular imagination, as well as over the minds of more sober observers. Thus, it may be necessary to *assume* that England could have, under the most extreme circumstances, become that survival of medieval times, an autocracy born of the marriage of monarch and church, the ideal of Christendom, as it were. Locke is determined to prevent this, and his argument as to the constitution of the commonwealth is designed to employ the single, irrevocably *secular tradition* of political theory, that of natural law. Even though that tradition had itself been absorbed by the Catholic church, it remained strangely secular in its implications. It never became entirely the province of souls rather than bodies. It was refrigerated by Catholic theologians, with their evidently Roman inheritance and their determination of respect for every living human being as a recipient of grace, almost in order that someone like Locke, the perfect empiricist, could thaw and employ it.

Such being the case, what does Locke make of the general

tradition of political theory in its authoritarian bias (with the suspect exception of Aristotle, who may be seen to be arguing natural law at one point and Platonism at another, though his political theories remain less authoritarian than some of his conceptions of human nature and the soul)? And where, *ever,* do we find such weight given to "the majority" (par. 132) that Locke has already been at some pains to establish as the legislative *force* of society? There is no sense of the "wise," to use a concept employed by both Aristotle and the Stoics, as some kind of elite who alone possess a workable and influential understanding of the realities of human life. In Locke, it is his "majority" who have "the whole power of the Community" and who "may imploy all that Power in making laws for the Community from time to time; and Executing those Laws by Officers of their own appointing." In this case, Locke says, "the *Form* of the Government is a perfect *Democracy."* On the other hand, power may be *put into* the hands of a "few select men" or even into the hands "of one Man," which is oligarchy in the former case and monarchy in the latter, whether hereditary or elective. The majority render into whatever hands they *choose* the legislative power, for what term they decide, in the "Common-wealth," by which Locke insists must be understood not "any Form of Government" but any *"Independent Community,"* which is his initial attempt to describe the retention of sovereignty in the majority of the people. It is authority that is given or granted, not sovereignty transferred.

Chapter 11 immediately proposes to discuss the *"Extent of the Legislative Power"* that is "given" (in other words, the introduction of positive law to that community which is the basis of government though not its form). The first and most fundamental positive law is, therefore, the establishment of the *"Legislative* Power," the *"first and fundamental Natural Law"* which is to govern even the legislative itself. The limitation upon the legislative power is the principle that its employment is designed for *"the preservation of the Society . . .* [and] of every person in it." The form of the legislative must be established and remain unalterable "in the hands where the Community have once placed it," in order that no other body, power, or edict, of whatever form, may overrule the legislative or enact laws, since it is the only body that operates with *"the consent of the Society."* Over the community, "no Body can have a power to make Laws, but by their own consent," he repeats almost at once (par. 134).

He then proceeds to demonstrate how this legislative cannot, under any circumstances, exercise an "arbitrary Power" over any person in the community, since no one had such an arbitrary power in the state of nature, and therefore cannot "transfer to another more power than he has in himself." Further, the legislative cannot "assume to its self a Power to Rule by extemporary Arbitrary Decrees," rather "whatever Form the Common-wealth is under, the Ruling Power ought to govern by *declared* and *received* Laws." The legislative cannot appropriate the property of individuals in the community either, since "the preservation of Property . . . [is] the end of Government." It *must* be remembered here what Locke intends by the idea of "Property"—lives, liberties, and estates—even though he sometimes uses the term to refer principally or even exclusively to possessions. In indicating that the legislative power has no arbitrary authority over a man's possessions, then it can hardly have any authority over his person or liberties without the same consent. However, we should by now be aware that Locke often uses the notion of *property* ironically, as a means of introducing a persuasive or seductive element into his argument, as if tempting the more conservative landed interests of his own time into agreement with his most radical proposals. He employs this method in paragraph 138, since he goes on to suggest that "variable" assemblies which are subject to "dissolution" have less opportunity of becoming arbitrary and seeking to affect property without consent, but "there is danger still" in those forms of government which employ a permanent assembly or a single person that the authority will come to consider itself "to have a distinct interest from the rest of the Community." In other words, Locke has clearly indicated his preferred form of government, a representative assembly whose political color is the choice of the majority to fulfill its views in the enactment of laws, and which is subject to regular dissolution and therefore reelection. And he has done so under the guise of defending property rights, just as he employed the idea of property initially to extend it to include rights, liberties, and personal safety.

He then proceeds to the thorny, especially in the seventeenth century, problem of *taxation.* Here one must recollect that the power of Parliament over the prerogative and executive authority of the monarch resided in Parliament's powers of granting supply (i.e., the royal income for the pursuance of government and foreign policy). On that basis, the legislative must itself receive the taxation, since it is the basis of the constitution or *form* of government, and certainly only the legislative may raise taxes, since they are the basis of the community's consent to government. Locke introduces this idea before discussing the nature of the executive, of course, just as he has introduced the necessity for increased, even extraordinary, powers in time of national emergency (par. 139). What is termed a command economy then exists, since it is the entire community which is at risk. Taxation is recognized by Locke as necessary for the functioning of government, and recognized as something that must be subject to consent, such consent admitted by all rational individuals as an essential element in their consent to government itself.

At the end of the chapter, Locke reiterates that "the *Legislative cannot transfer the Power of Making Laws,*" because "the People alone can appoint the Form of the Commonwealth." However, as he recognizes, we have established just such a *form* of the commonwealth, the government of the community by consent, and it is with that fact of government that we have to deal in Chapter 12.

"Of the Legislative, Executive, and Federative Power of the Commonwealth" runs the title of Chapter 12, and it opens with the statement that the legislative, which has in its hands the making of laws, need not itself be "always in being, not having always business to do." The execution of the laws that have been made, however, requires the existence of some permanent authority. Yet he has already seemed to suggest that the "Legislative" possesses at least some of the powers of an "Executive," in Chapter 11, since they have "the Power of Governing," et cetera. But what is *government* if it is not the executive as well as the legislative? The distinction between the two functions of a government (of whatever form, it requires 'rules' and their obedience) is one that Locke now makes clear upon rational and moral grounds. These two functions must be kept separate, for "it may be too great a temptation to humane frailty apt to grasp at Power, for the same Persons who have the Power of making Laws, to have also in their hands the power to execute them." Locke is of course concerned with the circumstances of 1688–90 in a very real and immediate sense, and the debate concerning the limitations upon prerogative power and executive authority as residing in the monarch. He intends to remove *all* prerogative authority, and make such authority an aspect of the legislative. Executive power may, or may not, remain in the 'person' of the monarch, but there can be no such thing as a royal *prerogative*, since that allows a residue of legislative function to remain with the executive power. However, his distinction between the functions or arms of government is by no means limited to its immediate context. An elected assembly with legislative but *no* executive power is, in Locke's view, the most accountable and least dangerous or arbitrary form of the commonwealth, each of these powers being in some controllable manner subject to an authority outside—primarily, the sovereignty and consent of the community.

Foreign policy Locke terms the *"Federative* Power" of the commonwealth. This is, he claims, a much more spontaneous and flexible form of authority than the government of the commonwealth itself, and must be much more left to the judgment and acuity of the wielder of such authority, who is, of course, subject to the community. Standing, positive laws cannot successfully anticipate every contingency in foreign affairs. Locke falls back upon a contemporary solution to the question, uniting the executive and federative powers of the commonwealth in the same authority, as was the case in the monarch's executive powers and his control of foreign policy as the most significant aspect of his prerogative power. William's desire and need to embroil his new kingdom in his European struggles against Louis XIV would have been known to Locke, and it seems something that he is prepared to countenance, at least by omission from his strictures upon federative power. However, after James II's behavior toward the commonwealth and his prerogative government and attempts to pack Parliament, and Charles II's secret subsidies from Louis in anticipation of a pro-French foreign policy abroad and a more arbitrary government at home, it is understandable that Locke might, by omission at least, not object to William's intended foreign policy. The Stuarts had *control* of foreign policy from the vantage of prerogative power, without "accountability," to use a modern euphemism. Such a circumstance would not exist under Locke's favored form of the commonwealth. However, the most important issue raised by any description of the form of a commonwealth, whether approved by Locke or not, remains to be dealt with—the question of *"the Subordination of the Powers"* of that commonwealth, a question which he addresses in Chapter 13.

There can be "but *one supream Power,"* and that is the legislative, claims paragraph 149, "to which all the rest are and must be subordinate." However, the legislative itself is described as a "Fiduciary Power," which means that it is of the nature of a *trust* and must retain the confidence of the community. It is "to act for certain ends" and there "remains still *in the People a Supream Power* to remove or *alter the Legislative,* when they find that the *Legislative* act contrary to the trust reposed in them." This supreme authority or *sovereignty* is never transferred or surrendered, merely 'loaned'. And it cannot be appropriated, since it is at that very point that the people may remove or alter their legislature. Here we have the core of Locke's theory of government, and that element in it which so evidently appealed to the Founding Fathers, who had both the necessity and opportunity to begin government anew. Their obsession with checks and balances between the legislative and the executive derives almost entirely from Locke's theory of the subordination of powers in a constitution and the continuing residence of supreme power in the community.

"In all cases," Locke however claims, "whilst the Government subsists, the *Legislative is the Supream Power.*" This is the necessary precondition of stability and "settled Law" in the commonwealth, and has been (and must be) consented to if *any* form of government is to occur other than that of arbitrary authority. Having established this point, he proceeds to examine the function of the executive power and takes the most familiar, and likely, in view of 1688–90, form of that authority, the monarchical person, who is to be described and defined as *"Supream Executor* of the Law." He allows that such a monarchical person might have some 'share' of legislative power, also, as would be, and had been, the case in seventeenth-century England—but that only serves to subordinate this supreme executor, like the legislative body, to the sovereignty of the community. The supreme executor may demand and receive *allegience,* but that means, says Locke, no more than *"Obedience according to Law,"* which, if violated, since everyone is subject to the law, including the executive, by this 'person', removes all obligations of obedience to him, which is exactly what he has said of the legislative if it abuses its authority.

At this juncture, in one of his most pointed, if metaphoric, references to Hobbes and his metaphoric description of the absolute monarch as the "sole Person" in the commonwealth, the "personator" of all his subjects, Locke describes the "Supream Executor" as no more than the "Image, Phantom, or Representative of the Commonwealth." He is "acted by the will of the Society, declared in its Laws; thus he has no Will, no Power, but that of the Law." If ever he should "act by his own private Will," he removes all obligation from himself and need not be obeyed. Apart from its clear and deliberate imitation of Hobbes's central image of the monarch, reductively become a mere ghost or "Image" to represent the substance of the community, Locke is evidently intent upon describing the very necessary limitations upon royal authority, or any kind of executive authority *distinct* from the legislative. Of ministerial and other more minor powers and persons, Locke indicates only that they "are all of them accountable to some other Power in the Commonwealth."

Locke's intent concern with the legislators' potential to "lay and carry on designs against the Liberties and Properties of the Subject" and any manner of their disregard of their trust or fiduciary power is a measure of his grasp of recent history and the comprehensiveness of his design of a just commonwealth answerable to its individual members, at the very least to a majority of them in choosing a legislative of a particular color or program. Parliament in the 1640s, the Stuarts and Cromwell and the major generals are all proscribed by their illegitimate extensions or appropriations of authority. The subordination of each of the various powers in the commonwealth ensures against "mall-administration" of the laws, which form the supreme authority under the community. Even if the legislative is not always in being (and here Locke is concerned to demonstrate the "Power of choosing" of the people as to their representatives in the legislative), the curb upon the executive remains, so that the use of "Force upon the People without Authority, and contrary to the Trust put in him, that does so, is in a state of War with the People, who have a right to *reinstate* their *Legislative in the Exercise* of their Power." This is as much a stern warning to William as it is a comment on the behavior of Charles and James. Indeed, it is at this point that Locke recognizes that "the true remedy of *Force* without Authority, is to oppose *Force* to it." ("No Taxation without Representation" would seem to sum this passage up just as succinctly.)

He now proceeds to outline the limitations upon the power to call or dissolve the legislative, and the manner in which the legislative shall meet and continue, before recognizing the necessity for periodic revision of the franchise which will take account of circumstances when the "*Representation* becomes very *unequal* and disproportionate to the reasons it was first establish'd upon." This authority, to revise the franchise, may rest with the executive power, acting "for the publick good in such Cases." This does not amount to the dissolution of government, the final act in the drama of trust and betrayal, when force may be opposed, but necessarily must be taken into account in the original form of government. He makes some interesting and novel comments on "unequal subjection of the rest" by means of "part or party" which, however, should not necessarily be understood as entirely prophetic. Rather, Locke intends that just representation of all should prevail in terms of the franchise and the nature of electoral units and divisions, rather than the merits of proportional representation, though this is not necessarily excluded from his scheme. He concludes the chapter with "the People shall chuse their *Representatives upon* just and undeniably *equal measures* suitable to the original Frame of the Government," in order that "it cannot be doubted to be the will and act of the Society."

X

What Locke has to say on the subject of Prerogative has already been dealt with in his discussion of the manner and necessity of the subordination, the checks and balances, of the various powers within the commonwealth, under the sovereignty of the people, and we need not, therefore, delay over Chapter 14. Chapter 15 is, however, a more necessary and wide-ranging reiteration of some of his principal themes—"Of Paternal, Political, and Despotical Power, considered together." He begins with the claim that "the great mistakes of late about Government [have] arisen from confounding these distinct Powers one with another." He returns to a more abstract level of discussion in this recapitulation. Paternal power has limitations of maturity in the child and cannot reach "at all to the *Property* of the Child," as he has previously remarked. Political power "when in the hands of the Magistrate" (the executive power being that of the supreme or preeminent magistrate) is "to preserve the Members of . . . Society in their Lives, Liberties and Possessions," and so is subject to severe limitations, and derives from and *"has its Original only from Compact* and Agreement, and the mutual Consent of those who make up the Community." *All* other forms or degrees of power are thereby rendered as "Despotical" and arbitrary, for this "is a Power which neither Nature gives, for it has made no such distinction between one Man and another; nor Compact can convey, for Man not having such an Arbitrary power over his own Life, cannot give another man such a Power over it." Finally, Locke reminds us that "by Property I must be understood here, as in other places, to mean that Property Men have in their Persons as well as Goods." Such a reminder is timely, and significantly ignored by Locke's critics of a certain Marxist or collectivist temper.

I do not propose here, toward the conclusion of this long essay on Locke's *Second Treatise,* to consider the discussion of relations between separate commonwealths that Locke engages upon in Chapter 16, nor his discussion of usurpation and tyranny in chapters 17 and 18, except insofar as they are displayed in their inevitable solution in Chapter 19, the final chapter of the treatise, which is entitled "Of the Dissolution of Government," by which, of course, Locke means the constitution, the *form of government,* original to the commonwealth and consented to by the community. It is here that he approves, as we might anticipate, the stance of Parliament in 1642, and its subsequent course of action against the personal government of Charles I, which, in Locke's terms, was an attempt at arbitrary absolutism by dispensing with the supreme authority of the legislative by not summoning Parliament between 1629 and 1640. Locke does not, as we have already seen, repose sovereignty either in the executive or the legislative arms of government, only certain limited and defined degrees of authority or "Power." Therefore, the Long Parliament, as it intended to become sovereign (as the Levelers never tired of remarking), was as much an arbitrary form of government as the personal rule; as was the most recent abrogation of the limits of royal authority by James, and his brother's dalliance with Louis's subsidies with the intent of doing without the legislative and reincarnating his father's personal, prerogative rule. All of these experiments—and certainly that of the "single Person and Parliament" of Oliver Cromwell as Lord Protector, which was, in reality, the beginnings of a military dictatorship—fall outside the scope and legitimacy of Locke's described, *just* commonwealth.

It does not seem to me that it is a question of stance or perspective as to the purpose of Locke's final chapter. It cannot be regarded both as a defense of 1642 and as an acquiescence in the 1688 attempt to ensure the continuity of the monarchical principle or of oligarchical government. It is a defense of the recent past and the right of lawful rebellion against an unjust ruler that is intended to *limit* royal authority, to indicate the nature of a new constitution. Locke cannot be regarded as radical in his understanding of 1642–49, but conservative in his attitude to William III and the motivations of his supporters, which were, largely and even among Whigs, concerned with continuity rather than novelty or justice. There were no questions of extension of suffrage, reform of the franchise, equality, merely a redistribution of factional power in an unrepresentative Parliament and the continuity of that partnership between Crown and country which nowhere receive any support from Locke's theory of government. That a century and a half of political and social progress was lost, until 1832, because of 1688–90, was precisely because Locke's outline of a just and new constitution was *not* put into practice and remained theory—mere ideas—until 1776 in Philadelphia when certain American colonies declared their independence.

To begin his discussion, Locke distinguishes between the *"Dissolution of the Society"* by conquest from outside and the *"Dissolution of the Government"* which occurs *"from within."* The crucial test of circumstance is the alteration of the legislative, by the usurpation of its power by another of the arms of government, principally the executive, or by the establishment of some other form of arbitrary government, or by the behavior of that legislative in an unconstitutional manner. All these are themselves the *conditions* rather than the preconditions of dissolution, and this distinction is crucial because it recognizes the sole *sovereign* power in the commonwealth, that of the people. To act against that sovereignty is already to have acted to dissolve the constitution, thereby the stigma of rebellion applies to the forces that have seized power and employed it arbitrarily *rather than* to the people who resist such a seizure. The people cannot, in any circumstances, be rebellious, except in that they attempt to subvert the constitution themselves, never as *resisting* arbitrary authority in any form by any persons. Locke describes the various instances of dissolution by the neglect or abuse of authority by those empowered before concluding that "in these and the like Cases, *when the Government is dissolved*, the People are at Liberty to provide for themselves, by erecting a new Legislative, differing from the other, by the change of Persons or Form, or both as they shall find it most for their safety and good."

Having progressed in his description of the just commonwealth thus far, Locke has only one principal objection to meet, which is that of his contemporaries and that most fearful to Hobbes and most authoritarian theorists then and since, which is, "To this perhaps it will be said, that the People being ignorant and always discontented, to lay the Foundation of the Government in the unsteady Opinion, and uncertain Humour of the People, is to expose it to certain ruine." And it is here that he reposes his trust in the members of his community, asserting that people are not incessantly factious or rebellious and that nothing short of a "long train of Abuses, Prevarications and Artifices" will "rouze them" to throw off the unjust government and institute another more to their liking. He refutes the authoritarian argument, the whole Platonic tradition of the "wise" as sole repositories of authority, since they alone are qualified to exercise power, by means of this simple, profound assertion. Another argument he might have employed is that since such a democracy has never been tried, there is no proof that the people are undeserving of their natural and inalienable sovereignty. Paragraph 229 asserts that "the end of Government is the good of Mankind, and which is *best for Mankind*, that the People should be always expos'd to the boundless will of Tyranny, or that the Rulers should be sometimes liable to be oppos'd . . . ?" thereby removing the debate to the level of government itself, its "end" or purpose. At such a level, only those who agree with the former proposition regarding *tyranny* can deny the sovereign right of the people to dismiss their unjust and arbitrary governors.

XI

In conclusion, it need only be said that Locke's *Second Treatise of Government* is entirely radical in intent and content, since it departs entirely from the 'practice' of the commonwealth as he observed it in seventeenth-century England, paralleling the arguments for suffrage, accountability, and the limitations upon authority that only the Levelers expressed as a political program. It is a lucid and entire refutation of Filmer—the royal apologist whose appeal was to the tradition of divine right of Hobbes, the apologist of absolutism and the prophet of European government for the succeeding century and more—and of Cromwell, Charles I, his sons, and of the consequences in *practice* of 1688, that less than glorious revolution. In place of the prevailing wisdoms of absolutism or factional or "fixed interest" government, Locke describes the most profoundly democratic commonwealth. He refutes party without the equality of representation he finds essential, he defends rebellion when authority is abused or appropriated, and he opposes the as yet nascent concept of the state, which may be regarded as the elevation of government and the form of the constitution to the sphere of sole and arbitrary sovereignty, such as Hobbes extolled.

Further than this, Locke's theory of government may be seen as opposing history, especially in the sense of tradition or *evolution*, long before such quasi-metaphysical interpretations such as those of the German Romantics, Hegel, and Marx were formulated. The "commonwealth," the government of political society, is made and remade continually by the act of consent and the possibility of change rather than evolution. Tradition, and therefore history, Locke quite rightly identified as the armament of absolutists everywhere. For him, history was *recent* history, the history of democratic ideas as expressed by the Levelers and as embodied, through all the vicissitudes of history and residence, of natural law theory as derived from the Stoics and Cicero. As Dickens claimed near the close of *Bleak House,* in the voice of the dying Richard Carstone, himself ruined and worn down by the 'tradition' of that infamous Chancery suit of *Jarndyce* v. *Jarndyce,* "I must begin the world." And this is precisely Locke's message concerning government, that it is, and must be, possible to "begin the world" of political society—not once, but again and again.

Hence the necessity of suitable celebration (and lament over unfulfilled history) at the tercentennial of the publication, anonymously, in 1690, of the *Two Treatises of Government.* Three hundred years later, it is possible to admit, even to celebrate, that some political societies have developed or been modeled with some regard to Locke's theory of government; and it is a cause for lament that, toward the close of our collectivist century, so many more have treated the theory with disregard, dismissal, and contempt. For countless millions, history has managed to postpone, disguise, dismiss, or find inappropriate Locke's insistence on the sovereignty of the members of a community and the capacity for change in the political order that need not obey the dictates of history itself, or the prescriptions of either and both materialist and metaphysical philosophies, which have little or no place in the formation of a political constitution.

BEHOLD THE SEE (MONSTER): THOMAS HOBBES AND HIS *LEVIATHAN*

To REGARD THOMAS HOBBES and John Locke as proponents of the two most significant traditions of political theory, as my introduction suggests, and therefore as arch-antagonists is in no way excessive. Whatever else Hobbes's intent, he is concerned with the construction of a *state,* just as Locke is concerned with its prevention, and in this, at least, they are true antagonists. Their influence upon subsequent thinkers and the history of political theory into our century is inestimably great. To understand them is to understand the extent and the limitations of ideas of political society.

Hobbes's exposition of the 'fiction' of civil society and the insistence that it must be regarded as the "naturall state" of human beings in social circumstances occupies the longest and most essential section of *Leviathan,* written largely during Hobbes's self-imposed exile from England during the Civil War and published upon his making his peace with the Commonwealth in 1651. His exposition begins, however, with "The First Part, Of Man," and with the circumstances of human nature that establish both the necessity of government and the exact, and inevitable, nature of civil society. For man is not altered (nor finds it necessary to 'adapt') within society; rather, human beings merely 'express' their natures in society. It is necessary, therefore, for Hobbes to convince us of the truth of his image of this essential human nature as revealed in social activity, cohabitation, and behavior.

Human nature, like everything else in the universe, is matter; moreover, matter in motion. This was a position Hobbes arrived at as early as the 1630s and expressed in his then unpublished *Short Tract on First Principles.* The Galilean assumption that *motion* was the 'natural' condition of the universe rather than *rest,* influences Hobbes's entire view of human nature and society, and as such cannot be overemphasized. It is the essence of his political philosophy, of *Leviathan.* His materialism was thereby able to accommodate a model or paradigm which satisfactorily explained human nature in material terms but which also rendered human nature entirely at one with the *material* universe being explored and defined by the new natural sciences. Human nature may thus be understood with the precision of a science, and political (and therefore social) theory may be rescued from the woolliness and theological assumptions of so much of its recent history. It is therefore not inappropriate to regard Hobbes as the first 'modern' exponent of a *science* of society, which is what he deliberately set out to create, rather than another proponent of what we might term the Platonic tradition of a search for a *rational* society, one rationally apprehensible, rationally based, evolved through reason, but not necessarily obedient to a scientific paradigm accepted as true at the time of writing. For example, Plato's theory of forms does not everywhere *inform* his view of society. In Hobbes, however, the science that is paradigmatic thoroughly and entirely explains not only human individual nature but the demonstration of those natures in motion around, and reacting to, each other.

Since motion is the principle upon which the material universe is based and through which it operates, then such a model requires human nature to be regarded not simply from the point of view of *behavior* but *as* motion itself or the result of motion. Thus, in Chapter 6, Hobbes describes the two kinds of motion to which human nature is susceptible and which it demonstrates—"Vitall" and "Voluntary." The former includes "the course of the Bloud, the Pulse, the Breathing," as well as "Nutrition, Excretion," et cetera. In other words, those motions where "there needs no help of Imagination." *Voluntary motions* such as "to go, to speak, to move," et cetera, motions primarily, as he first describes them, of activity and physical in origin, are those that occur "in such manner as is first fancied in our minds." He elaborates this idea in the following claim:

> That Sense, is Motion in the organs and interiour parts of mans body, caused by the action of the things we See, Heare, et cetera; And that fancy is but the Reliques of the same Motion, remaining after Sense . . .

He concludes that it is

> evident, that the Imagination is the first internall beginning of all Voluntary Motion . . . These small beginnings of Motion, within the body of Man, before they appear in walking, speaking, striking, and other visible actions, are commonly called Endeavour.

This is not, unlike Locke's epistemology, in any sense a *sensationalist* interpretation of human nature or behavior. Indeed, we are not here dealing with an epistemology at all, rather with an ontology, a theory of being, an attempt to describe the nature of existence rather than of knowledge about ourselves or the world. It is a materialistic ontology, furthermore, which means that Hobbes is asserting a complete and essentialist explanation of human *nature* rather than human *apprehension,* and one which assumes that phenomenally observed behavior has direct and unavoidable causal connection with parallel or 'like' activities within the human individual.

Hobbes continues his explication by defining two kinds of

"Endeavour," that which "when it is toward something which causes it, is called Appetite or Desire . . . and when the Endeavour is fromward something, it is generally called Aversion." The simple and mechanistic nature of Hobbes's system is already clearly apparent in this, as is the interconnection of the whole system. Man is to be regarded as a creature who reveals himself in motion or who is the expression of motions of aversion or appetite. Man's activity is inseparable from his nature, but that nature is to be understood solely in terms of his activity. What is also significant here, and which we must consider later, is the essentially physical or amoral view that Hobbes takes of the bases of human *nature*, rather than simply of *behavior*.

The remainder of Chapter 6 of *Leviathan* develops this basic idea. Appetite is synonymous with love, and aversion with hate. Hatred is related to "the presence of the Object," while desire occurs at its absence. Other than basic appetites, those connected with "Vitall Motions," "Appetites of particular things, proceed from Experience." Human nature's capacity to alter its apprehension of what is desirable or hateful is accounted for by the fact that "because the constitution of a mans Body is in continuall mutation, it is impossible that all the same things should always cause in him the same Appetites and Aversions." At this juncture, it is necessary to remark the obvious, that Hobbes predetermines the growth or maturity of human nature and its apprehension of the world by the simple, material expedient of *mutability*, itself a synonym for motion. The fact of "continuall mutation" is unquestioned but is clearly a process derived solely from a motion within or by the human being. From the response of appetite or aversion to the world arise, naturally, the concepts of good and evil, words which describe our aversions and desires, "there being nothing simply and absolutely so; nor . . . to be taken from the nature of the objects themselves," as he concludes. While this, of course, is reminiscent of various idealist theories, and even parallels empiricism to some extent, the purpose that Hobbes has in mind here is *not* to define the subjectivity of moral judgments but to establish the certainty and inclusiveness of the material reality of the world and man within it. Subjectivity becomes here apprehension in material terms of a material universe. Appetite and aversion are material (i.e., 'real'), proceeding as they do from a material premise of universal motion, while the moral concepts which are employed to describe or discuss human activity and *motive* are alone regarded as 'subjective' (i.e., remaining in the realm of language), a descriptive device distinct from the material reality of the desires and aversions that prompt such moral description and in no way explanatory of the motions of the bodies that human beings are, which motions are their *real* motives.

Hobbes proceeds to describe "Pleasure" and "Payne" as the "appearance or sense of Good; and . . . of Evill," much as a classical utilitarian might have done, and demonstrates that the whole gamut of response and feeling in human nature derives from this simple model of the human emotional framework; in large part, he describes a development of language rather than of experience. They are little more than other names for familiar things, multiplications of the few basic appetites and aversions. What occurs in the remainder of Chapter 6 is little short of the destruction of all moral apprehension of human feeling and action, which, as will be seen, is a vitally necessary part of Hobbes's system or 'scheme'—and this writer uses both words advisedly with regard to *Leviathan.* "Hope, Despayre," et cetera, as well as "Benevolence, Anger, Courage," are all defined within the scope of the simple, mechanical propositions which began the chapter. For example, "Constant *Hope*" is defined merely as "CONFI-DENCE of ourselves," with "Constant *Despayre*" as the opposite of that confidence of and in our selves.

Proceeding from this, Hobbes brings his argument to bear on the concept of "Deliberation," by which he means reflection, rational *weighing* of alternatives, the reflective capacity. Deliberation, for Hobbes, is "the whole summe of Desires, Aversions, Hopes and Fears, continued till the thing be either done, or thought impossible." In other words, reflection is an *activity* like any other, a prolongation by virtue of human reason of the process of acting or of responding to a desire or aversion. However, in order to provide the materialist limitation with regard to this recognizable capacity for reflection in human beings, what Hobbes might justly describe as 'hesitation before action', he goes on to say that "in *Deliberation,* the last Appetite, or Aversion, immediately adhering to the action, or the omission thereof, is that wee call the WILL; the Act, (not the faculty) of *Willing.*" Neatly, therefore, and universally, he contains man's rational capacity within the framework of activity, since deliberation is nothing more than a further degree of response to things or experiences and is defined as arising from the appetite or aversion *immediately adhering,* thereby describing deliberation as little more than a *serial hesitation* which, in its outcome, adopts that response to the action which immediately follows deliberation. Human rational capacity never returns to an earlier response or idea to inform its activities, it merely hesitates until some overriding appetite or aversion dissolves the whole process of reflection.

This is, of course, only Hobbes's initial brush with the reality of human reason, but it is inclusive and dependent upon his earlier description of the gamut of human response as it arises from a few basic emotions, which themselves arise from the two basic responses of appetite and aversion. *"Will is* therefore *the last Appetite in Deliberating."* This is Hobbes's encapsulation of human rational or reflective capacity, as well as of human nature's capacity—nil—to become dispassionate or objective in its responses. The decisive mechanism of human reason is will, originating in desire or aversion, whereas in Locke it may be regarded as some kind of moral capacity which apprehends experience and whose *judgment* predicates response rather than is derived from it. Hobbes interposes a substitute for reason which he terms will, a description not of a moral or even intellectual faculty but of response to the goad of experience and emerging as a series of desires and aversions. Indeed, *in*action is itself a response rather than a denial of response, a form of aversion.

It is at this point that Hobbes reverts to a linguistic—more properly etymological—discussion, especially of reason as opposed to deliberation—"Reasoning is in generall words; but Deliberation for the most part is of Particulars." This again reduces the rational capacity to an activity or a means of activity, rather than, as stylized by almost all philosophy recognizable as such, a reflective capacity obeying that principle of *rest* which had been refuted as an explanation of material reality by Galileo.

Hobbes's employment of etymology must be remarked at this point, though it will be returned to. He is concerned to shear language of its accretions, to the extent of disabling their currency, allusion, and association. The derivational employment of language that he persists in employing is again part of the system he is developing, which requires that the moral enrichment of the language employed by political and ethical theorists who preceded and surrounded him be bankrupted and recast as a devalued currency applicable only to materialism and the paradigmatic terminology of the Galilean revelation Hobbes had undergone. The 'scientific' regard Hobbes has for language is designed to purify it of accreted and distorted ethical senses and usages—not in order that it be reemployed for a similar purpose but that it *remain* divested of any capacity to express such meanings.

Hobbes concludes his crucial Chapter 6 with the following:

> Life it self is but Motion, and can never be without Desire,
> nor without Feare, no more than without Sense.

In this, he completes the foundations of his great edifice. The system seems self-enclosed and self-evident, though that perhaps owes as much to sleight of hand as to any discernible scientific evidence or even abstract logic. Hobbes has argued from premises he himself has *applied* to human nature rather than derived from observation. His conversion to scientific materialism, of course, is derived from geometry rather than from a more empirical method, from the formulaic rather than the observational. Hence the peculiarity and the 'inevitability' of his methodology, plus the strangely geometric Q.E.D. at which he arrives at the conclusion of the chapter—"Life it self is but Motion," which is the point from which he began and from which he did not depart to incorporate empirical evidence of any kind or degree. Indeed, the progress of Hobbes's argument in Chapter 6 is self-evidentially assertive, as in school geometry textbooks of a bygone age, where the diagram preceded the proof—to the extent that Hobbes's discussion is not a substantiation at all but an explanation of an unseen but nevertheless incontrovertible diagram of the truth.

It is necessary to remark even this early in any examination of *Leviathan* that Hobbes's materialism is deliberately subversive of what he often contemptuously refers to as the "schooles" (i.e., the moral philosophy of his own and earlier times). Locke is, of course, an empiricist and therefore without subversive intent as regards precedent ethical philosophy, indeed, he is their cultural inheritor. Hobbes, however, cannot be content with any sign of continuity, with any tradition of ethical or social philosophy, since his is a 'new' method entirely, a scientific approach to what had *previously* been an ethical preserve. He intends to break with tradition, to the extent that his linguistic concerns are as subversive and redefinitional as his ideas.

An example of this is the manner in Chapter 6 in which *rest*, the lack of motion—which may be regarded as the great supporting principle of ethical philosophy, since it is so regarded by Hobbes and since it implies and encloses a notion of *reflection* and detachment which "Wille" does not—is equated with "Contempt," a state of indifference between appetite and aversion, love, and hate, referring to "those things which we neither Desire nor Hate . . . CONTEMPT being nothing else but an immobility, or contumacy of the Heart, in resisting the action of certain things." In fact, this is a crucial passage in *Leviathan*, since it typifies Hobbes's linguistic methodology and the subversive extent of his materialism. Detachment, therefore, is equated with contempt, *or*—in materialist terminology—with things to which we are indifferent, unimportant or irrelevant things.

However, in breaking with ethical tradition—or the tradition of ethics as a distinct sphere of philosophy, to be more precise— Hobbes is intent upon *replacement* as well as redefinition. As a materialist he intends to define human capacities and experiences, and human attitudes to experience, as *material* 'things'. This means not only is human nature totally dependent upon *objects* of desire or aversion, and therefore upon the experience or at least imagination or secondhand reporting of experience, but human capacities have all the solidity and limitation of *physical bodies;* governed by motion but governed even more by their physical existence and their total explicability in physical, material terms. As yet, Hobbes has extended his materialism only to human emotions—but he has already defined human nature as *solely* emotional and governed by emotional response (will) rather than by any moral-reflective capacity. He has also, of course, subverted the whole idea of man in the detached or philosophic sense. Human nature is responsive to experience, yes, but to communal experience, it would appear from the inventory of human emotions contained in Chapter 6. Thus, Hobbes's materialism is at odds with, and entirely opposed to, any *ethical* consideration of political society, a consideration which Locke regards as de facto to any human combination in a society. *Civil* society, however, will be founded upon principles other than the ethical, as Hobbes proceeds to demonstrate.

"Deliberation" is not an innate, or even educable, moral capacity, it is an expression of the eventual and eventually responsive will. The weighing of appetites and aversions is not a recognizable process or undertaking, merely a period of waiting for a sufficiently imperative trigger to the human responsive capacity, which outcome we then *will*. As if to emphasize the inclusive materialism of Chapter 6, Hobbes remarks at the end of his exhaustive inventory, especially inclusive of "passions" we might consider, ethically, as disinterested, benevolent or moral, that emotional terminology is but the "voluntary significations of our passions: but certain signs they are not; because they may be used arbitrarily . . . The best signs of Passions present, are either in the countenance, motions of the body, actions, and ends, or aimes, which we otherwise know the man to have." Again, this is not an empiricism based upon observable or experienced phenomena, rather a materialism which assumes that the physical activity and expression of human nature is *all*-sufficient, the sole basis for comprehending human nature.

II

At the outset of Chapter 10, Hobbes having meanwhile demolished human intellectual capacity, reducing it to little more than a capacity to finely (or obliquely, depending upon degree of "Witte") calculate self-advantage, as he had earlier demolished the ideas of freedom and "Free will" in Chapter 5, we discover the heading "Of POWER, WORTH, DIGNITY, HONOUR, *and* WORTHINESSE." The first sentence reads: "The POWER *of a Man*, (to take it Universally,) is his present means, to obtain some future apparent Good." The title of the chapter and the arguments it contains establish the question of "power" as of essential importance to any discussion "Of Man." "Worth," "dignity," and the rest are to be understood as aspects of power, or the consequences of power, rather than as distinct human attributes. The whole chapter depends upon the conflation of the idea of *power,* and the word itself as "signifier" into the demonstration or acquisition of power in the sense that we would most readily understand it, in *social* terms (wealth and influence), then into the transmission, as it were, of such power into the hands of a governor or sovereign. It is in Chapter 10 that the purpose of Hobbes's demolition of any ethical framework to political theory first becomes apparent, when we are left with a 'de-ethicalized' language to cope with conceptions of the *organization* of political society. "The Greatest of humane Powers, is that which is compounded of the Powers of most men, united by consent, in one Person, Naturall or Civill . . . such is the Power of a Commonwealth," Hobbes claims a paragraph later. We have thus begun the discussion of a political society by directly discussing the "Faculties of Body, or Mind" and "Riches, reputation, Friends" which we may regard as the province of a *civil* society. Hobbes has, however, already outlined the nature of a satisfactory political organization, even as he begins to define the nature of power, worth, et cetera. To remark his technique here is sufficient, peculiar as it is and much as it demands explanation—but Hobbes himself is not yet ready to explain. So we must consider Hobbes's definition of "the *Value*, or WORTH of a man," which is, bluntly, "his Price; that is to say, so much as would be given for the use of his Power."

Hobbes has, of course, perennially been regarded as the great cynic of modern political theory, except perhaps until Marx, though in the latter there is an almost ecstatic contemplation of unalienated human nature. Such remarks are legion in *Leviathan*, but to regard them merely as the epithets of a masterly stylist with a cynical view of human nature is to misunderstand and diminish Hobbes. Hobbes is, indeed, by no means a cynic, or even a realist. He is an apologist for authority of a particular kind and a materialist whose interpretation of human nature is not only systematic but *must* be so. It must also confine itself to the visible end of the human spectrum and deal with human activity, patterns of human behavior which may be extrapolated to the "generall." Therefore, when Hobbes elevates power and value, worth and honor to preeminence in human experience, he is preparing his description of civil society *and* of the authority that subsequently becomes requisite to produce *order*—and he does so *before* any description of society as such—even before his discussion of the central idea of man's "naturall state" in Chapter 13.

It may be as well to consider chapters 5 to 12 of *Leviathan* as a concentrated and systematic reduction of what may be termed the potential of human nature. Beginning with his examination of "Freedom" and "Free will" in Chapter 5, where these arrogant conceptions are reduced to the formula of "free from being hindred by opposition," together with his initial attack upon the rational capacity of man, Hobbes engages in a progressive diminution of human capacities, especially those which the seventeenth century regarded, traditionally and currently, to distinguish man from the rest of creation. We have already seen in Chapter 6 the schematic derivation of the whole gamut of human passions, instincts, and feelings from the basic, magnetic opposites of attraction and repulsion, and in chapters 7 to 9 he mounts his assault upon reason, knowledge, and "Faith," all of which prepares for the two chapters (10 and 11) which develop his notion of material man and the limitations of such a creature, before the assault is renewed upon the two remaining, and now firmly interconnected, bastions of Aristotelian, Judeo-Christian, and Stoic thought—religion and natural law theory. Therefore, chapters 10 and 11 contain an essential element of the argument; while appearing to promulgate a 'real' view of human nature acting in the world, they do in fact further diminish the notion of rational, philosophical, reflective man; indeed, they present a *type* of human nature that is to be regarded as both essential and universal.

"Dignity" is thus the "publique worth of a man, which is the Value set on him by the Common-wealth." As for "Worthinesse," it is described as "a particular power, or ability for that, whereof he is said to be worthy: which particular ability, is usually named FITNESSE, or *Aptitude.*" Hobbes is presenting as preeminent those virtues which might be termed the civic virtues, and not necessarily cynically or contemptuously. They are of significance to the society, especially to the "Common-wealth," the institutions of government and order in a community. Power is the object of human appetite, worth is the measure of power, dignity is the dignity of office and position, and worthiness is the aptitude to employ those virtues civically. There is, of course, a naked and curious parallel with Plato's discussion of civic virtues in the *Republic* here—but Plato extends his discussion to other areas and degrees, even kinds, of virtue in his guardians, and the philosophic and rational qualities of all human beings are not in doubt, though the elite of the guardians will, of course, possess such qualities in greater abundance. Hobbes, however, is concerned *not* to derive civic virtues from such universal and ethical principles, but from the practice or appearance of such virtues in *action.* His models are derived from existing society, not from the necessity of an ideal republic. We are dealing here with courtiers rather than guardians. This may be regarded as the object of his successive diminution of human scope and capacity. The limitations of human reason and human knowledge allow only the narrowly (or shallowly) material appearance or *enactment* of the civic virtues for discussion.

In Chapter 11, Hobbes addresses the subject of "MANNERS," by which he intends to signify "those qualities of mankind, that concern their living together in Peace, and Unity," and *not* "Decency of behaviour," the *"Small Moralls"* of table manners, forms of address, et cetera. However, the diminution continues simply because Hobbes calls the qualities required for social existence "Manners," well understanding that the term is a diminutive unless applied to the "Small Moralls" alone.

Be that as it may, he begins by asserting that "Felicity of this life" cannot consist of repose of the mind or of desire or appetite satisfied. Further, there is "no such . . . utmost ayme nor . . . greatest Good, as is spoken of in the Books of the old Morall Philosophers." Felicity is, instead, "a continuall progresse of the desire, from one object to another." This first paragraph of the chapter encapsulates Hobbes's method and his materialism. Moral philosophy (which he is to freshly assault in Chapter 13, his great *putsch* for the citadel) is dismissed as erroneous, while the materialist view of eternally restless, ever-desiring human nature is again emphasized. The essential purpose of human nature is to "assure for ever, the way of his future desire." All man's voluntary actions (Chapter 6) are intent upon this. Power to fulfill desire is the necessary object of human activity, so that Hobbes claims that "I put for a generall inclination of all mankind, a perpetuall and restlesse desire for Power after power, that ceaseth onely in Death." This is, of course, one of Hobbes's most famous dictums, and it is the essence of his 'scientific' materialism as applied to the study of human nature and society, since it perfectly fulfills the molecular and egocentric nature of man as matter alone and provides a single, essential principle of human actions, as well as standing as a direct opposite of any and all conceptions of man as Aristotle's "rational animal." Finally, it is an essence of human nature that can only be expressed in action, man as matter in motion.

From this observation, Hobbes proceeds to regard all human activity as "desire," something he has already claimed but now proceeds to prove. Love of the arts and "Desire of Knowledge" contain no more than a "desire for leisure"—further, it is the first emphasis upon the desire for "some other Power than their own" by men, a protective power. "Desire of Ease and sensuall Delight, disposeth men to obey a common Power," he claims. This is, in part, the preparation for Chapter 13, where the infamous "warre of all against all" makes its appearance. For the moment, it is necessary only to remark that Hobbes is employing his characteristic technique with regard to the discussion of society, dealing with the material reality (the contemporary, existing structure) before undermining the philosophical, moral, ethical, or theological foundations of that contemporary reality, leaving only the *material* surface.

Hobbes also broaches the "Love of Contention" that he regards as an essential element in human nature, that competition for "Riches, Honour, Command" which regards all other individuals as objects placed in the way of the self's fulfillment of its desires. Hobbes, therefore, is beginning in Chapter 11 another and second process of diminution, as he has previously developed with regard to individual human capacities and potentials— namely, the diminution of society to a universally competitive, warring state which requires, more than anything else, the application of authority, of a "soveraign Power." This process of diminution reaches its climax in Chapter 13, where the "naturall state" of men is conflated with the reality of their social existence without the government of "some other Power than their own." However, we have not yet quite reached the war to the very death of unrestrained egos. What he has begun, however, is to develop that sublunary view of human nature, having stripped it of its illusions of philosophic, ethical, and rational capacity, that culminates in the description of the "naturall state"—men are governed by will and desire, and what they desire is power. Other men are objects in the way, to be competed against and defeated. Hobbes's model of human nature is the "animal" in Aristotle's compromise between the creation and the gods. The chapter is filled with terms such as "revenge," "hurt," "tumult," "torments," "kill, subdue, supplant," another of Hobbes's subtleties of language, since the object of the vocabulary is to predict and predetermine Chapter 13, rather than to actually signify the contents of Chapter 11.

It need only be remarked that in Chapter 12, "Of Religion," Hobbes demolishes the last pretensions of theology, since theology is man's attempt to explain causes, even to the "worship of Powers invisible." Hobbes is depriving human nature of but one illusion, since religion originates in man and may be summarily regarded as, in Hobbes's view, man's attempt to explain his existence, on the one hand, and as a desperate invention to supply that peace and order that is so absent from civil society.

In chapters 5 to 12 of *Leviathan,* therefore, Hobbes is engaged in the task of unfolding a phenomenal world and describing its activity, though not in any empirical sense but as reductively self-evident. He successively denudes his portrait of human nature of moral capacity and of its moral vocabulary, its *signification* in the world. That phenomenal world, composed entirely and solely of matter, becomes, in Chapter 13, the "naturall state" of man and of his society in its preinstitutional or pregovernmental reality. What he has also done is create the expectation of hidden *laws* or the desire for law, for "some other Power than their own," which he can later reveal in human nature and therefore in society. The inevitability of such hidden laws, rather than their arising from human reason as an artifact or construct, is, of course, essential to his argument. The task of political theory, as practiced by Hobbes, is the exposure of these inevitable laws, analogous to those of the natural sciences of his time and to the material universe, behind phenomena and underlying them; law is not a *decision,* a system arrived at by virtue of human reason. That capacity of reason has been dismissed by Chapter 12, so that

Hobbes's *principle of self,* the operation of will and desire, may serve as the origin and basis of the *principle of order.* Self-benefit, in natural law or "original position" theories of society (those of contract and/or consent), assumes the necessity of *mutual* benefit in the form of social organization to be adopted, and Hobbes parallels this idea with extreme subtlety and subversive intent. Self-benefit in his view of human nature is essentially antigovernmental and essentially competitive; it cannot be antisocial, since only in society is it demonstrated. However, it must contain the potentiality of government and order. Therefore, this corollary of the unrestrained, willing, and desiring self in a world of matter *must already exist* in the kind of authority human society already experiences, *not* in some metaphor of the origin of society by consent or by any process of decision to begin a political society in another form. (Hobbes discusses contract and consent later in *Leviathan.*) Sovereign authority exists, and has existed, as the form of government for human society and has fulfilled another archetypal *desire* of the self, that for "peace," not justice, since Hobbes is barely concerned with the concept of the good or the just society, only with the ordered society suppressed into peace. Hobbes's logic argues from human nature *as it is* to society *as it is* and thence to government *as it is.* Government is the expression of the greater (or greatest) will and desire, embodied in the authority, the superior "Power" which controls those powers of the competitive self.

It may be said, indeed, that the events of the Long Parliament as immediately preceding the Civil War were an aberrant attempt of men to act as if their natures were other than Hobbes describes, and that the ensuing chaos, the "vacuum" which "Nature abhors," was the direct result of such a fictitious attempt to follow natural law theory, to remake political society. The recognition of the necessity of order, of authority sufficiently powerful to thwart the desiring self, arises in human nature out of fear—of disorder, chaos, especially of death itself. This is where natural law theory is paralleled to the point of extremity. Fear of death replaces in the pantheon fear of intrusion upon liberties, upon that (metaphorical) complete freedom of activity, rights, and liberties that the man outside or preceding society enjoys. Following that metaphor, Hobbes is later to claim, produces only chaos, because natural law theory does not recognize human nature as it really is, nor the mechanistic *necessity* that is the law of a material universe. Therefore, order is the fulfillment of an *implicit principle* in human nature and the universe, that of the desire for life in a dangerous, violently competitive world. As natural law theory talks of man in the "state of Nature," Hobbes speaks of "natural man" and, just as the ego cannot will or desire its own death (in Locke, it is a matter of not *consenting* to one's own death), since it would contradict *the natural law of self-preservation,* the primary, and perhaps in Hobbes the only, natural right, that to life, the ego cannot therefore exist in a state of constant danger, since that contradicts or at least permanently threatens this *law of nature.* This is the basis of authority, the desire for self-preservation.

Natural law theory has never presented human nature or human political society as a paradigm of any of the natural or physical sciences. It is not materialist, though it is certainly empirical. Essentially, it accepts an ethical element in human nature, together with a rational capacity. It recognizes an equivalence of selves in congregation as the basis of society, and the emergence and necessity of a principle of mutual benefit by means of which society coheres and operates and out of which its institutions develop. The "state of Nature" or "original position" is a metaphor which preserves the concept of *choice* and the capacity to *design* political society. Hobbes's "naturall state," being a material condition, must provide all the evidence or phenomena of which human nature and society is composed. Therefore, it remains to the theorist only to uncover or reveal the hidden laws that explain the nature and *behavior* of the phenomenal world, laws which can be discerned *only* in the phenomenal world.

However, in Hobbes's "naturall state," and he means to emphasize both words, we find his most subtle parallel of natural law theory. Just as natural law theory assumes society to be for the preservation of freedom, security, rights, and liberties that the individual might enjoy outside its inevitable constraints, Hobbes has as his master principle *self*-preservation, the preservation of life itself. He conflates rights, liberties, freedoms, and duties into the single principle that the individual is concerned only with the desire for life and with the accretion or seizure of power in order to secure the continuance of life. It is in this mechanism of the ego, this willing and desiring, that Hobbes discovers his single principle. Human nature, thus viewed, predicates not the quasi-anarchical society that Marx also witnessed and excoriated, but the proto-political society expressing a "wille" and "desire" toward and for order. He has developed, through chapters 5 to 12, an apparently insoluble problem—the unrestrained ego's apparent acceptance of *government*, its instinct toward order, when everything he has claimed for human nature would appear to suggest the opposite principle. But, the *master principle* is that of self-preservation, which therefore allows only one kind of system, that of absolute authority, *"soveraign* Power," the rule of prerogative and the combination of what has become known as the executive and the legislature in one body, together with that third member of the institutional trinity, the judiciary. Therefore, chapters 5 to 12 of *Leviathan* are reductive to an inordinate degree, eventually fitting human nature to a universe explicable entirely in terms of matter in motion and describable in geometrically analogous formulas. It is then possible for Hobbes to erect the idea of one preeminent desire for the prolongation of life itself; all other desires are subordinated by this effusion of self-preservation under the constant and consistent threat of other selves. In Chapter 11, Hobbes explains the essence of the desire for power in human nature by a negative, when he says: "He cannot assure the power and means to live well, which he hath at present, without the acquisition of more," while he remarks of society that "there is no other way by which a man can secure his life and liberty," still in subversive tandem with natural law theory but with one half about to break from the other. Also, "the voluntary actions, and inclinations of all men, tend, not only to the procuring, but also to the *assuring* [my italics] of a contented life." This claim precedes that concerning the "perpetuall and restlesse desire of Power" quoted earlier.

Hence, Hobbes has planted the mines beneath the tunnels and windings of natural law theory by means of which he hopes to explode the theory, to hoist it with its own petard. Human nature cannot help but act upon the imperative of the master principle of self-preservation and therefore resolves upon order, on the preservation of desire, otherwise eternally thwarted by other selves and their possibly predominant desirings, by the suppression of *unrestrained* desire. There are only two "desires" from which to choose, that of desiring itself and that of the desire for life—given that choice, what rational creature would choose any but the latter?

All this obeys Hobbes's materialist strictures, since nothing can be further reduced in a material universe beyond the principle of continuing existence, but it also anticipates much of what Hobbes has to say in chapters 13 and 14 concerning natural law theory. And there lies before Hobbes still, in Chapter 12, that final assault upon the last citadel of ethical political theory. Empirical, idealist, essentialist, and collectivist theories may all, in their fashion, presuppose some rational capacity in human nature which will evolve, invent, or subsequently modify or change political society. Hobbes's materialism does not. Instead, it supposes that rationality enters, stage left, *only* in terms of authority. Reason is the exclusive preserve of the "soveraign Power."

Meanwhile, the truly Trojan horse is within the Greek citadel, and the "topless towers" of Stoic, Roman, and Judeo-Christian tradition are endangered, as Hobbes proceeds to the attack in Chapter 13.

III

Nature hath made men so equall, in the faculties of body, and mind; as that though there bee found one man sometimes manifestly stronger in body, or of quicker mind then another; yet when all is reckoned together, the difference between man, and man, is not so considerable, as that one man can claim to himselfe any benefit, to which another may not pretend, as well as he.

Thus Hobbes begins Chapter 13, to which he gives the title "Of the NATURALL CONDITION of Mankind, as concerning their Felicity, and Misery." This seeming expression of *equivalence* (which is politically far more important than *equality*, which is capable of the grossest distortions and systemizing) as regards human beings is in no sense a political statement but rather a moral observation, and a pejorative one at that. It is entirely in keeping with Hobbes's earlier examination of human nature and the motions that motivate individuals. This form of equality is reductive, translatable only as all men are much the same, whatever their circumstances—equally *alike*. The placing of the observation in the opening paragraph of the chapter, beneath a chapter heading which is itself a mocking paraphrase of natural law theory, is intended to continue the undermining of that theory, already begun by confining any discussion of human nature within the straitjacket of appetite or aversion.

From this it is then simple to reduce the structure to a single, overriding appetite, that for life itself. This *life-appetite*, as it might be termed, its inevitable corollary being the overriding aversion to death, is what now emerges in Hobbes's theory to supersede or dominate all other appetites. The life-appetite is the motive or motion behind the restless, unceasing desire for power, because the object of all power is *security* against the threat of danger or death. Power is the strength of 'life assurance' for the individual. The urgency is biological rather than moral, the energy expended to protect life itself rather than anything more esoteric or ethical such as rights, liberties, freedoms, choice. Motion is the *law* of existence, and the appetite for life the strongest expression of that motion. After all, the absence of motion, *rest*, has one remarkable similarity to death in its lack of motion.

Thus, Hobbes's *equality* is no more than an identity of *all* human natures, a biological, or in Hobbes's case a psychological, fact erected as the essence of a moral system and a political theory. Because of the significance of this master principle of human activity and motive, we are in fact dealing with a materialist *metaphysic*, something that has no connection with materialism per se and which is the opposite of empiricism. And, whatever its ethical or theological-metaphysical origins, natural law theory had become, in ideas of political society, an essential part of the empirical attitude.

Hobbes now proceeds with what is, essentially, a nonhierarchical view of society, one without the pyramidal structure of feudalism (despite Hobbes's often archaic and intensely traditional views of human nature and political society) in which men recognize their basic similarity and equivalence of "ability." From this, he claims, "ariseth equality of hope in the attaining of our Ends," which itself leads inevitably to men desiring the same thing, and since "they cannot both enjoy, they become enemies; and in the way to their End (which is principally their owne conservation, and sometimes their delectation only,) endeavour to destroy, or subdue one an other." This inevitability is designed, deliberate, inescapable, and one of syntax only, and it is another of those maxims that encapsulate Hobbes's method as well as his essential theory. The destruction, or at least complete subjugation, of others is the sole route to the satisfaction of our appetites, which principal and overweening appetite is our own preservation. This is the beginning of that "warre of all against all" which this chapter and those which succeed it seek to render irrefutable. Individual beings in a material universe constantly and dangerously collide with each other, intent upon harm and self-preservation through harm to others. To paraphrase the earlier metaphor regarding materialism, men are particles of an identical substance or expressions of one master principle, which is that of material objects in motion, and their lives are demonstrations of molecular likeness, all behaving and acting in exactly the same way, out of the same motives or motions.

Hobbes continues: ". . . from this diffidence to one another, there is no way for any man to secure himselfe, so reasonable, as Anticipation; that is, by force or wiles, to master the persons of all men he can . . ." until, Hobbes says, there is "no other power great enough to endanger him." It might be remarked here that Hobbes can be regarded as employing clichés that were habitually applied in the seventeenth century to the *relations of nations* and countries, making them serve his analysis of an internal or 'national' society. There is an even greater, and more traditional, convention of thought he employs in describing the State, as will be seen, but it is necessary to understand that at least some part of the peculiar power of Hobbes's *Leviathan* springs from the archetypes he employs, as here. The macrocosm of Europe or the political 'world' is now an image of the microcosm, the internal condition of states. This condition of society, at war out of a desire for security, says Hobbes, "ought to be allowed," since it is necessary "to a mans conservation."

Immediately following this view of human relations, and now clearly justifiable, Hobbes remarks: "Men have no pleasure, (but on the contrary a great deal of griefe) in keeping company, where there is no power able to over-awe them all." He continues by referring once more to men requiring to be valued by others as they value themselves, then proceeds to outline the three "principall causes of quarrell" which, unsurprisingly, spring from "Competition," from "Diffidence," and from "Glory," paralleling much of what he earlier said of *"Desire."* Then, at once, he springs upon the but half-prepared reader his most infamous dictum, "that during the time men live without a common Power to keep them all in awe, they are in that condition which is called Warre; and such a warre, as is of every man against every man." This, then, is the essential and continuing condition of civil society, yet within the observation as first stated lies the solution, prepared for by Hobbes's equation of *"Power"* with "security," with self-preservation, and with *"Peace."* The nature of war, he tells us, is not in actual fighting but in the "known disposition thereto," and therefore his vision of a warring society need not demonstrate any actual conflict, only the "known disposition" or potential to such. Society might look very calm on the surface, for the most part and for most of the time, but if *conditional* circumstances such as men's efforts at wealth, glory, worth, dignity, et cetera, can be identified, then we, with Hobbes, are correct in determining society to be at war of the most internecine and destructive kind. Hobbes proceeds to describe the condition of society in such an actual, or *potential,* state of war, concluding with his other most infamous remark that human life becomes "solitary, poore, nasty, brutish and short."

Despite the above, Hobbes is determined that this be seen as no unnatural or immoral state but rather as the "naturall condition" of men, for he says: "The Desires, and other Passions of men, are in themselves no Sin. No more are the Actions, that proceed from those Passions, till they know a Law that forbids them." It is at this point, of course, as he implicitly rejects any idea of an innate or original moral capacity, whether described as a conscience or as some other ethical agency in human nature, that Hobbes attempts to dispatch natural law theory, which suggests if not claims a moral capacity that is *natural,* and a sense of *law* deriving from human nature rather than from education or imposition. For Hobbes, none of this has the slightest validity. Men are motivated by their passions, *moved* by their appetites or aversions. They must be taught ethical, or at least unselfish, behavior, not necessarily by means of their moral education, which is how natural law theory would assume a moral sense was instilled, or its innate qualities illuminated, but by what Wordsworth called "the impressive discipline of fear"—by a superior or "soveraign" power governing their actions.

Hobbes now introduces the most irrefutable proof in support of such an order and in demonstration of men being ruled by no innate motives other than appetite and passion. Without a "com-

mon Power to feare," "peacefull government" is impossible; witness the depredations of a "civill Warre," the utter collapse of
organization and order—of political society itself. Hobbes, however, introduces rather than discusses the idea at this point, in
another of his preparatory declamations to be taken up in a later
chapter as if already proven. There is no place in *Leviathan* for
the Scottish legal system's verdict of *not proven;* the principles
upon which the book bases its arguments are proven by previous
insertion into a different context, to be extracted and extrapolated
at a subsequent point. Thus, "civill Warre" is another of those
principal ideas to which Hobbes is later to return but which serves
as self-evident syllogism at the point of its introduction, since he
immediately proceeds to describe the international condition of
nations, remarking that the international condition of constant,
though implicit, war that exists between monarchs is healthy in
itself as upholding the "Industry of their [i.e., kings'] Subjects,"
so that "there does not follow from it, that misery, which accom-
panies the Liberty of particular men."

One should remark, at once, the closed nature of the argument,
proceeding from statement to generalization to conclusion but
returning to initial principle, so that at no point does empirical
qualification or doubt intrude. Hobbes has expanded the analogous argument to the inclusiveness his system requires, in that
international relations (remembering that foreign policy and the
right to wage war against foreign enemies had always been regarded, even by Parliament, as the prerogative of the monarch)
has become a mirror of internal circumstances, and their reproof.
The state of war, absolute and enduring, at least by implication,
is projected *morally* into the international sphere, while acquiring
an immorality when practiced at home, *within* the nation-state.
There it is a dissipation of the "naturall condition" of civil society.
Hobbes then introduces the idea of a contract or desire for a
contract or treaty in civil society, analogous with a treaty or
concordat between nations, at which point he concludes Chapter
13 with the remark that "the Passions that incline men to Peace,
are Feare of Death . . ." (together with a desire for "commodious

living") resulting in reason suggesting "convenient Articles of Peace," as if we were drawing toward the end of some war between separate and aggressive nation-states, which is the purpose of the analogous relationship of foreign and internal wars which occupies the concluding section of this important chapter.

In Chapter 14, Hobbes proceeds to discuss "NATURALL LAWES," but before we consider his observations we should observe that in Chapter 13, by expanding the argument of the "warre of every man against every man" to the level of the *inevitable*, Hobbes has justified as well as dignified the idea of the war of survival, as any nation is asked to conceive of its wars— never as wars of aggrandizement or aggression, which is how he describes human society "without Lawes." Men may *appear* to be moral creatures, but only in circumstances where they admit the authority of a superior power, of a kind, especially, capable of waging successful foreign wars.

The implication for natural law theory is evident, that of the de facto existence and success of "soveraign Power" in history, especially recent or even contemporary history, as solely responsible for the existence of moral behavior, for human activity that may be termed ethical, imposing *law* where naturally there is none. It is, therefore, a kind of historical proof, even though history is hardly discussed in *Leviathan*. The most recent space of history is sufficient example, when compared with the contemporary chaos of civil conflict, for the decade of Hobbes's exile furnishes the sternest proofs of the stark opposition of chaos and order; the rebellion or revolution of the Civil War is a breakdown of order rather than a war *about law* and the residence of the executive power and the possession of sovereignty. Hobbes has a traditional or historical perspective upon the events of the 1640s in England, and that perspective is indicated by one crucial signifier—*rebellion*. In other words, the Civil War is an attempt to overthrow legitimate authority. It is not a 'new' event, but another of those illegitimate attempts to seize power by violent means, the most recent example being the Pilgrimage of Grace and the incipient threat of like rebellions that rumbled above the last decade of Elizabeth's reign.

Hobbes thus reveals himself as a Platonic materialist, another traditional model or archetype underlying his analysis or science of society in that any rebellion against order or authority is incipiently *anarchic* (and inclusive, though unstated here, of Plato's proposition that democracy is the next worst thing to anarchy— something applied by many traditionalists to the more radical ideas of the Levelers and others during the 1640s and the Protectorate). Thus, anarchy is the result of "civill warre." Hobbes takes no account of the aspirations or deprivations of those rebelling, or the nature of their government, so long as it resides in an authoritarian monarch. Therefore, there is no distinction of kind from a foreign war of oppression and subjugation; of degree is another matter, since a "civill warre" is war of the most intolerable kind.

It must be remarked at this point that Hobbes shares with Plato a dread of civil unrest that would seem to motivate much of the theorizing about the nature of the state in Plato, even perhaps overriding his concern to establish a model of the *good* or *just* society, in which of course Hobbes has only an incidental interest. Both philosophers imply a geometric inversion with regard to popular liberty whereby the degree of popular freedom seems to encourage an inverse ratio of dissent, democracy, and thereby anarchy, though one must remember the critical distinction between Plato and Hobbes—which is that Plato assumed that a new and even ideal state could be *begun* and established, while the whole thrust of Hobbes's theory is that no such beginning anew is possible; indeed, all beginnings are merely ends, the collapse of or war against the established, functioning, and correct form of government, that of the kind of monarchy Plato would have shudderingly rejected. Hobbes, as a materialist, assumes the contemporary and historical existence of the *right* form of government, just as Hegel was to do in his evolutionary theory of history. What exists is the best that can be expected, because predetermined. Hobbes is not quite so rigorous a historical determinist, but materialism certainly leads him in that direction. The effectiveness of the monarchical state—perhaps he did not, after all, know too much about history—is its own justification; indeed, its very *existence* as matter is its justification. Therefore, de facto predominates, in Hobbes's scientific deference to empirical reality. His intention, to apply the rigors of science to an investigation of political theory, apprehends contemporary reality as if it were evidence of an entirely objective and implicitly continuous kind. What this then allows him to do, and what he has already begun to demonstrate, is impress a range of traditional conceptions and practices as evidence of his *first principle*, that men behave as examples of matter in motion. In other words, contemporary political reality, and the reality of history, require only the uncovering of this first and inclusive principle in order to be satisfactorily and systematically explained. But the field of study must be the contemporary, phenomenal political universe, which contains both past and future, as well as present, the redundant, the nascent, the emerging and the *wrong* in conjunction with the *right*. And, just as precedent or *tradition* must most easily occupy the analyst of any contemporaneity, so it is with Hobbes. Hence, tradition is as much *fact* as contemporary experience. Durkheim poses many of the same problems, in his search for the nature of the conscience collective. History, indeed, achieves something akin to the status of unchanging phenomenon, interrupted by such chaotic eruptions as rebellion and civil conflict. History reduced to the material of materialism, as it were, can be no more than scientifically objectified phenomena, without relative weight or significance, and in such an equation, tradition must secure favor.

Hobbes emerges with a first principle which explains history, tradition, and the contemporary—the principle of chaos and order, of *ego* and *authority*. Tradition exhibits the workings of that theory, its *balance*, while contemporary circumstances (1640–1650) display an imbalance, the rebellion of egoistic forces against authority. This fits Hobbes's model as an illness in the *body politic*, a phrase itself traditional and fraught with significance for Hobbes; indeed, it may be regarded as a key metaphor, since it suggests a material representation as well as a wholeness or entity with regard to the state or the nation. And 'bodies' have 'heads', as will be seen.

To return to Hobbes's implicit state of war in society, any overthrow of an existing order by rebellion or revolution must be regarded as an *actual* state of war (as indeed it is) *and* as opposing that end of all human desires, "for PEACE." This is the contradiction and the paradox of Hobbes's thought, one he expertly conjures with, that human beings are by nature aggressive, competitive, and violent, yet their chief desire is for peace, for a *life* that offers at least one equivalent with death, peace. The acquisition of power for the purpose of security becomes the maxim that power *means* security, which is a direct invitation to consider the degree and kind of power that might *guarantee* peace. Therefore, finally, the actual realization of the condition of *political* society, as opposed to that dangerous, quasi-anarchic circumstance, civil society, lies in a single and sovereign power, one of whom all are in awe and who is superior to all other powers and aspirations to power. Only power has the ability to awe men into moral conduct, the removal of all *executive* power from all men—save one. The struggle for such executive power is a human motion, and in political society such executive power must reside in a supreme "Person"—who may quell all other persons into *rest,* being himself alone in *motion.*

As a result of this closed argument, forever returning to the point of its inception, any attempt to *seize* the executive power is made in obedience to mere human nature and *not* in obedience to the necessities of natural law theory or any differing ideal of political society. There can exist no other such vision that has validity, since all of them are grounded in human nature, all of them dissipate or *share* that sovereign power which alone prevents, through awe or fear, a competitive, destructive exercise of power by disparate individuals. They are, in short, no more than rebellions. The executive cannot be diluted, because to do so is to surrender to the essential passions and appetites of human nature—to *civil* rather than *political* society. Long before Hobbes reaches his discussion of the "Common-wealth," he has already begun to establish the inexorable fact that to share the executive power is to return to a "feare" of the power of others over oneself.

However, it must be admitted that this section has been seduced into an imitation of Hobbes's own method, anticipating subjects that have not yet been fully explored, and anticipating them with epithetical certainty, what is more. Therefore, we should return to a consideration of Chapter 14, "Of the first and second NATURALL LAWES, and of CONTRACTS," in which Hobbes demolishes that great Hellenic edifice of natural law theory in order to erect an imitation behind the facade of *contract theory*.

IV

In *Behemoth,* ostensibly Hobbes's history of the English Civil War, he observes that men "became acquainted with the democratical principles of Aristotle and Cicero, and from the love of their eloquence fell in love with their politics, and that more and more, till it grew into the rebellion." In *Leviathan,* Hobbes is more circumspect in his accusations, but his argument opposing natural law theory is of a seamless garment with his description of the democratic anarchy that possessed England in the 1640s. He begins by defining *jus naturale* as the "Right of Nature," claiming that it represents "the Liberty each man hath to use his own power, as he will himselfe, for the preservation of his own Nature." By liberty, he signifies "the absence of externall Impediments," which is little more than a gloss on Locke's "perfect freedom" of the "state of Nature." *Lex naturale* or natural law is that precept discovered by reason that a man may not be "destructive of his life" or remove the means from himself of preserving his life. Hobbes's definitions, crucial to his argument, are evidently reductive since the tradition of natural law theory assumes self-preservation almost as a 'pre-right' or 'ur-natural' law and is essentially more sophisticated than Hobbes suggests, concerning itself with rights and liberties, with the *equivalent otherness* of others. Natural law theory was a recognition of others' individuality as identical to our own—whereas Hobbes reduces it to its egoistic roots.

He proceeds to distinguish *rights* and *law*, which natural law theory also attempted, but only in order to identify the former with the latter, to coalesce natural law with natural rights, out of which *positive law* and a system of government may then develop. Hobbes, however, intends that the terms be understood as opposites, just as "Obligation, and Liberty" are opposites. This is the essence of the Stoic and Roman effort, to identify together natural law and rights and regard the opposite of that position as a system of law which does not incorporate natural rights. However, having already described the "naturall condition" of men, Hobbes demonstrates that natural right allows that "every man has a Right to every thing." From this position, the fundamental natural *law* is *"to seek Peace, and follow it,"* and the "summe" of natural *right* is *"by all means we can, to defend our selves."* At this point, in reconciliation of these opposites, Hobbes introduces the idea of *contract,* which is essential to all natural law theory, though Locke, like his classical forebears, refers to consent rather than contract—the fact that Hobbes is soon to substitute the term *covenant* is of the utmost significance, of course. The reconciliation of natural law and natural rights must be based upon agreement, some form of contract between the aggressive, egoistical individuals that compose Hobbes's civil society, and the means of so doing must lie in their mutual recognition of each other's power and their incapacity ever to achieve so much personal power that they are never again threatened and so that their "Peace" will be assured and unbroken. The discussion of how this is to occur comes later in *Leviathan;* for the moment, it is necessary to understand that the schism between rights and laws that may be regarded as *natural* is Hobbes's most potent weapon, since both right and law may then be regarded in a materialist sense, attributable to human nature as he has defined it. In neither right nor law is there any inherent or even implicit recognition of the law and right pertaining to others. Reason, as we have seen earlier, is merely a method of apprehending personal advantage and not a moral agent. In the "state of Warre," Hobbes says, "every one is governed by his own Reason."

What Hobbes has done, and what becomes the keystone of his structure, is to substitute, or identify, a natural *instinct* for a rational apprehension of right and law. His natural law and right of nature are the *instinct* to self-preservation, the biological necessity which employs human reason to further its urge. Natural law theory is, of course, vulnerable to this kind of scientism, because it has always relied heavily upon what may be termed the divine or at least ennobled example, the idea of rationality as something distinctly human and unalloyed by the animal element in human nature, a capacity man derives from the deity. At least, natural law theory would seem to be vulnerable, if it is indeed based upon some deistic notion of human nature. But is it?

The idea of the *appeal* of natural law theory, which really should be understood as being a theory of natural *rights* rather than *laws*, to "right Reason," to man's rational-moral propensity, is an element in the tradition. But in actual fact such an appeal is only a demonstration of the 'naturalness' of the theory. Locke's "common sense" is sufficient to recognize and accept the theory, which is self-evident, of the *personhood* of other members of a community, if that community is to function. It is at this point that "right Reason" may become active in the formulation of *positive law* which, as closely as possible, will mirror or reflect natural law (i.e., that conglomeration of rights and liberties that the individual would enjoy if he did not submit himself to the restraints of society for his own and others' benefit). Natural rights theory claims only an equivalent personhood for all members of the society. All Locke claims is the idea that men can discern and *will* law, which is what Hobbes, except in a single act of *covenant*, denies them. Locke does not assume a presocial condition, except as an intellectual model or as exhibited in the virgin territories of the Americas, but he does assume what may be termed a *componential* society—the membership as *individual* components of the community.

Hobbes recognized, in the statement with which the section opened, that natural law theory was intensely democratic, and indeed that was the basis of his objection to it. The theory is radically opposed to the monarchical-hierarchical form of government that was traditional in the English constitution and personified in Charles I and Cromwell. The ideas of natural rights and law promulgate equality and equivalence, together with, as we have seen, the traditional theory's tendency to combine the concepts of rights and law together. Hobbes's strenuous effort to make them once more distinct is the essence of his attack, making them preconditions for imposed and absolute authority and reducing them to an instinct to self-preservation. There is, in Hobbes's civil society, no model of how society should function and be governed. Civil society is, essentially, lawless until law is imposed, much, as we shall see, as the appetites and desires are controlled or repressed by some superior agent—or by the fear of prosecution under the law. Thus, law is not an invention that mirrors the aspirations of the members of the community, except insofar as it is the solution to their primary desire for safety and "Peace."

Having defined the fundamental "Law of Nature" and the "summe of the Right of Nature" as distinct from one another, Hobbes proceeds to examine the surrender of *"this right to all things"* for the sake of ensuring peace (i.e., the notion of contract or consent essential in natural law theories of society and government). As he says, "Right is layde aside, either by simply Renouncing it; or by Transferring it to another." This is a direct paraphrase of one of the basic tenets of natural law theory, as is the implicit acceptance thereafter that a man "is said to be OBLIGED or BOUND" and that it is "his DUTY, not to make voyd that voluntary act of his own." However, when Hobbes comes to sum up this contract, or resignation of rights, he claims that the motive for a man acting thus is "nothing else but the security of a man's person, in his life, and in the means of so preserving life, as not to be weary of it." Later in the chapter, indeed, Hobbes concludes that only two forces operate upon men to abide by contracts, "a Feare of the consequences of breaking their word" or "a Glory, or Pride in appearing not to breake it." The reductive argument again devolves upon the basic human motivations outlined in earlier chapters. Out of a desperation of "Peace" being achieved by any other means, men are reluctantly obliged to evolve some form of contract which will ensure their mutual safety from one another. The derivation of the idea of contract lies in fear of others and their "Power," which is not necessarily entirely opposed to the tenets of natural law theory, rather than in a recognition of their personhood. To return to what was earlier claimed as Hobbes's essential analogy of internal society, that of intersocial relations, contract is defensive, to be regarded as a peace treaty between warring elements.

Hobbes assumes in social man a recognition of the necessity for order, for a restraint that must be imposed. As he proceeds to demonstrate forcibly in Chapter 15, "Of other Lawes of Nature," such questions as "Justice and Propriety" do not come into existence *until* the "Constitution of Commonwealth" under a "coercive Power." In the absence of such a power, men will not perform their "Covenants" or contracts. This, of course, assumes that no code or system of law exists in civil society without the intervention or creation of a sovereign authority who makes the law under which the society will operate and in so doing become a commonwealth. Natural law theory begins with the recognition that *law* in a "Commonwealth" precedes *authority*. This is perhaps both its fiction and its value as a theory, that law must be regarded as perhaps more essential and more continuous than any particular *form* of authority. The progress of Hobbes's argument assumes the necessity of the imposition of justice and law. Its evolution, or even its primeval admission as a necessity by the community, is ignored—as is the possibility, as will be seen later, of ever changing or ameliorating the authority charged with the creation and execution of the law. Because his argument must move by an inexorable, reductive logic to the necessity of absolutism and a static rather than evolving society, Hobbes must assume universally selfish human motivation and the desperate recognition that authority is required to enforce security and "Peace." The transfer by contract is of power, and it is permanent and irrevocable.

One further point. Hobbes's notion of justice is of a body of law and a degree of authority necessary to deal with flawed human nature; it is a corrective or *moral* law, which all law plainly is not, especially that of contract, rather than a solution to the inevitable problems of communal existence. Justice becomes, therefore, the coercive power of the state to suppress human inclinations to the bad *and to do nothing more,* rather than Locke's notion that although positive law must take account of human propensity to evil, a system of law is and must be designed to be *just* to all, to preserve rather than suppress, to recognize rather than disqualify. Most importantly, it evolves rather than is developed. Natural law theory is, as Hobbes rightly recognizes, participatory and equivalent, while his own theory of authority produces an equality of constraint, recognizing the personhood of the "single Person," the figure of authority, and of no other. As he says, "the definition of INJUSTICE, is no other than *the not Performance of Covenant.* And whatsoever is not Unjust, is *Just."* The performance of contract or covenant must necessarily be enforced, and that enforcement is justice. Covenants, indeed, are only such when there is a "Civill Power erected over the parties promising." Hobbes thus identifies the *law* with the *authority of the law,* which his human individuals would not consent to without the "impressive discipline of fear" of punishment for nonperformance of contract, such punishment to be executed by the "Person" of the executive power. And it is this conflation of the legislative and the executive, their being one and the same "Person," that is at the heart of Hobbes's argument, just as *the distinction between* the legislative and the executive is the essence of natural law theory, where the members of the community are represented by the legislative and the executive may be regarded

more often as a *judiciary*. Hobbes wishes this trinity of powers—
executive, judiciary, and legislature—to be a "single Person," the
sole person. Natural law theory assumes that the legislature precedes the executive in importance, and is *of* the membership,
deriving power and content from them.

Hence, though natural law theory and Locke posit a "state of
Nature," it is an attempt to combine the idea of 'according to
nature' with the concept of law, and therefore of justice. Natural
is not that which derives from a "naturall condition" in Hobbes's
sense, but rather that which attempts to counter any theory that
derives from an 'unnatural' condition, that of imposed law that
takes no account of *choice* as the basis of law. Law, therefore,
must as closely as possible approximate to 'nature'. In Hobbes, it
is an agreement by the individual to the *force* of law rather than
the acceptance of just laws.

Law approximating as closely as possible to nature, on the other
hand, assumes that the desire for law *and* for a legislature *and*
judiciary, is distinct from a *transfer of power to the executive;*
envisaging rather a reposing of authority rather than a transfer of
rights or power. Hobbes argues that power exists *before* law, and
therefore that law can only spring from power. His right of men
"to do any thing" is indeed power rather than rights, the arbitration between separate *rights* rather than *powers* being justice. A
created but artificially greater power is the basis of all law in a
community.

Hobbes's fiction is that a state of civil society can and does exist
without law, thereby requiring the willing of a restraint of power
rather than a guarantee of rights. The fictional model is therefore
more abstract and untenable than the "state of Nature," which
is a model only for *the condition of the individual* rather than
from some presocial existence. Hobbes's model, however, cannot
exist outside society, since it is the "naturall condition" of society
itself, requiring to become a State. It cannot exist under any
circumstances, not even in the Americas in the seventeenth century, since such a total war of individuals does not represent any
kind of society or community—it is not quasi-anarchical, it is

chaos. However, as an anarchy of separate powers requires not so much law as a superior power, any agglomeration of *individuals* might well be assumed to require an *arbiter* rather than a ruler, an agreement to regulation and to rules rather than a submission to rule. Even Hobbes's aggressive and egoistic individuals would surely, possessed of reason, at some time agree to regulation rather than power, otherwise they would continue forever to seek such power for themselves.

Thus, the surrender of power into other hands is not a paraphrase of the will to regulate *human relations*. Rather, Hobbes identifies a will to regulate human *behavior* rather than their *interactivity*, not all of which exists at the level of life and death, power and despoliation. In that sense, he is the repressive, reforming, 'Elect' element in Puritanism rather than its sense of the sanctity of individual conscience and its attempt to divorce church and state.

That will to regulate *is* natural law theory—the recognition that what a person requires is no more than arbitration of his social encounters and dealings, while he can continue to attend to his own personhood, which is self-regulating or answerable to his conscience—the genuinely radical Puritan stance. In Hobbes, unlike natural law theory, there is no such private person within social man, because in a materialist sense, there cannot be. Man is no more, or less, than matter in motion, the expression and expenditure of power. And Hobbes envisages not an executive entrusted with the execution of the law, but an executive *power*, one of such enormity that it will awe those individual atoms of motion into *rest* and thereby provide that hidden, scientific law which will explain how materialist man as mere matter can create such artificial and unnatural things as *law* or government—or even exist in social circumstances without an endemic and endless anarchy. Having wished to apply science to the study of politics, Hobbes is forced to fit society to the Procrustean bed of there *having to be an explanation* in terms of governing, universal, *scientific* laws.

Hobbes remarks of the "justice of an Arbitrator" or "Distributive Justice," that it is also "a law of Nature, as shall be shewn in due place." The due place occurs within the same chapter (15), and during his discussion of this question of arbitration or *judgment*, Hobbes proceeds, as we might expect, to demolish the argument for a judiciary which is separate from executive power by devolving the argument once more to his view of human nature, in preparation for his monarch or governor. One might well suspect by this time something of divinity or at least "divine right" in such an extraordinary and unnatural person, meaning that, since such arbitration requires independence and lack of bias—true indifference—ordinary judges and arbiters may be regarded only as entirely and usually subject to the fallibilities of human nature.

Hobbes sums up Chapter 15 in the following way:

> . . . Morall Philosophy is nothing else but the Science of what
> is *Good* and *Evill*, in the conversation, and Society of
> mankind. *Good*, and *Evill*, are names that signifie our
> Appetites, and Aversions; which in different tempers,
> customes, and doctrines of men are different . . . And divers
> men, differ not onely in their Judgement . . .

This statement introduces, or reintroduces, that essential relativism which is one of Hobbes's fundamental intellectual attitudes, while finally he remarks, in closing the chapter, that "Law, properly is the word of him, that by right hath command over others."

V

Chapter 16, "Of PERSONS, AUTHORS, and things Personated," is perhaps the strangest and most archaic in the whole of *Leviathan*. Amid Hobbes's modernity and his scientism, it reads much like an Elizabethan speculation upon the *metaphorical* implications of acting and matters theatrical and their possession of allegorical or symbolic significance. And indeed, allegory is what Hobbes intends, and symbolism is part of his purpose in remaking the notion of personhood *into* a metaphor, in order that he may describe society and its members in terms of acting rather than activity, as a pretense or fiction played out on a stage. Such an appearance then requires a corresponding or underlying reality to substantiate the *personation* that is the condition of human government.

Hobbes's materialism is here at its most immaterial and literary, the individual now being regarded merely as a phenomenon or the mere appearance or manifestation of reality, while the hidden or underlying law or *principle* that governs the phenomenal world is to be personified and expressed in the person of the *lawgiver.* Hobbes is exploring a metaphysical distinction between appearance and reality for the sole purpose of signifying that the material universe's laws govern the commonwealth by analogous means—the trick is to discover the hidden or concealed principle, and this he proceeds to do.

He distinguishes between a "Naturall Person," whose words and actions are his own, and a *"Feigned* or *Artificiall Person,"* whose words and actions are those of another. He then defines via the Latin *persona* the equivalence between an *actor* and a *person,* a crucial conflation in view of what follows, which is nothing less than the demolition of the concept of the person as *other than actor* (i.e., as contemplative, rational, moral). Personation becomes personhood. He proceeds then to indicate that "Artificiall" persons have their words and actions *"Owned"* by another, who is the "AUTHOR," in which case, he says "the Actor acteth by Authority," and that "the Right of doing any Action, is called Authority." This is another, and perhaps one of the most significant, of Hobbes's employments of the reductive or diminishing purity of language. Authority plainly means far more than the ownership of his words and stage directions by an author, but that is what Hobbes reduces it to here, in order that *authority* becomes part of the whole metaphor of *personation* with which the chapter is concerned. Hobbes harnesses terms together by derivation rather than usage or current signification, or even by redefinition, which one might expect in a philosophic context. Language is the tool of his system rather than of his examination of reality.

The impersonal world is not directly *personable,* except by figures who derive their authority from such things, as a rector in and from a church, a "Hospital by a Master," et cetera. These figures personate the impersonal, claims Hobbes. He has taken the metaphor, already, to the level of "Covenant" by representing the idea of an *author* as authority, whose agreement to the covenant is necessary for it to be binding—the actor cannot make the covenant without the authority of the author. He continues by discussing the personation of God by Moses, Christ, et cetera—who possessed the authority to speak on behalf of God, to reveal God's authority and his *law.* From this, he proceeds to define the "Multitude" as *"Many"* and therefore not capable of personating themselves, since the concept of the *person* applies to only one, not to many. He is thus arguing toward a position where personation or *representation* is expressed in a single person or authority, but the analogy of Christ's personation of God is wickedly significant. Christ is the *authority* of the Christian church, its testament, its spirit. Christ is the *reality,* especially to the Puritan temperament, of which his church is the representation, the appearance. Thus, though Hobbes appears to be working toward a designated authority or representative which sounds democratic, he is developing the distinction between the *appearance* (actors, people, the members of civil society) and the *reality* (the *person,* the sole authority). The central element of the whole metaphor of the chapter is the *person* of Christ (and the concept, which is implicit throughout the second part, of the divine right of kings) and his authority derived from God. Yet Christ's intercessional and spiritual authority is not metaphorical but real, more real than the spiritual status and intercessional authority of his priests and church, and especially of his worshipers.

Therefore, men 'surrender' their *authorship* to their representative, their actor or personator. But the personator is, by Hobbes, regarded as the *"One* Person." Thereby, Hobbes has reduced the "multitude" to the status of actors without authority and elevated the personator to the status of *person*. The linguistic trap snaps shut at this point; the metaphor has fulfilled its purpose of reversing the *real* idea of elective representation or contract to make it mere *appearance*, the subordinate function of actor rather than author, whose authority now resides in the "Person," not in the "Multitude."

He concludes the chapter by demonstrating any plurality of representatives as ineffective, contradictory, *without authority*. A single, sole authority is therefore necessary. Of what kind and degree Hobbes will demonstrate in the second part, "Of COMMONWEALTH."

Hobbes might have made the discussion of representation much easier than he does in Chapter 16; his purpose, however, is not to be lucid but rather diffuse and metaphorical. The sleight of literary hand in which he engages is the total surrender or transfer of authority to a personator—but not an actor, one should note. The idea of the actor or personator is subtly erased during the central metaphor of the *authority* of Christ, after which point Hobbes refers only to the person, artificially created by covenant though that person may be, and thereby made to represent the multitude, but nevertheless *assuming* their agglomerated authority and thus reducing them to the role of actors, expressions of activity (their previously described condition in civil society and as matter in motion). Evidently, Hobbes's argument required this dense, diffuse excursion into metaphor and abstruseness *at this point*, before he passes directly to the first chapter of the second part of *Leviathan*. The metaphor is linguistically reductive, and theatrical. It concerns appearance and reality, and the terms have altered their objects of signification during the chapter. The ideas of *author* and *actor* have been reversed—which was Hobbes's purpose.

VI

Hobbes begins Chapter 17 with the claim that "Covenants, without the Sword, are but Words," words not as signifiers at this juncture but as mere, empty breathing orchestrated in vocal noises. He also remarks that:

> The finall Cause, End or Designe of Men (who naturally love Liberty, and Dominion over others,) in the introduction of that restraint upon themselves, (in which we see them live in Commonwealths,) is the foresight of their own preservation, and of a more contented life thereby; that is to say, of getting themselves out from that miserable condition of Warre, which is necessarily consequent . . . to the naturall Passions of men, when there is no visible Power to keep them in awe, and tye them by feare of punishment to the performance of their Covenants.

It is evident here that the preconditions of the *nature* of the commonwealth that Hobbes envisages and promulgates have already been entirely established in the first part, "Of MAN." Hobbes's political society or state depends entirely upon his materialist view of human nature and the reductive argument that such natures must be subjugated by a superior, or "soveraign" power, which—according to Chapter 16—must be expressed in a single person, the reason being that, "notwithstanding the Lawes of Nature, (which every one hath then kept, when he has the will to keep them, when he can do it safely,) if there be no Power erected . . . every man will and may lawfully rely on his own strength and art, for caution against other men."

Therefore, the preceding eighty-five pages (in the original edition) of the first part may be regarded as being encapsulated, reductively and deterministically, in these three remarks at the outset of Chapter 17. The demolition of natural law theory is already so complete that Hobbes might almost forbear to observe that "notwithstanding the Lawes of Nature, . . ." et cetera. The laws of nature are complied with by individual men just so long as they remain unthreatened by others, just so long as there is an equilibrium of *power to do harm* between all the members of a civil society. However, such a situation is 'ideal' and hardly the experience of Hobbesian man in his social circumstance, therefore and thereby the coming into existence of a commonwealth.

In his description of the origins or necessity of a political society, he dismisses first of all the quasi-original position of a "small community" by employing again the prerogative of the monarch and the imagery of foreign policy, whereby small societies are too weak to defend themselves; therefore we are to deal with larger, more defensible communities—in which instance the members of his civil society "can expect no defence, nor protection, neither against a Common enemy, nor against the injuries of one another" without the direction and intervention of a "Civill Government." The proof of the necessity of government is that governments exist and must therefore be necessary. To suppose that men were capable of obedience to the laws of nature without downward pressure upon them would obviate the need for any form of civil government. Otherwise, "there would be Peace without subjection." Positive law, therefore, is to develop from subjection to a lawgiver (perhaps the introduction of Moses in Chapter 16 is thus explained since he was simply *personating* the deity) because *natural* law only operates or is obeyed under the strictest and most rigorously peaceful or subjugated circumstances. Man has less than free will to obey the laws of nature, since he is intent upon enacting his natural rights in his "naturall condition," and therefore never achieves the pacific circumstances where he will remain obedient to the laws of nature.

Hobbes continues with the observation, or maxim, that "the only way to erect such a Common Power . . . is, to conferre all their power and strength upon one Man, or upon one Assembly of men, that may reduce all their Wills . . . unto one Will." Out of this covenant arises the notion and reality of a commonwealth.

It might be pertinent to remark here that the notion of *covenant* rather than contract becomes of increasing and exclusive importance in this second part and that it is intended to embrace not only the Mosaic covenant between God and his chosen people but also to include the nascent nationalism of the English in the seventeenth century, another obviously chosen people, together with the idea of election so significant to certain rigid sections of the Puritan outlook.

Individuals surrender or transfer their power to a single person, and "this done, the Multitude so united in one Person, is called a COMMON-WEALTH, in Latine, CIVITAS. This is the generation of that great LEVIATHAN, or rather (to speake more reverently) of that *Mortall God,* our peace and defence." Hobbes, it is evident, feels that all qualification or necessities of proof by empirical assessment are no longer required. He can press on with his exultation in the absolutist state with hardly a sidelong glance. This great Leviathan, because he "hath the use of so much Power and Strength conferred on him, that by terror thereof, he is inabled to forme the wills of them all . . ." In him, Hobbes adds almost unnecessarily, "consisteth the Essence of the Commonwealth," because the multitude have by covenant made "themselves every one the Author" of this actor or representative. This single person is to be termed, according to Hobbes, "SOVERAIGN" and is to possess *"Soveraigne Power."* It is not surprising that the fate of "every one besides" is to be "his SUBJECT."

During the remainder of Chapter 17, Hobbes merely continues the analogy of society as successfully representable by intersocial models, in defining two kinds of "Soveraign Power," one by seizure and submission to "Naturall force" and the other by the voluntary action "when men agree amongst themselves" to establish the supremacy of "some Man."

As might be suspected, there appears to be very little difference between "Commonwealth by *Institution"* and "Commonwealth by *Acquisition,"* except at the point of origin—one is impositional at its outset, the other voluntary, which is Hobbes's nominal regard for the tradition of natural law theory, but that point of origin is itself sole and entire, the whole idea then becoming synonymous with a commonwealth established by seizure, since both kinds become versions of absolutism, the distinction between them being removed by the statement that "they that have already Instituted a Common-wealth . . . cannot lawfully make a new Covenant, amongst themselves, to be obedient to any other, in any thing whatsoever, without his permission." Once the status of subject has been adopted, there is no recantation of such a status, under "Him that beareth their Person." The metaphor here makes its reappearance, and the reversal is operational—the *person* and the *subject,* which is itself another of Hobbes's linguistic triumphs, another example of his etymological propaganda on behalf of absolutism, since we are now dealing with a subject-object relationship in the metaphysical sense, the objective being the more 'real', the subjective being only that expression of appetite and desire exclusive to civil society and to human nature.

The covenant is such that the sovereign, also, is bound by it (it appears, momentarily, to be an agreement among equals), so that he cannot resign his sovereignty, which is good for all of us to know, but which in fact only congeals the state in the condition in which it originates, without opportunity or hope of change or evolution. Hobbes then proceeds to indicate the grounds of monarchy, the extent of its power, always being *just* through exercise of that power and *obedient to the enactment of* its created and promulgated laws rather than obedient or subordinate to the law itself. The sovereign is the sole judge of what is good, whether for the defense of the realm and the peace of his subjects, as regards "what Opinions and Doctrines are averse," but, primarily, "is annexed to the Soveraigntie, the whole power of prescribing the Rules, whereby every man may know, what Goods he may enjoy and what Actions he may doe." In other words, Hobbes has not only gathered back to the sovereign all the traditional elements of the king's prerogative but has accrued to the institution of monarchy, the "single Person," the functions of the legislature, the judiciary, and the executive rather than that evident sham, the "King-in-Parliament." Absolutism has never, in actuality, been quite so absolute as Hobbes would make it.

There is nothing in chapters 17 and 18 that has not been predicated by the first part, and they require little further expansion, as Hobbes turns his attention in Chapter 19 to the kinds rather than degrees of government that are available, thereby following once more his Platonic model, albeit in his very individual way. It is not surprising to learn that oligarchy, democracy, aristocracy, tyranny are all prey to self-interest, and only the "Soveraign Power" in one man, above such weaknesses and villainies of human nature, upon which Hobbes has expended so much time and effort, guarantees that degree of indifference we demand from government in the hope of justice. Thus, at the end of the chapter, we are left with the irrefutable fact that in "Monarchy, the private interest is the same with the publique" and, further, that in terms of the *succession,* which, in any other form of government, means a new covenant or contract, Hobbes claims that "there is no perfect forme of Government, where the disposing of the Succession is not in the present Soveraign." The whole chapter, indeed, has led to this point, but in the main its content has been the ascription to the person of the monarch a more than human indifference and sense of justice, an ideal personhood, one distinct from the individual human natures which compose civil society. Why this should be so hinges upon the *rest* or "Peace" of absolute power itself. The monarch alone is a fully human person in the state because he alone is above the motions of appetite and aversion and the desire for power and obedience to the life-appetite, all of which his subjects express and by all of which they are moved and motivated. Hence, the monarch *is* the sole person in the state, the only truly, traditionally *human,* being—more than that, he is no longer Aristotle's rational animal, but all 'spirit'. In Cleopatra's words, he is

> fire and air; my other elements
> I give to baser life

and, as such, is ennobled above mere humanity, itself debased below the traditional model by becoming a creature merely of appetite and aversion.

The idea of the *model* or analogy, which has threatened Hobbes's argument like a broken bone sticking through the skin on many occasions, must now be remarked. There is, indeed, a model for Hobbes's state, and the model is that traditional, quasi-medieval and certainly theological model of the "rational animal," itself inherited from Aristotle and preserved in natural law theory and in Aquinas, Augustine, and the humanism of Erasmus (though to varying degrees)—the model is the image of man as part animal, part angel. In Hobbes's state or "Common-wealth," the model serves to grant the capacity of reason to the monarch, and "animal spirits" to the "Multitude," the subjects of the monarch. The rational capacity and even moral instinct of the individual is wholly ascribed to the person of the monarch, while those other elements of passion, desire, and instinct are wholly credited to the subjects. This is the final and complete model of the state in *Leviathan,* and Hobbes's underlying or metaphorical justification of monarchy and absolutism, that *the state alone is the whole* and that the monarch is the 'head' (reason) of the state, while the members of civil society are the 'body' (its emotions and passions and appetites). And, as in the traditional archetype, just as the reason controls the passions, so the monarch is obligated to control the subjects—to describe and enforce the law which he, as the reason, has created—as legislature, judiciary, and executive.

In Chapter 20, Hobbes proceeds to describe his two forms of "Dominion," by acquisition and institution, as "PATERNALL" or "DESPOTICALL," but he is able to conclude that "the Rights and Consequences of both *Paternall* and *Despoticall* Dominion, are the very same with those of a Soveraign by Institution." In the following chapter, he comes at last to *"the* LIBERTY *of Subjects,"* which discussion he begins by echoing a much earlier statement, claiming that "LIBERTY, or FREE-DOME, signifieth (properly) the absence of Opposition; (by Opposition, I mean externall Impediments of motion)" rather than any sense of freedom from constraint or freedom from injustice or oppression—what natural law theory enshrined as natural rights, liberties, and freedoms. As he says, "when the words *Free,* and *Liberty,* are applyed to any thing but *Bodies,* they are abused." From this protestation, Hobbes proceeds to define, and confine, natural rights and liberties within his envisaged and perfect commonwealth and to those liberties that the sovereign will *permit*. ". . . [F]rom the use of the word *Freewill*, no liberty can be inferred to the will, desire, or inclination, but the liberty of the man; which consisteth in this, that finds no stop, in doing what he has the will, desire, or inclination to doe."

Hobbes then proceeds to indicate that "Feare and Liberty are consistent" and that "*Liberty* and *Necessity* are Consistent." The proof of this is a pattern of causation which proceeds, ultimately from God's will, had men the wit but to understand the chain of causes, and perceive *necessity* in their 'free' activity and willing. ". . . [T]hey can have no passion, nor appetite to any thing, of which appetite Gods will is not the cause."

The theological implications of this statement need not be considered, but for our purposes it is necessary to understand the determinism that governs human activity *as a preparation* for the determinist state and the absolute nature of the sovereign power's authority. He continues: "But as men, for the atteyning of peace, and conservation of themselves thereby, have made an Artificiall Man, which we call a Common-wealth; so also have they made Artificiall Chains, called *Civill Lawes*, which they themselves, by mutuall covenants, have fastened at one end, to the lips of that Man, or Assembly, to whom they have given the Soveraigne Power." The concept of the artificial man, the *created* power has, naturally, its Biblical flattery and constriction. The people create, godlike, this sovereign power, but also there is a *transference* of that godlike power. Further, the image of civil or positive law as a chain issuing from the artificial power's lips is a substitute causality and determinism equivalent to that which Hobbes has already outlined and which is quoted above. The individual will, which is supposed only out of ignorance to be truly free, is governed by a divine determinism and in a theological analogy; the sovereign civil power imposes an equivalent determinism upon the individual members of the commonwealth—so that Hobbes may conclude that "the Liberty of a Subject lyeth therefore only in those things, which is regulating their actions, the Soveraign hath praetermitted: such as the Liberty to buy, and sell, and otherwise contract with one another; to choose their own aboad, their own diet, their own trade of life, and institute their children as they themselves think fit; & the like."

The individual is thus, subsequent to the sole and original contract or covenant, removed from the process of lawmaking and decision making, of power and influence and choice, except for those material freedoms, which have often seemed the sole permissible freedoms of a great many modern democracies, at least from a jaundiced standpoint. Further, the significance of positive or "Civill" law in Hobbes's scheme is always secondary to that of the sovereign power. It is not the *law* that is fixed, irrevocable, impositional, but the presence and authority of the *lawmaker,* the monarch, the "Artificiall Man" who embodies the state and assumes to himself all authority in all matters of government, law, rights, and liberties. It is the Hegelian model of the "rational State" that springs most readily to mind, the creation, imposition, and deification, or at least sanctification, of another and absolute level of authority (or, as both Hobbes and Hegel would distinguish it, another and greater level of liberty or freedom).

In order to complete his pillage and final sack of the citadel of natural law theory, Hobbes now proceeds to discuss the ideas of, in particular, Aristotle and Cicero, though within a broader historical discussion of forms of government. Quite rightly, he identifies the freedom of the *polis* in Athenian political theory, rather than any more peculiar freedom of the individual, though he does call it the "Liberty of the Common-wealth," which is not, in his terminology, identical with the *polis* or *civitas,* though he claims it is—because we already have the reversal of metaphor in our author-actor image, *reinforced* now, or perhaps given substance, by the metaphor of the artificial man or created power. This person signifies and indeed *embodies* the commonwealth, so that we are talking about what Plato and Aristotle would have understood as a tyranny. There is *no* suffrage in Hobbes's state, however much he, and others, would wish to expose the limitations of suffrage in Athens, Rome, or anywhere else. The Greek *polis* did not mean a single "soveraign Power." He says, of both Aristotle and Cicero, that they have been misunderstood and their ideas misapplied, as follows: ". . . it is an easy thing for men to be deceived, by the specious name of Libertie; and for want of Judgement to distinguish, mistake that for their Private Inheritance, and Birth right, which is the right of the Publique only." The problem with Hobbes's interpretation of "publique" and *polis* is that he is deliberately misinterpreting natural law theory as it clearly existed and was promulgated in the works of Aristotle, the Stoics, Cicero, and all its other adherents and apologists. In assuming to natural rights and liberties no more or less than an anarchic form of individual-centered democracy, Hobbes is attempting to indicate that Aristotle and Cicero were merely antimonarchical rather than opposed to a sovereign power.

It is a short, heavy step from Hobbes's destruction of natural law theory and notions of individual rights and liberties to statements such as "To resist the Sword of the Common-wealth in defence of another man, guilty, or innocent, no man hath Liberty . . . [it is] destructive of the very essence of Government." And only a further small step for mankind to arrive at the destination of: "The Soveraignty is the Soule of the Common-wealth." This was, remember, the "Artificiall Man" which men themselves created. The *human model,* which has been the basis of Hobbes's metaphor of the state, his analogous structure, here achieves its apotheosis, casting its shadow back across the second part, and fulfilling the prophetic reductionism of the first part of *Leviathan.* That absent or denied rational-moral capacity, that spiritual element of Aristotle's "rational animal," is here revealed to reside in the "Soveraignty," the absolute power of and in the state. Hobbes continues: ". . . which, once departed from the Body, the members doe no more receive their motion from it." Presumably the pun upon *anima,* the soul, and *animation* is fully intended, as is the whole theological import of the complete sentence. It is of the utmost significance to grasp how subtle and complete Hobbes's literary-metaphorical use of language has been throughout *Leviathan,* and to grasp the purpose for such consistent usage, which is to imbue the sovereign power, by Chapter 21, with all that "divinity [that] doth hedge a King" so as to present the weightiest and most dignified defense of the divine right of kings theory and thereby, through the religious allusiveness of the language to diminish the members of civil society (and the commonwealth) finally to the position of bodies, material beings animated by the absolute, sovereign power of the central authority, which Hobbes intends to be a "single Person," a monarch. His materialism, too, becomes metaphorical in its stance, the idea of men as matter in motion now being dependent upon some first cause or *primary motion,* which is imparted by the sovereign power. The chain of causation we noted above is quite definitely literal at this point, proceeding from the primary, animating power of the monarch, so that as the "Common-wealth" is analogous to the individual, as he is finally and irrevocably identified with the state, the monarch is analogous with the inner or hidden motions that are motivating forces in the individual and which cause, as Chapter 6 so clearly expounded, the bodily and emotional movements of individual human beings. *Only* the state, in the person of the monarch, has this animating power in the commonwealth; not only is he voluntary and vital motion, will, appetite, and aversion, but he is also the "soule."

Therefore, the absolute authority has subsumed to itself not only the material properties of the individual members, and is the sole person and author extant in the commonwealth, he is the motivating force of the state, its spirit in a very metaphysical and not at all materialist sense. Hobbes's work may fairly be judged as an apostrophe to absolute monarchy by this observation alone, since his whole argument leads to this juncture, where the metaphysical metaphor of the "Soul" is to be regarded *literally.* The state has become a kind of incubus, a stealer of souls, reducing the individual members of civil society to automata within the state, only living a determining rather than determined existence at the level of a *civil society* and *not* at the elevated level of the "Common-wealth." The parallel with Hegel, though a century and a half earlier and in another country, is remarkable and thorough.

It is at this point where one may leave detailed discussion of *Leviathan*. The remainder of the second part culminates deterministically (or derivatively in an entirely determinist sense and pattern) in claims that the commonwealth may only be disbanded by the success of an enemy in a foreign war and subsequent conquest, which comprehensively dismisses the whole decade 1640–50, together with much that preceded it during the reign of Charles Stuart, and the necessity of "Obedience" by the subjects of the monarch, since anything less will inevitably lead to the destruction of the "Concord of the People" and the dissolving of the state itself. Fear of consequences, it should be noted, is a consistent theme or motto in the first two parts of the book. To "speak evill of the Soveraign Representative," naturally, is "how great a fault," since it would diminish the aura of divinity and infallibility that ought to surround the absolute power. Finally, in Chapter 30, we arrive at a position where "by a Good Law, I mean not a Just Law: for no Law can be Unjust. The Law is made by the Soveraign Power, is warranted and owned by every one of the people . . ."

It is not within the scope of this essay to consider the third and fourth parts of *Leviathan*, since they do no more than glance at, or extenuate the necessity of, a commonwealth or state, while reserving the main might of their argument specifically, it seems, to arouse that reaction which labeled Hobbes an atheist in his own day—and, one suspects, has endeared him to successive generations of secularists and materialists, as if these were appendages to the argument, an acceptable curriculum vitae. Hobbes removes the discussion here to the level of metaphysics—or at least to that level of metaphysics then prevailing, the Christian, Protestant religion and its factionalism in the first half of the seventeenth century, an important factor in the development of the urgency of Parliament to partake of the executive and legislative functions. To assault and conquer the prevailing *root* or wellspring of secular, individualistic, democratic theories of political society occupies all but half the effort and space of *Leviathan*, as it predictably should, since Hobbes is engaged in a task of resurrection as well as the greater task of mystifying and justifying what one may, without qualm, term the future of Europe. Hobbes is only reactionary with regard to the politics and events of the period 1630 to the date of publication and may be regarded as in the vanguard of political thought again by 1655, with the emergence of the "single Person and Parliament" and that single person losing his ever-shortening patience with the parliaments of his governorship.

Hobbes is the prophet and apologist, even the propagandist, of the immediate and even the medium-term future for two irrefutable reasons. This Nostradamus of political theory predicted the two often indissoluble, nascent, but improbably powerful ideologies of the following centuries, those of absolute monarchy and the nation-state, the latter perhaps only in metaphor, since he employs the idea of a nation engaged with other nations as an analogy of his aggressive, anarchic civil society. And because Hobbes is of the future, as Locke was to be of the past—and of a much farther, though as yet fragile, future, it becomes necessary before taking our leave of the heady language and headier claims of *Leviathan*, to consider some more abstract implications and influences of the book and the consistency and ideological nature of Hobbes's argument; for it remains of crucial importance both to understand and to reject the political theorist from Malmesbury as we journey from there to where we are.

VII

It is necessary in any summary of Hobbes's argument and the schematic arrangement of *Leviathan*, for which earlier works often seem to be little more than sketches, to indicate that, like the theory he is defending—kingship's divine right to rule in absolute terms—Hobbes's imagery of the sovereign power derives from tribalism rather than from more recent and sophisticated theories of political society or the state. This is the point of conjunction between his own ideas and those of Hegel, who was able to muster, and learn from, erroneous theories of the collapse of the Roman Empire and the torchbearing qualities of those Germanic tribes insulated within its boundaries and then cast into the darkness that followed—while, of course, brandishing aloft a consciously passed torch of civilization or, even more significantly, the torch of the evolutionary idea of self-consciousness. Both philosophers of society employ, however consciously, images of a primitive but wise tribal system, which contains no hierarchy, no pyramidal groupings of status or order, merely the simplest model of social organization, that of members and leader or 'chief', often, so anthropologists tell us, endowed and imbued with spiritual qualities and significance, even to the extent that 'The King Must Die'. The model of Hobbes and Hegel alike requires membership, which is itself a distinction, but also a symbolic and absolute leader. In this, both thinkers are utterly radical, and also entirely ideological, in the sense that that definition implies and indicates the expression of a closed system of thought with an overriding purpose which is entirely, or at least in great part, nonempirical and has little or no requirement to answer or account to the political facts of the current situation or society. The radicalism of Hobbes and Hegel lies in their escape from current theory, in their divergence from contemporary assumptions— while their *error* lies in their assumption that past and more primitive *models* of society can be assumed to be ideal. In other words, by appropriating to current or recent circumstances an ideal that either can be realized or is in the process of realization, they approach political theory from a distinctly metaphysical position. There is an attempt to *fulfill* or *complete* the empirical by means of a closed system, by a model or ideal.

Nascent states require apologists, even propagandists. Hegel and Hobbes understood their times better than most, and were predictive or prophetic from a deep understanding of history and the contemporary. The European context informed their theories, and both of them, to a great degree, represented the future rather than, strangely and contradictorily, glancing backward to the past, to tradition—even though they relied upon the metaphors, fictions, and realities of past societies as evidence of the correctness and inevitability of their theories. But, from their materialist or idealist standpoints, there is no necessary connection between their metaphysics and their politics. Hegel need not have arrived at his *form* of the state from his notions of the idea or spirit *(Geist)* or from his interpretation of history and its evolution. The "rational State" is still a special plea for the Prussian state of 1800–1820—for the status quo's evolution, as it were—ascribing idealist-evolutionary *necessity* to that particular time and place and government. Similarly, Hobbes discovers a chain of causality-necessity to justify and make inevitable the absolute monarchy he wishes to promulgate. Hegel allows the macrocosmic idea-spirit to manifest itself at its highest yet attainable degree of self-consciousness and realization in the Prussia of the hundred years before and including his own life and thought, identifying the German nation as a chosen people through the theory of world-historical peoples, just as Hobbes, employing conventional Puritan and even Elizabethan images, could conceive of England in the seventeenth century as containing a similarly *chosen* race. For Hobbes, and not dissimilarly for Hegel when he came to consider the empirical details of government, the chosen people come to be truly embodied in the chosen person, the single expression of the collectivity.

Tribalism requires a complete identity of the members with the collective organism, and it is to be regarded as an organism, which is perhaps why Durkheim's evolutionary analogies fit so well with his investigations of aboriginal tribalism; Weber was able, from this, to fashion the idea of the kind of charismatic or absolute leader we have discussed above as indicative of, or necessary to, tribalism. The state has become, been assumed into, the idea of the *nation* by 1800 (to choose an arbitrary date), in large part due to the France of Louis XIV, which became the France of the Revolution and Napoleon. European absolutism, already arising rather than entirely nascent in Hobbes's Europe, had largely triumphed in France. Absolutism may be regarded as the tool, the forerunner, or the precipitant of *nationalism*. What nationalism possesses, on the other hand, that links it with tribalism is what may be termed an exclusivity; the nation, like the tribe, but not necessarily like any political society, possesses a communal identity which unites rather than distinguishes individuals—indeed, which supersedes any sense of identity confined to individuality in favor of a national identity. For Hegel, this condition is as necessary as it appears to be in Hobbes's argument. For Hegel, the "world-historical people" are regarded as inheriting the evolutionary torch of civilization after the fall of Rome, while in Hobbes we have the model of foreign policy to define the essence of identity with the state and with the presence of the king as leader, having assumed to himself, as Weber might have put it, the charisma of leadership of the community or tribe during war; so that there is a process, in both Hobbes and Hegel, of deliberate mystification of the principle as well as person of the leader, out of the necessity of *distilling* and 'spiritualizing' the community, something that Britain understood quite distinctly during the last war, in the persons of the king and queen, and especially Churchill, not to mention German loyalty to the Führer. All those mentioned acquired an identity *expressive* of the nation. Thus, it may be said that the nation becomes the state by a process of distillation, and that political theory that is desirous of a state usually, though not invariably, chooses the option of identifying the community with its leader. Conversely, the identity of the members of the community is best or most elevatedly expressed in *their* identity with the nation. All of which has little or nothing to do with conceptions of individuality and equivalence, those bases of any theory of democratic political society.

Any conception of such a society, and of the place of its members within it, is based—like natural law theory—upon equivalence and is therefore also grounded in some kind or degree of nonconsummation with the collectivity, some retention of personal identity above, below, within, or beyond national, tribal, or collective identity. Therefore, even in the Greek *polis,* there is a sense of identity with the collectivity that does not exclude the privacy or individuality of moral activity. The *polis,* however, may be regarded as another road to the state, especially in regard to its conflicts with Sparta and other, larger conflicts which required the exercise of the 'leader principle' and the partial suspension of the limitedly democratic constitution. Also, the very fact of the size and compactness of the city-state encourages an ever-closer identity with the community, the nation. During conflict, it is *loyalty* that becomes the chief virtue, something Hobbes understood with remarkable clarity in his employment of foreign policy as a viable analogy of the mechanics of an 'internal' society.

It is only in the Stoics that the tendency is away from the conception of the community toward individual suffrage, toward democratic equivalence in a political society.

The passage from what might be termed a *residual tribalism,* the feudal condition of the medieval period in Europe, to the absolutist state of the eighteenth and nineteenth centuries, occurs when feudal forces may well be losing ground or are confronted by new economic and social forces, but while feudal magnates still possess much of their authority and influence and surrender this to a strong central authority in cohering around it, as is the case in the France of Louis XIV and in nineteenth-century Prussian Germany. The tribal leadership passes from the fragmented, unstable power groupings of feudal estates and territories, not necessarily with, or without, conflict of a prolonged, internecine nature, to the central authority, which cultivates its embodiment of the 'people' or nation; but without the existence and survival of the feudal forces to become a court (i.e., the new, deputed executive) such centralization would not occur and the state would not, in the terms that it did in France in particular, have come into existence at the beginning of the modern period of European history. A similar, though less extreme, oligarchical system occurred in England after the Glorious Revolution of 1688, when the Whig landed interests dominated political life and power, and the cause of suffrage and reform was suspended for more than a century, until the 1830s, in fact. The collusion, and the real authority to collude effectively, of the landed class at the evening of feudalism produced a set of conditions in which democratic political society was unlikely to emerge and the notion of the absolutist state with its central government, its limited or pseudo-suffrage (patronage), its mystified and even deified monarchical figure appeared as a radical development of the status quo rather than of change. The monarchical ideal is the *national* version of the feudal ideal, with power and authority (the 'trinity' of executive, legislature, and judiciary contained in the 'one') at the apex of the pyramid but with an absence of rights and suffrage at the base that was peculiarly feudal—even as it was the future of Europe.

Thus, as advocates of sovereignty, both Hegel and Hobbes are of the future, highly attuned to the political and social circumstances of their times. Both of them feared suffrage's dilution of authority and order, to the extent that both exercized this procedure of mystification, of elevating the monarchical figure, as embodiment of the state, to the status of analogous or intercessionary divinity. The sacerdotal and instructional functions of the monarchy are as important to Hegel and Hobbes as the judicial and executive functions. Both, too, have an ideal view of the state, a determinism that claims that evolutionary forces predicate an arrival at perfection, or, in Hobbes' case, the suggestion that tradition illustrates political society's having already arrived at the perfect form of the state. Both thinkers desired, and required above all else, the cohesion and coherence of society, which to both of them indicated the necessity of a mystical element or force in the nation, expressed by the state itself or by the leader/monarch. To return to the Hellenic world for a moment, Sparta may be regarded as the perfect hierarchical state, as well as the perfection of the tribe, with its two kings, its warrior elite, and entirely different *idea* of political society to that expressed, however haphazardly and often contradictorily (in imitation of the Spartan model on many occasions, often when in conflict with the latter) by Athens. Similarly for Hobbes and Hegel, there is a symmetrical perfection in hierarchy, central authority, a coherent, national aggression, and the leadership principle.

In Hobbes, this process is dignified, for the purpose of 'beginning' the absolutist state and in order to include the tradition of natural rights in his argument, by the *covenant* which the people make with the sovereign power. The covenant, however, is strictly a single occasion, a complete transference of power to the monarch, and thereafter abiding under, and identifying with, his authority.

In both Hobbes and Hegel, though with quite different individual emphasis, the concept of freedom is equivalent to the idea of *belonging,* and in that sense it is akin to the Athenian idea of the *polis.* It is a freedom *from* both human nature itself and the aggressive competitiveness of civil society, a process that in Hegel is understood as self-realization by identification with the State, just as in Hobbes there is a personation of the members by the Author, the "Artificiall Man." In Hegel, the *Idea* and the State become synonymous, while in Hobbes the same equivalence is granted to the Person and the State. It is an idea of freedom that equals *identification* and not identity. While Hegel's Idea is gradually realizing itself through history, Hobbes's ideal is a realized perfection, an existant. Both of them represent what might be termed a subversion of the idea of Christendom into that of the state, making a political society whose foundations are some *national* equivalent of a spiritual or spiritualized community. For Hobbes, there is a degree of modernization of the divinity that hedges kingship, itself a medieval-feudal-Elizabethan convention of thought, for that divinity, postulated as embodying and expressing the community, is the representation of a *community of faith.* In this, while Hobbes displays a deep understanding of the nature and political implications of Puritanism and may be regarded as Puritan in his stance, he is attempting to counter that division between church (spirit) and state (political society) which was essential to radical English Puritanism, without envisaging the theocracy of Calvin. Neither Hobbes nor Hegel may be said to be proponents of a secular society or secular politics, which may be regarded as a necessary precondition of any democratic political society which confines its authority to the empirical, phenomenal sphere of the relations of law governing men in a social context, while omitting any metaphysical concept of community, 'likeness', identification, and any ethical system based on assumptions of essential similarity between human individuals. At the level of civil society, which is the level and degree of privacy and individuality allowed by the political ideals represented in Hobbes and Hegel, there is only an essential, simple-principle replication of a 'single' human nature, conditioned and determinist and entirely predictable. As a result, elevation to a spiritual plane is the purpose and object of the state.

VIII

Some mention has already been made of Hobbes's peculiar and systematic employment of language, but further examination of this aspect of *Leviathan*, its linguistic skin, so to speak, does assist in identifying Hobbes as a propagandist rather than an ethical or political philosopher.

In the simplest sense, it is a language fit for material bodies, for man as matter in motion. It is simple and also simplistic, entirely dependent upon a reductive etymology which has as its purpose the divorce of his essential or key terms and significations from their accretions *and* from their philosophical-ethical origins. Hobbes employs the vocabulary of theology, of moral philosophy and of political theory, of Puritanism and of the established church, of democracy and absolutism, but in this peculiarly and erroneously 'original' sense, redefining in terms of supposed linguistic *roots* the vocabulary and terminology of the disciplines and spheres of enquiry he parallels. In so doing, he subverts the vocabulary to his desired materialist 'purity' and function. In that sense, Hobbes employs a rhetoric. It may be so termed as a distinctly purposive approach to language the devices and techniques of which are informed by a single purpose, and a celebratory one at that. It expresses, too, a closed argument, since the object is always in view and clearly known, rather than exhibiting an exploratory use of language which one might more easily associate with an enquiry into political theory and human nature. He reinvents English almost as radically as Milton did with the Latinism of *Paradise Lost,* producing a truly materialist language.

Hobbes envisages his rhetoric as part of a structure as taut, inclusive, and systematically sound as ever Augustine did in *The City of God,* in which the signifying power of language is entirely controlled and determined in order to expound and celebrate a theory or royal absolutism. Language is definitive, encapsulatory, and reductive, just as his syntax is that of certainty, predetermined by his view of human nature and the necessity of absolutism. There are no diversions, no qualification, no *dialectic;* rather, a *rhetoric,* a device of persuasion rather than philosophical inquiry. In this, Hobbes is medieval or Elizabethan more than he is a man of the seventeenth century—though not only in this is he such. Plato provided a synthesis, the original of the dialectic, of the two approaches in his dialogues, but Hobbes has the need only for rhetoric, which is why so much of his argument is ahistorical, since contrary theories and evidence have little or no place in rhetorical practice. Ciceronian rhetoric was disputatious, a question of proof by disproof which it shared with Platonic method, while Hobbesian rhetoric is peculiarly English, sixteenth-century, and literary, relying crucially and centrally upon notions of appearance and metaphor as analogous to substantive reality. Hobbes may also be regarded as, in one sense, a very subtle Platonist, if one takes the view that Plato was more of a rhetorician than a political-moral philosopher in the *Republic,* and also as a very poor one if one takes the opposing view of Plato. In Hobbes's dialectic, antithesis is all but absent, represented only as occasional asides, while thesis and synthesis have an inevitable and irrefutable consequence the one upon the other. This is how Hobbes is able, through the use of the literary artifice of *actor* and *author,* appearance and reality, to arrive at a model of human nature to represent the state, not merely to be a metaphor of it.

Such a view of Hobbes does not necessarily invalidate his materialist view of human nature, upon which he predicates the necessity of absolute authority (that may be invalidated by other means), but to ignore the rhetoric of *Leviathan* is dangerous, because it is in his employment of language that Hobbes indicates that his purpose is that of assertion rather than enquiry. His is an art of persuasion rather than exploration. And that rhetoric places itself at the service of an ontology, a theory of being, rather than an epistemology, a theory of knowledge, from which point Locke begins. Hobbes has an essentialist view of human nature and of political society, but, because of the rhetoric, one may feel oneself confronted with the situation of the chicken and the egg. Is the ontology designed to support the theory of absolutism—to prove the necessity of a sovereign power without suffrage or redress—or is the progression to absolutism as a solution to the problem of civil society *only* necessary because of Hobbes's pessimism regarding human nature and its moral incapacity? In either case, Hobbes's absolutism is only necessary because of his materialism, and his materialist view of human nature is flawed—merely rhetorically irrefutable, with a merely *apparent* causative necessity.

It may therefore be remarked in conclusion that Hobbes, the prophet of European absolutism, was perhaps no more than reacting against humanism's revivifying of what amounted to the corpse of natural rights theory. Hobbes was waging a war on behalf of an idealized *tradition* of absolutism, in support of a *literary* view of monarchy rather than the feudal reality, perhaps, in fact, attempting to invigorate that mystification of the Tudors—the 'Tudor myth'—and supply it to the Stuarts, who had manifestly failed either to exploit it or demonstrate any capacity to maintain it. In short, he is restating the tradition of the divine right of kings that Shakespeare was so eloquently able to dramatize in the tragedy of *Richard II* and dismiss so violently in *King Lear.*

VERY RATIONAL NOTIONS: DESCARTES, SPINOZA, LEIBNIZ, AND KANT

IN ORDER TO COMPREHEND THE PROFUNDITY of the change in philosophy brought about by Hegel, and which via Marx to a large extent determined the future of the science of society and provided the prevailing wind of political theory since the beginning of the last century, it is first necessary to return to what is regarded as the previous cataclysm in philosophical enquiry brought about by Descartes and the rationalists. Here, it is theories of knowledge, or epistemology, rather than ethical or political thought that is of the essence. Locke's major work of philosophy was itself an empirical epistemological enquiry, the *Essay Concerning Human Understanding*. Both Continental rationalism and English empiricism derive from the same intellectual presuppositions, and both strains in seventeenth- and eighteenth-century thought may be said to extend and support the concept of *self* which becomes the basis of so much of what is termed 'liberal' theory. Both strains are deeply influenced by mathematics and the new physical sciences—as were the theories of Hobbes, the great 'illiberal'.

What Descartes (1596–1650) offered philosophy was a universe of doubt, a profound and total skepticism concerning what we can know and prove. The paradigm of his method was mathematics, and, as Hobbes did more imperfectly, he sought the kind of simple maxim or proposition from which to begin argument, theory, and proof—the proof of knowledge itself, of what we can successfully accept as 'real'. *Je pense, donc je suis (Cogito, ergo sum)* is the most famous claim in philosophy, but it is important to realize that it comes at the end of the lightless tunnel of doubt. It is the only thing Descartes claims he can possibly *not* doubt. From this indubitable beginning he can proceed to conceive of the infamous dualism inherent in man and his universe, that dualism of mind and matter, a mind distanced from, and unique within, empirically perceived reality. What follows, inevitably and crucially for philosophy, is the separation between the human mind and its own body, its emotions and feelings as well as its physical existence, and between the perceiving mind and the more 'secondary' reality that it observes. There is detachment and division such as the Romantic movement in the following century in Germany attempted to redress, identifying man as being at one with the whole of creation, with nature. It is also a significant negative influence upon the materialists of the eighteenth-century French Enlightenment who, in dismissing the dualism, dismissed 'mind' altogether in favor of 'matter' as the sole constituent of the universe.

In Descartes, Aristotle's "rational animal," man, becomes divided into mind, including will, and body. What also occurs is that *feeling* is subordinated to *reason,* as it is in Locke and in most theories that elevate human reason to primacy, but in a peculiarly definite and definitive manner. Feeling, emotion, affection, desire, indeed become alienated from mind, from the *cogito* which is the 'real' self. Thus, we have a concept of self that is wholly rational and essentially divorced from body and from the matter that constitutes the reality that surrounds the self. At the same moment, Descartes is providing a fundamental concept of selfhood that places man, or at least his mind, at the center of the universe.

Rationalism is, profoundly, opposed to the strain of philosophical enquiry described as empiricism, because knowledge of the world is derived *a priori*, by the operation of reason alone, rather than through sense-experience of the world. Therefore, rationalism cannot avoid positing an entirely different view of human nature, that of dualistic man, divorcing mind from body, as opposed to the empirical view that man cannot *know* without the operation of the senses (i.e., an 'undivided' man capable of rational thought, much more akin to Aristotle's conception). As Descartes adopted the paradigm of mathematics, so it might be suggested that Locke's method was closer to the new physical or natural sciences, closer, at least, to our idea of the scientist observing and examining and only subsequently theorizing.

Because of the influence of Descartes's theory of man as a dualism of mind and body, it is necessary to regard his epistemology as having become, or possessing the status of, an ontology, a theory of being or existence. It is by this means that his influence extends itself into social and political theorizing, into ethics. Whatever the essential intent of his theorizing, its effect is to create a system of thought profoundly influential in every field of inquiry. Moreover, it was a system which created a vast and continuing opposition to itself, whether in materialism or in the 'whole being' ideas of the German Romantics or in the "natural man" ideas of Rousseau. Descartes's influence, in this negative sense, cannot be overestimated. Reaction against his ideas may be more significant for theories of human nature and society in succeeding centuries than the direct influence of Locke or Kant. His unflinching vision of reason alone in a universe of matter, separated from it in capacity, nature, and kind—and superior to it—stalks all philosophy which follows, and the *doubt* that is the fundamental presupposition of that reason effectively divorces philosophy from any and all paradigmatic influence of theology. Among much else, Descartes's theories were the most significant of the influences at work upon the ideas of the *philosophes*, the materialists of the Enlightenment, far more influential, indeed, than was Locke, for whom a primacy of influence is often claimed.

What cannot be derived from Descartes with any great success is a clearly formulated ethical theory, which might lead to social and political theories. There is a great deal that is implicit, most significantly the pressure toward not only autonomous but isolated individuality as a precondition of behavior, and socialist thinkers have been reacting against such a concept and moral and political thoeries that employ it ever since Descartes, and their refutations and condemnations continue. In the second member of the great trinity of rationalists, Spinoza (1632–77), we do in fact discover such theories, and distinctively 'liberal' theories, at that. Like that of Descartes, his methodology was entirely deductive; it is also true that Cartesian dualism persists in his remarkably complex and difficult theories. Also like Descartes, his paradigm was mathematics, since he believed that truth lies in a few axioms of thought which cannot logically be denied or refuted. These axioms must be uncovered and stated, then applied to the field of interest of the individual philosopher. We are dealing, therefore, once more with an epistemology—What can we know, and how?—but Spinoza applies his own dictum and examines the sphere of ethics by means of his epistemological theories.

There is something all but pantheistic in his basic concept of *modes* as the ultimate units of reality (ideas are more accurately described as "modes of thought" for example), but the result of his inquiries is to posit a single, infinite substance in the universe, rather than to emphasize the dualism of reality. Mind and matter are separate but not different, since they are simply different attributes of the single, infinite substance, which Spinoza identifies with God. Thus, though his thought is notoriously difficult and abstruse, what Spinoza achieved in ontology was a subtle and complex reintegration of the individual with the world. Spinoza's thought was regarded in his time as atheistic, principally because God is no longer identified as the creator but as the "infinite Substance" of which human beings are attributes or modes— expressions, as it were. Spinoza may be regarded as refuting that notion of the individual, isolated self that is implicit in Descartes, what may be termed a merely epistemological self, by his notion of the single, universal substance. This gives any notion of self an ontological rather than epistemological status, the status of *being*, not merely *knowing*. This enables Spinoza's ethical theories to remain of a piece with his metaphysical postulates. Man is at one with his 'world' and active in it, therefore capable of, and requiring, an ethical dimension.

He also denied the concept of free will in favor of a deterministic view of the operation of universal laws such as science was capable of exposing. However, the concept of freedom is not necessarily denied by his determinism, and it forms an essential element of his ethical theories. Man possesses freedom in the employment of reason to subdue his "passions," and this concept of positive freedom, though it may be regarded as dualistic in its view of reason versus emotion, is considered by Spinoza a very real freedom. Freedom becomes, in fact, the equivalent of the primacy of reason as a human capacity, a position not unlike that of Locke and especially close to that of Kant in his view of the "moral Reason." Indeed, the Fifth Part of the *Ethics* (1677) is entitled "Concerning the Power of the Intellect, or Human Freedom."

Freedom in Spinoza may be seen as the state of not being subject to the effect upon us of external objects via our passions, and to that extent it is a rationalist view of human nature that predominates. However, it should also be remarked that the ontological basis of this conception is the idea that all human beings partake of the nature of the single, infinite substance, so as to restore to individualism an equality of importance appertaining to each and every individual. Thus, in the *Ethics* and in the *Tractatus Theologico-Politicus* of 1670, we discover Spinoza's acceptance and employment of both natural law theory and the concept of natural rights and liberties much as they are to be found in Locke. Spinoza's view of government is remarkably empirical. The idea of consent in government and of individual liberty, without which there can be no true consent to be governed, together with free speech and religious toleration, all are emphatically promulgated, together with a concept of sovereignty as residing in a democratic assembly and not in monarchy. All stem from the primacy of reason and the necessity that reason enjoys freedom in its exercise. It is possible to add that human nature, as an attribute of the 'divine' substance, is awarded a dignity and significance that distinguishes *each* human being, a concept that must underlie all political and social thinking that desires to be considered democratic. The concept of substance integrates man not only with his world but with his fellows as other 'expressions' or 'attributes' of the single, universal substance.

In the third of the great rationalist philosophers, Leibniz (1646–1716), we discover a very different basic concept of an infinity of substances in the universe, which he 'atomizes' in the idea of the monad, and more significantly for the purposes of political and social theory there is a far less radical and individualistic interpretation of society and the state. Leibniz, while insisting on the freedom of the will, was nevertheless a determinist in presupposing a God who had in his omniscience both created and determined the behavior of all the substances (monads) in the universe. From this, his political theories derive, in the form of an idea of the "common good," of the organization and determination of human interaction in imitation of his ontological theory. Thus, Leibniz begins from a legalistic standpoint and attempts to develop a universal jurisprudence, but one which is founded in analogous imitation of the relation of God to his creation (i.e., the inevitable inequality between the ruler and those who rule, something familiar and comfortable to Hobbes). The fundamental implication of Leibniz's view of a natural and inevitable inequality is the dismissal of natural rights, and there are also implications in statements such as "government belongs to the wisest" that are Platonic in their ancestry. If not a single monarch, then definitely a ruling caste, those most skilled and wisest in their employment of reason. There are *degrees* of rational endowment in human beings. Leibniz had read Locke's *Two Treatises* and had quarreled with the English philosopher's assumption of the "equality of rights of man." Leibniz also rejected the idea of consent or contract in any discussion of the origin of society and government.

Based upon his assumption of the necessity of a rationally wise ruling caste, he can claim that "the end of democracy . . . is to make the people themselves agree to what is good for them," while also observing that "Arbitrary power is what is directly opposed to the empire of Reason . . . [it] is found not only in Kings but also in assemblies." Leibniz's state is safeguarded from tyranny by the government of the wise and therefore moral. Liberty is to be guaranteed by the state, but there is a curiously Hobbesian, and nineteenth-century, mistrust of democracy in his views. His emphasis on public welfare and his view of justice as charity tempered by wisdom is what might be termed 'socialist' rather than 'liberal', to use two rather inappropriate labels to characterize the bent of his thought, except that we may thereby distinguish him from seventeenth-century English liberals who emphasized natural rights rather than social well-being. He may also be regarded as conservative in his attitude to revolution when he remarks that "the evil of revolt ordinarily being incomparably greater than that which causes it." One cannot but be reminded of Burke's horrified denunciations of the French Revolution in such an observation.

It is possible, and not misleading, to regard Leibniz as, in many ways, a precondition of Hegel's philosophy. It is a rationalist position that is pronouncedly conservative and social, rather than liberal-individualistic, as even the most superficial comparison with Spinoza exhibits. It is also intensely derivative of time and place, a 'prenational' Germany such as still encompassed Hegel. Like Spinoza, however, Leibniz demonstrates an ethical and political preoccupation which is largely absent from Descartes and which brings both rationalists closer to the strain of English empiricism. Leibniz is a polar opposite of Descartes, since his universe is the best possible universe; willed and created by God it could not be otherwise—a universe of certainty rather than doubt. Since this assumption underlies his ethical and political thinking, he could hardly be radical in his view of government.

European rationalism displays, in Spinoza and Leibniz, a derogation of emotion and feeling in favor of reason, but in the ethical concerns of both there may be perceived a nobility of ideal regarding those emotions that are inevitable in human interaction in the public world—charity, freedom, sympathy must all invest the "spirit of society." In Spinoza, it issues in radical form in a restatement of natural law theory, while in Leibniz it is conservative. In the best of all possible worlds, radical change in society is a difficult idea to justify!

For the narrower purpose of discovering the ancestry of Hegelian thought, we must return to the political circumstances of Germany in the seventeenth and eighteenth centuries. The Thirty Years' War and the fragmentation into hundreds of small political units of a hereditary, and occasionally electoral, governmental nature is the condition of pre-nationhood. Upheaval and carnage and political fragmentation may be said to inculcate a yearning toward the condition of a state, together with a deeply conservative attitude to political change and to the nature of government. Centralization implies a centralizing force or magnetism and a central, usually single, authority rather than a more liberal system. It is also possible to assume that this yearning might manifest itself in a 'spiritual' manner, in the kind of idealism of approach we find in Plato's republic or in the old concept of Christendom (i.e., the emergence of a style of political thinking that seeks models of society, perfect organizations or organisms supremely regulated and structured and closed to change or evolution). We can, at the least, remark that Leibniz exhibits many ideas we later discover in Hegel.

If the above is something like the case, then despite Leibniz's search for a universal jurisprudence it is the ethical, the 'idealist' vision of society that predominates in both Leibniz and Hegel, rather than the constitutional strain of thought exhibited by Locke. There are unquestioned assumptions about *good* having to be imposed and regulated and a movement away from the necessity of rights and liberties toward what may be termed prescriptions for the morality and function of authority. Social theory becomes centralized in the concept of authority, and it is usual in such theorizing that the central authority is that of the individual ruler, a monarch. By analogy with the physical sciences of the seventeenth century, the greater mass of the citizens of a society becomes merely fragments, drawn by the central and greater mass of the ruler. One may also remark the similarities between such theories and the authority of the Catholic church and the Pope. There is an emphasis upon free will but a greater emphasis upon authority, even in matters that determine the destination of the essence of human nature, the soul. Protestantism, through Luther and Calvin, with its emphasis upon individual responsibility for the condition and destination of the soul, is opposed to such centralization and is therefore a more radical analogy for political theory than philosophical or doctrinal systems that seek to define the nature of authority rather than liberty.

It is not misleading to suggest that the majority of the main strands of eighteenth-century European thought may be witnessed in the theories of Descartes, Spinoza, and Leibniz, though they represent metaphysics rather than empirical inquiry. Their identification of mind and matter, or substance, or monads, fulfills the requirement of metaphysics in identifying the basic and universal nature of reality in a single principle. They consider elements and aspects of reality in separate and exhaustive detail, but nevertheless their attempt is to satisfy the criterion of considering reality as a whole. Though Kant, himself a metaphysician, began his inquiries seeking a place and legitimacy for metaphysics itself, he did so not in response to the seventeenth-century's rationalism but to the—by his time—pervasive influence of the materialism characteristic of French 'rationalism' during the Enlightenment. The influence of Locke and the empiricists was, fortunately, strong in Kant, which enabled him to assume the radicalism of Spinoza and Locke himself and to avoid the authoritarian idealism of Leibniz. Superficially, it may be remarked at this point that Hegel had obviously read Leibniz and misread Kant, who was, despite his effort toward a new metaphysic, too honest an empiricist to be able to dignify authority with any 'ideal' qualities.

The significance of Rationalism for political and social theory before Hegel is best indicated by the exhaustive moral philosophy of Kant and its negative influence upon the Germany of Hegel and *Sturm und Drang.* The apostasy from reason had already proceeded too far for Kant to recall the faithful to a system which, while elevating human reason and demoting human passions, nevertheless provided one of the definitive and most humane theories of human freedom in Western philosophy. Whereas Locke's influence upon philosophy in England as well as upon Kant was immense, Kant's influence as an ethical and social thinker in Germany was virtually negligible, unless one accepts the notion that his third major work, *Critique of Judgment,* was a major influence upon German Romanticism and the idealists who preceded Hegel. Kant's concept of the Sublime and claims for the significance of art do not, nevertheless, contain any influential ethical-political theories such as appeared in the *Critique of Practical Reason* and were ignored or refuted by his successors.

Rationalism had, at best, followed Leibniz rather than Spinoza, or else degenerated into French materialism or the vague and idealistic notions of German Romanticism, where art replaces reason as the object of all piety and harmony. The harmony of man with nature seems attractive, especially when contrasted with Cartesian dualism and the chill of the universe of matter inhabited by mind, but it exhibits that same magnetic pull toward central authority or some central and common principle, as in Rouseeau, as Leibniz and Hobbes present. By its originality, novelty, and identification with scientific inquiry, itself a pervasively influential 'novelty' in the seventeenth century, Rationalism only *appears* to break with metaphysical tradition (as exemplified in theology). Its ethical and political legacy is not the radicalism of Spinoza but the detachment of mind from body and from matter in general of Descartes, or the political conservatism of Leibniz and its pressure toward central authority, its prescription, indeed, that political theory should address itself to the nature of authority—the governor, not the governed—and away from natural rights and liberties. In that sense, Rationalism is a precondition of Hegel and Marx, as, most strangely of all, is Hobbes.

II

Immanuel Kant's style is conventionally regarded as academic in the pejorative sense, dry and difficult, but usually by students who have not had the misfortune to encounter the oceanic verbiage of his preeminent successor in German philosophy, G. W. F. Hegel. It is, perhaps, the profoundest error of nineteenth-century social and political thought that, despite his comparative clarity—pellucid clarity by any rational standard—Kant (1724–1804) was ignored, to the benefit of Hegel, without doubt one of the direst of influences on political inquiry, certainly with regard to Germany and therefore, given her history, upon Europe in the twentieth century, though it may be as facile to blame Hegel for Hitler as it is to condemn Marx because of Stalin, though both are conventional maxims of opinion one should examine before dismissing. There is implied some declension of thought that may not be entirely erroneous. No such genealogy of theory can be ascribed to Locke, not even as a forefather of capitalism.

Kant's theories are complex and his proofs exhaustive. Like Descartes and Spinoza, he attempted to discover what might be deduced *a priori*, without the necessity of sensory experience. To that extent, he is the true heir of the Rationalists and a genuine metaphysician. Strangely, however, the essence of his system resides in the most liberal of ethical values. Whether he was aware of the true nature of his task or not, the pursuit of metaphysics as a means of ascribing and describing *essence* and the comprehension of reality as a whole, an entity, was not an ontological or epistemological pursuit, as it had been primarily for the rationalists, but an *ethical* endeavor. Kant, beginning with the task of "illuminating the inherent moral sense that all men possess," is engaged in justifying, to the degree of doctrine rather than theory, liberal human, social, and political values. In doing so, he arrives at the *categorical imperative*, the notoriety of which is second only to Descartes's *cogito* in the history of philosophy, and it is possible to assert that his whole edifice of thought is designed and pursued in order to so arrive. His effort is circular. To paraphrase T. S. Eliot, it is an effort to arrive at the place where he began and to know the place for the first time. From his background as the son of a harness maker and a family sincerely Pietist in outlook, he derived a basically commonsensical view of divinity, moral apprehension, and human reason. It was to make these universal principles into such as deserved the designation 'metaphysic' that his three *Critiques,* of *Pure Reason* (1781), *Practical Reason* (1788), and *Judgment* (1790) labor—and not in vain.

What Kant derived from his background and upbringing, and what remained with him, may be termed a universal sympathy toward human nature together with a view of human moral worth that was undistinguishing and unselective. His ideals presumed the capacity of all human beings to engage their "moral Reasons" in the task of existence, though not necessarily to the same degree. However, he accorded to all human beings an equality of worth and uniqueness, as is demonstrated by his concept of human beings as *ends,* above and beyond causality and the laws of nature as explored and defined by science. Human beings are *things-in-themselves (noumena* rather than *phenomena),* but they are, in a more important sense, that of ethical behavior, *ends-in-themselves* rather than merely *means,* and as such not for the use or exploitation of other human beings—and there are *no* exceptions. Unlike, as will be seen, the French Enlightenment, Kant deliberately did not elevate reason as exemplified in scientific inquiry. In fact, he deliberately placed upon scientific reasoning the same kind of limitation that Locke did, and for the same reason, that he could not abandon his faith in favor of a materialistic outlook, and instead elevated what he termed the "moral Reason" as the primary and most profound human capacity. In a parallel of Descartes, he began his odyssey of inquiry by asking what it was that the human mind could know of reality, though the *object* of such inquiry was not epistemological as it was in Descartes but ethical (i.e., What can we know that will enable us to live, and to live with others, morally?). It is a question he felt impelled to ask and to answer in the face of the theorizing of

Hobbes and so many others, where human nature is viewed pessimistically as the "slave of passion" and human society as a war of all against all. The empirical persuasiveness of the notion of rampant egoism as the reality of human nature, which any thinker in any age is in danger of finding overwhelmingly true, unnerved and repelled Kant, giving a sense of urgency, perhaps even desperation, to his inquiries. Such ideas simply *had* to be countered and defeated. For him, even the emergent utilitarian theory, so pernicious in its influence on eighteenth- and nineteenth-century liberalism, of the "greatest happiness" principle, was insufficient for Kant—indeed, he regarded ideas such as happiness as the highest good as a corruption of morality, of that true freedom he believed was only possible in the full exercise of the moral reason and the subduing of desire and the emotions, much as Spinoza had postulated in his *Ethics*.

Thus, we may observe what have earlier appeared to be contrary strands of philosophical inquiry yoked together by Kant. His deductive methodology derives from Descartes and Spinoza and seventeenth-century Rationalism, while his 'values' stem from the influence of Locke, Berkeley, and Hume, the English empiricists, another way in which Kant stands at the crossroads of modern social and political theory, and perhaps the most important way. Unfortunately for our century, Hegel doubled back on Kant and switched the signposts at an earlier crossing, misdirecting all of us. Kant had read and was influenced by Hume's ideas on causality, and he was not without interest in the natural sciences. However, as has been remarked, he was determinedly aware of the limitations of scientific reasoning, just as he was aware of the attractiveness of the theory of causality by its very illustration in the sphere of scientific inquiry. But, for him, causality excluded religious faith, and above all it reduced human beings to 'things' or *means* rather than "ends-in-themselves." Therefore, any true apprehension of human nature must regard it as being somehow not subject to causality. Hence he termed his philosophical outlook "transcendental Idealism," signifying the transcendence of the moral reason over the iron law of cause and effect.

Essentially, the method he expounds in *Critique of Pure Reason* distinguishes between two sources of knowledge, what Kant terms sensibility and understanding. By means of the former, we receive information concerning reality, and by the latter we think. The process of "understanding" classifies and orders what may be described as 'mere' experience. He defines twelve categories, which he regards as the minimal conceptual apparatus a human being requires to make sense of the world. It is this he terms transcendental, and it is this that is metaphysical in his system, since the categories or concepts relate to the operation of reason alone, as does the attempt of the whole *Critique*, even though the concepts cannot be applied to anything beyond the subject of sense experience. Kant dismisses what he terms "speculative metaphysics." Though the method and object seem close to those of Descartes, Kant assumes that there is no need to prove the existence of the world outside the self, since reason "assumes an objective world" in its very self-awareness.

The *Critique of Practical Reason* continues the explication of Kant's system, applying his conception of the *a priori* operation of reason to the field of action (i.e., moral action). It is here that he expounds his most famous maxim, which he termed the *categorical imperative*, the profoundest rule of moral action, in the form of an *a priori* proposition. "Act only on that maxim which you can at the same time will to become a universal law." This forms, for Kant, not so much a principle in itself (in practical terms, a value), but that which underlies and by which human beings may judge moral values. It is a *test* of principle. Unlike the categorical imperative, Kant posits what he calls hypothetical imperatives, which he designates as promptings and injunctions we may choose to take notice of and act upon with a particular aim in mind. They do not, since morality cannot be founded upon the wishes or inclinations of the individual human agent, constitute true moral principle or prompt real moral action. Only the categorical imperative can do so. The concept of *duty* is introduced by Kant to describe true moral activity, but the term has served Kant's system ill, with its pejorative implications and its suggestion of *duty to* or *duty imposed*. Kant is defining only a duty to self, to the moral reason.

The clearest and most profound principles of Kant's system of transcendental idealism lie in the autonomy of the moral reason within each individual human being, to the extent that he ascribes to the capacity of human reason the derivation of all moral law. The moral universe, for Kant, is centered upon human capability rather than prescribed moral systems, including those of theology. His clearest restatement of the significance of each individual lies in deriving from the categorical imperative the concept of men as ends-in-themselves, which forbids human beings from using others as means. It is the most profound, and radical, statement of autonomous individuality, and perhaps the last great such assertion in European philosophy. He even speaks of "the kingdom of ends" which, though a somewhat drab and unemotional idea, describes the community of independent and essentially equal judges of conduct which is the basis of any 'ideal' social organization. It bears no resemblance to the rule of the wisest we find in the Platonic tradition.

Reason, for Kant, has made human nature unique and has removed it from causality. The concept of freedom does not apply to any sphere in which natural causation is universal, he claims, meaning the world apprehended by scientific inquiry and scientific reason. As a metaphysician, of course, Kant distinguished that external world as 'appearance' and human reason and its operations as 'reality'. The reality we apprehend outside our minds is mere *phenomenon*, and the limitations of our verifiable knowledge of the world never allow us to glimpse the *noumenon*, the reality, except the 'reality' of our own reason and its operations. Thus we are handicapped and incapable of speculative metaphysics, which must thus be abandoned as a branch of philosophy, but we are by the same limitation *noumena* ourselves, in our moral reasons. We are removed from that causality which is the principle governing the world of phenomena.

It can be suggested, not entirely erroneously, that Fichte, Schelling, and, finally, Hegel, in all seeking to 'complete', or rectify the errors of, Kant's system, misunderstood the dualism of phenomenon and noumenon, disregarding the noumenal reality Kant had granted to individuals and therefore to selves who, being equal, unique, and uniquely *alike*, represent a noumenal 'world' to be comprehended. Hegel, especially, went beyond Kant to posit an idealist theory in which the world can only be regarded as 'real' insofar as it is imbued with our own intellectual activity—which reduces the noumenal condition of *others*. In so doing, Hegel and his fellow idealists fatally undermined the concept of self in subsequent German thought.

Thus, as in Spinoza, we can perceive Kant arriving at a conception of freedom or even free will for human nature in a world that is otherwise governed by the determining factor of causality, those universal laws science has apprehended and revealed. The dualism of man as rational creature and creature of passion and desire is reasserted and, again as in Spinoza, there is in Kant a necessary emphasis upon such a dualism. Reason must govern our actions if they are to be truly moral actions, and if we are to be truly free in our actions; otherwise, the stimulus of the phenomenal world on our sensibilities and desires will *cause us to act* on our impulses. We shall then become obedient to our egoistic wishes and desires and never achieve true moral action. We will have become less than a noumenon, less *real*. As important, others will no longer be ends but only means, subordinate in some way or other to ourselves.

True freedom lies solely in the exercise of the moral reason, or moral "Will" as Kant often defines it. It is the only means of self-determination and the only way in which we are true to the reality of our human natures. Only by *dutifully* following the dictates of our moral capacity can we achieve thought or action which is not determined by some consideration external to our selves. Even our passions are external to our real selves in this sense.

The *Critique of Practical Reason* was published in 1788, the year before the cataclysm of the French Revolution and almost a century after Locke's *Essay* and the *Two Treatises*. It is, together with Kant's more popular *Groundwork of the Metaphysic of Morals* (1785), perhaps an even more radical document than the writings of the English empiricist. Indeed, in Kant's severely noble conception of human nature lies the last, and perhaps profoundest, statement of the value of autonomous, individual human nature, directly applicable to social and political thought as well as to ethics; it was one that was swept aside, even away, by the thought and subsequent influence of Hegel. The foundations of his great edifice had been rotted from beneath, like the piles under some huge Venetian palazzo, by the slow tides of materialism in France, the 'revised' empiricism of David Hume, and the *Sturm und Drang* of German Romanticism. Indeed, that *Sturm* might well be seen as causing the flood tide of Hegelian rhetoric and speculation that altogether swept away the individual in philosophical thought.

FRENCH CONNECTIONS: MATERIALISTS, REVOLUTIONARIES, AND OTHERS

It HAS FREQUENTLY BEEN CLAIMED, and often accepted, that the empiricism of Locke was a distinct and profound influence upon French thinkers of the eighteenth century, such that it has become a maxim of historians of political theory. It is perhaps more illuminating to consider the thinkers of the Enlightenment in France as *materialists* exhibiting an inheritance that derives as much from Descartes and Spinoza and exaggeratedly influenced by a peculiarly narrow conception of the capacities and purposes of human reason, than as the successors of Locke. True, they shared many of his social and political values. What they had abandoned—Cartesian dualism in favor of a universality of matter—was, however, far more significant for our purposes. Rather than the inheritors of empiricism, they were the forerunners of French Positivism. Reason had become an implement of comprehension rather than the source of individual human uniqueness. Human reason as the essence of human identity ceased to be a philosophical assumption.

It is also a truism that there is little that is original in the theories of the *philosophes* of the Enlightenment—for example, their 'liberal' values derive mainly from Locke and the English empiricists—but in making any assumption about that unoriginality, the historian of ideas seriously mistakes the effects of the basis of those adopted values, materialism itself. In d'Holbach's (1723–89) setting-out of the theories of materialism in his *System of Nature* (trans. 1796), materialism means simply that the entire universe, reality, consists of matter and that there is a fundamental continuity between man and nature or all nonhuman reality. The Cartesian dualism of mind and matter is miraculously healed. Reason becomes a means of understanding that continuity rather than the distinction between man and nature or between the *noumenon* of Kant (Descartes's *cogito*) and the phenomenal reality of everything other than man. Reason no longer retains a distinguishing *moral* function, as it does in Locke and was later to have in Kant, nor is it the means of arriving at *a priori* knowledge. Instead, it is an implement for understanding the reality outside the self. From being *moral* reason, it becomes *scientific* reason, and the assumption thereby arises and is commonly held among the *philosophes* that understanding of the laws governing reality derived from the explorations of science will achieve completion at some future date and that the subsequent scientific worldview will be, in itself, the solution to all human problems. The belief in scientific progress becomes absolute, and of absolute value. It is this fundamental alteration in the basis of liberal values that assists in ameliorating those values, producing in both France and in eighteenth-century England the beginnings of utilitarian liberal ideas, and even more significantly assists in altering those conceptions of human identity based upon natural law theory and natural rights, or in the concept of the *person* or rational man, or even the individual as an *end-in-himself.*

Given that reason is an implement of comprehension and of progress, the French Enlightenment employs the implement, and the 'value' given it as the means of human progress, in a concerted examination of eighteenth-century French society. The attitudes of French thinkers cannot be separated from their basic and shared anticlericalism, atheism, or vague pantheism. To do so would be to misunderstand the direction of much of their thought and almost all its vigor. Reason is the enemy of revealed religion and of its exponent, the Catholic church, and thus becomes 'enlightened', an instrument of rejection and progressive truth. What occurred was that reason became assumed and self-evident, even familiar and commonplace, but its *function* was to dispel the myths and errors of religion and of the grossly hierarchical society that was eighteenth-century France.

French society was rigidly divided into classes, principally nobility and peasants, with the bourgeoisie a poor and undervalued 'middle' class. It was this class that adopted and cherished the ideals of the Enlightenment and identified themselves with it most closely. The absence of a framework of rights in law for any but the nobility rendered the concepts of natural law theory more speculative and abstract than was the case with Locke—rendered them newly 'ideal', as it were. Their embrace by Voltaire and Montesquieu was an example of all but divine revelation. They had about them an almost mystical quality of self-justification, even as materialism was reducing the uniqueness of the individual agent and beneficiary of natural rights. Social and theological criticism became the paradigm of Enlightenment thought before Rousseau, in conjunction with an unquestioning belief in scientific progress. The importation of empirical liberal values was of huge significance, and need not be brought into question. The reason for their appeal, in France, was in no measure cynical, rather visionary. But, in their adoption by the *philosophes,* they became self-justifying by their opposition to existing social and political circumstances. They became a myth against the myth of absolutism. The result of this deification is to idealize the concept of the individual, also, so that the individual becomes typified and abstract. Epistemological concepts and theories, in Descartes and Spinoza, offer up the uniqueness of the individual reason, in their separate ways, but there is no epistemology in French materialism, only the *virtue* of reason as against faith. Human nature is not distinct from reality, all is matter, and therefore man cannot possess a distinguishing faculty or capability such as the rationalist idea of reason. He possesses reason in order to understand and to reject, rather than to *be.*

Locke's empirical inquiries into epistemology in the *Essay* are such that we might describe them as psychology as much as philosophy. They have an innate tendency toward individualizing human nature, whereas materialism, in its effort to effect radical change in society and the apprehension of society and politics by individuals, must assume and propagate the concept of reason in its employment as an implement of condemnation. Reason is there to 'do' something—especially the task of condemning through ridicule. Reason becomes 'wit' and not a definition of identity. Hence, it cannot develop a comprehensive theory of government or of society, such as that of Locke or Kant, because it is directed to rejection, not construction, and is a property of education and demystification, not of explication. The allied concept of scientific progress confirms the assumption that 'matters will come right'—an echo of Leibniz's best-possible-universe idea—the more reason comprehends. Further, the buoyancy of liberal values, evident to *any* reasoning person, is enhanced by the discovery of utilitarian man, who is a sensory being, a 'scientific' definition.

Therefore, it is not in the lack of originality that the Enlightenment is a reversal of empiricism and the concept of the autonomous individual but in its assumptions about reason's function as a human capacity. Locke's theories depend, in Hamlet's phrase, upon reason being "that Godlike reason," and in Kant they depend upon a conception of dualism between appearance and reality and the *a priori* capacity of human reason. In d'Holbach and the other *philosophes,* assumptions concerning reason are based upon the history of scientific discovery, enlarging and becoming more comprehensive throughout the century. We are left, therefore, with the contradiction that the Enlightenment promoted liberal values and "inalienable rights" more vigorously than perhaps any other movement in modern history, while at the same moment abandoning any metaphysical or 'idealist' conception of human nature, best exemplified in its faculty of reason. Whether 'religious' or 'rational', Locke, Spinoza, and Kant share an idealistic view of human potential, and therefore of the potential of any and *every* individual human nature.

Of the three clarion calls of the Revolution, the one which is missing from Enlightenment materialism is equality. The oneness of man with the rest of creation is not despicable, but its idea of equality is latent rather than active and real. Rather than human nature being elevated by materialist equivalence between man and nature, man's nature becomes merely common to all men. Materialism makes the equation one of man's equality with the universe rather than the equality of individuals marked off from the physical universe, or even from their own passions and desires. Materialism is anti-individual because it admits only of the common denominators of human nature. The paradigm of reason active in scientific discovery dominates materialist theories of human nature; *applied* reason, operating on the material universe that surrounds us, becomes the 'spirit' of reason; reason becomes the opposite of faith, a means of dispelling myth and illusion rather than a means of discovering the truth, for the assumption has already been made that certain liberal values are self-evident. The effort required to become and remain a morally reasoning being has already been dismissed. Isn't it obvious? becomes the watchword of liberal values.

None of the above, of course, invalidates the potential to popularize, at least among educated men and women, liberal values and what Locke would have termed "natural rights," and in that sense, perhaps, the influence of philosophical ideas upon history may be glimpsed. If the obviousness of liberal values rather than the rational effort toward them and toward justifying them implies danger for the future, it also demonstrates the power of the ideas themselves, once popularized, in an autocratic state. Philosophy-become-journalism possesses a vast power for radical change, though few of the *philosophes* were at all radical, their borrowed ideas only radical in France. However, given the social and political reality of France during and after the reign of the Sun King, another myth to be demolished by the operation of reason, it was inevitable that some kind of utilitarian theory would arise, as indeed it did. The "greatest happiness for the greatest number" principle, which Bentham codified for English culture, had an irresistible appeal for French thinkers who had imbibed liberal values from across the Channel. It must have seemed the perfect solution to society's ills, a thread that could wind through their theorizing and social criticism, or a cell of certainty. It was reinforced, should it need any reinforcement, by the unquestioning belief in the progress of science, that paradigm of rational outlook and inquiry. The heady moral rectitude it inspired was irresistible to the educated bourgeoisie.

Reason has, however, by this genealogy become a means of perceiving what is conventionally termed enlightened self-interest. Thus is has lost the almost somber rectitude with which Locke and later Kant endowed it. It is no longer the single human capacity capable of directing moral action, of subduing the passions, or of understanding reality. And because a profound change has occurred in the idea of reason itself, a corresponding change has occurred in ideas of human nature. The autonomy of the individual has been discarded or mislaid, and with it the necessity of achieving an individual moral rectitude. Instead, as the Revolution was to prove, the imposition of perceived values becomes all that is necessary to individual reason. Liberal values are self-evident, since values are self-justifying if they oppose the contemporary reality of society. Therefore, the perceivers with the clearest sight are elevated above those more myopic, selfish, or deluded. Individuals begin to be differentiated as to the degree to which they are ends-in-themselves, at best along Platonic lines (the wisest should govern) and at worst as the suppression of those individual moral reasons that oppose the new wisdom.

It remained to Rousseau to initially oppose this subtle and unstated collectivism and finally to exalt it in the theory of the social contract and the idea of the "general will." Before him, however, we can only witness the contradiction of materialism in

France, that it promulgated with the utmost wit and vigor the liberal values of Locke's writings while diminishing the status granted to individual human nature. All theology, like all metaphysics, has a collectivist magnetic pull, but at the same time it dignifies human nature with a 'soul' or a "moral Reason"—it establishes the commonality of human nature and the uniqueness of the individual in the same idea. Materialism is disqualified from such a contradiction. *Soul* no longer remains a viable concept, since it is the progeny of superstition and revealed religion, while *reason* has been reduced to its scientific application or to use as a weapon against the oppressions of society and the church. There is no *essence* remaining to dignify human nature. This pervasive materialism makes Kant's search for a defensibly metaphysical position both urgent and necessary. He understood the full cost of the dethronement of reason from that position of governing eminence in human nature.

The values so widely promulgated by the French Enlightenment become the *property* of those accepting their rational, self-evidential truth, which means they became, as Marx observed, the almost exclusive property of that articulate but powerless class in French society, the bourgeoisie. The values that Locke and Kant considered the product of reason, whether empirically or metaphysically uncovered, and which were the property of every rational human being—indeed the foundation of all moral, just action—became acquired and subsequently promoted as an identification, even a product, of attitude and class. Liberal values are no longer universal but particular; reason itself becomes evidence of social and political discontent.

Rationalism and materialism confront us, therefore, with two distinctly opposite interpretations of human nature. In rationalist theory, reason is the distinctive quality of human nature; and the ideas of natural law and natural rights are conveniently and happily subsumed into the concept of the primacy of a 'moral' reason; reason evidences a moral essence which is identified almost entirely with what we must conventionally term 'liberal' values. In rationalism, as in Kant, the employment of human reason is the sole means of evading that principle of causality which science continued to demonstrate was everywhere and in everything, the *law* that governed reality. To avoid causality—the subordination of human reason to mere matter—was synonymous with freedom; the only 'true' freedom. In materialism, however, reason is merely a faculty of apprehension, directed outward from the self toward the world, especially that reality explicable in terms of scientific laws. The materialists regarded all reality as scientifically knowable, as *real* rather than *appearance,* and man as another element of *matter* in that reality. In effect, causality applies to human reason as it does to the world of 'things'. Man becomes, or begins to become, a rational *thing.*

However, both approaches arrive at the upholding and expression of liberal values. Both rationalism in Europe and the English empirical philosophers insist that these values demonstrate the separation of human reason and, therefore, individual human nature, from the rest of creation, the world of appearances of things. The materialists arrive at identical values not by any theory of reason or natural law but because the significance of science and scientific law in a totally material universe suggests that it is the laws of nature that are rational, even 'just'. For this reason, human society should also demonstrate 'laws'. Human society can be neither unjust nor irrational unless it is a wrong conception of society. Autocracy and religion, both uniquely identified together in eighteenth-century France, are against the laws of nature, therefore they are irrational. Justice, freedom, natural rights appear far more suitable as laws of society. Natural law becomes the law of nature revealed by scientific reason.

From this basic position, Helvétius (1715–71), who influenced Bentham, posits his theory of the "greatest happiness" principle, the utilitarian amelioration of liberal values. The object of human activity, even and perhaps especially, of moral conduct, is the enjoyment of as much pleasure as possible and the avoidance of as much pain as possible. Human beings must, of necessity, pursue their self-interest. Helvétius assumes he is making a scientific judgment of human nature here, ascribing to self-interest a governing and lawlike role in society comparable with that of the principle of motion in physics. Since man is social rather than solitary, the only rational standard of conduct is the greatest good for the greatest number. It is almost unnecessary to point out that the Hobbesian concept of unregenerate man peeps through the specious structure of his argument. At one point in his main work, *De l'esprit* (1758), he remarks: "Good laws are the only means of making men virtuous. The whole art of legislation consists in forcing men, by the sentiment of self-love, to be always just to others." Out of this egoistic conception of human nature is developed the consequent idea that self-love makes the seeking-of-pleasure–avoidance-of-pain the essence of human nature. It is easy to remark the vastness of the change in the materialist conception of human nature when one observes the extreme view of human psychology Helvétius accepts and promulgates. Liberal values are the product not of human reason but of legislation, and the idea of natural rights has, in this extreme, become no more than *just* legislation. The secularization of reason has been completed in Helvétius's utilitarian theories, as has its separation from self and its importance as a concept embodying personal identity.

Except, it might be argued, for Rousseau. *The Social Contract* was published in 1762, only four years after *De l'esprit.* Rousseau (1712–78), the most influential of modern social and political thinkers before Marx; Rousseau the democrat and individualist— surely his influence means that liberal values became universal once more and natural rights reestablished? The violence of Rousseau's opposition to the Enlightenment thinkers must have redressed the balance, surely, especially since Kant himself admitted the degree to which Rousseau had impressed and influenced him regarding the idea of the moral will's superiority to mere scientific inquiry.

There are, indeed, good and solid grounds for regarding Rousseau as the real inheritor of Locke's ideas, as well as being their most influential popularizer; many similarities between his ideas and those of Kant can also be inferred—except that behind Rousseau's often-contradictory and often-changing views is a conception of human nature that precludes any real emphasis on personal liberty in the sense of liberal values having an essential application to the individual. As Rousseau remarked in a chilly paradox, men "will be forced to be free," a perhaps more onerous and limited conception of freedom than Kant's stern moral duty.

Rousseau's initial assumption concerning human nature is that men are "naturally good," while he also assumes that men hardly differ in the essential human nature they exemplify. There is no observable contradiction in these two assumptions, but a direction is suggested toward the concept of the group rather than the individual; a direction that Rousseau pursues toward his central idea of the "general will." His bold assertion that "a thinking man is a depraved animal" establishes the intensity of his opposition to the thinkers of the Enlightenment, as he raises to primacy over reason, knowledge, and the progress of science the virtues of benevolent feeling, good will, and reverence. What he posits is the universality and significance of what have been described as the "common feelings." The assault of the materialists upon *piety* in religion and social structure required a counterattack, so that, as Rousseau exclaims of them, "they smile contemptuously at such old names as patriotism and religion, and consecrate their talents and philosophy to the destruction and defamation of all that men hold sacred." It is perhaps not entirely surprising that this puritanical element in such a radical becomes evident. Rousseau, rightly, regarded the *philosophes* as elitist. Like Kant, Rousseau determined to limit the deification of scientific reason, confining it, as Kant did, to the phenomenal world rather than to human nature, and this is indeed the crucial divergence between his ideas and those of the Enlightenment. At such a juncture, Rousseau would seem capable of a genuine redefinition of natural rights and of "moral Reason," as against the utilitarianism of Helvétius and the general stance of the materialists. In the outcome, what did he do?

It is still possible to claim that, in rejecting the ideas of the materialists, especially in their developing view of human nature as motivated by self-interest, Rousseau is serving the cause of rational individualism which alone provides a certain basis for the liberal values adopted by the *philosophes*. However, in the crucial claim in *Émile* (1762) that "it is the common people who compose the human race; what is not the people is hardly worth taking into account. Man is the same in all ranks; that being so, the ranks which are most numerous deserve most respect," we may hear a fore-echo of Marx's passionate denunciation of laissez-faire capitalism and see an image of his angry compassion. So we may also suspect a movement toward the concept of the group or the class rather than the individual.

At this point, it must be remarked that many historians of philosophy have attempted to distinguish between the radical individualism of early works such as the *Discourse on the Origins of Inequality* and his other essays of the 1750s, and the theories advanced in *The Social Contract* (1762). An essential lack of consistency of argument and theory tends to obviate such a simple progression of ideas. Nevertheless, it is the later theories, when Rousseau has tethered his "noble savage" within the bonds of society, that require closest examination. His reaction was against the materialists, but theirs was, as he quite rightly identified, a theory of society governed by inevitable self-interest that did not descend from Locke but from Hobbes, the arch-authoritarian; and, though Hobbes is not of direct concern at the moment, it is essential to regard Rousseau's reaction as against theories which envisaged unfree *societies* rather than unfree individuals. Rousseau was impelled to posit a theory or model of a genuinely free *society*, and it is in that undertaking that his originality and influence lie. The materialists had all but assured, by their unquestioning optimism regarding science and the application of reason to society's malformations, that any reaction against their absolutism of thought would take its form as a social theory, rejecting reason but more critically rejecting all conceptions of the 'good' as inextricably bound up with the concept of the autonomous moral agent, the individual. In Rousseau, assertion combats the negations of the materialists. If their ideals are opposed, then the undercurrent of their thinking must also be damned. Liberal values, the preserve of *every* individual and the basis of theories of society, may be imitated or recast by Rousseau, but they become applicable to the group, to society. The appropriation of those liberal values as the exclusive property of the bourgeoisie, as their manifesto, by the materialists resulted in the development, in Rousseau's writings, of other values, values more universal and applicable to the whole of society, to every individual, but only as *member* of society.

Rousseau's works mark one of the most prominent watersheds in the history of the theory of natural law and natural rights, also one of the most significant watersheds of what may be termed the history of the individual in social and political thought. It therefore must be clearly understood that Rousseau's radicalism was a reaction, though not 'reactionary', and that his principal theories originated in a rejection of the materialism of the Enlightenment and the clothing that that materialism had given to Locke's values. Kant attempted, at a huge intellectual effort and with greatness of mind, to snatch both reason and liberal values from the flames, but his effort was too late and largely in vain. The history of political and social theory was already on the long road of collectivism.

Rousseau's debt to Plato and the tradition of Plato is as important as the similar debts of Hegel and Marx. Plato helped him rescue a theory of the moral worth of the *group* and enabled him to envisage society as the chief agent of morality and moral action. Society becomes, in Rousseau, the originator of men's ideas about themselves and of their behavior. The "noble savage" cannot be truly free or truly human until he is incorporated in the larger organic unit of society. Men are drawn together into a society or group innately and instinctively. Nothing else but their essential need for society is either innate or fundamental about human nature. Everything else is the *product of society.* As he remarks: ". . . we begin properly to become men only after we have become citizens."

What results, in *The Social Contract,* is the rejection of what might be termed civilized egoism, such as the materialists presented, with their utilitarianism or "greatest happiness" principle, in favor of Rousseau's vision of the *just* society where, as has been remarked, men "will be forced to be free." The principal idea of that work is Rousseau's theory of the "general will," the concept that a society or community has a corporate personality and that the expression of that corporate persona is the general will. Society is, of course, assumed to be *organic*, and the moral standards of the general will have a validity for all members of society *as a whole*. "The body politic, therefore, is also a moral being possessed of a will; and this general will . . . is the source of the laws, [and] constitutes for all the members of the state, in their relations to one another and to it, the rule of what is just or unjust." Governments are obligated to provide welfare, to remove gross inequality, supply liberty under the law, and also create a system of education which will educate children to become "accustomed to regard their individuality only in its relation to the body of the state." The opening paradox of the work is, of course, famous: "By what inconceivable art has a means been found of making men free by making them subject?" Not, we might observe, through liberal values.

Rousseau's use of paradox is by no means entirely unlike the dialectical approach of Hegel and his most famous student. More than either, there is the essential collectivist primacy of the group or society over the individual and the resolution of the problems of identity and moral activity in the *direction* of society itself. There is a clarity of declension from Rousseau via the Positivists to Durkheim, but the affinities with Hegel and Marx are only a little less marked. Freedom is perhaps for the first time since Hobbes defined solely and utterly in terms of what is *allowed* by the whole, the group. Rousseau remarks that: "If the state is a moral person whose life is in the union of its members . . . it must have a universal and compelling force, in order to move and dispose each part as may be most advantageous to the whole." Natural law and the rights of autonomous *individuals* have disappeared from the spectrum, as if illusory.

Rousseau, however, felt the tug of individual and inalienable rights throughout *The Social Contract*, hence the paradoxical and contradictory nature of much of his theorizing. He seems driven to oppose everything vaunted by the materialists, including individual rights and liberties so pertinent to French society in the 1760s, yet understands not only the attraction of natural law theory but feels its 'rightness', senses it as an aspect of justice and the 'good'. But that good had been made synonymous by the materialists with the good of a particular group within society rather than with society as a whole; thus the weight of his angry theories and his profound compassion for the unpropertied and unconsidered that suppressed his lingering, affectionate instinct toward what are distinguished as the values of individualism. So, finally, he can conclude that ". . . whoever refuses to obey the general will shall be compelled to do so by the whole body. This means nothing less than that he will be forced to be free."

In conclusion, we may observe simply that values formerly associated in philosophy with the primacy of the individual have now become the property of the whole, of society or even the state. Natural law theory, with its equality of emphasis upon the importance of individuality and the rights attaching thereto, and upon the universality of all men, effectively comes to the end of its journey from the Stoics to the eighteenth century. Just as Locke was influential upon all European thought at the beginning of the century, by its close the influence of Rousseau and Hegel is far greater than that of Kant. The autonomy of the individual as moral agent cannot be recovered even by his efforts. The torch has passed to collective theories of human nature and human liberties, to a newer and social theory of identity. Materialism had particularized as the possession of a group or class the values inextricably bound up with the whole history of natural law theory and, in rejecting such appropriation, Rousseau invested the "general will," the organism of society as a whole, with moral purpose and the capacity to morally instruct and determine which had previously been the function and preserve of the individual moral reason and was for a final time to be reemphasized in Kant.

It is little less than a revolution in social and psychological thought, and it is of the greatest significance for that more practical revolution that began in 1789.

II

To understand the nature and profundity of the change in philosophical conceptions of the self and identity, the decline or dismissal of natural law theory, it is necessary to consider not only the ideas of the French materialists but also those of perhaps the most influential British philosopher, certainly of the eighteenth century, David Hume. From him as well as from them derives the assimilation of natural law into what we have already learned to call liberal values—together with the appropriation of natural law and reason by an elite, even a philosophical, discipline. The universality of reason becomes the notion of scientific reason or the opposition of rational skepticism to faith and superstition. Reason becomes divorced from theism and identity becomes as much a matter of tradition and what Hume denoted as "custom" as it does of reason. Reason itself becomes—albeit of the greatest significance—only one element of human identity. In this process of qualification, natural law theory becomes utilitarianism by the end of the century, and human identity is conceived of as primarily social—derived from society, responsible to society, belonging and dependent rather than consenting and individual. At best, the liberal values derived from natural law theory become the insistence of a particular group or kind of government, while at worst they become the exclusive property of government or class—or, finally, denied and rejected precisely because they have become such a 'property'. All these changes occur between 1690 and 1789.

It is the rational materialists who divorce reason from any and all theistic conceptions of the universe. Revealed religion is merely a bundling together of the darkest superstitions. Science uncovers universal laws of motion and matter, the hitherto secret rules which operate upon and behind reality. Science explains to men what they are and what forces control them. Religion keeps them in ignorance. This enveloping skepticism is the fundamental characteristic of materialist thought, but materialist thought itself, as we have seen, becomes the 'property' of a particular class or group in eighteenth-century France, the bourgeoisie. The values ascribed to natural law theory become the property, likewise, of rational skepticism, a proposal for political unrest, agitation, and change. If at times in history the province only of lawyers and clerics, natural law now becomes the protestation of the ignored and clamorous intelligentsia of the bourgeoisie. Rights and liberties become, for the first time, maxims of political change rather than precepts of law or concepts in ethics and epistemology. In such an appropriation of the 'good' by a particular group is implicit the inference that those outside the favored group, class, or attitude of mind, are of less significance, of inferior importance. There is no longer an automatic and axiomatic assumption of universal equality. There are degrees of personhood and differences of identity.

Other assumptions of a theistic or essentialist nature appear to occupy the vacuum left by the denigration and dismissal of faith and of the universality of reason and, at least partly because of the previous appropriation of natural rights as a political platform, such essentialisms derive from conceptions of social rather than individual man; or, theories regarding history, the state, or the "general will" appear as the justification of natural rights. New and stranger gods are elevated to the pantheon. It is a revolutionary change in the conception of human nature, which itself posits a revolution to fulfill the promise of such a change. Robespierre claimed that "our will is the general will" when describing the Jacobins. Reason and natural law have become exclusivities and, in that especial period of French history, the dictatorship of those who had most radically appropriated the universal concepts of natural law. The equality of variation and difference in human belief and activity, proscribed only by the necessity not to infringe the liberty and *identity* of others, becomes a prescriptive theory of identity and society which must be imposed from above by the dictatorship of those who recognize the 'good', who possess the correct notion of human identity and wish to ensure its exemplification by all members of the social organism. Unregenerate man makes an unwelcome reappearance on the philosophical stage, a creature of appetite and desire, of surpassing and dominant ego, *incapable* of reason. Such a creature must be constrained not by reason but by those of us possessing reason.

There is a return to the *polis*, to the idea of those who *belong by right* (i.e., by the qualities that distinguish them from others, make them extraordinary) and more than an echo of Platonic theories of the state. Others, outside the *polis* by virtue of their unregenerate or ignorant natures, must be reeducated, changed into model citizens, otherwise ... The church had never ascribed that kind of 'outlaw' status to any human being—between the stirrup and the ground there was time for repentance, for the seeking of grace and the hope of salvation. Now, however, the possibility of real and utter unregeneracy had arisen. Reason, and therefore natural law and natural rights, is distinct, meagerly distributed in human nature and society, powerless, radical. It *knows* the 'good' and seeks to establish it—by force, if necessary.

Science was, of course, at the same time enforcing a prescriptive view of human nature, at least by analogy. The universal laws and systems and types, the organic nature of life and its government by simple, fundamental principles all produced a pressure toward essentialism in the laws governing human nature and human society. Such 'typing' of human nature posits the necessity of change, of conscripting and conditioning human nature to exemplify those ideal laws.

History, too, and the study of history, becomes scientific, or at least imbued with the progressive scientific spirit. History was no longer cyclical but evolutionary. Plato, Aristotle, the medieval church all conceived of the wheel-like progress of history, the return to the same point, the rhythm of rise and fall and new beginning of men, societies, civilizations. Science was, on the other hand, evolving, growing, adding to men's knowledge of themselves and their world. Among the many outmoded beliefs the broom of science swept away was the conception of history current until the seventeenth century. History, in the eighteenth century and culminating in Hegel's theories, demonstrated, like science, human progress, a movement forward, not the cycle of repetitions that men had assumed until then. In Positivism at the end of the eighteenth century and early in the nineteenth, science had become the sole means of progress in social and spiritual terms. It must be stressed that even without the excesses of Positivism the study of history contributed to the fundamental change in theories of human identity, even if only by uncovering more and more of man's social past and conceiving of the vaster, collective movements and changes of history as those which most significantly exemplified human nature and the nature of society. The ahistorical concept of consent as the original basis of social organization cannot be supported historically and, taken literally, is refuted, and *society* assumes a primacy over all notions of the *individual.* History emphasizes, in its evolutionary as much as in its cyclical form, the continuity of basic human nature. The emphasis, therefore, becomes more firmly and irrevocably placed upon the social and historical influences upon that basic nature, to the extent that, in the theories of Hume, we arrive at the predominance of social factors and influences in any analysis or understanding of human nature and, especially, human values. Values become historical and social, and basic human nature is most clearly exemplified in primitive societies—*natural man* replaces the idea of *man in a state of nature,* as in Locke's theory. Social man takes precedence over individual man. Natural man, outside society, or without society to restrain and educate him, is an irrational creature motivated by selfish passions.

Fundamentally, what occurs in the empirical and materialist thought of the eighteenth century is that the divorce between human nature and causality was obscured, healed as if it were something necessary but broken. Kant's great effort to put man above causality came too late. The popularization of science as a paradigm of rational human inquiry, the evolutionary, progressive conception of history, together with the gulf opened between theism and reason, conspired to subject man to laws similar to those of science; man became governed by society and, more significantly, by history. Natural law and the "moral Reason" became subject to the iron law of cause and effect, and, at the end of the century, there remains no influential conception of man as other than matter and thereby subordinated to the scientific laws governing all matter. Cyclical history never posed a threat to individuality such as progressive history provided, since in the thought of the Stoics, the Roman legal theorists, and the Church, the rational individual was not only given a unique soul or significance but was granted the freedom of a detachment from history, from material 'life'. The capacity to negate causality or to overcome it continued to be propounded. During the eighteenth century, man became subject to history.

III

The influence of David Hume upon the course of empirical philosophy in England and the rest of Europe was profound and lasting. The most significant effect of his ideas of human nature was to invalidate the theory of the primacy of reason in human response, decision, and activity. In so doing, he is diametrically opposed to his only rival to philosophical preeminence in the century, Kant. Hume, however, was far more influential upon the subsequent history of those values embedded in natural law theory. In summary, Hume's conception of human nature, so reasonable and empirically 'realistic' as it seems, amounts to the assertion that reason is but one capacity of human nature, and then not the governing faculty. Men are as likely to act upon their feelings and desires as upon reason—though, importantly, his human being is no Hobbesian man, since human nature is as often prompted by goodwill and benevolence as by egoism and selfishness. However, the values inherent in natural law theory are

derived from such benevolent and sympathetic feelings and responses, and are derived from human nature as it is rather than
the province of the truly rational human being. Society is itself
founded upon a clear understanding of human nature, rather than
upon abstract principles.

Hume posited the influence of tradition and what he called
custom on human nature and thus on the form of human society
that evolved through history. He was skeptical of the universal
principle of causality, but nevertheless supposed that human nature seeks to observe or even construct causality as a basis for
action. What we can truly know, and therefore use to guide our
decisions and actions, is minimal; nevertheless, convention and
custom instruct us to expect repetition (i.e., because an effect has
occurred numerous times before from a particular cause, it will
occur again). Causality or *necessity* is something we associate with
the phenomenal world rather than an accurate description of its
underlying reality. We may observe that in Hume, empiricism
becomes entirely secular, however careful he was to avoid direct
charges of atheism, and that therefore reason is divorced from any
theistic conception of reality. Human nature is examined in what
must be described as psychological terms, and the outcome is a
limitation of human rational capacity.

Hume upheld the values explicit in the Glorious Revolution of
1688 and the 'tradition' of liberal (comparatively speaking) government and the constitutional circumstances then established.
What is implicit in his work, however, is the claim that such
values are derived from human nature as it is and at its best and
that therefore their only validity is that they are human and that
they 'work' and have successfully existed for a long time, as custom and tradition. Such liberal values as society demonstrates are
valuable because of the benefits they bestow on man in society;
the origins of English utilitarianism are here. That Hume might
have scorned the views of nineteenth-century utilitarian liberals
does not mitigate the effects of his annihilation of natural law
theory and the primacy of the "moral Reason."

Hume's effort was to make human nature, empirically observed and dissected, central to any philosophical inquiry. His objective was as far-reaching as Descartes's attempt at the utter revision of philosophic practice—and he succeeded. He assumed, always, that human nature was everywhere and in every age similarly constructed and motivated, and he allowed the significance of tradition and habit far greater importance than any philosopher before him. As such, he is the archetypal empiricist, recording and expounding what he observes to be 'true' of human nature and human society. In so doing, he revolutionized even empiricism. Hume was skeptical, though not cynical or pessimistic. A compromise with the ideal which was satisfactory for most of the purposes and activities of human life was perfectly possible and was demonstrated by the United Kingdom of his day. It was his very reasonableness that was so persuasive and influential, but its effects are to remove from empirical political philosophy any concept of consent or of contract, individually recognized. Locke's theory of political society based upon consent is dismissed; also individuality and its responsibility and paradigm as moral agent also disappear. Hume cleared the ground, more effectively than Locke ever claimed to have done, of natural theology and rationalist deductive moral systems—of metaphysics. He reversed the philosophical forces opposed to French materialism. Enlightened self-interest becomes the moral force of human nature; a degree of benevolent sympathy operating in society is the principle of human interaction. Hume removed 'ideals' from the language of 'values'. His empirical realism is one in which human nature is thoroughly socialized, where the causality of tradition and/or custom governs behavior and held values. The perception of rights and liberties accommodates itself to personal benefit, so much the opposite of Locke's granting of equivalence to other individuals and to Kant's stern concept of the duty that governs moral perception. Any kind of essentialism is foreign to Hume's thought, so that the essential human potentiality of moral reason is dismissed and, with it, natural law theory and any idea of inalienable rights. What follows, in the history of political and social ideas, is the appearance of a new essentialism in idealist philosophy—or, contemporary with Hume, the social essence of the general will and the social contract in Rousseau. Social man makes his appearance, and the human essence is to be discovered therein. For Hegel and Marx, the struggle against individualistic conceptions of human nature has already been won by Hume's devastating reasonableness. For the English utilitarians, too, the battlefield has already been claimed.

In Hume's ideas, natural rights become the expression of human nature, losing their universal validity, becoming rather than the province of the individual moral reason the concern of society, tradition, and history. This is unsettling—and the proverbial breath of fresh air—just so long as Hume's skeptical but basically optimistic view of human nature holds good and sway. But, Hobbesian man, that creature of unrestrained ego, waits in the wings, ready to become the measure of human nature, the maxim by which government must assess and regard the individual. Hobbesian man, the individual of Marx and Hegel, as a view of human nature allows, even invites, the assumption of government or even of society as the repository of values, sweeping individuality aside. After Hume a different psychology of human nature becomes the maxim of ethical and political philosophy, and it is a view that is far less optimistic than was Hume's skeptical analysis. The principle of *benefit* from human activity and interaction is established, then distorted into a Hobbesian, pessimistic analysis of human motivation. Both Kant and Locke recognized that unrestrained ego and selfishness lay beneath the rational activity of man, while Hume regarded such things as aspects of a human nature that would probably choose to act benevolently rather than viciously. Without optimism, and without the primacy of the moral reason, a pessimistic view of human nature can look only to prescriptive versions of man in society, to means of regulating the unrestrained ego of the individual. The prescriptive burden is removed from the individual and given to society or 'government'; that is the essence of Hume's legacy. The only radical revision of Hume that is required is, in fact, the assumption that tradition and custom are not benevolent but malicious.

Marx, therefore, was able to turn the full savagery of his con-tempt upon a concept of individualism undignified by the con-cept of moral agency—upon what became, after Hume, the utili-tarian liberalism appropriated by the bourgeoisie in France and the capitalist middle class in England—upon laissez-faire eco-nomics and economic individualism which would have been anathema equally to Locke and Hume.

We may view the beginnings of that return to the necessity of essence, of the spiritual dimension assumed to be inherent in social man, in the theories of Rousseau, befriended by Hume, who became the object of Rousseau's suspicious ingratitude. Rous-seau's reaction against the scientism and rationality of the En-lightenment prefigures so much in nineteenth-century thought after Hegel, and its point of origin may be traced to a similarity of view regarding human nature as is to be found in Hume. There is an essential optimism in Rousseau's regard for sentiment and that base of feeling that derives from the small or family group—cooperation, affection, sympathy, et cetera. Rousseau opposed such ordinary sentiments to reason as promulgated by the *philo-sophes*, just as Hume had opposed his view of human nature to natural theology, innate rights and liberties, and the primacy of reason. Rationality, for Rousseau, was a minor, even a vicious, characteristic of human nature. But Rousseau's ideal of sentimen-tal man is, by definition, a social being; otherwise, how would such idealized sentiments arise or be given expression? The idea of the 'common man' has also appeared, not in a political sense as proletarian or peasant but simply in the encapsulation of common or usual sentiments and feelings as best or 'good'. The theory of the general will as a political principle derives from this back-ground of assumptions about human nature. Rousseau's effort to recapture liberal values from the intelligentsia reinvested empiri-cal or materialist man with the spirit of the general will. The consent or compact that was the basis of society became the government of the general will.

The theories of both philosophers, Hume and Rousseau, are self-evidently influential, not only upon later political and social thinkers but upon their times. They may be seen, not without distortion but with a degree of truth, as providing the paradigm of human nature upon which nineteenth-century political theory was based; or they may be regarded as the last true descendants of Locke before the amelioration of natural law theory into *mere* liberal values becomes so distinct from Locke as to become hardly recognizable. They do represent the last European influence of English or French thought, in political terms, before 1793, after which French influence was wholly negative and the influence of the English utilitarians hardly less so. With the French Revolution, *Sturm und Drang,* and principally Hegel, the true home of influential political theory moves east to Germany.

THE WHOLLY
(RATIONAL) GHOST:
ROMANTICS, IDEALISTS—
AND HEGEL

THE REVOLUTION OF 1789 in France was responsible for producing, outside France and in the history of the most influential political and social theories, an almost entirely negative influence, just as it also provided, as the revolt of the American colonies did not, a model for future revolutions, especially that of 1917. Lenin learned as much from the period 1789–1796 as he did from the economic theories of Marx, though it must be added that even here Marx had already represented the revolution in France as a paradigm of such occurrences, despite its bourgeois origins. However, though the significance of the Revolution has been remarkably overexplored on the occasion of its bicentenary, it is possible to remark that many of the millions of words written to celebrate the anniversary were of muted tone, not widely different from the reactions of contemporaries outside France, especially among philosophers and theorists. Thinkers were busy demolishing the myth of *Liberté, Égalité, Fraternité* and the struggle for freedom and justice even before that myth had acquired its rich patina of age.

What, in essence, near-contemporary reaction and much current speculation perceived, with the hindsight of the Bolshevik Revolution to assist it, was not what we might term the historical necessity of the uprising of the 'mass' against their exploiters, the causality that linked social and political conditions in the France of the eighteenth century to the outburst in revolt and violence against such conditions; rather, they forged the causality of Revolution and Terror, something Lenin determined would be repeated, fulfilling cause and effect. Instead of the circumstances before 1789 giving rise to the events of that year, 1789 became the *cause* of the events of the following years, especially of the Jacobin-inspired Terror, in which the Revolution, in the infamous phrase, "devoured its own children" rather than the comparatively small number of *aristos* who were guillotined. This lesson in causality was not lost upon the Bolshevik leadership and appears to have been recalled to mind by the Chinese leaders much more recently, if events in Tiananmen Square are anything to go by.

In England particularly—rather than in France, where the traditions of Positivism show a remarkable continuity of development on either side of the Terror—we see what it is sensible to call a conservative reaction only in the case of the political theorist Edmund Burke, though one may assume, to a degree, that he was as much a follower of Hume as he was a horrified observer of the queues for the guillotine. In Germany, the reaction of historians, of thinkers labeled Romantics, and chiefly of Hegel were too complex and too influential to merit any such easy label, though their principal reaction was, as with Burke, one of horror at the bloodletting, the social and political chaos, and at the determined, ruthless dictatorship of the Committee of Public Safety, that dictatorship of the bourgeoisie. A new, radical, and *effective* autocracy seized and held power, and its governmental method was that of suspending all civil and individual rights and silencing all opponents by the terrible expedient of removing their heads. It was theories of *government* of any and every kind that suffered during the Revolution's continuation and unfolding. Events before 1789 became ignored. The meaning and significance of the Revolution was not to be found in dry, academic social history or abstruse theories of government, rather in the tabloid, technicolor atrocities of a small group of madmen creating, and then feeding from, an atmosphere of national fear, suspicion, and self-preservation (Hobbes's "war of all against all").

Reflection on the years 1796 to 1815 can as easily be summarized by Beethoven's response to Napoleon's acceptance of an imperial crown by renaming his third symphony as by any other single instance. Napoleon both fascinated and repelled even those whose countries he conquered or with whom he was at war. But one may well suspect that his fascination as a "great man" was more significant than his legal and governmental reforms—the way he 'ran' his empire. Napoleon, succeeding the fall of Robespierre and the period of the Terror, represented another, radical, easily mythologized autocracy, one which made the chaotic home of the Revolution the greatest power in Europe. In that lies his significance, whether evident or implicit. The modern, efficient, aggressive national state was symbolized by a single individual for perhaps the first time since the era of the Sun King. The impact of such imagery upon the diffuse principalities and electorates of Germany, the nation without a state, is all too easily imagined. The intellectual influence of the Revolution might, without undue distortion, be said to reside not in its ideals of democracy or the "general will" of Rousseau—in freedom and justice—but in its hypnotic balance of tension between anarchy, dictatorship by terror, and effective central authority. In that sense, and that sense only, the Revolution was not a 'new' event in history, rather a further performance of past political ideologies—a hurried, garish replaying of some of history's vast footage, offering the same, inevitable choice between chaos and order, between democracy and authority. Given the recent vivacity of the Terror, together with the demonstrable efficiency and power of the autocratic nation-state, it can be no surprise to find in Hegel and his contemporaries a reaction against democratic government and natural law theory, or 'liberal' values; a reaction the extent of which is to regard the entire course of human history as culminating in the authoritarian national state, though this is but one influence in a complex transmission of information from a preceding generation to what became known as the idealist philosophers, of whom Hegel was preeminent.

Materialist thought did not, either systematically or succinctly, express any radical reorganization of society in the sense of a remodeling. Voltaire and others were prepared to allow some kind of monarchical authoritarianism, with the eradication of clerical influence and the principal abuses of the aristocracy curtailed and their privileges abolished. For them, the institution of liberal, rational, self-evident values was possible without a radical change in the way society was governed. Enlightened self-interest, if given scope, would alight birdlike on those same values and implement them. Any rational awareness of a concept such as liberty perceives that such freedom is in the interest of the self, and therefore it becomes a political principle; in benefiting the self, it benefits all other selves. Limited government is better than autocracy, naturally—but limitation of the present system will be sufficient to enshrine liberal values in government and the law.

However, implicit in the optimism of the materialists and their absolute faith in reason and science is the necessity of radical change. France remained what we must term feudal in structure and government and in any sense of justice or individual liberty; its inertial resistance to change was massive, centuries-hardened, and strengthened by tradition and myth. However placid or even indifferent the *philosophes* might have been toward questions of political program and the detail of social and political change, their outlook and basic assumptions imply reconstruction, a new model for society. There was no basis of common law, of parliamentary tradition and representation, no tradition of limited monarchy; the elements that would allow any kind of continuity or provide the bases of gradual, political change simply did not exist. Therefore, change would be, of necessity, revolutionary, a complete remodeling of political society, to effect the kind of constitutional guarantees sought by the forces of Parliament in the 1640s in England. The Revolution must ensure the imposition of those values upon a recalcitrant social reality by radical, complete change.

What we have arrived at here is the difference between ideas of freedom, liberty, rights, and justice and the recognition of them. Natural law theory, with its emphasis upon the equivalence of individual human natures, has become materialist theory, where matter is the sole component of the universe, and which has accomplished the appropriation of the values inherent in natural law theory by a single class in society, the intelligentsia. There is little or no admission of equivalence of individuality or of the capacity of universal reason to recognize and support such values. Therefore, the class possessing the belief in such values must come to power in order to impose them on society—to remake society as necessary. Within the shell of Enlightenment optimism there is a tiny, hungry worm of pessimism regarding 'ordinary' human nature. There is an elitism, the sense of distinction between those who apprehend via reason liberal values and the progress of science and who thus reject contemporary French society and those who do not. The Terror may be regarded as a *trahison des clercs* more profound than any other in French history; it was a terror inspired by lawyers, writers, schoolmasters. The Jacobins were ideologues rather than reformers, dealing ideologically in human types and theoretical generalities. The ubiquitous term *citoyen* exemplifies this tendency. Rousseau's primacy of the citizen over the individual achieves its apotheosis in Jacobin regimentation of society through terror, the imposition of a 'rule' of human nature and behavior: the imposition, in effect, of everything—utter autocracy. In reacting against the classifications into orders and estates characteristic of feudalism, the Jacobins were incapable of accepting and upholding the concept of the individual.

It may be remarked that materialism worked like an acid on French society, causing it to dissolve and crumble and to become the object of disillusionment and anger, however impotent. But an ideologue was required to provide a basis of opposition, an alternative *social theology*. Rousseau supplied that lack. The heady prophetic strain in his emotional, disorganized theorizing was intoxicating to those who would assume the leadership of the reorganization of society. Rousseau's views of civilized egoism, of the exploitative nature of French society, his belief in "common sentiments" and the essential brotherhood of man—as well as in the corporate personality of society itself—gave point and *content* to the frustrations and anger of the critics of French society. "The social order is a sacred right which is the basis of all other rights," Rousseau claimed in Book One of *The Social Contract*. Whatever was actually meant by the statement, it cannot conceivably be regarded as a promulgation of individual liberties or of the concept of the autonomous individual. Any implication of equality is not the equality of equivalent moral reasons interacting in the context of society or of Kant's "kingdom of ends."

Rousseau also rejected representative government. Government was to be simply an agent of the general will, the people as a corporate body. It is not too far a step, and it is more than implicit in Rousseau, to the idea of government by a minority dedicated to the expression of the general will, Robespierre's "despotism of liberty against tyranny" (1794). Rousseau would have been appalled by the actuality of the Jacobin Terror, though he would probably have agreed beforehand that they were 'just the men for the job' as regards government by the general will.

We might remark, in conclusion, that the fundamental optimism with which the Enlightenment regarded the progress of science and which produced Positivism and the beginnings of our science of society produced in the years following 1789 a 'scientific' attitude to the reshaping of society—detached, experimental, certain. The materialists never, unlike Locke and Kant, rejected the application of scientific laws and models to human nature and behavior; thus could they contemplate the reconstruction of society in a different image, whatever the individual dissent and cost.

Though the influence of ideas upon political upheavals may be exaggerated with some ease, especially with the hindsight of 1917 and its theoretical explanation by participants and succeeding apologists, the ideas and theories that derive from the French Revolution and its subsequent course are of direct concern. Dictatorial conceptions of freedom and government, the rational opposition to *all* existing social and political institutions, and the radical change of emphasis regarding the collectivity and its absorption into the concept of the *state* are all preconditions of the Revolution, just as they are conclusions drawn regarding the revolutionary period and its successor, the empire. Ideologically, Rousseau provides an equivalent to the political significance of Napoleon in that basically he restated in a novel and immensely attractive guise a perennial agreement. As Napoleon renewed in radical costume the image of central authority and the national state, order succeeding chaos, so Rousseau's ideas embody the principle of the sovereignty of a central authority, a collective order, a vision of a social order expressed by the collective, ensured and imposed by a group of true believers.

What the Revolution achieved, outside France and in the history of political ideas, was a revivification of the concept of the nation-state, controlled by an authoritarian central power or legislature, together with the assumption of the primacy of the social, rather than the individual, identity of human beings. Most strangely and paradoxically, it proselytized the doctrines of authoritarian government and *national* identity rather than those of democracy and the liberty of the individual.

II

Sturm und Drang may be regarded as either the initial manifestation of German Romanticism or primarily as the literary and poetic aspect of that Romanticism which came to embrace historical theory and philosophical inquiry in Germany and the rest of Europe at the end of the eighteenth and the beginning of the

nineteenth centuries. It is contemporary in appearance with
Kant's three great *Critiques* but is, because of its opposition to
or attempts at 'completion' or supplementation of those *Critiques*, of greater significance for the course of nineteenth-century
social, political, and ethical theory. This is despite the relatively
minor significance of the major figures of philosophical Romanticism in Germany—Fichte, Schelling, Herder, Schlegel, et cetera—beside the importance of Kant in the history of ideas. For
our purposes, it is more necessary to understand the German
Romantic movement and the rise of Idealism as the predominant
strand in German philosophy, itself the metaphysical or abstract
aspect of Romanticism, than to comprehend much of the *detail*
of Hegel's thought. It was the influence of *Sturm und Drang* and
Romanticism upon Hegel that make him significant as a conduit
of metaphysical inquiry to Marx, the materialist metaphysician.

Kant, to the Romantic generation, startlingly and freshly influenced by Spinoza's ideas as they were, had failed to recapture
metaphysics, that "queen of the sciences," as a truly valid—
indeed, as the most valid—branch of philosophy. They judged his
work as incomplete and as manifesting the Cartesian dualism in
another form by his distinction of the *noumenal* and *phenomenal*
realities of the world, the former of which was "unknowable," a
position that no 'true' metaphysician could accept. In his *Critique
of Judgment*, which deals with aesthetic theory in the main, Kant
himself attempts some healing of the chasm between the noumenal and phenomenal. Spinoza's "single Substance," universal as
it was conceived, seemed to offer a genuinely metaphysical single
principle or whole and unified explanation of reality. There was
utter certitude in such a concept as well as a meaningful and
satisfactory completion, rather than refutation, of Kant's divisible
reality. To the task of rendering Kant's ideas as true metaphysics
and describing a fully *knowable* world, the Romantics and the
Idealists, for the terms are, to a large extent, interchangeable once
we consider the philosophers who belonged to the Romantic
movement, dedicated themselves.

Though much of this seems, at first sight, distant from Marx and even from Hegel's *Philosophy of Right,* any preliminary study is required to comprehend, and demonstrate, the *metaphysical imperative* of the Idealists and their affinity with the Romantic movement, especially as regards Hegel, which imperative is transmitted to Marx and to the social and historical theorists both within and outside Germany in the nineteenth century. Thus, in dealing with his social, economic, and political ideas, and with those of Hegel, his great predecessor and mentor, we must be clear that we are dealing not with a science, nor with empiricism or ethics, not even with political theory, but with a burgeoning and sustained desire to render reality in satisfactorily metaphysical concepts, to describe all of reality in a constrained, peculiar, urgent, and almost hallucinogenic metaphysic that informed theories of history, art, literature, and politics. To understand the collectivist ideologies that have dominated our century, at least until its final decade, one needs to understand the *ideological defeat* of seventeenth- and eighteenth-century individualist theories, not merely their historical failure or superannuation. In so doing, it is necessary to remark the triumph of metaphysical theories of nations, peoples, classes, history itself, over theories of political society composed of equivalent individuals.

It is important at the outset, therefore, to understand the idealization of the Greek city-state as an expression of what was perceived by the Romantics to be the Athenian–Hellenic metaphysic or *harmony* (see below). Thus, the ordered and embracing ethos of the Greek *polis* or community of citizens becomes something to be striven for, to be recaptured. In recovering this ideal of the city-state, the Romantics and Idealists, and the Arcadian aspect of Marx's theories, are seeking to raise political and ethical theory to the status of metaphysics, to *incorporate* these subordinate branches of speculation in a single philosophic theory. Political theory becomes merely an aspect of a controlling and unified metaphysic, not a means of allowing men to live harmoniously within a system of laws whatever their opinions, notions, beliefs, worldview, or even essence may be. The Romantics are recovering Plato's theory of Forms in attempting to complete Kant's ideas.

Political theory, therefore, becomes in its most influential strain in the nineteenth and twentieth centuries, a derivation of, or extrapolation from, a metaphysical basis, divorced from its empirical past. Similarly, we are dealing with a problem of identification, which does *not* presuppose the resolution of identity in the individual person, as Kant pursued in allowing the dignity of "ends-in-themselves" to every human being. In any empirical, political, or even ethical discussion of human personhood or identity, there is no metaphysical absolute, no harmonization of the human being with a single, universal principle of reality; rather, the assumption is that every human being is *unique,* a self, rather than solely an aspect of the universal.

The influence of Spinoza's idea of substance, as opposed to Leibniz's innumerable monads, has been noted, but the effect of the consequences of the Revolution (its Terror and Empire) is also of the greatest significance upon the Romantics. In response to the aftermath of 1789, the rejection of rationalism, of the capacities of individual human reason, seemed the only course open to men of intellect—artists, writers, or philosophers. Human reason had been demonstrably shown to have failed the greatest challenge, that of remaking political society in the image of Reason. For Kant, the solution was to divorce the individual moral reason from the material or phenomenal world, to define the *a priori* capacity of reason and reflection. Kant understood the distinction between rationalism and its manifestation in eighteenth-century France as materialism. The Romantics did not. They identified the rational (moral) capacity itself, together with the distinction between the *noumenon*—rational man as Kant allowed him to be—and the phenomenal world as an ultimately tragic error of philosophy. Materialism had denied any incorporeal capacity to human thought and rationality, while Kant had failed to identify the universal principle that metaphysics, perforce, must assume underlies reality.

Both strands of eighteenth-century thought were in error, to the extent that dualism of any kind was abandoned, just as a *materialist* unity of substance was rejected as the parent of the

Terror and the cause of reason's alienation from the other human capacities of feeling and emotion on the one hand and of man's rational alienation from the rest of creation, or reality, on the other. Dualism becomes *harmony*, or at least the search for harmony. In *Sturm und Drang*, this is apparent in the promulgation of a love of nature and in full-fledged Romantic thought identification with the "spirit of Nature," and thence to the universal Spirit that is the metaphysical reality of the universe of the Idealists. In brief, scientific rationalism was turned out of doors in favor of Art, the Sublime, Beauty, Spirit—any Hellenic concept suggestive or explanatory of harmony between Man and Nature. Whatever theories were in circulation before the Revolution which displayed a tone of antirationalism became of exaggerated importance (e.g., Baumgarten's *Aesthetica* of 1740). Sensuous experience and *feeling*, as perhaps in Rousseau, replaced the 'coldness' of rational thought and inquiry as essential to human experience. Though this initial outburst of Rousseau-like emphasis soon became absorbed into the grander schemes of the Romantics and Idealists, its importance should not be underestimated. There is a sense in which Hegel and the other Idealists reacted emotionally as well as intellectually against the Kantian doctrine of *noumenon* and *phenomenon* and against the chill of the Cartesian dualism between thinking man and his alien universe of matter. Romanticism's emphasis upon feeling, emotion, response, spiritual harmony, was attractive in a subtler sense as an alternative to rationalism than as a merely intellectual opposition.

Spinoza's pantheistic lack of division between man and his world is eminently suited to the Romantic temperament and yearning, for the Romantic ontology is an attempt *not* to distinguish between subject and object, noumenon and phenomenon, appearance and reality. The basis of existence is the identification of man with all reality, without distinction between him and Nature. Briefly, the universe is entirely *spirit* rather than composed entirely of *matter*. Instead of Kant's deification of Reason, we are confronted in Romanticism with the deification of Nature, of which we are indivisibly an element. After the Terror, the reductio ad absurdum of reason divorced from feeling, of Man from Nature, the necessity of a spiritual interpretation of reality became paramount and most generally acceptable.

In both rationalism and Romanticism, the concept of *freedom* is essential (see below), personal moral freedom, a degree of autonomy that allows the fulfillment of the individual. Indeed, there might seem only a difference of means rather than ends. The problem arises, however, with the translation of these different bases of the concept of freedom from speculation to political society; Kant's "kingdom of ends" can become, after Romanticism, Hegel's idealization of the national state as the expression of the "world-spirit" or *Weltgeist* to the degree that individual identification with the social and political organism of the state *is* the only real freedom. It is this conception of political freedom that Hegel develops from the influence of Romanticism and which he handed to Marx.

Rationalism (let us say Kant) views freedom as expressed and upheld by the exercise of the individual reason, which is a moral agent. *A priori* deductions which guide human behavior morally can be made by the exercise of reason and give rise to the idea of the categorical imperative and the sanctity of other individuals. In Romanticism, the metaphysical status of feeling rather than reason is extolled. Pantheistic or agnostic, there is a spiritual reality in Nature *as* in Man, and the sense of elevation of the human being over the reality around him, whether by a Cartesian dualism or by the capacity of the moral reason, is decredited and denied. The burden and duty of moral activity concomitant with the possession of moral reason becomes the 'duty' to respond to the equivalent 'spirit' of others, and freedom becomes some version of unity with the universal. The translation of universal into *collective*, as freedom becomes a political concept based on Romantic ideas, is if not inevitable, then probable.

A further factor in the artistic theories of the Romantics in their search for a universal and paradigmatic notion of *harmony* has its influence upon the political theory of the early nineteenth century in Germany and elsewhere, and that is the idealization of Greek art, sculpture, and artistic theory as a model of the Sublime, as the perfect manifestation of the spirit of Art, unsurprising in view of the Romantic idealization of Hellenic culture and society of the classical period. There was a similar and inevitable idealization of Greek theories of political society and of Plato in particular, rather than of the Stoics and the Cynics. History becomes, in a sense, a perspective upon synthesis, a kind of Arcadianism as regards the classical Greek achievement in the arts and politics. A reincarnation of the Greek synthesis (in political terms, the city-state and the rule of the wise, et cetera) is promised in Hegel as being superior even to the model, particularly in Art. And the very mention of models should lead us to conclude, or at least to postulate, that whereas the model of rational inquiry was either mathematics or the empirical sciences, the model of philosophical inquiry at the beginning of the nineteenth century is based upon the harmony of Man with Nature. In political theory, the concept of the State supplants that of the model, Nature, as the object of harmony, man *with* the state rather than the harmony of men *within* something that might be termed the state.

The justification of such a transposition of terms lies in the assumption of 'image' or 'likeness', as with reason in Locke and Kant and the theologians being the more finite image of the Divine Reason. The individual is a reduction or image of the larger collective, the state. His harmony with the collective is therefore his identity and his freedom. Harmony with existence becomes harmony with social reality, especially in Hegel, who assumes a moral superiority in Prussian monarchical absolutism and the ordered state that resulted from it, and therefore there is this chilly, strange conservatism at the heart of radical Romantic theory, when transposed more or less intact to political society. Such a transposition requires the employment of the fullest sense of harmony and the universal spirit, too. Almost a century later, Durkheim was still able to talk, in all seriousness, of the "sacred" element in society itself. Such a view will take political and social theorists a great way down the road toward assumptions as to the significance of society and social conditioning on human psychology, even to the extent that concepts such as freedom and liberty arise *only* within a social framework (Rousseau) and are the *gift* of the collective (Hegel *et al.*).

In other words, the paradigm, model, or construct has been altered from science to the idea of Nature, particularly in its spiritual manifestation. Therefore, as in Rousseau's early work, unregenerate or unsophisticated man becomes an ideal—the man of feeling and sentiment, the man of instinct, as Marx and Engels both look back toward some quasi-Arcadian image of man, preeminently social but classless and free, with which man in the future will again identify in the recovery of his species-being. He becomes, this unspoiled human being, the *origin of the species*, the benchmark against which Rousseau and the Romantics were able to measure the corruption, delusion, or "alienation" of modern man, who must recover his harmony with existence. In Schelling (1775–1854), existence must aspire to the condition of Art, but, more importantly, any valid philosophical inquiry should aspire to such a condition. It is in Art that the mind becomes truly and fully aware of itself. Schelling was the most influential philosopher of the Romantic movement, and we should remark his definition of the purpose and nature of philosophical inquiry if only to fully realize how disparate such a concept is from Kant's attempt to reinvigorate a metaphysics founded upon the application of reason.

I have thus far, of course, talked of the German Romantic movement and that group of philosophers known as Idealists as if they espoused the same principles; to a large extent, such a conflation is justified, despite the archetypal Romantic figure, the heroic–tragic *individual.* The poets and dramatists of *Sturm und Drang* do, indeed, espouse the drama and the heroic nature of individualism, but their vision is grounded in the notion of individuality as deracination, as longing, expressed in the metaphor of the life search, the journey. The individual is seeking enlightenment, fulfillment, the Sublime. Above and beyond everything else, it is a self-dramatization, the idea of the artistic individual or the individual-as-artist; to have become labeled 'Byronic' is perhaps a disservice to George Gordon, Lord Byron, who died serving in a war of independence, but is apt in describing the way in which the Romantics themselves characterized, but never endorsed, individuality. Rather, Romanticism sought communion with the world, community, with truth that lay outside and beyond the individuality of the seeker, above all with the Spirit of Nature. This destination may have been termed the "Sublime" rather than the "Absolute" or "Spirit" of Hegel and the other Idealists, but it represents a parallel concept of the universal, the underlying, single reality. Idealism and the Romantic movement both envisage a select or 'super' individual who perceives, or, tragically, fails to perceive, a unity with existence, with the single spiritual reality that pervades and animates the universe. And both to that extent are engaged in an attempt to heal or circumvent the Cartesian dualism that, dramatically and completely, separates human beings from the nonsentient world of matter in which they exist.

Further, to understand Idealism it is not necessary to assume that Fichte, Schelling, Hegel, and others in any sense rejected the objective reality of the world in positing the notion that the world as we perceive it *is* the reality of the world. What is intended by this central tenet of Idealism, as opposed to the reality of the world extraneous to the self as held by other schools of philosophy, characterized as "dogmatism" by Fichte, is merely the supposition that the world out there is 'mindlike', is informed by the *same* animation or spirit as the world of the self. Idealism is directly opposed to any sense of the exclusivity of human reason or, in an older expression, human *soul* and to the *mere* materiality of the rest of the universe. *All* reality, including ourselves, is expressive of the same spirit or *Geist*, the same soul. Thus, it is the task of the individual (in Idealism the philosopher as against the Romantic artist) to recognize, to apprehend and reveal, the universal spirit or principle. The metaphor of the journey or search is one which informs much of Hegel's work, even at its most abstruse, but it is necessary to remember that in both Idealism and Romanticism the search is one for *fulfillment,* a journey of self-realization, the terminus of which is the harmony of the individual self with the world, the human world of others *and* the semi-sentient world described by both as Nature.

And, just as the world is mindlike, expressive of the animus of the human being, so the individual is worldlike, part of the unity of reality, an aspect or expression of the single, underlying principle that informs the universe. The end of search and journeying lies in an identity fully admitted and shared between men and the world that surrounds them. To become one with the world, which is us and of which we are an integral aspect, is fulfillment—is freedom. The epistemology that allows the Idealists to perceive the world in this fashion is also an ontology, a mode of being rather than simply knowing. Thus, in another sense, the Cartesian dualism is healed, for to the Idealists the *division* between men and their world was annulled by the simple proposition that there was a single, Spinozian reality of which all real or apparent things were aspects or expressions; though the underlying reality was not the "single Substance" of Spinoza—rather, for the Romantics, it was the concept of the Sublime, to be approached through, and only through, art, as the Greeks had most notably done, while for the Idealists, similarly Hellenophiles, it lay in the universal Spirit or Idea. Descartes's division was a delusion. The task of philosophy was not to change the world but our understanding of it.

The task of philosophy was, therefore, that of metaphysics, not of ethics, political theory, logic. It was, in the title of Hegel's first great work, to demonstrate the phenomenology of the universal spirit, to make the phenomenal and noumenal worlds one, indivisible. In thus concentrating the task of Idealism, there is a reduction in what one might term the necessity to account for, and to direct, the empirical *behavior* of human beings, as if the journey and the search become the only meaningful *activity* in the world. Kant and, of course, Locke must account for human behavior and consider the ethical sphere of human activity—Kant's "moral duty." Idealism admits no such requisite, but the onus upon Kant occurs precisely because the phenomenal world is distinct from the noumenal or 'really real' world. There is no ultimate harmony, no metaphysical 'joining' with the universal which has its own unstated but certain *moral* quality for Kant, except in his religious faith, which itself would have forced him to become a moral philosopher. Therefore, the phenomenal activity and manner of human life is of the greatest significance, just as, paralleling the argument in simplistically Christian terms, one may say that our phenomenal activity is the expression of our moral nature, but also the only means by which our spiritual destination is decided. There is nothing else knowable than the phenomenal, *ethical* sphere of human behavior and activity, which includes thought, feeling, motive. For the Idealists, the ethical and therefore political sphere of activity and theory is of small importance. It may either be ignored or discussed by means of an ideal paradigm, a political model of the universal—especially a historical, 'real' model.

In other words, what we have in Idealist political theory, if such a term can be used at all, is the necessity for a paradigm, as Art had become a paradigm rather than a fulfillment in the Idealist pantheon, akin to the old notion of Christendom, a spiritual community realized in phenomenal social and political terms. And the Idealists found their model in ancient Greece, itself a complete paradigm for the universality of Nature, Art, and humanity, at least in their eyes. It is a collective, with an ideal of citizenship—the Greek *polis;* political society is *not* a composition of individuals, it is an expression of the universal principle, the Spirit or Idea, a manifestation of harmony. Thus, political society itself becomes mindlike *as an entity* and not by virtue of its component parts. It is the task of the individual, by analogy with his spiritual search for harmony with the universal, to *identify with* the community, the political reality—in Hegel, the "rational State." It may be objected that *all* Western political theory looks back, in one way or another, to Plato, Aristotle, Athens—even Sparta in some extreme instances, perhaps—but the weight of concern is with the theory and the practice, *not* with the metaphysical or universal principle being 'realized' in ancient Greece.

The ideal of the Greek *polis* thus is revived to occupy what is little less than a vacuum at the heart of Idealist ethical and political thought, the need to discover an aspect of the universal harmony in politics, a smaller harmony within the greater. It was, too, the ideal of the greatest poet and dramatist of the Romantic movement, Schiller, in the sense that for him it represented the individual woven into the fabric of society, and therefore, of reality, in harmony with—because *of*—the political community. It was, of course, a rather misty view of the idea of the *polis*, of that deliberate circumscription of political life within the walls of the city-state, while outside barbaric and degenerate man still violently roamed. Political society was a closed community in that it accepted that *only within* such a community of citizens were men capable of political behavior, of civilization, perhaps. Further, there is little or no notion of any inalienable equality between human beings, merely an equality that exists solely in political terms, as members of the *polis*. Otherwise, men are distinctly unequal. Further still, men were only to be regarded as free in the presence of their peers, as members of the *polis*—with the inevitable corollary that those who did not belong were not free or to be regarded as such. Freedom lies—and this is the crucial lesson that the Idealists and their Romantic peers *did* learn above all others—in *identification with the community.*

There is thus in Idealism no place for a phenomenal theory of political society which allows, as is the case with Kant and Locke, not to mention the Stoics, the existence of a noumenal world of individual theory, motive, and intellectual apprehension which is not the concern of the political society until its laws and governance are challenged through a challenge to the individuality of others. A thousand, a million, ideas of the Absolute or the Spirit in a democratic, phenomenal political society do not appeal to the Idealists—such merely perpetuate Kant's division of reality.

Much, or even all, of this coalesces in the Romantic–Idealist notion of "true Freedom," which is itself essential to any political theory that corresponds to the tradition of natural law theory or to democratic principles. Freedom, however, is not merely negative freedom, that of the absence of restraints associated with limited government, nor even what we might call positive freedom. This is the concept one would find in a Bill of Rights or a constitution of the rights and liberties that are guaranteed and protected by the legislature and executive of the political society—though the term may be used in other, less applicable senses, which might contain some suggestion of self-realization or fulfillment, though not in any sense that the Idealists would have understood those ideas. Rather, the notion of freedom is an abstraction, indicating *solely* the idea of self-fulfillment, of belonging rather than remaining individual and separate. This is, indeed, what Hegel and others, but most notably Hegel, term "real" or "true" Freedom, even the "only true Freedom." It is a submersion of self in the selflike universal, the achievement of harmony with the universe. Freedom is no longer synonymous with certain rights and liberties, indeed with *Liberté, Égalité, Fraternité,* in any realizable or concrete sense; it is the destination of that journey of self-realization. In Hegel, it *is* the Absolute, the Idea, the Spirit. In what may be regarded as the greatest, most breathtaking act of semantic subversion in the history of Western philosophy, the notion of *freedom* itself becomes divorced from theories of political society and from ethical philosophy, to become an epistemological idea, an understanding of reality rather than a description of human circumstances, attitudes, and activities. It is not an *ideal* in the sense that we understand the term, but an *idea.* It is a spiritual and intellectual escape from Cartesian dualism and from Kant, the idea of freedom as an expression of epistemological *understanding* of the universe rather than as an ethical or political *circumstance.* Acting upon the principle of "Freedom" in the Idealist sense means achieving an ontological harmony with the absolute, the universal principle, not a recognition of the equivalent individuality of others which alone guarantees the freedom of each individual.

In short, the idea of freedom as a condition of individual rights and liberties, of the recognition of equivalence between autonomous individual moral agents, has been so altered that it eventually degenerates into that later nineteenth-century conception of *Innerlichkeit,* or withdrawal of the self from the world into an interior, subjective, artistic reality, so potent a feature of Weber's pessimism. Freedom, for the Romantics and Idealists, becomes a spiritual concept that describes self-fulfillment, not a *precondition of fulfillment,* since those who are not free cannot *be themselves.* At the same time, it has been removed from the sublunary, empirical sphere of political theory; it has been recaptured by metaphysics. This may, without undue distortion, be regarded as a further manifestation of the Romantic reaction—what we should term the Idealist reaction—against the materialism of the French Revolution and its aftermath. Instead of a political empire, arising from the fire and blood of the Terror, there is a spiritual empire of all men, a vast harmony of men with each other and with their material universe and the spirit that flows through everything. The ideals of the Revolution become the misty visions of universal harmony on a spiritual plane where political society is, at best, unnecessary and, more realistically, little more than a microcosm of the universal spirit granting men their identity rather than guaranteeing their rights and liberties. Freedom becomes divine, the meaning of human existence rather than a desirable condition of earthly justice. In Hegel, the idea of freedom becomes the essential expression of the Will (or Idea) in History—the whole purpose of history. Romantic–Idealist theory eventually comes to conflate the two ideas of harmony with Nature and spiritual freedom into the central concept of the freedom that derives from harmony with Nature. The declension of this idea into the notion that freedom derives from a parallel, utter identification with the state is implicit in the sentient quality granted to existence or Nature. The State, too, is possessed of, or is an expression of, Spirit.

Finally, German Romantic and Idealist theory, chaotic and hazy in outline as it often is, presents throughout an adaptation of the idea of freedom as a process of historical evolution toward perfection. It has already been noted that scientific progress created, in Positivism especially, the analogous idea that history itself exhibited a similar evolutionary movement forward and upward, toward the 'ever-better'. Idealism thus possesses a certainty in the future, an optimism toward what is to come. It demonstrates that progress and radical change can be achieved without violent revolution, and perhaps this is the real and abiding legacy of Romantic thought, this evolutionary idealism, the influence of which is to be found in the founding fathers of the science of society, with the possible exception of Max Weber. It is certainly to be found in Marx, especially in his turning away from revolution in his later theories of progress toward the classless society and the disappearance of the state.

In Hegel, as we shall see, another aspect of evolutionary Idealism is displayed, though not necessarily with the utmost rigidity, and that is the notion that the evolution of history has already, in one sense, been fulfilled in the present—we have arrived at the only 'good' available to us at this point in the Spirit's self-realization in History. Therefore, the present moment is both good and necessary, and for Hegel it is the modern nation-state, the German nation-state, particularly. History as a spiral motion in Hegel allows cycle and evolution to coexist, a fact essential to Hegel's proof of the meaning and lesson of history.

History, in conjunction with science, displaces the individual almost entirely and also has a subtle effect on the idea of causality. Causality becomes constraining and paramount, but it has also now become a positive force, a promise of progress and betterment. Determinism becomes optimistic, perhaps for the first time in the history of ideas. A study of history diminishes the significance of individual lives, evidently, just as radio astronomy diminishes the significance of a single planet orbiting a single yellow star, but history invested with "Spirit," with an evolutionary *and* sentient meaning—exemplified in society or the State—is dangerous more than it is diminishing. In conjunction with heady ideas of freedom of the spirit through identification with existence or Nature, there is not simply a reduction of the importance of individuality. The significant phrase is *identification with*, of course. Even theology posits a relationship between each individual and the infinite or divine that is meaningful and of the utmost importance. Each human soul is uniquely valuable, however many millions have lived and died, however vast the perspective of history. Now, existence or Nature, society or the State, allows no free will or any other form of uniqueness to the individual. Each individual life is no longer unique, it is merely a role, an identification with the processes of history and its product, the modern state. *Purposive* history has arrived, not merely evolutionary history.

In the idea of purposive history, the only freedom possible to the individual lies in merging with the larger purpose; but, just as the peculiar Romantic conception of freedom had to be defined, we similarly need to identify exactly what kind of 'divinity' we must so completely identify with—take our identity from. We are discussing not a perfect, personal God but, eventually, a modern nation-state—to be precise, not even Germany but prenational Prussia under Frederick the Great. Christian theology assumed a merger with the divine after this life; Hegel posits such a merger here on earth—with history and the collectivity he terms the State.

But Hegel's ideas are shared, in part and in interesting and influential ways, by two other German philosophers in particular, Fichte and Schelling. Both were contemporaries (and the latter a friend) of, and in correspondence with, Hegel; both philosophers influenced him profoundly.

III

It has already been remarked of the principal Idealists—Fichte, Schelling, and Hegel—that what they sought, above all else, was a unitary explanation of reality, some essence behind all appearance—in Kant's terminology, a *common* and universal noumenon, and in the poet Hölderlin's description, the "spirit that is in everything." They were systemizers, assuming that there could be discovered some essential explanation of all experience, knowledge, and reality, and it was largely on this basis that they objected, Fichte most immediately and systematically, to Kant's division between the self and the world, which for Kant could be no more than a world of appearances. To achieve the healing of that dualism the Idealists posited, in Fichte's theory most succinctly, the ego as the "ground of experience." It was not the rational ego of Kant nor the passive receptor of the empiricists but what Fichte described as the "active ego," inextricably intermingled with reality, imposing itself upon the world of experience, to a degree 'making' that world of experience in its own image. As Fichte claims in *The Vocation of Man* of 1792, "Not to KNOW but to DO, is the vocation of Man." For Fichte (1762–1814), there were only two possible responses to the world, that of the realist, or "dogmatist" in his terminology, and that of the idealist. The philosopher's response, more profound than that of the ordinary man, is idealist, while realism remains the province of nonphilosophical response to and understanding of the world.

From this "ground" of the active ego, the philosopher proceeds to expand his understanding of reality, exposing the analagous nature of the world to the ego, the "I." In effect, this means that the identifiable, knowable qualities of the "I" are to be discovered in reality outside the self. Gradually, relationships and parallels, images and analogies are uncovered, until the point is reached where all of reality may be explained in relation to the individual ego, which is perceived as sharing in the spirit, the *Weltgeist,* that pervades and is the essence of the world. This "world-spirit" sounds, of course, remarkably like a restatement of the Romantic aesthetic of the human spirit in harmony with the spirit of Nature, as indeed it is.

Essentially, all three Idealists rejected Kant's assertion that there was much in reality that could only be experienced phenomenally, the noumena of the objects and others in the world being undiscernible to philosophers and to the individual moral reason. Kant's moral reason has become "spirit," and man is now conceived as a whole rather than as Aristotle's rational animal or the Rationalist concept of a dualistic nature of reason and passions, mind and body, which the influential Spinoza shared with Descartes and Kant. The human being is a spiritual creature, his reason an instrument of understanding in harmony with his sentiments, feelings, and psychology. A comprehensive understanding of reality no longer excludes the rational ego from the world. Instead, the world is infused with the ego, displaying in varying ways and to different degrees the spirit that is fully realized and expressed by the individual ego, which *operates* rationally but *is* spirit. Therefore, while Kant and the Rationalists, and even the empiricists, were unable to ascribe reason to animals and 'things', the Idealists are able to allow some element or degree of Spirit to be realized in organic and inorganic Nature.

The Idealist reaction was also opposed to Rationalism's divorce between reason and the passions or sentiments, especially acute in Kant's stern and difficult imposition of moral duty, and to the exaltation of rational inquiry and scientific Positivism exhibited by the materialism of the French Enlightenment. In rationalism and in empiricism, there is, for the Idealists, an unacceptable passivity regarding the employment and operation of the reason, to which they regard Kant as still adhering. The *activity* of the ego is what fascinates and concerns Fichte, Schelling, and Hegel. Therefore, in its *activity of thinking,* the ego of the Idealists is capable of producing *experience* and not merely understanding or reflection. Briefly, Descartes's *cogito* becomes Fichte's *ego* and "I think, therefore I am" is conflated to the existence of the ego-of-itself. Thinking is no longer reflection, it is experience. Also, because of this, there can be no kind of reality that is distinct or separated from the ego that experiences it. Whereas empiricism posits, at least by implication, a 'real' world that is experienced, the Idealists assumed no distinction between the subject of the experiencing agent and the objective world being experienced.

Further, Fichte and Schelling assumed that the ego was innately a moral agent, again contrary to Kant's conception of the effort of moral duty for the rational being, the necessity to achieve the categorical imperative in making any moral decision or taking any moral action. Men are regarded by the Idealists as innately, though imperfectly, moral in their essential, nondualistic natures. This leads, as we shall see, to a strangely Hobbesian view of the State as possessing the right and duty to perfect the ego's moral imperfection by the exercise of its authority. This in turn assumes the moral quality or essence of the State itself, which is where Hegel enters. Idealism therefore abandons all previous theological and Rationalist views of human nature, of reason versus passion, mind and body, good and evil, and for Fichte at least, the present imperfections of the ego are simply a stage in its evolution toward perfection.

It is, however, in the work of F. W. J. von Schelling (1775–1854) that we find the most remarkable similarities to Hegel's principal theories. The two philosophers were friends and correspondents, and Schelling anticipates much of Hegel's method as well as many of his views. It is, perhaps, best to begin with Schelling's idea of the "absolute ego," which he regards as being "unconditioned by the world" of objects and which is posited through the idea of freedom. He distinguishes his position from rationalism by casting himself as diametrically opposed to Spinoza, who, Schelling claimed, considered that "the world [the object as opposed to the subject] was—*everything;* for me this is true of the *ego.*" He continues: "For me the highest principle of philosophy is the pure, absolute ego . . ." The title of this early work was, unsurprisingly, *Of the I as Principle of Philosophy* (1795).

Schelling further argues that Spinoza has been misinterpreted, in that "dogmatists" have regarded his Substance as referring to the world, whereas Schelling believes Spinoza was, in fact, describing the absolute ego as the single, universal stuff of reality. He also argues that "dogmatism," and we must regard this term as here including both materialist and empirical philosophy, encourages passivity and "denies all free causality in me," while idealism encourages man to assert his freedom against the objec-

tive world. To Schelling, previous philosophy stressed the detachment of the ego from the world, while in effect, the absolute ego
is both affected by and affects reality. In no meaningful sense can
it be divorced from objective reality.

Where Schelling is the precursor and perhaps the tutor of
Hegel is in the idea that the absolute ego is evidenced in the world
in particular and significant ways—in Nature and in History.
Space and time provide the evidence of the operation of the ego,
as we might well expect, until we realize that the inevitable
corollary is that Nature and History also exhibit the *qualities* of
the absolute ego—they are possessed of "spirit" just as the ego is.
Schelling is thus the almost-complete Idealist and certainly the
entire Romantic, since it is in the work of art rather than in the
moral action (as with Kant) that the pinnacle of the ego's expression is achieved. Schelling's system leads to an aesthetic philosophy opposed to any scientific or mechanical view of Nature, and
it is in this that he displays the reaction against materialism and
rationalism at its clearest. Nature is invested with the "I" or ego,
albeit at a lower level of consciousness than is the case with
human beings. Nature is nonmechanical, inexplicable in terms of
natural philosophy. In History, too, the spirit evidences itself.
History is no less than the expression of the spirit in time. In his
Essays on the *Idealism of the Science of Knowledge* (1797) he
proposes a "history of self-consciousness," while in the *System of
Transcendental Idealism* of 1800 he suggests that history reveals
a "progressive series of intuitions through which the I rises up to
consciousness in the highest potency." Thus, in Schelling's
thought, not only is there the postulate that both Nature and
History reveal organic, mindlike qualities but the assertion that its
manifestation or operation in history is superior to the mindlike
quality of Nature; mind is at its most primitive and unrealized in
Nature, though present, while in History it is more "potent."

Schelling's most significant ideas, however, concern neither
Nature nor History—rather, they lie in his aesthetic ideas. His
claims concerning history are little more than extensions of some
of the commonplaces of Romantic thought, evidenced most

clearly and influentially in the works of Herder and in the concept—so significant in Hegel's development of it—of the
Volksgeist, the national spirit of a people which must be recognized and accommodated as the essence of any social organization
or state. Herder was also influential in attacking the empirical
view of experience, positing, like Fichte and Schelling, the active
nature of the human intelligence. Schelling's aesthetic is of equivalent importance in establishing the "ground" of Romantic-
Idealist thought.

He regarded the philosophy of Art as the pinnacle of his transcendental idealism. He claims that "the objective world is just
the original, the as yet unconscious poetry of the spirit; the universal organon of philosophy—and the keystone of its entire vault—
is the philosophy of art." What is an ethical bias in Fichte's
thought becomes increasingly in Schelling an attempt to system-
ize knowledge and experience—the interpretation of reality—by
means of an aesthetic. To such a degree, indeed, that he can also
claim that "the state ought to appear as a work of art." Schelling's
political ideas are scattered and undeveloped in the main, but
where he does emphasize the political sphere it is from an aesthetic standpoint—more importantly, the State possesses an organic unity and mindlike qualities and potential, just as is true of
Nature and History. The state is not a means to an end but has
some of the qualities of an end-in-itself, a *realization* of Spirit, the
absolute ego—and it should not be viewed as existing to promote
general well-being or to protect rights and liberties, just as Nature
cannot be conceived to be 'there' to benefit man.

Thus, Schelling's fragmentary ideas add another figure to the
Trinity of mindlike realities in the objective world—Nature, History, and now the State are all realizations of the universal Spirit.
What Schelling achieves, though only in outline, is a transcendental philosophy, an embracing account of objective reality and the
human mind, a vision of harmony and identity throughout reality.
Man is not a noumenon surrounded by phenomena but an ego
or spirit recognizing in objective reality similar qualities of spirit.
It was this theory that Hegel extended and rendered systemati-

cally. To reiterate, therefore, as Kant had imposed upon himself the task of discovering whether metaphysics might not be reinvigorated and returned to her position as "queen of the sciences," so the Idealists, most particularly Hegel, set themselves the task of restoring unity to philosophy, to the affirmation of a single, true metaphysic, to discover the Philosopher's Stone of the single underlying principle of reality. Fichte, Schelling, and finally Hegel sought and found the solution in the mirroring of the human spirit in Nature and History.

Further, whereas Kant, in the tradition of ethical philosophy, assumed that human nature required the development and cultivation of a moral instinct, Idealism implicitly posits the idea of a moral *environment*. Schelling especially assumes the innate or basic moral rectitude of human nature, which is naturally reinforced by the instructive mirrors of Nature, History, and the State. The weight of emphasis has shifted like a huge ballast, so that there is no 'difficulty' about moral activity, no effort or duty attached to moral action and instinct, just as there is a decline of any meaningful concept of the individual. Cartesian dualism and its subsequent manifestations distinguish human nature and thus *individual* human nature; the recognition of the universality of mind or what may be considered mindlike in objective reality reduces that sense of uniqueness, responsibility, and free will, all of which are fragments of the cosmic rubble which gravitationally comes together into a concept of the individual. In Schelling— and in Hegel—the state itself can be viewed as mindlike and therefore *moral*. There is little or no examination in Idealism of the 'good' state, as there is in Plato, because the state is no longer an artificial construct, a product of human association but rather is a further manifestation of Spirit or the absolute ego in objective reality.

In Hegel, this refusal to posit a *theory* of the state is justified by his insistence that speculation as to the future and the 'ideal'— in the sense that we would normally understand the word—is impossible to philosophy, since the realization of Mind in History, though progressive and evolutionary, can only be understood in retrospect. And since to understand this process is the *sole* task of philosophers, speculation on future, purely man-made blue-prints of the state or political society are idle; man-centered and man-constructed ideals that do not attend to the reality of the progress of Mind—or Spirit—in History are incapable of success. There can be, therefore, no 'merely' human ethical or political theory. Not only does the state assume a greater significance, even an independence of individuals, it is removed from the sphere of ethical and political discussion, just as nature is no longer the province of the physical or biological sciences. And history, mean-while, has become the progressive manifestation of Spirit, a grad-ual revelation, for Schelling, of "the Absolute." It is ethical in-quiry that suffers in the hands of the Idealists, but it is ethical notions that are significant in determining human activity—asso-ciation and, crucially and for most of the history of philosophy, human awareness of self.

As we shall see more clearly with Hegel, from this lack of ethical theory, where all reality is harmoniously of one substance or essence and therefore ethical distinctions regarding politics, society, and history have become unnecessary, springs what can only be described as the notion of the *sentience* of the State. The state is no longer the product of human beings in the sense that it can be restructured, altered, done away with, limited, changed. Likewise, history is to be regarded as an expression of Spirit rather than, in its traditional ethical or even its cyclical interpretation, providing a pattern of enlightenment and political instruction. History has become progressive, developing a gradual and ascend-ing manifestation of *Geist.*

Ethical history demands *choice* on the part of human natures, by the operation of that rational faculty man is presumed to possess. Whether that choice is free, or conditional and limited, the choice is there and is arrived at by decision between alterna-tive actions. Idealism largely avoids such considerations, and the state becomes an end-in-itself, an entity as little open to ethical judgment as nature.

IV

The following observations on Hegel are preliminary and are attempted in the light of his Romantic affinities and borrowings, together with an emphasis upon his view of history. Hegel regarded himself, like Fichte and Schelling, as somehow completing Kant's system, and in the sense of the Romantic idea of *harmony* his was another and contemporaneous attempt at recapturing the Hellenic ideal, especially when one considers *The Philosophy of Right* (1820), the work of his maturity in the sphere of political theory.

It may be necessary to observe here, even if we are not, at present, concerned with the peculiarities of Hegel's version of idealism to any great extent, that his notion of the *world* as an 'out-there' and subsequently an equally *real* constituent of the cosmic reality, is individual even beyond the strictures of Fichte and Schelling. What Hegel regards as 'real' in the world outside the self is the evidence supplied by the world of the operations of human intelligence, especially philosophic inquiry, through history. Which means that the 'really real' aspect of the world apprehended by the individual intelligence is that which displays the accumulated wisdom of the ages. The world of politics, society, the state is far more 'real' to Hegel than the natural creation, the individual psyche, the accidents of everyday living. Where intelligence—the realization of mind in the world—can be perceived, there reality is to be found.

In such a radical position, Hegel rejects, of course, much of the accretion of Romanticism around the kernel of human reason. However, this does not make Hegel a successor to the rationalists. His conception of what exactly demonstrates the workings of human intelligence upon 'brute' nature and brutish man alike is peculiarly Romantic. The world that surrounds the individual human intelligence presents an overload of precepts, strictures, and formulations which, when one comes to his theory of political society—the work of other human intelligences, especially those of philosophers, particularly Plato—more than counter any tendency toward a consideration of political society as anything other than an ideal and *ordered* construct, and especially as the construct of the great mass and weight of past philosophers, as they best and most profoundly express the activity of human thought (*Geist*) *upon* the 'world'. The world is not our idea of it, perhaps, but in Hegel it is what we *make* of it through philosophy.

However, it is our task here to illuminate the nature of Hegel's optimism with regard to history and thus toward the state as he perceived, anticipated, and concluded its necessary appearance, constitution, and functions. Both history and the state, as he interpreted them, are the material against which Marx posited his own theories, in a clean, dialectical opposition to Hegel's opinions.

Marx's imitation of Hegelian dialectic (see below) caused him the most profound problems in attempting to obviate its optimistic determinism, such that it is an intellectual reaction that causes him to embrace the notion of revolution. He is brought to the pass of having to imply, if not promote, the idea of revolution as the *Weltgeist* of history, in order to free human activity from Hegel's conclusion that the future is unpredictable except that it will be the next or further manifestation of Spirit in History. In that sense, the dialectic, whether his own as borrowed or the Hegelian original, failed Marx, since Hegel's view of history is 'amoral' while Marx's was fundamentally imbued with moral outrage.

This section must also demonstrate, albeit cursorily, Hegel's mature reaction to the events of the Revolution and its aftermath, to learn from its 'history' and even to approve the idea of a nation in arms that came into being with the Empire, while rejecting what he considered the motivating ideology of that revolution.

Further, we must attempt to understand the power over Hegel's thought of German historians such as Herder, together with the fact of the absence of a truly 'German' history, even as Hegel was attempting to display the Germanic races as the "world-historical people" succeeding to the legacy of the Roman Empire. For his German history, he was required to borrow heavily from Romantic notions of the *volk*, the people of superstition and 'naturalness' in communion with Nature, tribal and—in an important sense—obeying Rousseau's dictates regarding the unsophisticated.

Beyond, or behind, Hegel's adopted and extrapolated notions regarding history lies that other perennial problem-solution of the Romantics and Idealists, that *sentient* quality or essence given to the 'world' but in the sense here that such a wholeness of the world, including the world of men, impairs the capacity for political change, since greater forces than the individual or the collectivity are *purposing* the world. It is here that Hegel displays the extent and depth of his disillusion with the French Revolution, in that 'man-based' efforts at change in political society are doomed to failure. History, for Hegel, is unalterable, because of the Spirit invested in it and becoming realized through its progression, and that element of determinism is important not only as metaphysic but also in the effect it has on his cogitations upon political society. What is called the course of history cannot be changed by human intervention—human beings must understand history, that much is true, but only in order to harmonize with it. To *apprehend* reality is the purpose of *all* philosophy. (It is little surprise that Marx's infamous thirteenth *Thesis* against Feuerbach reads as it does, that philosophy *can* change the world—and history.) Hegel's ideas concur, strangely and appallingly, with those of Metternich and the forces of conservatism and restoration who met at the Congress of Vienna in 1815. Hegel becomes, albeit within a Prussian neo-state a century behind France and Britain, an apologist for the status quo.

In conjunction with any examination of Hegel's notion of purposive history, a recognition of his equation of the Idea, as revealed in and expressing itself in history, with the concept of Freedom is necessary. What happens in this equation is that freedom cannot be equated with the novel, the new, with man-inspired efforts to alter, even by revolutionary means, the conditions of his political society. Constructs and constitutions are *not* the bases or even the implements of freedom. It is little wonder that Marx was obliged to oppose revolution to this quadratic of determinism, though he was driven by Hegel's exclusive categorization and definition, and his clear appreciation of the realities of the aftermath of the French Revolution, to propose as the instrument of change "the class that is not yet a class," in order to escape the Hegelian dialectic's proof of the unalterability of history and thus of the future as determined by history. A *collective* revolution might, for Marx's purposes, oppose successfully the Hegelian anathema pronounced upon the individualism of the Revolution. Marx, it may be remarked, conceived of the notion of an evolution of revolution, a more and greater collectivity of revolution, until the whole of civil society was in revolt against the pertaining social and economic circumstances—all of which may be only Marx's attempt to defeat the strictures, and thus escape them, of the Hegelian dialectic. In this sense, perhaps preeminently, it is necessary to understand Hegel, in the means and ways by which Marx attempted to escape him.

It is also necessary to recognize Hegel, in any preliminary study, as the parent, in philosophical terms, of the nation-state, and the parent, too, of the assumption that, for the first time in political history, political society is greater than its elements of law, constitution, suffrage, et cetera—that it is nothing less than an expression of Spirit. The inevitable association of this idea with collective theories of the state is immediately obvious, since the State as an expression of Spirit, as has been suggested, requires identification with it and identity in its terms. Together with Hegel's view of inevitably purposive history—which gives the form of the state an ethical approval—this notion of the state as the expression of the *Weltgeist* precludes ethical judgment of the apprehensible, empirical political society that any human being finds himself or herself within. Hegel's is the greatest promulgation since that of Plato of the *polis-* man, the citizen, the recipient of identity from the political organization of which he is a member. It is Hegel, even above Plato, who makes a metaphysic and an ontology of political identity.

For the above reasons, I have not, in this preliminary survey, identified the detail of Hegel's 'ideal', in his terms *real,* state, since the exact kind of state he supported may be better described in the history of Prussia during the period of his lifetime. Instead, I have attempted to demonstrate the philosophical (i.e., metaphysical and ontological) presuppositions which make Weber's *power-state* inevitable as a result of Hegel's theorizing. An absolutist state such as Hobbes would have totally admired is inevitable, given Hegel's attitude to history and to the Romantic-Idealist notion of Spirit.

It is on matters such as these that we must concentrate—as well as upon that other and equally thorny Hegelian problem, the matter of the dialectic.

V

No recognition, however cursory, of Hegel's significance and influence as a Romantic, Idealist, and philosopher of the state, can afford to ignore his peculiar and original methodology, the dialectic, which he suggested was borrowed from Platonic dialogue but which, in fact, functioned as a closed system of argument in a fundamentally different manner. As will be noted in the instance of Marx, the residue of already established views and their incomplete dismissal forms an important element in the triadic progression characteristic of the founder of dialectical materialism. In place of what might be termed a 'simple' response or reaction to current theory, there is the cumbersome and often suspect solution of the *synthesis,* the retention of at least elements of current thought and attitude—particularly, the retention of unquestioned *conventions* of current thought, especially if those are themselves radical responses to previous conventions—as part of the final position.

The conventional attitudes and assumptions we might at the outset expect Hegel to have adopted *without examination except by* the triad of thesis, antithesis, and synthesis may be found in the ideas of his contemporary (though in publication earlier) Idealists. And since they systemized as well as inherited a great deal that was current in Romantic theory, any focus upon Hegel must admit the importance of concepts and ideas significant to Fichte and Schelling as regards History, the State and the interrelation of the *subject* (the "I") and the *object.*

The dialectical method is fraught with problems, not least because the method is not based upon the Platonic model of the dialogue; its purpose is a totally dissimilar one. The Socratic dialogues are not intended to discover one final synthesis of reality, though it might be argued that Plato often had just such a consequence in view, but to examine an aspect of reality as closely and fully as possible. The Hegelian dialectic, however, is designed to become its own paradigm, since all scientific paradigms— mathematics, physics, even the putative biological sciences that seem to lie behind early French Positivism—had been rejected in the rejection of Kantian dualism. The dialectic is constructed triadically to become inclusive. Hegel's assumption that all philosophy arrived at his own theories, that he was the culmination of philosophical inquiry because he had unified all branches of philosophy under a single system, added great weight to the method and justification of the dialectic in the presupposition of culminative truth. The *thesis* may be regarded as being the 'current'-'past' of philosophical theory and the *antithesis* its opposite, with the final *synthesis* preserving the elements of truth in both thesis and antithesis. Hegel's claim that the dialectic was the only fully philosophical method of progressive argument, and his rejection of rationalist and scientific deductive reasoning and all traditional forms of logic, invest the dialectic with great authority—for Hegel, at least. But it must already be evident that since the thesis is only questioned by its antithesis, which may not be an opposing school of contemporary thought at all, or a validly opposite, fully evolved theory, the weight of the synthesis may well lie with the assumptions inherent in the thesis, which are those of immediate inheritance rather than of more distinguished longevity, especially remembering that Hegel, with all his compendious knowledge of the history of ideas, was as combative and tendentious as his disciple Marx. That being the case, the dialectic satisfied only by its apparent and commodious inclusion of other views, though *all* other views are open to qualification or rejection, and even while it may be employed to reject much of Romantic theory or to quarrel with Kant, or to restate Schelling's and Herder's ideas of history, its *synthesis* must be regarded as complete, comprehensive, final, but also *residual.*

Even a cursory acquaintance with Hegel's major works, *The Phenomenology of Mind* (1806), *Science of Logic* (1812–16), the *Encyclopaedia* (1817), and *The Philosophy of Right* (1820), exhibits a far more significant context that he might himself have assumed; his philosophy is a matter of immediate inheritance, of current conventions of thought and the Idealist-Romantic urge toward system on the one hand and *harmony* on the other (i.e., his philosophical inheritance was far more recent and limited than the compendiousness of his sources might lead his readers to believe). The posthumous *Lectures on the Philosophy of History* and *Lectures on the History of Philosophy* both reveal that the sense of summation was greater than the sense of the independence of previous thinkers and their ideas. The dialectic, like its creator, regards the elements of the thesis and the antithesis as mere grist to the mill of the final, and *conclusive,* synthesis. The novelist R. L. Stevenson once remarked that it was "better to travel hopefully than to arrive," but Hegel's whole philosophy is concerned with arrival. Evolution stops, fulfillments abound, patterns are resolved—especially in the sphere of history, which one may take either as the central concern of Hegelian thought or even as its paradigm—assuming that one already possesses Hegel's interpretation of history, its 'meaning', in order to make history paradigmatic. History is at the very core of Hegel's theories, for, just as the dialectic is itself progressive but also inclusive, while deductive and inductive argument, being progressive, are limited by their rejection of 'falsities', history becomes progressive, but not evolutionary in some kind of ascending curve or line. History is, dialectically, of the nature of a spiral, in that in its progression, which Hegel's predecessors had affirmed, it is also, in the manner of that former 'notion' of history, the cyclical pattern, returned to some previous point—though at a higher level. The synthesis is the spiral movement of history, since this incorporates those elements of truth in the former theories, the cyclical and the progressive. This becomes especially important when dealing with Hegel's view of the state, because the modern state, in some better way and by means of the spiral of history, recaptures and improves upon that most ideal of historical periods and its institutions, classical Greece, and therefore the Greek city-state and its notion of the *polis* and of *citizenship*.

Almost all Hegel's principal ideas have this pattern of progression by spiral (the method of the dialectic itself), so that all his ideas may be seen, at least in one sense, to be governed by history, at least by the spiral progress evidenced in history. Thus, in his central concept of Mind itself, we have not only Schelling's gradations of mindlike qualities in History and Nature, together with the progress of Mind in History toward the Absolute, but the progress of Mind toward "self-consciousness" through history, toward fulfillment, together with the synthesis of all manifestations of Mind in objective reality as aspects of a single Mind, the *Weltgeist.* Herder's *Volksgeist* is another, though genuine rather than erroneous, manifestation of the single Mind. To ascribe a set purpose or predetermination to all this might be too dismissive of a great philosopher—nevertheless, one cannot but entertain the sneaking suspicion that Hegel's philosophical task, self-imposed, to sum up all previous philosophy and synthesize it into a single, inclusive, universal system is not itself the result of synthesis so much as of thesis and predeliction.

The dialectic, therefore, is not in any sense syllogistic but is, according to its author, a "true logic." It is, in a sense, relative and 'historical', since by the application of the dialectic all philosophy contains some truth and some falsehood. But the means of extracting the truth from varied or opposing theories requires a perspective, as it were. Thus, ideas must be viewed historically or from the perspective of Hegel's idea of the gradual revelation of the progress of Mind in the world. By the dialectic, such progress never abandons its past entirely but retains what there is of truth in past 'facts' and past ideas. Hegel argued in the *Lectures on the Philosophy of History* that man's concrete or factual history was as much a progression as the history of ideas. Therefore, history itself is the *process* of synthesis. Hence its significance as regards Hegel's entire system of ideas. *All* his ideas exhibit the same methodological examination and resolution, but they also all have to 'do' with history. It must be remarked that the dialectic, in its synthesis, does not so much retain aspects of empirically observed historical circumstances or reality but rather elements of thought, philosophies, *ideas*. Hegel's dialectic, modeled to some extent, especially in its purpose, upon that of Kant, is truly and literally *synthetic*. In other words, it functions in an *a priori* manner as to its operation and conclusions. It *imitates* a means of reasoning toward *a priori* certainties, as Descartes and those he influenced had done, while it proposes to discuss politics, ethics, history. Nature, in short, is not merely the empirically apprehensible world of human behavior but is that which Hegel would represent as an aspect of the universal Mind or *Weltgeist,* which may be discussed in *a priori* terms, in imitation of Kant. Therefore, Hegel is able to adopt what is, essentially, an *a priori* methodology in order to subsume the empirical branches of speculation into an embracing metaphysic. It may be remarked that Marx's dialectic is a similarly intellectual exercise, despite the introduction of empirical 'facts' in order that the dialectic serve a more *scientific* function than does that of Hegel.

To demonstrate the method and purpose of the dialectic in its attempt to complete Kant's system by providing a final and successful synthesis which will obviate any necessity to resort to the dualism of noumenal and phenomenal worlds, a passage from the Introduction to Hegel's *Philosophy of Right* will suffice. In it are encapsulated many of Hegel's principal ideas, and a small-scale demonstration of the manner in which the dialectic can be both inclusive and subtle, revealing and deceptive. In paragraph 7 of the Introduction, Hegel is discussing the *Will* as the "unity of both these moments" of self-consciousness as related solely to the Understanding. "Will is free," he has claimed in paragraph 4, and is the "point of origin" of right, which may well seem little more than a paraphrase of most ethical philosophy of an 'individualistic' kind. The moments of "self-determination" or "self-conscious-ness," as he refers to them elsewhere, occur as the *ego*—Schelling's "I," but what must be understood in a purely philosophical sense as rational, *thinking* self rather than as Hobbesian or Freudian ego—which becomes aware of itself, abstractly in the "first moment" and then concretely, *realizing* itself in the sense that it regards itself as actually in the world, "determining" itself as real. This may be regarded as Hegel's paraphrase of abstract or *a priori* thinking and *a posteriori* understanding based upon observation of empirical reality. It is necessary *always* to remember that Hegel characterizes his thinking as idealist, that the conception and understanding of the world is what is most real, and that therefore the debate about the nature of reality is a discussion of the operation we call thinking. Thus, those who attempt to distinguish the "will as another special faculty" which is distinct from "thinking" are in error, Hegel claims.

The third moment of "self-determination" by the will occurs when what Hegel *now* describes as "the universality which has the particular as its opposite" becomes "the particular which by its reflection into itself has been equalized with the universal. This unity is individuality . . . in accordance with its concept; indeed, individuality in this sense is just precisely the concept itself." The difficulty of the dialectic is obvious here but also quite remarkably effective, for what Hegel has achieved is to reconcile the individual with the universal and the metaphysical with the empirically apparent by the triadic progress of the three "moments of self-determination of the ego," a synthesis which claims that *only* in harmony with the universal is there any real or "true" individuality. Further, he has established that the will or the ego—for our purposes the two may be regarded as *stages* of the self, so that the will *becomes* the ego when the synthesis is reached and identity itself is achieved at the point of synthesis—has the capacity to establish the first two moments, which are related to the Understanding, but it does not become a true will or *ego* until "it is this self-mediating activity, this return into itself," for "the will is not something complete and universal prior to its determining itself and prior to its superseding and idealizing this determination." Prior to this synthesis, the will is capable only of being regarded as having the capacity to "abstract [itself] from everything" or as "determined in some specific way either by itself or by something else." These two stages of "moments" of consciousness of the self or person equate with metaphysics and empiricism in the past but are insufficient to account for the purposiveness of Mind in History and the progress of philosophical speculation. Therefore, the third and synthetic moment is that of the will becoming the true ego or *mind* by its self-awareness, its awareness of the world, and then its reconciliation of the abstract and the particular, the universal and the individual.

Hegel circumvents Kantian dualism by asking an ontological question in place of an epistemological one. If we suppose that Kant asked 'What can we (metaphysically) *know?*' then Hegel asked 'What *are* we (metaphysically)?' But Hegel's ontology must be characterized as possessing the qualities of an epistemology—it is a 'thinking' ontology or theory of being, a series of ascending recognitions of a single *existant* which is universal and yet particularized in each individual mind. And, in each mind's *knowing* is its *being.* There is no division between thought and experience because thought *is* experience, the only "true" experience. Therefore, the object of experience, the apprehensible world, becomes the property of the intellect, and Kant had to be in error in persisting with the notion of a world divisible into noumena and phenomena. The world as it really is is our thought of it, our intellectual experience–understanding of it, and therefore nothing can be hidden from us, there can be no unknowable, 'real' reality. The triadic progress of the dialectic, with its stages or steps of understanding, must in its synthetic outcome provide a *full* description of reality, since it is describing the *full* process of our thinking about the world. (The medium is the message, as someone once remarked.) Synthesis is *self-evidently* true by virtue of retaining elements of both thesis and antithesis and because it is *now* while other theories, epistemological or ontological, are *then*, past and partial in their truth.

Hegel, in this brief paragraph, demonstrates the method, the difficulty, and the comprehensiveness of the dialectic. The essential quality of the dialectic is that any particular demonstration of the method, as in paragraph 7 of the Introduction, is a demonstration of the process of self-realization in terms of the intellect. From the Understanding, which is partial, to the will, which is capable of rational apprehension of the abstract and the particular, we proceed to the ego, or true will, which "determines itself" in relation to both abstract and particular but can also finally harmonize or "equalize with the universal," recognize the identicality of the universal and the individual.

Therefore, when Hegel speaks of reason as "Mind" (*Geist*, which may also be translated as "Spirit"), he is—in the larger progress of the dialectic—employing the method of paragraph 7. *Mind* may be regarded as Kantian only if the dialectic remains unemployed. Once we begin to speculate dialectically, we arrive at the notion of *the progress of Mind*—in its microcosmic sense of "self-determination" and then in its macrocosmic application as the progress of Mind in History. On the larger scale, and especially in *The Philosophy of Right*, history as purposive, revelatory progress is the paradigm of "self-determination," those stages of intellectual understanding leading to the achievement of the concept of the individual.

Thus the spiral movement of history, in recapturing the Greek *polis* in the modern State, has as its antithesis in history precisely that period which we saw permitted the development of natural law theory—the loss of the Greek city-state and its associated concepts of citizenship and government; leading to what Hegel, critically, termed "isolated individuality" or the "unhappy consciousness," where Stoicism declines into skepticism, which asserts only the isolated nature of the distinct individual. Hegel's idea of Mind may be to some extent the equivalent of Schelling's

absolute ego, but he travels much further than his younger contemporary in asserting the role of history in the progress of this
universal, single Mind. He says, in the *Phenomenology*, that
human history is "conceived history, the recollection of the Absolute Mind and its graveyard, the actuality, certainty and truth of
its throne, without which it would be forever alone and devoid of
life." In the *Phenomenology*'s last two parts, Hegel sketches the
progress of philosophical thought from earliest religions, forms of
nature worship, through the Greek idea of God in human form,
then Stoical rejection of God in favor of human self-knowledge,
such skeptical humanism to be succeeded by Christianity which
unites the human and divine in the person of Christ and which
eventually gives way to modern philosophical theory and its understanding of this very progress toward self-enlightenment and
the fuller recognition and expression of the Absolute Mind. Hegel
parallels Schelling, but his synthesis is arrived at through the
fullest exploration of human history, and he systemizes it to demonstrate what Schelling did little more than assert, that history
was progress toward the full realization of the absolute "I." It
would seem that for Hegel, Kant cannot be rejected, as he was
by both Fichte and Schelling, on the simple basis of refutation
by opposition. Instead, there must be the characteristic and necessary synthesis—but already the synonymous nature of History
and synthesis is perhaps apparent. Kant cannot be entirely in
error, but the emphasis now lies as much on Kant having thought
in the past as it does on the fact that his theories are, in essence,
untenable. History is the paradigm and the *present* is the moment
of synthesis.

Further, purposive or progressive history, in the sense that
historical periods exhibit Mind to the degree to which they are
capable—but always in a progressive, upward spiral—cannot be
judged as just or 'good' or 'free'. The terms are inapplicable to
societies and governments which are no more than stages of a
journey toward synthesis. Fichte requires the empirical and contemporary world to be the 'worst of all possible worlds', for only
by that means may man as a moral agent realize most fully his

"active moral ego." For both Schelling and, especially, Hegel this must represent the 'best of all possible worlds', since there is an inevitable *progress* of Mind–Spirit in the world, demonstrated in History. Fichte retains a sense of the Kantian moral essence or "imperative" with regard to human nature and society, even though his view of history is determinist; history remains morally evaluable—which is not the case, except in special and distinct circumstances rather like the Positivists' periods of transition or crisis, with Hegel's view of history. For Hegel, the only periods in the history of ideas—and therefore, of society and of human progress—which may be judged to be 'bad' or 'corrupt' or non progressive are those periods when the "unhappy consciousness" reigns, when men lose touch with Mind as it is manifesting itself in the world, and when, especially after 1789, they attempt to reconstruct (i.e., *oppose*) the determinism of history. Cyclical history contained a moral dimension together with a sense of inevitability; Hegel's determinism, optimistic as it is, is amoral and nonethical, in discussion and examination of just those spheres of human activity that most seem to require an ethical perspective.

Hegel's notion of *Geist* is the equivalent of the Romantic conception of the Spirit of Nature, in the sense that such a spirit pervades the whole of reality, including man himself, and *harmony* with that Spirit is the goal of the human being. Hegel's *Geist* is his universal principle, the essential reality; and all reality, as in Schelling, displays levels of expression and possession of *Geist*, in human beings, levels of *awareness* or "consciousness" of the Mind–Spirit. History discloses the progress of Mind and also man's awareness of Mind, just as contemporary human beings display degrees of consciousness, with the philosopher at the apex of "self-consciousness." Thus, history is the gradual realization of *Geist*—*by* men and *through* men in an upwardly spiraling movement toward not only the 'best' period of history but toward the greatest awareness in man and his 'world' of *Geist*. Our knowledge of *Geist* and our realization that we share in that universal Mind become our freedom, and in being free we have crossed the abyss that Cartesian dualism opened at our feet, dividing the rational, finite being from the universe he inhabits.

When such an objective is applied to the study of History, Art, or Nature, as Hegel applied it, historical epochs not only become far more significant than smaller, more finite periods, but also such epochs possess a nonethical but what Hegel might have called a deeply *moral* function, since they demonstrate the kind and degree of self-realization of *Geist* in the epoch, culture, society, or State under examination. Hegel was perhaps the most informed of philosophers regarding both history in the concrete and the history of ideas, but his interpretation of both history *and* ideas is based upon this embracing premise of *Geist* and its "march through the World" or historical realization. In other words, he insists that the prevailing philosophies of past epochs are their essence and, moreover, assumes that the cultures and societies of the past were *obedient* to the prevailing ideas of their culture and did not run counter to them or enact very different philosophies. It is tantamount to an act of faith; at least it is acceptance of the dominance of the history of *philosophy* over the history of *events* and societies, to so believe. Furthermore, it offers no ethical assessment of the relationship of a culture to its participants or a government toward its subjects. Slavery in the Greek city-state is, quite literally, irrelevant, as presumably is the lack of embodiment of Christian ideals in the laws governing the treatment of human beings by those who governed them in the Middle Ages. It is in this sense that purposive, epochal history allows Hegel to regard the state, the collectivity, as paramount and inevitable, neither just nor unjust, good or bad—simply, like art and nature, an expression of *Geist.*

None of this might matter very much if Hegel had not been a political thinker of great influence or if Karl Marx had not been among his methodological disciples. But, because both are the case, it is necessary to understand the essence of Hegel's system and his view of history in order to understand the pedigree of his political observations; the origin of his optimistic determinism, his promulgation of inevitability, his assertion of the predomi-

nance of the state over the individual, and his disastrous removal
of political thought altogether from the sphere of ethics. Before
Hegel, political theory either derived from, or was contained
within, an ethical framework. This is easiest to observe in the
ideas of government and social organization of a Christian thinker
like Augustine—who, like Hegel, believed history to be the gradual revelation of a divine scheme. Locke and the Stoics will serve
the purpose more clearly, however, in that the manner in which
they suggest society be organized and the rights and liberties to
be granted to citizens devolve from their sense of ethics.

In the *Lectures on the Philosophy of History,* Hegel remarks
that "in the state alone has man rational existence," and there are
countless similar remarks throughout his works. To understand
his idea of the state in detail, however, we must begin with his
adaptation of Herder's term, *Volksgeist.* For Hegel, there are
what he calls certain "world-historical peoples" evidenced in history in whom is expressed, with varying degrees of adequacy, the
Spirit–Mind itself. As he claims: "World history is the presentation of the divine, absolute process of Mind [*Geist*] in its highest
forms, of this progress through stages whereby he attains to his
truth and self-consciousness about himself. The forms of these
stages are the world-historical *Volksgeister.*" Prehistorical organization, at least in Hegel's sense, is represented by tribalism. The
first great epoch, of course, is the classical world, which evidences
what Hegel calls *Sittlichkeit,* or ethics; but what he means by it
is the *ethical harmony* concomitant with the individual's identification with the community, especially with the Greek *polis.* Such
identity or harmony is, for Hegel, the essence of the ethical.

It should be remarked at this point that Romantic aesthetic
theory regarded the Greek world as exemplifying the perfection
of art, and incorporated in that evaluation was an idealized view
not of Greek democratic experiments but of the essential unity
of the individual and the community, men's identification with
the city-state. But for Hegel, since the past, however admirable,
cannot be 'ideal', what is only *partially* realized in the Greek *polis*
is the notion that all men belong, or need to belong, to the

community on equal terms. Thus, to fulfill the *dialectical* progress of History, the Greek world must decline into a division between the individual and the state, to give rise to the idea of the *individual* itself. *Geist* must progress by this means because the Greek city-state is parochial rather than universal. Here, Hegel quite correctly identifies Stoicism with the growth of what he refers to as "universal individualism," the recognition of individuality *and* universality.

However, in this period, that of the Roman Empire, the individual cannot be truly united with the state, and thus the birth of Christianity, with its idea of community in the universal Catholic church. Such a community, however, is itself unsatisfactory because it does not reunite the universal individual that succeeded the Greek *polis* with the state. The next eighteen hundred years have the task of providing this new unity, recovering by means of the dialectical or spiral progress of history the Greek *polis* in a new, rational, and *universal* sense in the modern state. The "world-historical people" who exemplify and fulfill this movement are Germanic. Hegel here means the Germanic peoples who brought about the collapse of the Roman Empire and who were the founders of the modern nations of Europe. The Germanic barbarians were conscious above all of their independence of authority, but this must be united with the sense of community exhibited by the Christian church and the ancient world. It is Hegel's assumption that such a unity has been achieved in the modern, monarchical state, which preserves the private individuality of men and the essential community to which they must belong to achieve full self-consciousness and complete, rational freedom.

It is not difficult to perceive how this pattern of "world-historical peoples" exhibits the pattern of the dialectic, the synthesis of individuality and community being the modern, rational State. Hegel must account for the emergence of the concept of the individual, and he does this with profound insight; but he also regards such detached, noncommunal individuality as the "unhappy consciousness" and therefore as the antithesis of the ancient Greek sense of the *polis* which acts as thesis but which is also partial in its realization of *Geist* in History. Thus, an incorporation of the "unhappy consciousness" within a renewed and adapted *polis* or community (State) is the ideal synthesis, the resolution of the whole of History. There is, however, a pressure toward synthesis in this manner that is contemporary with Hegel rather than historical—the outcome of the French Revolution and its decline into the atrocities of the Terror, which Hegel, appalled, must explain. He does so in terms of the Enlightenment and in terms of the inevitability of history.

Briefly, Hegel regards the theorizing and materialism of the Enlightenment as leading to an attempt to rebuild or re-create society according to the dictates of human will alone, obeying the "moments of the Understanding," in spite of *Geist*. This he calls "unconditioned freedom," which he contrasts with the genuine freedom which is achieved by the recognition of man's unity with *Geist* in the world. Unconditioned or absolute freedom assumes that the rational, *individual* will is the supreme power and authority in the world and is therefore destined to failure because it refuses to recognize the universal Spirit–Mind. It attempts to change history in a radical way and thereby disobeys the inevitability and determinism inherent in both history and the dialectic. The Terror is the inevitable result of the Revolution because, once it has destroyed all the existing institutions, it turns in what Hegel calls "the fury of destruction" upon its own children, those who do not accept or who dissent from the rigid, new orthodoxy. By separation from and denial of *Geist* in favor of the supremacy of the rational will, human energy is merely destructive. The attempt to impose principles upon a society without acknowledgment of the conditions that pertain in that society, its customs, and the disposition of its members, in fulfillment of the merely rational will is bound to encounter opposition, and that opposition or dissent must, like all contrary elements, be destroyed. In that sense, the individual rational will operates 'logically' and through a process of simple refutation, rather than by dialectic means. It has not sought to retain elements of the *thesis* but instead is simple *antithesis* rather than *synthesis.*

In his reflections on the Terror, Hegel is remarkably and astutely prophetic of political terror in general, predicting its inevitability with regard to all sudden and radical political change. He does, of course, disregard the denial of individuality expressed by pluralism or dissent which might also lie at the basis of any explanation of totalitarian oppression, since such a conception of individuality is unsatisfactory as regards his system. Nevertheless, it is Hegel who best articulates among his contemporaries not merely the appalled horror of humane observers outside France but the underlying motivations that gave rise to the Jacobin dictatorship and Terror.

Radicalism in any form, we may safely conclude, is unlikely to make an appearance in *The Philosophy of Right,* in which work Hegel expounds his view of the rational state, the synthesis of historical development. But what kind of society does he propose and what ideas of political society does it contain? What of the individual, his rights and liberties, as a citizen of this state?

Hegel's analysis of the state naturally proceeds by means of the dialectic. The thesis, briefly, is the family, the antithesis what he terms "civil society," and the synthesis is embodied in the idea of the State, the higher community, membership in which Hegel regards as true freedom. His view of the family is not of a microcosm, simply as one element of the dialectic, and therefore he distinguishes the bonds of the family as being those of *piety,* of affection, respect—the unity provided by feeling and the sense of immediate community. This, in the triad of the dialectic, will survive in the synthesis, since it offers a context larger than that of the individual. The family is viewed not as an agglomeration of individuals but in a very traditional sense, both socially and philosophically. *Piety* as a philosophic idea has its roots in Roman political thought, as distinguishing actions not based upon contract or upon any voluntary choice by the agent, while in tradition the family was regarded as hierarchical, even patriarchal. Hegel gives due weight to both meanings in the thesis of the family, for both are important in the attitudes expected of the citizen in the eventual synthesis.

The antithesis in Hegel's triad is *civil society,* which he regards as that association of individuals which most fully expresses their individuality, in trade, commerce, and the like, what Marx would term the "bourgeois economy." Inherent in this view of civil society is Hegel's instinctive suspicion that human nature is Hobbesian in its unfettered individualism. There are many indications in his writings that support such a view. Man is selfish, egoistical, unmoral if not immoral. Hegel allows such tendencies a degree of license in the commercial world. However, we are dealing here only with the antithesis, the necessary accommodation of the individuality that was so important to the Stoics and to Roman legal theorists and which, for Hegel, is an essential part of the progress of History. In the synthesis, we arrive at Hegel's theory of the State, except that he has already included what we might term a class system, though he uses the more traditional term "Estates." Economic man is differentiated into certain estates—the agricultural class, the business class, and the civil service class. Naturally, the first equates most closely with the family, the second is the most individual expression of human nature, and the third, concerned with the good of the community as a whole, tends toward the condition of the State itself.

Men are therefore in the sphere of civil society, individuals; but their need for cooperation in this sphere is already leading toward the community that will become the State.

The State, however, for Hegel must become a unity, rather than simply the antithesis's aggregation of groups, classes, or estates. As in Schelling, it is one of the trinity of witnesses to the progress of the universal Mind, and, like Art and Nature, it has mindlike qualities. For Hegel, these are evidenced in and derived from an assumption of unity in the synthesis, in a view of the State as organic and as an organism. In order to fulfill such strictures, a certain type of social and governmental organization must emerge that is monarchical, hierarchical, ordered, settled, probably illiberal (i.e., a modern version of the *polis,* a Greek city-state admitting everyone to membership of one *degree* or another). Indeed, the image of the State that Hegel adopts is extremely traditional. It depends upon acceptance of 'place' and 'function'. A dialectic of German social thinkers might have as its thesis Hegel, its antithesis Marx, with Weber to provide the synthesis.

Again, it seems opportune to stress at this point the inherent and developing inertia of the dialectic, which allows into its triadic construction not only some, but many, unquestioned *assumptions*. And because history—cultures, epochs, and societies—is the analogy as well as the raw material of the dialectic, thesis and anithesis allow not only selectivity but also the sin of assumption. Thus, in dealing with the State, as with much else, Hegel has preconditioned the synthesis, as the example of his use of the notion of *piety*, above, indicates. But the largest and most profound assumption of the dialectic method when dealing with political and social questions is that the state is in any way the realization of *Geist*, and the synthesis of the historical process. Being regarded as such, it is presented as a fulfillment rather than a stage or moment. Thus, the modern state, not necessarily but probably Prussia, comes as synthesis to *demand* recognition and obedience. It has also become an entity, separated from its members, an *organism* which demands men's loyalty and membership and confers their only real freedom upon them when they recognize in it the expression of Mind (i.e., become "self-conscious" with regard to the State and their relationship to it).

One may remark here that often in *The Philosophy of Right* there would appear to be a contraction of the concept of Mind, so that it is made to signify *only* human intelligence itself, not human intelligence as it 'answers' some cosmic intelligence present in the universe as a whole—at least, human intelligence as displayed in the history of philosophy. Hegel never disclaimed belief in a *Weltgeist* or admitted to apprehending it solely in terms of human intelligence's interference in, and shaping of, the 'world', but that may have become his final position, by 1820. Thus, it may be necessary to read the following observations aware of this 'dualism'—are we to suppose that man is equating with some separate and universal 'Mind', or are we presumed to understand that it is the mass of human, but philosophic, intelligences that have operated throughout history that 'modern' individuals must align themselves with? For our purposes, it is necessary only to remark that for Hegel no human intelligence can, or should, make itself ahistorical, detached from the *mind of the past* or from the *mind that surrounds.*

Such is the certainty with which Hegel presents the modern State as his synthesis that he can claim in *The Philosophy of Right* that "The state is the divine will in the sense that it is Mind present on earth." It is possible, without entering the realms of fancy, to regard Art, Nature, and the State as the triad of another dialectic, one left unstated by Hegel—at least in quite the following way—but which sees Nature as thesis, Art as antithesis (Nature given perfect, if man-made and artificial form), and the State as the synthesis of both, the successful combination of nature and artifice.

Where Hegel was most 'modern' in his view of the State was principally in the idea of a governing class, which he earlier distinguished in his estates of the realm, the civil servant. It is here that he is in closest communion with Weber almost a century later. Yet even this might be said to be a mirror of Plato's Guardians. The sense of hierarchy in Hegel's rational State is pervasive and inescapable—freedom lies not in particular rights and liberties, about which he was vague in the extreme, but in submission to, and fulfillment of, one's place or station in society. The radical or revolutionary state, by contrast, represents disorder, the defiance or ignorance of *Geist.* For example, he refers to the principle of universal suffrage as an "atomistic and abstract point of view," because people are representing themselves as individuals here rather than as members of some smaller community within the larger community of the State, remembering that the individual is viewed in the context of the family or of commerce, both of which negate what Hegel called, detrimentally, "absolute freedom" (i.e., the freedom to do as one wishes—Hobbes's anathema, too).

In his envisaged legislature, the landed estate or class is, of course, extremely significant. It has an independence of commercial fortunes and of the Crown by virtue of landed property which peculiarly fits it for public life since it is "independent of favor, whether from the executive [the Crown] or the multitude." Hegel assumes no *self*-interest on the part of this group. They form the upper house, while the lower house, though representative, is drawn by appointment from the various corporations, associations, and the like of "civil society." The members of these two houses are not to be seen as delegates or representatives of those who have sent them but rather as *organic,* in some way working for the "common good." As an element of the synthesis, they must obviously be changed from being merely representative of the groups outlined in the thesis and antithesis.

We need only note Hegel's attitude to war and bear in mind Kant's *Perpetual Peace* to understand the Prussian nature of much of Hegel's thinking about the state and to qualify his vision as reactionary, illiberal, suspect. The state must obviously be, for all men, the object of powerful attraction, especially through the sentiments of patriotism and loyalty. And war becomes, as he says, the call of the State upon its members to preserve the unity that is the State and their relationship with it "at the risk and sacrifice of property and life." In other words, war is *the* occasion upon which the state demonstrates its superior importance over that of its members, whether groups or individuals. Hegel's basic attitude to war lies in the idea that "just as the blowing of the winds preserves the sea from the foulness which would be the result of a prolonged calm, so also the corruption in nations would be the product of a prolonged, let alone 'perpetual' peace." It seems a desperate pity here that Hegel's philosophy had abandoned the physical sciences as a paradigm of method, otherwise he might have been better acquainted with the action of tides. War, too, is defended on the grounds that other and surrounding states, especially France and England, are *not* realizations of the rational, modern State but aberrations or survivals of older forms, and this shows Hegel's particularism most clearly.

The conclusions to be easily drawn, from the above examination, of Hegel's particular and detailed political theories hardly require statement. They may be left below the "self-conscious" level. The line of descent, especially through Marx, of many of the notions, especially those which require obedience to the state and which must subsume individuality into some larger group or interest, are wearily, even horribly, familiar at the end of our collective century. To pillory Hegel is too easy and perhaps unfair—also perhaps unnecessary. He was the prisoner of method, and the method's flaws, once exposed, may be left to do their own damage to the theories, indeed to the entire system. Beyond that, Hegel should be remembered as the nonethical theorist, or perhaps as the optimistic determinist. However one attempts to characterize him, his work, and his later influence, one should remain aware of the essentialism that drove him to develop both the method and the synthetic ideas that were the result of the dialectic. The single, universal principle of his philosophical system, *Geist*, is by its nature and definition supramoral, above ethical judgment. So is that manifestation of *Geist* that most affects and influences—and has control over as well as responsibility for—the system of law and government, the State. The conservative, hierarchical, 'fixed' legislative and executive he envisaged to perform the work of government is significant precisely because it is the structure best suited to the necessity of *belonging* to the state, of men finding their identity within it and on its terms. Political society, an artificial construct based upon consent and contract, necessary only insofar as it regulates social interaction while enabling individuals to affect, even effect, their own lives, has become in Hegel not the brutish and brutal power state some have observed but rather an aspect of the divine—a wholly rational *Geist*. That being the essence of Hegel's State, it is unnecessary to ask what kind of state is being worshiped, enough to abhor that the ceremony is taking place at all.

SALAD DAYS:
MARX BEFORE *CAPITAL*

Anyone confronting the thought of Karl Marx must at least begin to feel like Childe Roland as he "to the Dark Tower came." There cannot, surely, be anything new to say of Marx's theories and their influence; neither can there be, as the compromises so long awaited actually begin in Eastern Europe and elsewhere, any pressing need to disinter the great thinker's bones for yet another autopsy. And yet, there is, conversely, always something new to observe and remark—even if it is only to recognize that a process of rehabilitation of the arch-authoritarian, Hegel, is taking place as a form of mild acid to clean off the accretion of blame that Marx's bust in Highgate Cemetery has acquired. However robbed of completeness and universality—even of its pretensions to 'scientific' method—Marx's system has now become, it remains still to be confronted and understood.

The early writings of Marx, those which either became lost in the mist or which never struggled into the light of the published day until the past few decades, have been the object of much recent study, much of it confirmatory, even congratulatory. The fact that so much of Marx's early writing was not published until long *after* his influence was predominant and assured does not disqualify these works from inclusion in a discussion of Marx's basic and abiding ideas of politics and society, not to mention human nature itself; indeed, since they so underlie and inform *Capital* and *Gründrisse*, they provide an entirely necessary illumination and commentary, an X-ray outline, rather than merely a skeleton, of Marx's most consistent and influential theories, in fact. This body of work, largely completed before *The Communist Manifesto* of 1848, the work of Marx and Engels, is substantial and has given rise to accusations of inconsistency and acclamations of consistency in the longest term; to recognitions, above all, of Marx's abiding concerns and the early formulation of theories that remained central to his thought, even if no more than epigrammatically presented in a welter of diatribe against men now completely unknown, like Stirner. More than anything else, these early works have brought to the forefront of discussion of Marx the indebtedness he always acknowledged to Hegel. The real problem with much examination of these early works is that Hegel has become regarded as little more than the springboard from which Marx jumped, arced, twisted, and performed his perfect entry into the water of the history of ideas, its main current, in fact.

Marx's debt to Hegel is often regarded as one of methodology (i.e., the dialectic) rather than of ideas, except, perhaps, with regard to his idea of history, but only in the broadest sense that Marx, like Hegel, regarded history as displaying a certain evolutionary pattern, so that it might be divided into epochs which conveniently illustrate the progressive development of those factors determining human history and the progressive stages of human society. Other than the dialectic and history, Marx is regarded as reacting against Hegel, of refuting and finally dismissing him. Which, of course, sounds remarkably clear-sighted and 'philosophical' and not at all like the obsession that Marx's whole system and basic assumptions really display toward Hegel's ideas.

Marx's earlier writings do display an evident desire to refute systematically and *completely* Hegel's idealism with what he termed his own materialism, which means that he required his own system to 'answer' that of Hegel at every point and turn—to strangely balance it. It was no more or less than rejection by total opposition, and by 'total' one has to infer at any and every level and the 'countering' rather than dismissal of every significant idea. The second problem is that Marx continued to employ certain assumptions that he inherited from Hegel and which he felt no cause to analyze or reject. These assumptions or propositions, many of which were not original to Hegel (some of them are displayed in Hobbes's political theories), are in some cases metaphysical, not merely philosophical but of that realm of philosophy Marx was determined to renounce, and in other examples psychological. Marx's view of human nature may be accounted for differently, but it is essentially that of Hobbes without the imposition of some fulfilling greater entity (Hegel's rational State and Marx's "species-being"). The decision as to what exact weight to give to the abiding influence of Hegel over Marx depends upon the degree and kind of assumptions that either remain unquestioned or which are made directly and solely to answer a proposition of Hegel.

It is not difficult to begin with the assertion that the derivation of Marx's system lies in Hegelian idealism, a metaphysic itself deriving from an opposition to and qualification of the work of Kant. Metaphysics, of its nature, deals with what Kant would have described as the reality that lies behind appearance. Marx, proclaiming himself a materialist, though distinguishing himself from the tradition of French materialism, opposed idealism, especially where there is any assumption that it was trading with the divine or exalting Mind, as in Hegel, where it elevates both rationality and the primacy of 'thought' of all kinds over 'activity' or the sense experience essential to empiricism. It was the religiosity of Hegel's idealism that Marx rejected, and the principal reason he termed himself a materialist. Marx would, above everything, deal with the sublunary world of human beings and their actions, their societies, and their circumstances.

His dilemma was that much of his equipment and assumptions—even the object of his inquiries, to establish a 'system'—

while belonging to the essentialism of metaphysical inquiry are applied to a sphere of analysis itself incomplete and nonmeta-physical (i.e., the empirical sphere of political activity and theory, of society and economic life). To the sublunary manifestations and concerns of this sphere Marx brought not only the tools but the *demands* of metaphysical inquiry—a search for underlying, hopefully 'single' principles which would completely explain the 'world', expose the 'truth' that *must* lie behind appearance, the sense-apprehensible reality that is as 'real' as we are ourselves. Marx required an analysis of political society and economic life that would be as verifiable as a law of natural science. What he actually and unconsciously sought were explicatory principles which would have the force of metaphysics or theology.

In other words, what Marx achieved, as I hope will be apparent from the subsequent examination of his earlier writings, some of them in conjunction with Engels, that indeed-fallen angel, was a *transposition* of Hegelian idealism to a distinctly empirical sphere of inquiry. He did not refute Hegel so much as replace his ideal-ism with an essentialist metaphysic of his own. His concepts have a direct relationship of opposition to the principal ideas of Hegel's system, rather than being ideas arising from examination of the empirical sphere of current politics and society. Of course they can be seen in this light, but the conclusions that Marx drew finally, and time and again, are such as to 'balance' ideas in Hegel rather than to prescribe 'empirical' solutions. As witness to this, it may be remarked how Marx became increasingly separated from the society that surrounded him after 1849, when he settled in England after exile from Germany. What historians are pleased to call, with little or no dissent except from Marxists, the great Age of Reform, Marx seems to ignore. At least, he does not allow it to influence his theories of both present and future. No reshap-ing or amelioration of the essential bases of his system occurs after 1849, however importunate empirical evidence may be to the contrary. History changing in unexpected ways, bourgeois democ-racy beginning to put its house in order, the benefits of enlarged suffrage and the reform of constituencies, the postponement of mortality and improvements in health—none of these dismayed Marx from continuing to impose his system upon empirical reality in the manner of Procrustes, except that Marx's definition of 'revolution' embraces—at times—periods of peaceful, radical social change as well as the violent upheavals and redirections of forceful revolution, though this, too, may be ascribed to Hegel rather than to Marx's sojourn in England after 1849.

It may be useful to adapt as a starting point the first sentence of Dickens's novel *A Tale of Two Cities.* For Hegel, with his view of purposive history, his own time was "the best of times" because it was inevitable and simply the appropriate period in the gradual realization of absolute Mind in history. For Marx, his lifetime was "the worst of times"—though the future would alter that perspective, violently or by evolutionary change—because of the method of production of capitalist, bourgeois society which enslaved and alienated millions of human beings, indeed, had divided society into countless individuals and into that "warre of all against all" which Hobbes describes. For Marx, it was a time when violent revolutionary change was demanded, though it must be remarked that his earliest recorded responses to the political society around him should be described as democratic rather than revolutionary. In opposition to Hegel's idea of the absolute state, Marx posited the concept of the 'absolute' community, his vision of the perfect society.

If we examine Marx's early writings in order to elicit his attitudes before 1848 toward a small number of essential considerations, we can, from these earlier works, understand the essential force and purpose of Marx's system—why he required a 'system' rather than an ideology, a political or sociopolitical program that could operate upon capitalist society and change it by process of legislation, prescriptive and proscriptive. Marx required of his work a redefinition of idealism, nothing less, the transposition not simply of Hegelian method and concepts to other spheres of inquiry but a metaphysical system that was entirely 'materialist' and which would utterly and entirely refute or replace the Hegelian system. Marx, however, was Promethean in more than one sense. He defied the old gods who still ruled, incarnated in Hegel's thought, idealism, determinism, and that admiration for the authoritarian, modern nation-state and for the curse of nationalism. Acutely and quite properly, Marx especially despised that latter object of worship. Yet it was those same gods who chained him to the rock, and the bird that fed daily on his liver had Hegel's features.

In other words, there is a case to be made for regarding the whole impetus and systematic nature of Marx's thought as being designed to counter Hegel's system, rather than arising from empirical inquiry. It is *synthetic* in the Kantian sense in relation to the ideas of others; it is not a synthesis of observed realities. This becomes most apparent in Marx's view of history itself, which is a dialectical synthesis of Hegelian and other ideas of history. It is the view of a philosopher rather than an economist or historian, and an attempt, like those of Kant and Hegel before him, to synthesize all philosophy into a single system. Thus, while engaged in the utter refutation of Hegel, Marx is also engaged in a synthesis of his and other ideas, together with their adaptation to the empirical spheres of economics, politics, and society. The origins of such concepts as alienation, historical materialism, "civil society," and "species-being" are outside Marx, in the work of Hegel and Feuerbach in particular. Marx adapted these concepts to the spheres of inquiry he wished to pursue, but he also regarded his system of ideas at once as a synthesis of his forerunners' thinking *and* as a refutation of them, so that in *The German Ideology* he and Engels could claim that the work was written to "settle accounts with our former philosophical views," as if it marked a decisive break with the past. To understand that it was no such watershed seems to me one of the tasks remaining to analysts and critics of Marx. The massive construction that is *Capital* and the ideas that inform *Gründrisse* and his other mature writings remain an attempt to replace the Hegelian 'worldview' and account of reality with one of his own, in terms that Hegel would have understood and by means of a method that he would have recognized. When empiricism was required of Marx, idealism dominated his thinking and methodology.

II

In beginning to construct his systematic refutation of Hegel, Marx accepts, on the one hand, Hegel's ideas of the egoism of individuals and individualism, though he somewhat alters his view of Hegel's "civil society." This intermediate stage between the family unit and the state was the sphere in which men carried out their commercial and competitive activities. Marx's view of civil society was of competition and exploitation, of the complete expression of egoistic individualism, of the *alienation* of men from themselves and other men. It is this term that exists at the core of Marx's view of human nature and society, and it is necessary at the outset to understand what Hegel intended by its employment. In Hegel, it is represented by two terms—*Entaüsserung,* meaning 'objectification', and *Entfremdung,* or 'self-estrangement'. Both terms are required to describe what Hegel identifies as the progress of absolute mind through history. Mind, which is the 'reality' of the world in its progress toward self-consciousness, *objectifies* itself in the world—in a special sense 'creating' its world. However, moments of 'self-estrangement' occur when Mind realizes that the 'world' it has objectified is and can be no more than an illusion. This produces an estrangement of Mind from itself, followed by an eventual return to itself. By such means, Mind progresses toward complete knowledge of itself. I have referred here to Mind in the sense that Hegel reserves for 'absolute' or universal Mind, though the process toward self-consciousness is undertaken by every individual, by classes, groups, by societies, and cultures—such is the meaning of history for Hegel.

For Marx, in a materialism opposing itself to this idealism, *alienation* becomes something both different and analogous. In

Marx, the essence of human nature lies in *activity* rather than thought in a quite simple and complete counterpoint to Hegel. Human beings are sensuous, active, empirical creatures, not the abstract, philosophic creatures of *The Phenomenology of Mind.* Marx expresses his view of essential human nature on numerous occasions before *The Communist Manifesto* of 1848, but a lengthy quotation from his *Critique of Hegel's Dialectic* contained in what are termed the *Economic and Philosophical Manuscripts* of 1844 encapsulates the idea, as follows:

> Man is a directly natural being. As a living natural being he is on the one hand equipped with natural vital powers and is an active, natural being. These powers of his are dispositions, capacities, instincts . . . the objects of his instincts are exterior to him and independent of him yet they are objects of his need, essential objects that are indispensible for the exercise and confirmation of his faculties . . . he has real, sensuous objects as the objects of his life-expression. In other words, he can only express his being in real, sensous objects.

In the above can be seen Marx's refutation of the primacy of thought over activity, together with his idea that the human essence is a matter of expression rather than response. Thought and reflection imply a passivity toward the external world and to experience, whereas Marx's human being is essentially his 'self-expression'; and that self-expression is equivalent to *production*, to man's work or *labor*. What Marx was to term man's "vital activity" or his "active function" was not simply the expression of his essence but the essence itself. Activity and labor and their 'products' are not, at least initially, narrowly confined to mechanical labor, to material products, but include ideas, works of art, societies, and cultures—everything, in fact. Marx expands the terminology of the classical economists in the act of employing them to embrace the whole of the external world as the 'product' of men. In so doing, he was engaged in the groundwork of his theories of political economy that resulted in *Capital.* He consciously adapted the current economic vocabulary to a discussion of Hegelian idealism, to extract the reality that lay behind appearance; from the outset, it was to be what might be termed a 'metaphysical' economics.

Crucial to Marx's discussion of human nature was a term he borrowed from Feuerbach, one of the 'young Hegelians', like Bauer, who had already begun the process of adapting or ameliorating Hegel's ideas and methodology to the discussion of social and religious questions. The term was *species-being*, because the other facet of Marx's image of human nature lies in man's essentially social rather than individual essence. By species-being, Marx created the equivalent, in a materialist sense, of Hegel's *Geist*, the essential quality of human nature that both distinguishes men *and* binds them together. Man is communal rather than individual by nature, and this is the essential description of man in both Hegel and Feuerbach. Marx adapts the term to materialist ends by extending its meaning to embrace the idea of human activity, labor, and production as the 'expression' of that community— which allows him to examine societies in history insofar as they fulfill or deny that species-being, in other words, insofar as they either do, or do not, "alienate" men from each other and from their essential selves.

As Marx announces in his lengthy review of Bauer's *On the Jewish Question* of 1843, with regard to the rights of man in any and every political sense:

> Thus none of these so-called rights of man goes beyond egoistic man, man as he is in civil society, namely an individual withdrawn behind his private interests and whims and separated from the community. Far from the rights of man conceiving of man as a species-being, species-life itself, society, appears as a framework exterior to individuals, a limitation of their original self-sufficiency.

He continues a little later:

> Political emancipation is the reduction of man, on the one hand, to a member of civil society, an egoistic and

independent individual, on the other hand to a citizen, a moral person.

The actual individual man must take the abstract citizen back into himself and . . . become a species-being; man must recognise his own forces as social forces, organise them, and thus no longer separate social forces from himself in the form of political forces. Only when this has been achieved will human emancipation be completed.

It needs no great perspicuity here to recognize a barely altered impersonation of Hegel's reverence for the Greek *polis,* the community, and for the individual's successful and necessary identification with the *polis.* This "little measure" of Marx's consistent and continuing indebtedness to Hegel will suffice as an emblem of the entire debt.

It is also necessary to recognize that Marx's view of individuality is that of Hegel and Hobbes, the *product* of what he terms "civil society," the product, in fact, of alienation. The Hegelian concepts of *objectification* and *self-estrangement* have been assumed into Marx's ideas and presented as the basis of social organization where individuality is either recognized, supported, or *produced* by the nature of that society. His use of the idea of species-being in relation to some ideal community of citizens is a direct counterpoint to the significance with which Hegel invests what he terms the "rational State." The community in which species-being is retained and successfully expressed is intended as the refutation of that exultation of the modern state. More than that, however, it is the essential expression of the human essence—even more, it *is* that essence. There is nothing *other* than those elements essential to human beings.

Where, in Hegel, civil society both displays and allows the expression of what Hegel regarded as an unavoidable element of human nature, individuality, in Marx's civil society such individualism is the very essence of alienation, the loss or disregard of species-being. Species-being for Hegel is expressed in membership of the state, a higher loyalty and fulfillment than membership of civil society. For Marx, community and civil society are opposed.

And where for Hegel membership of that community embodied in the state is contemplative, spiritual, 'philosophical', for Marx membership of the community that fulfills species-being is active, productive.

Marx may be seen, therefore, to have inherited that vast lurch toward a species of collectivism initiated by Hegel in opposition to Kant's fundamental definition of human beings as ends-in-themselves and as therefore individually unique and valuable. Marx completes the process Hegel had begun; species-being does not posit simply one (albeit the highest) kind of human fulfillment in 'citizenship' of some larger conglomerate such as society, nation, or state, it posits that citizenship as the *only* manner of human fulfillment. *All* other human activity and behavior is alienated, a distortion or exploitation of human beings.

Marx summarized much of his thinking about human nature in his *Theses on Feuerbach* of 1845, little more than pithy statements of his divergence from Feuerbach's "humanism," as Marx termed it. Thesis I claims that:

> The chief defect of all hitherto existing materialism . . . is that
> the thing, reality, sensuousness, is conceived only in the form
> of the object of contemplation, but not as sensuous human
> activity, practice, not subjectively.

In Thesis VI, he further claims that "the human essence is no abstraction inherent in each single individual. In its reality it is the ensemble of the social relations." Materialist philosophies in the past (and this includes the materialism of the French Enlightenment as well as that of Feuerbach) can only achieve, he says, "the contemplation of single individuals and of civil society." Finally, Thesis X asserts that "the standpoint of the old materialism is civil society; the standpoint of the new is human society, or social humanity."

As suggested above, Marx intended, from his earliest writings, to establish the vocabulary of classical economics on a metaphysical level, to employ its terminology to describe concepts traditionally the concern of metaphysicians, ethical philosophy, ontology, politics, and history, to use the vocabulary, in other words, in an all-embracing system of thought and to describe an inclusive theory of reality. The reality which he wished to contain was to be a mirror of what he wished to refute. He wished to answer Hegel thoroughly and completely, and accepted that Hegel's essential, essentialist, and holistic preoccupations were those he must properly address. Thus, even though his theories have been described on numerous occasions as a synthesis of Hegel and Feuerbach, they are both much more and much less than such a synthesis would contain.

For the moment, we should be content with the idea that Marx's view of human nature is not of man-within-society but of social man, not of man further and more greatly fulfilled in community but as capable of any kind of fulfillment, freedom, and true 'self' *only* in community. To further discuss the significance of the concept of alienation, even of "activity," it is necessary to discuss Marx's view of community in both ideal and real manifestations.

III

The terms *labor* and *production* have a more than merely economic inclusiveness when used by Marx. Or do they? Having expanded their signification, does he not then contract them to something like their meaning for Smith, Ricardo, and the other classical economists, albeit turning them against their former employers like weapons? His redefinition of these two terms is equivalent to his altered employment of Hegel's terms of *objectification* and *self-estrangement,* in an opposite sense. Marx contracted the capacity to signify of Hegel's means of describing alienation so as to conform to an economic and political theory and acquire precise meaning only within that empirical sphere, while he expanded the economists' vocabulary to metaphysical proportions. However, once we come to examine Marx's view of society, and therefore of human economic and political activity, we can discover that *production* and *labor* have a similar precision of application, such as is now the case with "alienation." There is a consistency at least of intent in this procedure.

In his review of *On the Jewish Question,* Marx remarks that "the perfected political state is by its nature the species-life of man in opposition to his material life." Given what has already been said regarding "species-life," there might seem little difference from Hegel's view of the state. However, it should be noticed that Marx does not oppose the spiritual to the material life, or the life of thought, but opposes species-life to all other categorizations. The expression of man's communal labor and production is his self-expression in its truest sense. It is on this that Marx erects his theory of alienation, which is confined to describing the divorce between man and the products of his labor caused especially and most completely by modern, capitalist society. Marx's definition of the human essence was designed very much with this 'inevitable' transposition or progression in mind. His dealing with Hegel and with Feuerbach in his early writings intentionally establishes a philosophical *ground* for his theories of political economy. He does not and will not separate or make distinct the various spheres of philosophical inquiry but rather subsumes them into a single system—so, communal man begins to appear to be wearing much the same clothing as 'economic man', as, a little later, species-being appears in the costume of the proletariat.

Indeed, what Marx would appear to be doing is making a distinct effort at systemization where no system, as yet, is being elucidated. It can be argued, not unfruitfully, that Marx's eventual system displays greater continuity of terminology than of ideas. Political economy is being fit to discuss all aspects and circumstances of human nature and the material world, not simply because the essence of human society is to be discovered in the economic means and relations of production in any given society but rather to describe a metaphysical interpretation of reality. However, any further discussion of this topic should be postponed until Marx's employment of and admiration for Hegelian dialectic can be considered.

For the moment, an examination of the section of the *Economic and Philosophical Manuscripts* which deals with "Alienated Labor" will reveal much of Marx's terminological method, together with the conjunction of his ideas on human nature and human society.

The theory of alienation and alienated labor as described by Marx is not difficult, focusing as it does on economic and social exploitation of one kind or degree or another. What is of greater significance is the retention by Marx of, if not the direct terminology then, the assumptions behind Hegel's language, his ideas. Therefore, it is necessary to remind ourselves of Hegel's terms, *Entaüsserung* and *Entfremdung*, objectification and self-estrangement. Marx is aware of both and employs both in his discussion of alienated labor. He employs the terminology to render an essentialist, holistic weight to the alienation of labor as *loss of self*, spiritual denudation.

Marx begins the section by observing that "we started from the presuppositions of political economy. We accepted its vocabulary and its laws . . . Using the very words of political economy we have demonstrated that the worker is degraded to the most miserable form of commodity; that the misery of the worker is in inverse proportion to the power and size of his production . . . and that finally the . . . whole of society must fall apart into the two classes of the property owners and the propertyless workers." Any counterargument would need to proceed on economic or social grounds, introducing empirical evidence, widening the area of discussion, et cetera. A philosophy would not be required to refute or qualify Marx's statement, hardly even a more empirical sociology, even though he is evidently making an observation about society as well as an economic system he detests.

A little later, he remarks that "the only wheels that political economy sets in motion are greed and war among the greedy, competition." Elements of psychology and implicit observations of human nature, but principally a notion of the social conditioning of human beings, are being presented. Again, we need have no resort (as is the case with much of Marx's greatest work, *Capital*—at least, Volume 1) to philosophical terminology or concepts.

Marx continues by then introducing the term alienation to describe the "monopoly and competition," "the separation of labor, capital and landed property," "private property," "selfishness," and "the value and degradation of man," and we may now begin to see the essentialist implications of the term itself. It is being made economically inclusive but retains its idealist or metaphysical dimension. To none of the ideas or economic 'facts' Marx has used need the term *alienation* necessarily be ascribed. He continues by claiming that "the depreciation of the human world progresses in direct proportion to the increase in value of the world of things. Labor does not only produce commodities, it produces itself and the laborer as a commodity." This idea is pursued in the statement: "The product of labor is labor that has solidified itself into an object, made itself into a thing, the objectification of labor. The realization of labor is its objectification." The juxtaposition of two sources of terminology, Hegel and the classical economists, is quite evident at this juncture, as is the method Marx employs not to confuse so much as conflate them into a single, systematic vocabulary. He continues: "In political economy, this realization of labor appears as a loss of reality for the worker, objectification as a loss of the object or slavery to it, and appropriation as alienation, as externalization." Thus, Marx has arrived at a satisfactorily inclusive idea of alienation through the exploitation of a capitalist economy practiced upon its workers, an alienation which depends for its universality of meaning upon the materialist reinterpretation of Hegel's idea of *Entaüsserung* as 'product' in an economic sense. The laborer is objectifying not merely his labor but his *self*, his "inner life," as Marx terms it a little later. As an analogy, he adapts Feuerbach's humanism regarding religion by observing that "the more man puts into God, the less he retains in himself." The employment of such an analogy is itself suggestive of the metaphysical purpose with which Marx approaches 'economics'.

Following these observations, Marx returns to his critique of the prevailing capitalist system of production, only to develop a second essential or metaphysical notion, that the "externalization of labor" results in "compulsory, forced labor," to the extent that we have *Entfremdung,* or self-estrangement in labor, the "relationship of the worker to his own activity as something that is alien and does not belong to him." It is, as Marx claims, "self-alienation." This is pursued in the distinction of a third kind of alienation, that which "turns his species-life into a means toward his individual life," which leads him eventually to conclude that "when alienated labor tears from man the object of his production, it also tears from him his species-life, the real objectivity of his species" and that this, in turn, has the "immediate consequence" of producing the "alienation of man from man," so that, in conclusion, "one man is alienated from another as each of them is alienated from the human essence."

The emphasis of Marx's ideas concerning alienation falls upon the second of Hegel's terms, that signifying *self-estrangement* (what we might most easily understand by the term alienation) rather than upon *objectification.* The introduction of the notion of the "human essence," however, with its inevitably metaphysical purpose, indicates that Marx's critique of contemporary capitalism not only strives to become sociology but aims at the status of philosophy. Elsewhere in his writings, Marx observes of Hegel that his summation of the traditions of philosophy requires that the task left to intellectual inquiry is to "realize" that philosophy in the world. This is perhaps the basis of his opposition to Hegel, not for the purpose of rejection but *application;* in other words, it is a dialectical opposition. But, in applying Hegelian idealism to the requisite degree requires a metaphysic rather than any form of empiricism.

Human beings, in Marx's theory, become alienated in the ways outlined above, and with the consequences illustrated. Alienation is, in economic terms, exploitation, the acquisition by the capitalist of the laborer's product, his externalization or realization of his labor and therefore of his species-life. Marx regards the laborer as remaining *free* only in his "animal functions of eating, drinking and procreating, at most also in his dwelling and dress." The only aspects of his life untouched by alienation are regarded as "animal." The problem with such a conclusion is that it uses the empirical circumstances of the industrial proletariat, regardless of their lack of education, and even of income, to a degree, as a model of human nature and capacities within a certain economic system; it uses the appalling circumstances of industrial life for the proletariat in the decades after the Industrial Revolution to describe the antithesis of the human essence. The spiritual consequences of an economic system are assumed to be universal and, later, to be irreversible and incapable of amelioration by political or social change.

Thus, in Marx's concept of alienated labor is invested the entire metaphysical cargo he inherited from Hegel and which he felt obligated to use.

Marx concludes this section of the *Economic and Philosophical Manuscripts* by extending the discussion to the subject of private property, beginning his observations by remarking that "just as he turns his production into his own loss of reality . . . so he creates the domination of the man who does not produce over the production and the product." The proletariat is regarded as in a sense creating the capitalist, rather than the other way around, since the capitalist does no more than appropriate the products of the worker. The progression of the argument is, of course, the progress of the *whole* argument, so that we are no longer dealing with a merely economic relationship, however distorted and vile, but with a spiritual relationship, a demonic partnership in which the essence of the laborer is possessed by the nonlaborer, as Marx terms him. "Private property is thus the product, result and necessary consequence of externalized labor, of the exterior relationship of the worker to nature and to himself." There is a pejorative use of the term "externalization" here, which has itself become a synonym for Hegel's objectification. If the essence of species-being is labor, and the product of labor is the means of objectifying that essence, then in the capitalist system there can only be the appropriation by *others* of that product and therefore that essence. But the whole edifice depends upon the conflation of the terms "externalization" and "objectification," to mean the same thing not only in economic but in moral or spiritual terms. Therefore, the materialist metaphysic *precedes* the analysis of the capitalist system, and always informs it, and the conclusions of the analysis are always referred back to the metaphysic which contains it. "Thus private property is the result of the analysis of the concept of externalized labor, i.e., externalized man, alienated work, alienated life, alienated man," Marx concludes, indicating precisely the necessity to use the term *externalization* rather than *objectification* so as to create the *object* that can be appropriated, an idea not even implicit in Hegel's notion of objectification. Further, the alienation that Hegel remarked as being a consequence of objectification is here the alienation of the divorce caused between man and his 'productions' by the intervention of an appropriating third party, the capitalist. The system imposes a method of production that is *intended* to alienate, to separate men from their 'products'. It is harsh but not necessarily incorrect to view Marx's whole conception of alienation as little more than an application of Hegel's idea of "alienated property," where property, in order to be given a relationship with its possessor, is infused with the "will" of that possessor. In this abstruse sense, Marx's idea of alienation is an almost exact parallel. The human essence—species-being rather than will—is somehow embodied in property or, for Marx, in product.

The bases of any economic system are, according to Marx, to be identified in the forces and the relations of production of a society. Periods of crisis occur when the forces of production far outrun or move beyond the relations of production. This is equivalent to those periods of crisis in the gradual objectification of mind in history posited by Hegel, and it is, Marx says, what happened to cause the breakdown of feudal society. Modern means of production emerged during the feudal period, changing the relations of production and bringing to the control of society a new class, those who controlled the new means of production—the bourgeoisie—who thus altered the relations of production to one of capitalist and wage-earning laborer. The process of objectification, in its narrow meaning of a period of historical crisis, or upheaval, always within a context of progress, becomes for Marx within this new, capitalist system a process of alienation, of self-estrangement. It was this application of Hegel's terminology that he regarded as essential to the 'metaphysic' of capitalist society. All societies in history are founded on domination of one kind or another, principally economic domination, but the distinction peculiar to capitalism is the limitlessness, as it appeared to Marx, of the means of production. And, as his section on "Alienated Labor" clearly confirms, he regarded this as a more hideous and more complete enslavement of man than had ever previously existed in history. His detestation for early capitalism's capacity to appropriate wealth through control of the means of production and its equivalent capacity to pauperize whole populations by those same means for the increasing wealth of the few can only be laudable, the demonstration of a greatness of spirit and a breadth of human sympathy evidenced by very few thinkers; but, the urge toward an essentialism inappropriate, or attached with the greatest difficulty and not a little tautology, to the sphere of political economy is an urge to produce the simplest, most universal models of human nature, behavior, and history.

There are two theories polarized within the capitalist system—a view of egoistic individuality that is Hobbesian or Hegelian and which itself is deterministic, and an interpretation of social mechanisms in terms of what has been described as base and superstructure. Marx, in identifying the controlling forces in any society, regarded all else as part of the superstructure erected upon the base of the economic system, the nature of the forces and relations of production. Politics, class, behavior, thought itself, all form part of the superstructure created from that base and erected to defend it. Essentialism produces determinism, in that sense, since a society's economic system dictates its culture and its attitudes to itself, and government is the means by which the controlling class retains control. Social change can only come from economic change and, because of the special nature of the capitalist system, it can probably only be changed by its violent overthrow and the imposition of a different, communist system. (At least, that was Marx's position in 1848.)

One may describe a theory as determinist if it disallows any capacity for choice, if the theory depends upon the inevitability of circumstances in its description of reality. Hegel's idea of history is determinist, and so is Marx's view of society, even in the sense that the revolution to overthrow capitalism must be a special kind of revolution, so as not merely to replace one ruling class with another. Society cannot be legislatively altered or improved, nor can this be achieved through altruism and a 'change of heart or mind', since human nature, within the economic system Marx is describing, is determined by that system. The essence of human nature, activity in the world rather than thought about the world, is at the mercy of the economic system which flourishes at any period of history or in any society. What Marx is saying of human nature is not that it is free, or even that it is conditioned by economic or social circumstances so that the *probability* may be posited of predetermined attitudes and actions, but that it is imprisoned by the economic system and may only change when and if the system itself changes. Capitalism's deterministic influence in shaping human nature is thoroughly evil, creating archetypal exploiters and exploited *and no other human capacities or attitudes.*

It is, of course, possible to ignore much of the above when reading *Capital*, Volume 1, and it is also true that Marx did not publish many of his early works in any other form than as newspaper articles—many of them were not published before 1931. It is, however, the case that many of the attitudes we find expressed for the first time in these early writings form part of the structure of assumptions which *Capital* displays, and it is for that reason that we should clearly understand exactly what 'philosophic' assumptions Marx retained in maturity. To that extent, the concept of alienated labor might be regarded as having a more profound influence upon his mature work than the theory of surplus value itself.

But, if Marx is such a determinist, if absolute control of the intellectual life of a society is demonstrated by the acceptance of the prevailing economic system, then how can Marx posit any kind of optimistic change in society—unless the means of production once more outstrip the relations of production, causing another crisis? How can there be any such occurrence as a *political* revolution?

IV

"We can easily see how necessary it is that the whole revolutionary movement should find not so much its empirical as its theoretical basis in the development of private property and particularly the economic system." This is Marx's claim in that section of the *Economic and Philosophical Manuscripts* bearing the title "Private Property and Communism." We would do well to bear in mind at this point Proudhon's infamous dictum that "property is theft," since it is certain that Marx did so. In this section, he dismisses, in fact, the kind of communism we might associate with the redistribution of property and that which attempts to remove the apparatus of the state, in favor of his own definition, which embraces the above but expands upon it in a manner metaphysically consistent with his observations on alienation. He claims this third kind of communism as "the positive abolition of private property and thus of human self-alienation and therefore the real appropriation of the human essence by and for man. This is communism as the complete and conscious return of man conserving all the riches of previous development for man himself as a social, i.e., human, being."

The term *property,* especially in its 'private' form, is crucial to this section and any discussion of it. Unlike the remark of Proudhon quoted above, Marx's view of property appears to be that of *appropriation* rather than theft—but only because property consists of the products of other men, the objectification or externalization of their essence. It might be objected that there is no necessity for Marx to go beyond Proudhon in defense of some kind of communist system, but that would predicate Marx as concerned with a political solution to the problem of capitalism, as Proudhon was, and Marx was uninterested in any legislative or political changes, since as such they would not accord with his identification of the *basis* of society, the economic mechanism. Hence, property becomes the possession of the essence of others, their expression of themselves from which they have been alienated by the relations of production. Marx describes property as the "material, sensuous expression of man's alienated life. Its movement of production and consumption is the sensuous revelation of all previous production, i.e., the reality of man." Few claims could be as essentialist as that, but the important point is to notice how private property has now become the *essence* of the economic system, synonymous with the forces and relations of production themselves. It is also based upon the simple and illusory model of no more than *two* distinct social classes, their division regarded at its most profound as being between propertied and propertyless. Only in this way can property be regarded as synonymous with the "appropriation of human life." On the one hand is great property and on the other absolutely no property—only by such a degree of distinction can the term property become the *absolute* that Marx requires rather than subject to at least some degree of relativism.

Property is, of course, the next of Marx's terms to receive the operation that has already been undergone by *production* and *labor,* the impregnation of vocabulary by the Holy Spirit of metaphysics. "Religion," says Marx, "family, state, law, morality, science and art are only particular forms of production and fall under its general law" (i.e., the law of appropriation from one by another human being, by one class from another). The products of what we might denote as culture or even civilization can indeed be appropriated—they are properties like books, paintings, china, furniture, even ideas, though they do not, in the case of ideas, faiths, and theories necessarily cease to belong to the producer; but they are not necessarily externalizations of the human essence which can then be appropriated in an act of theft to the detriment of the spiritual and emotional life of the producer. In "Private Property and Communism," however, Marx makes the following claim: "Thus all physical and intellectual senses have been replaced by the simple alienation of all these senses, the sense of having."

Possession is presented as a metaphysical condition or mode of being, an ontological proposition. Possession does not merely subordinate the five senses and whatever inner satisfaction one receives through them, but it *replaces* them, whereas to most of us it is evident that the sense of possession *derives from the other senses* which apprehend the object possessed. To relate the empirical apprehension of the world by means of the senses directly with the sensation of possessing apprehensible objects (and, more ridiculously, ideas, art, law, et cetera) is an assertion that is characteristic of Marx, to make a 'simple' word and its inherent 'simple' idea or signification as inclusive and universal in application as possible, so that, synonymously, it represents far more than its assumed capacity. In the case of possession, he has invested the idea with sensuous, active reality so that it *is* a human sense rather than a mental or emotional sensation prompted by sense experience.

In discussing "Money," another short section of the *Manuscripts*, Marx describes it as "the bond of all bonds" and therefore, by the dialectic of opposition which Marx consistently employs, the "negation of the negation." As he describes it, money automatically becomes the "universal means of separation." The Bible ascribed evil to the love of money rather than to the substance itself, but Marx makes no such error—money itself *operates* and functions, "changing fidelity into infidelity, love into hate, hate into love, virtue into vice, vice into virtue . . ." Thus, as is evident in much of Hegel's system, the *thing* possesses a sentient quality that operates in the world and is a value rather than a fact, possessing elements of subjectivity rather than remaining an object.

Together with this tendency of thought, it is evident in the discussion of private property that Marx is unprepared to allow any gradations of possession or wealth, since property as appropriation must be total and entirely alienating in order that the 'spiritual' effects are to be as dire as Marx claims. The idea of private property is divisible into total possession by a few and total lack of possession by the many. The idea is then further expanded, if only by implication, to become generic, to represent material reality, the world, which must therefore be *possessed in common*. Any degree of private property is the appropriation of someone else's essence, his expression in the world of his inner self. Man's externalization of himself in the state, in laws, in social institutions of any and every kind allows possession by others, allows the appropriation of self, the rendering of all forms of society as just another kind of property which can be appropriated and possessed by the few, the bourgeois capitalists. This is the final stage of the pregnancy of the term *property*, just as inclusive and universal, and just as distorted, as the term *production* and the idea of *labor*.

The model of political society that Marx offers in these early writings and in his 'empirical' work, *Capital*, is one which rejects all forms of the state and all social and political institutions, particularly those exhibited by contemporary reality but also those demonstrated in history. All societies and all political systems, even theoretical communism in its past or contemporary manifestations, are utterly rejected. "The history of all hitherto existing society is the history of class struggles." Therefore, all forms of political society embody and support such struggles and must be swept away.

Because human nature is instinctive and sensual, as opposed to essentially reflective or rational, human nature itself lacks the capacity to change *without* the changing of society, which unavoidably imposes its pattern upon human nature. The social and psychological stereotype or model that Marx establishes allows no capacity for, or possibility of, divergence from that model. Whereas Hegel distinguished the man of "civil society" as merely one *aspect*, albeit a lesser one, of human nature, Marx the sociologist is a more thorough determinist. And that view of human nature, and his ideas of political society and of the ideal community of the future, derive from his view of the *total negativity* of his contemporary reality. This is the purpose of the dialectic and the essential concept of the negation of the negation, which will be discussed more fully in another section. However, it must be remarked here that, for Marx, capitalist society represents the utter negative, and the negation of that negative is communism, the complete and entire opposite of contemporary reality. In this, of course, he entirely opposes Hegel's view of the "rational State," which is inevitably, according to his dialectic of history, the "best of all possible worlds."

Marx reduces human capacity and potential to a few simple generalizations, to socially determined stereotyping without the possibility of amelioration, while the economic and social system is reduced to similarly simple 'first principles'. He then proceeds to analyze both the contemporary and human history on the assumption of the 'fact' that the utter *negation* is unqualifiedly represented in his analysis. From this assumption, he proceeds to outline the "negation of the negation," the only alternative to this sordid, choking, vile social reality. But how, exactly, does he intend that such essential change occurs? Who is to abolish private property and how is this to be achieved?

V

"Communism is for us not a state of affairs which is to be established, an ideal to which reality will have to adjust itself. We call communism the real movement which abolishes the present state of things. The conditions of this movement result from the premisses now in existence." Thus stated Marx and Engels in *The*

German Ideology of 1845, which was written "to settle accounts with our former philosophical views." In many ways it is a summation of the early writings as well as a progression of theory. Much of its content deserves discussion in relation to Marx's view of history, but for the moment it can be assumed to confirm the assertions regarding communism, in Marx's particular version of that ideology, already presented in the *Manuscripts* and *The Holy Family* of 1844. Communism, the "negation of the negation," is the system without system to replace capitalism. The manner in which this is to be achieved and the forces that will realize it are outlined in some detail in Marx's earlier *Critique of Hegel's Philosophy of Right* (1844).

The means of change must be radical, violent revolution, as implied by the implacability of Marx toward contemporary society and by the description of historical revolutions as "partial" or class-inspired and class-benefiting, particularly that of 1789, which Marx correctly analyzes as a bourgeois revolution against the remnants of feudalism in French society and the economic system. The universality of the Declaration of the Rights of Man accompanying that revolution is, of course, merely part of the superstructure erected by the bourgeoisie to justify the economic and social system imposed by them. To change the system entirely requires a different kind of revolution, because a "purely political revolution" achieves nothing more than that "a part of civil society emancipates itself and attains to universal domination." Instead, "one class [must] stand for the whole of society, the deficiency of all society must inversely be concentrated in another class," and this class must be "a class that arouses universal scandal and incorporates all limitations; a particular social sphere must be regarded as the notorious crime of the whole society, so that the liberation of this sphere appears as universal self-liberation." What is occurring in this argument is by now familiar, a preparation of opposites which creates not only an obedience to the dialectic but also a revolutionary force that can 'universalize' the future revolution. This class must possess "radical chains" and be "a class in civil society that is not a class of civil society, of a social group that is the dissolution of all social groups, of a sphere that has a universal character because of its universal sufferings . . . This dissolution of society, as a particular class, is the proletariat."

Marx has previously identified class interest and the deterministic and inescapable force of class loyalty, and therefore defines the proletariat as a "class which is not a class" within civil society but excluded from it. Only by this means can the proletariat universalize the revolution that is to come and install a system which is not a system—communism. The dialectic requires such an absolute negation of the negation rather than that the pressure of empirical evidence supply such a conclusion regarding the proletariat. However, within the structure of the argument, regardless of its empirical basis, Marx claims that communism "differs from all previous movements in that it overturns the basis of all earlier relations of production and intercourse," which is the only resolution of capitalist society. This revolution will do away "with labor, and abolish the rule of all classes with the classes themselves, because it is carried through by a class which no longer counts as a class in society . . ." And the method of change must be revolution, he continues.

To rehearse the arguments relating to the circumstances which must prevail before the revolution can succeed, such as the increasing polarization of society into two classes, the increasing "pauperization" of the proletariat, the role of philosophers and radical thinkers, et cetera, is to reiterate familiar maxims. The revolution is inevitable . . . except when Marx assumes that by revolution one may also mean nonviolent radical change when the inherent contradictions of the capitalist system cause its final collapse from within, allowing a communist society to emerge. That, too, is familiar territory.

The mature Marx vacillated between the two solutions, never entirely abandoning either in favor of the other. If the course of history must be radically interrupted and diverted, revolution seems to be the only solution; if not, we may then suspect the influence of Engels (especially on volumes 2 and 3 of *Capital*, which he edited and collated), who actually coined the phrase "the withering away of the state." More, one concludes that revolution is merely an interim period, the break with history, the negation of the negation that is social and economic history, and that the resulting, but not necessarily immediate, communist society that succeeds capitalism must therefore be the final *synthesis*, belonging to history (i.e., the future) rather than to what Marx called "pre-history," the past and present. His empirical analysis of capitalist society, which he had not seriously begun before 1849 and the beginning of his exile in England, may employ most if not all of the dialectic assumptions we have already examined, but it produced in addition a theory of inherent and self-destructive contradictions in the capitalist economy which would serve the purpose, eventually, of the proletarian revolution, in effect replacing it. Whichever is the precise explanation for Marx's recurring hesitancy toward active, violent revolution after the failures of 1848, there is an inevitability concerning the sweeping away of capitalism and the ending of class struggle which he never abandoned. His certainties remain intact after 1848, as do his assumptions concerning society, human nature, and, most significantly, human history.

Hegel was a great philosopher of history and a historian of philosophy. The interpretation of history is the essence of his philosophy and the basis for his determinism, optimistic as that might be described. For Marx, too, history has a purposive, explicable meaning. For him, as for Hegel, it is the objectification of human nature, the expression of the abiding metaphysical realities of the human condition. But, it is a materialist view of history and, as such, is deliberately and consistently opposed—in dialectical terms—to Hegel's interpretation of the past.

VI

It is not history that presupposes a model of itself, but rather Hegel's interpretation of history provides Marx with a dialectical model. History is established by Hegel as purposive, as displaying a certain and inexorable progression, with the qualification that history operates spirally, in that it is cyclic in its return to a past set of circumstances; but it improves upon those circumstances, indicating progress beyond the past. Marx accepted the implications of the dialectic. For him, history was not random, eccentric, fortunate, but purposive; but nor was it cyclic, as the medieval image of history was represented, the return of a wheel-like motion to its original starting point, nor even spiral in its movement, because Marx extracted from the dialectic the notion of crisis, and from this nub extrapolated both back into the past and forward into the future, which Hegel claimed could not be predicted.

Marx's view of history is regressive. History develops and, in the medieval pattern, repeats itself endlessly, the repetition disguised in new forms but always exemplifying the basic characteristics distilled in the maxim of "history as the history of class struggles." Perhaps, though, we would be more equipped to understand Marx's view of history if we supposed *antagonism* as a suitably accurate translation of "struggle"—class oppositions and antagonisms being the essence of history for Marx. This in itself is a form of progress, though as has been indicated, Marx termed it generically "pre-history," indicating its endless similarity from epoch to epoch. However, it is important to realize what exactly he understood by, and extracted from, the Hegelian dialectic of history.

Hegel's was a history of the "progress of Mind through the world," an Idealist history. The measure of history was, for Hegel, the exemplification of thought, the objectification of the products of Mind. Thus, for example, the Greek city-state holds a special place of honor in his pantheon, the *polis* of Athenian voters and decision makers being the exemplification in civil society of the same degree of progress of Mind that displayed itself in the unmatched artifacts and products of the Greek artistic imagination. History is always, hopefully, returning to that point, though with the increased elevation implied by the metaphor of the spiral. In Marx, opposing his materialism as completely as possible to the idealism of Hegel, but by the same methodology, history is the demonstration of the objectification of man's essence, which is not Mind (as part of the universal Mind), but which is active, sensuous, and expressed in labor. The measure of history, for Marx, therefore becomes not *the degree of objectification*, which it might have become in materialist terms, but *the degree to which such examples of objectification are appropriated* by those who control the historical circumstances. To arrive at this derivation of the dialectic, Marx considered not Hegel's triadic notion of thesis, antithesis, and synthesis in history, giving the spiral movement or progress, but instead Hegel's idea of history's "moments of crisis."

For Hegel, Mind is always attempting to objectify itself in the social, political, and artistic circumstances of any society and is doing so progressively, eventually to arrive at a complete objectification of Mind in the world and therefore in history. However, objectification is itself a cause of detachment or "alienation" *(Entaüsserung* resulting in *Entfremdung)* between Mind and the objects it has embodied itself within. This is the cause of what Hegel termed the "unhappy consciousness," his idea of alienation being the realization in men that they are divorced from their objects. But this realization is itself a progress, and men (and the universal Mind) progress by this process, accepting the objectivity through realization and moving toward renewal, change, and the eventual repetition of the process of alienation.

Marx extracted from Hegel's dialectic of history the essence that seemed to him encapsulated in Hegel's idealism, that all societies represent more or less adequate representations of *something,* and that the change from one kind of society to another is apparent through crisis (i.e., Marx extracted the *dynamic* of the dialectic rather than its implicit *pattern*). Therefore, he attempted to identify the essentials of various historical societies, beginning with the one he could examine firsthand, the capitalist economy. In tracing its development, he discovered the relationship between the forces and relations of production and the changes produced by the engine of the forces of production. Modern capitalism developed the forces of production for itself during the feudal epoch and, in eventually throwing over those feudal relations of production, it emerged from its chrysalis in its adult form. However, in France, the moment of crisis was a revolution—the moment of change is, therefore, one of crisis, as Hegel suggested, but in a very *material* sense. Marx then extrapolated historically upon this simple pattern and the notion of rigidly class-divided societies that it engendered—relations of production necessarily implies primary producers and those who instruct or control.

Armed with these first principles, Marx was able to identify various stages of development of society—the Asiatic, which is not really Western at all but which was required to explain the dialectic as Marx envisaged it in truly universal terms, whereby the means of production are totally owned by the state; the ancient world which is based upon a slave economy (the relation of production); the feudal, which has as its basis lord and serf; and the modern or capitalist, which has the antagonistic relationship of the bourgeois and the wage-earning laborer. Essentially, these were the only distinctions between historical epochs and societies. As to the forces of production, the means of producing, these receive relatively little mention in Marx's analysis of past societies. Only with capitalism do the forces of production produce a moment of crisis unparalleled in history. The forces of production finally galvanize and alter themselves and society beyond previous imagination during the Industrial Revolution, creating two entirely new classes, the bourgeois and the proletariat, entirely alone in society and entirely antagonistic, the thesis and antithesis of modern society that will eventually produce the synthesis of communism. Since the wheel, the factory is the most galvanic force in industrial production and Marx may well be accurate in identifying the basis of an economy in its forces and relations of production—but he cannot casually and causally extrapolate that essence backward except by ignoring or minimizing the role of the forces of production and concentrating almost exclusively on the relations of production, which in reality means the class system typical of any past society.

Marx emerges with his own materialist dialectic of history, which in essence means that history displays a pattern of repetitions *whatever* forces of production apply within its economic life, until there is some galvanic change in those forces of production. This, in turn, leads to the contemporary exaggeration of the relations of production into a polarization of two classes, ever more antagonistic—to result either in collapse or revolution and the eventual emergence of Marx's version of communistic society, classless and laborless. Marx's view of history, therefore, may be regarded as regressive, except that 'change' does not imply 'worse' until the forces of production change as radically as they did in the Industrial Revolution. But the crisis of the present will worsen until it is resolved, violently or otherwise.

This materialist version of the dialectic of history does not depend upon the spiral movement of history. Rather, it depends upon identifying the antagonisms in historical societies (thesis and antithesis) and regarding all history, including the present, as "pre-history" and the future as synthesis of the antagonisms of history, in a nonantagonistic society, communistic and 'free'. The materialist dialectic, too, accepts the notion of objectification but employs it to describe the attributes of a society as objects which can be appropriated, become the property of the governing or controlling class. The notion of alienation by which Hegel signifies the disjointedness of men and their institutions at certain stages of historical development, however dramatic in certain ages and societies, becomes for Marx a description of spiritual denial or exclusion. Societies in history are structured upon those who work (e.g., the pyramids built by slaves and captives for the glory of dead Pharaohs). Those who work are inevitably and inexorably exploited by those who govern and own. This is true of history in its entirety. The necessity to produce a materialist metaphysic that would provide an equivalent to, or active partner of, Hegel's summation of intellectual history requires a similar kind of essentialism, one which is at the same time determinist and pessimistic. Men cannot alter their circumstances except by creating an entirely different form of society, one that history gives us no evidence of. Therefore, there must be a complete break with history. History has no synthesis of its dialectic in the Hegelian and triadic sense, except for the inevitable future. To and including the present, it displays only the antagonism of thesis and antithesis 'objectified' in terms of class antagonisms.

The synthesis of "pre-history" and its antagonisms lies in the future and its nonantagonistic, communist community. The interpretation of the past is achieved by the extrapolation of first principles derived from contemporary circumstances and the consequent identification of entirely similar antagonisms and class struggles, of exploitation, property, and "alienation" in each and every past culture. Once the essentialist doctrine of base and superstructure demanded by imitation of Hegel's idealistic interpretation of history—that is, the identification of the essence (base) that is displayed by all history, or is the movement of all history—is established and adhered to, as it was by Marx, then the *materialist essence* must lie in activity, in the economic pattern of a society, *and* all the significant elements of a culture or society identified and valued by Hegelian idealism must be relegated to the role of superstructure, to the *non*essential, if Marx is to counter it not only effectively but entirely.

What emerges from Marx's view of history, in regard to any examination of the history of ideas of political society, is the overwhelming powerlessness of human beings confronted by the essential mechanisms of society. The inability of political activity and of the polity to change or even to ameliorate the social and economic conditions of a society in any meaningful way is not only depressing but counter to the assumptions of the majority of political philosophers. Hegel, of course, saw no need to intervene—the progress of mind in an optimistic evolution through history was unquestionable. Therefore, the "rational State," authoritarian and hierarchical as it might be, strict and demanding obedience, was what ought to be expected and rejoiced in. For Marx, given the total pessimism with which he regarded capitalist society, there is no optimism in the deterministic forces of history and society. There is no hope beyond the circumscription of evolution or revolution, for, either after the revolutionary crisis of capitalism or following its collapse from within, the elements of the superstructure embodied in any and all conceptions of the state, the forces of alienation and appropriation themselves, disappear, to be succeeded by an idealistically communist society. Along with everything else, of course, the bourgeoisie will disappear. It is important to remark that Marx consciously uses the term *bourgeois* in its traditional sense, deriving from the idea of burgher or local governor, and by so doing conflates the idea of government and authority with the economic system the 'burghers' might be said to evince, capitalism.

Marx's conception of the dialectic, therefore, is quite deliberately opposed to that of Hegel. It is, in its original form, an analysis of history and of the present, but for Marx, while the whole of human history is proof of the dialectic, his examination of history is cursory when it ranges beyond the capitalist 'moment'. That this is the case may be demonstrated by Marx's significant use of the Hegelian term, the "negation of the negation," which in simpler language describes the antithesis as the negative and the final synthesis as the negation of the antithesis. In Hegel's view of history, the thesis may be equated with the Greek *polis*, the antithesis as individuality without a sense of the communal-universal, and the synthesis as the modern state. For Marx to have a thesis is to employ a cloudy Arcadianism rather than a historical actuality, to which not history but only the 'present' of capitalism acts as antithesis. It is the capitalist system that fully and really obeys the dialectic. The relationship between the forces and relations of production demonstrates the *profound* sense of opposition (thesis and antithesis) that is the basis of dialectic. The present is, for Marx, the most and *only* critical and crisis-ridden moment of history; the relations of production have diverged from the forces of production to the extent that the forces of production have become *owned* rather than merely controlled by the 'superstructure' of society; they have been entirely appropriated. It is here, as proof of the dialectic, that Marx's central theory of surplus value is most significant, as the empirical proof of the materialist conception of history.

The theory of surplus value is the *only* theory that Marx could possibly have arrived at. His employment of the dialectic in direct opposition to Hegel and his sense of horror at the villainies of early capitalism determine his economic analysis of society. Surplus value is the *exploitative* fact of political society, the demonstration of appropriation and therefore of alienation. It is not an inductive conclusion, it is deductive, argued from the first principles of Marx's conception of human nature. It is used not to describe the way workers may be treated by their employers under capitalism, nor even to demonstrate moral opprobrium at the degree of exploitation, but to prove that capitalism is basically a system which alienates labor. It is a *moral* agent, its effects spiritual and emotional. What Engels hailed as Marx's "great discovery" is, in essence, the outcome not of his economic studies but of his philosophical background, antecedents, and materialist stance. This, of course, creates the difficulty of the theory in economic terms, since Marx would not ascribe to the machine the capacity to produce this surplus value, only to the human worker. The essence of the discovery was that it was alienating and appropriative in *human* terms.

In the pattern and determination of the dialectic, therefore, Marx espouses as synthesis the simpler form of the "negation of the negation" (i.e., the future, and the emergence of a communist society) rather than Hegel's attempt to combine cyclical and evolutionary concepts in the spiral of history. Marx chooses the simple idea of the opposite. Thus his examination of the remoter eras of "pre-history" is perfunctory, to say the least. The past is simply a latent form of the present, and only the future offers distinct change. The capitalist present is the 'highest' expression of the negation; complete and utter transformation of the economic foundations of society alone will provide the 'positive', the "negation of the negation." Other than that, the past may be described as the regressive progress of the negative to its fulfillment in the capitalist system as the utter negation.

VII

Marx did not intend to create a science of society, rather a science of political economy. But suitably bearded in the patriarchal tradition, it was he who descended from the mountain with the circumstances of sociology inscribed upon tablets of stone. His influence was sufficiently enormous for him to be regarded as the preeminent founding father of the science of society. Even the generic term *sociology* is older than Marx, deriving, as does the infant science, from Comte and the other Positivists and from Saint-Simon, who had a more than passing effect upon the young Marx. Nevertheless, both of those eminent French social philosophers and the two figures who are discussed in another essay are of relatively minor importance beside Marx, their influence patchy or now disregarded. Which facts make it all the more important to understand that the science of society was, to a remarkable extent, *defined* by Marx, and that it was he who infused it with its spirit. What, precisely, then, did he do?

From the outset, Marx reemphasized and legitimized what Comte and others had already indicated, that any science of society that aspired to lay claim to scientific validity would be prescriptive rather than descriptive (i.e., what is now fashionably referred to as social engineering was one, if not the primary, function of sociology), which means that it would be, at least in part, an ideological discipline. Being deductive in its reasoning and conclusions, it imitated the natural sciences of the period in which it developed, but that imitation is itself partial. Marx (and therefore sociology) assumed the empirical validity of a method based upon a materialist first-principles or even *a priori* approach simply because its *subject* was empirical, the *facts* of society contemporary with the examiner or comprehensible through the study of history. We have already referred to the analogous spirit of metaphysicians as they sought to examine political society, but it is necessary to recognize that this is also the method of sociology, from its beginnings. The imitation of scientific method was de rigeur to the pretensions of the new science—but a more pervasive imitation was that of philosophy itself, especially metaphysics, as we have seen with Marx.

What Marx also established, beyond refutation, was the idea that sociology was to be, or to become, a moral instrument, with due and equal weight given to both terms. Therefore, it would be prescriptive, systematic, in the proper sense of describing systems or 'model patterns', and in Marx's case essentialist and metaphysical, even beyond the merely ethical, if we regard ethics as an empirical branch of philosophy and someway akin to a moral psychology—though ethics is, self-evidently, also prescriptive. The 'morality' of sociology, however, from its very beginnings, is of the essentialist, holistic variety, that which has no scent of relativism about it.

Further, Marx and subsequent sociology, reconfirmed in this misguided belief by the work of Durkheim, Weber, and many others toward the end of the last century and in this, regarded history as purposive. Saint-Simonians and Comtians did so, too. Not only is history explicable but history also explains the present. And given the vastness of the subject, the holistic approach to explaining *all* history by means of simple, essential principles is irresistible. Determinism lurks at this door, and Marx all but succumbs. His solution, complete and radical change in society, whether or not violent, has become a reflex of sociology rather than a subject for reflection. This obsessive adoration of the "negation of the negation" may even be considered as Marx's most dangerous and abiding legacy to our century—the conceit that *only* the most radical and/or violent alteration of society can produce progress or change that may be regarded as 'good'.

To misapply Kant's description of metaphysics as the "queen

of the sciences" to sociology (which status it has been largely granted in our century and our educational establishments, to the great detriment of political theory—or even empirical social thought), preeminence stems directly from the work and influence of Marx. And we may clearly see that, in Marx's theories, what has been assumed to be most empirical is, indeed, a metaphysic, albeit couched in terms of materialism, which should *not* be mistaken for empiricism.

In the work of Marx's two most distinguished successors in this science of society in the nineteenth century, Durkheim and Weber, whose work is generally conceded not to have been surpassed in our own century, we may encounter nothing that appears akin to either metaphysics or materialism. However, what we shall meet is the rump of Marx's theories—a disillusionment with capitalist society persists, paralyzingly. There is the halfhearted and often uncritical usage of such significant ideas as alienation and exploitation; there is the promulgation of the collectivity over the claims of the individuals composing a society, and, most disturbingly, there is that Hobbesian cynicism with regard to human nature that permeates Marx's writing when it is not concerned with idealizing the proletariat and exploiting it for the purposes of argument! Sociology was bequeathed pessimism, together with so much else, by Marx. But, primarily a spurious legitimacy of empiricism was given to sociology by Marx's successors, and that, at least, should be dispelled.

THE CHARISMATIC
COLLECTIVE: A SCIENCE
OF SOCIETY IN PLACE OF
POLITICAL THEORY

THE MAIN CURRENT of European philosophy may well have been, during the late eighteenth century, turning away from rationalism toward various manifestations of idealism and the influence of the Romantic movement in Germany; nevertheless, this new direction was by no means apparent before the advent of the works of Hegel in Germany and Comte in France. Before 1789, 'Romantics' such as Rousseau had been pressed to the service of both the Revolution and of French materialism, not least because they exhibited a preponderantly individualist framework of value judgments. Such a basis for philosophical speculation became impossible in the aftermath of the Terror and its succeeding Empire, and though the strands of nineteenth-century thought are many and various, they may be commonly distinguished as exhibiting a flight from reason as from a ruined citadel, put to the torch by the nation under arms galvanized by the Revolution and Bonaparte. To arrive at the theories and attitudes of Bergson, Nietzsche, and Freud and the music of Mahler and Strauss at the end of the century which began with Beethoven, the French Revolution, and materialism is to have made a great journey, and it would be convenient to discover on some intellectual map that the journey had been accomplished along one broad motorway rather than having been complex, difficult, and with many changes of direction and many minor roads. For our purposes, there *is* a motorway, if we consider only those elements of nineteenth-century thought which lead from Hegel to Durkheim and Weber.

That there is a Continental origin to the science of society is undeniable, but it ought also to be recognized that the abiding influence of that origin and its weight upon the discipline remained undisturbed during the course of the first hundred years of sociological inquiry. To understand the science must be to understand whereof it derived its basic tenets, validity, and methodology; but, to do so, a return must be made in this most empirical of human sciences to idealism and also to a consideration of the divide that exists between Saint-Simon, for example, and Hegel, and then and only then to Durkheim and Weber, via Marx, even if, finally, we must conclude that Marx's influence outweighed all others. What must be posited regarding sociology, and thus much of our own century's most influential thinking about politics, man, and society, is the kind of speculative environment in which it emerged as a distinct discipline. In doing so, we shall be forced to conclude that the most influential thinkers had abandoned, almost with cries of horror in Hegel's case, both individualism and the primacy of reason that are inseparable elements of natural law theory, *before* anything recognizable as a forerunner of modern sociology appears. Neither rationalism nor what may be termed 'liberalism' had reestablished itself before the fledgling social science had become inordinately influential. Indeed, English liberalism may be said to have welcomed the new science like a long-lost relative, speciously vouched for but whose credentials they omitted to inspect closely. Witness Herbert Spencer, whose optimism with regard to capitalism's capacity to evolve and ameliorate its own villainies rendered him disregarded by twentieth-century sociologists respectful of a Marxist tradition. The influence of this decidedly Continental upstart upon English and then American political theory demonstrates that the native empirical tradition of both cultures was incapable of resisting the superficial scientism and pseudo-empiricism of sociology. Marx, Durkheim, and Weber became the founding fathers not simply of German and French social thinking but of Western sociology; hence the fact that so much thinking about political society in the present century has been prescriptive, doctrinaire, idealist in the philosophical sense, and concerned with social engineering of a radical and inclusive kind. That aspect of social thought in Marx has already been discussed, but it remains to identify the same or similar tendencies in the thought of his two most significant sociological successors. Can they, too, be identified as 'metaphysicians', or do they offer a variant strain of thought? Is their framework determined, like the limits of a cage, by Marx, or do they present an alternative school of thought, as Max Weber supposed he did?

It has been claimed that much modern political thought, with its origins in the metaphysical or Platonic tradition, is distinctly illiberal in tendency, that it demonstrates a gravitational attraction toward a concern with the governance of society and the nature and role of the governors rather than a concern with the members of any governed society. In that, it is the distinct opposite of Locke's insistence upon limited government by the consent of the governed and the protection of the rights and freedoms of each member of the commonality or "commonwealth"—if necessary even from the illiberality of the governors. Much illiberal political ideology arises from collective theories of society or the state, from *identification* and *identity* (their conflation into a single sense of individual identity *through*, and only through, membership of the collective). Marx insisted on not only the primacy of the collectivity but a model of human nature which is imposed or cultivated by 'education' in the broadest sense of that term. He recognized that the role he and other like-minded intellectuals might play in his communistic society would be that of educators, a remarkably Platonic assumption. Empirical inquiry would disown such models and work inductively from the temporal evidence of human nature, assuming only its capacity to be 'better' or 'bettered' when encountering what Marx calls alienated man, those denuded and exploited victims of a social system. Empiricism would assume that social conditions must be changed—by legislation, suffrage, the enforceable recognition of equivalence among all individuals—while the metaphysical tradition of political thought would offer a model of social organization and an inculcated model of human behavior. Which tradition did Durkheim and Weber adhere to?

Briefly, they inherited a tradition of philosophy which had no gravitational attraction toward the idea of individuality. The science of society and its emerging methodology had been conditioned by both French materialism and German idealism—both either already being or exhibiting a strong attraction toward metaphysics; idealism is a manifestation of metaphysics at a certain period of history in a certain culture, that of prenational Germany, while French materialism was *not* the legitimate child of English empiricism, rather that child educated in a foreign tradition, that of French rationalism since Descartes. The claim that sociology implicity makes, of course, is to be an empirical sphere of inquiry employing the 'scientific' method of inductive rather than deductive reasoning.

However, it will be seen quite clearly in the case of Durkheim that we are dealing with that analogous employment of science either as paradigm or imitated methodology, conventionally *deductive* in its apparatus and reasoning. Sociology, at least in the case of Durkheim, develops a paraphrase of scientific method and accuracy, and in Durkheim's case the paradigmatic science was not physics, chemistry, or the *material sciences* that so affected French thinking but biology in its Darwinian manifestation. To anticipate a later section of this essay, Durkheim responded to society as to an *organism*, and assumed that society was as capable as an animal or other living organism of supplying evidence of *laws* governing its nature and behavior as well as demonstrating the principle of evolution anticipated by his predecessors and major influences, Comte and Saint-Simon. These discovered and elucidated laws would be as scientifically and universally valid, temporally and spatially, as were Darwin's conclusions concerning plants, animals, and the human body.

As such, Durkheim's methodology and assumptions differ widely but indistinctly from those of Marx. The object of both thinkers is to arrive at essential and underlying reality, at an understanding of social *laws*, the 'hidden government' of society and therefore of man within society. However, as with Marx and Hegel, there is again that tendency to assume that society is somehow sentient, humanlike or mindlike in its internal or underlying governance.

The resulting philosophy or 'atmosphere' of sociological inquiry in the nineteenth century, and in our own time, makes that quite crucial and irrefutable assumption of the greater *significance* of the collective over its individual members, not merely for the purposes of studying society but in regard to the nature of the membership of any society. Further, the 'essence'—for that is what is sought and defined—of individuality comes to be regarded as the harmonious dependence of the individual upon the collective. The degree and success of an individual's social conditioning is the measure of his individuality and his only *real* freedom. One need not bring to mind Orwell's nightmare, *1984*, here. A more proper analogy is with Plato's ideal republic and the Platonic tradition of political thought.

It may be observed here that liberalism as understood in its descent from Locke's political theory, and only partially as exhibited by Mill and the successors of Bentham, supporters or opponents alike, is nonhistorical, or perhaps ahistorical. Its values as derived from Stoicism are universal in their applicability, but they are neither conditioned nor compromised by historical circumstances or by an examination of history. Sociology, as a discipline, emerges after the discovery of *history as a purposive influence*, as a continuum, and its acknowledgment of history and concern with the influential past are significant. It is also determinist. This determinism is twofold, in that it emphasizes the weight of the collective against any gradualism which seems anodyne in a democratic society (the assumption that change can be made, that 'tinkering' with the mechanics of legislation and fiscal management and the rights and liberties guaranteed by whatever written or unwritten constitution pertains) and it also suggests and sustains a particular view of the history of the collectivity under examination whereby the evolutionary process, as morally neutral as Darwin's theory at best, but often regressive in a moral dimension, cannot be altered, checked, or ameliorated, except perhaps by radical or revolutionary change, which discontinuity requires a specific and single model of society and human behavior to succeed.

There is more to say with regard to the particularities of Durkheim's and Weber's theories and their contiguity with both atmospheric elements, determinism and pessimism—and the revolutionary answer or its unavailability, itself conducive to a deeper pessimism, but in the theories of the founders of sociology, just as there is a marked determination to uncover the laws governing the functioning of a society, there is a cessation of inquiry at the point where such laws appear to have been exposed, and what follows is simply extrapolation, the application of those laws and their derived antitheses to all societies and cultures. There is little or no inclination to revise those laws in light of changing circumstances—the child-scientist's inability to admit an error. In Marx's theories, English capitalist society remained unchanged from the 1840s to the 1880s, a somewhat auspicious period of social and political development. But then, Marx was always allowed the time lags of capitalism as it developed in different countries. Germany, for example, lagged far behind England in terms of both horrors and ameliorations. Therefore, his theories possessed a currency that could not, universally, be devalued. Durkheim, as will be seen, demonstrates a similar rigidity of theory in the face of empirical change.

To return to a metaphor that Durkheim evolves into a paradigm, the individual 'cells' that compose a society cannot hope to affect the 'organism', certainly not to alter it in any optimistic sense. At best, it is a class that must take this task upon itself. Parliaments and legislatures cannot hope to make real and improving changes since, among other things, they are part of a conspiracy against change or, in Durkheim, are at least too partial to possess the will to change. That pressure-after-suffrage that we recognize as influential, of course, figures not at all in the works of theorists who preceded the establishment of mass suffrage or who had abandoned it in absentia or simply lost patience with it.

II

It was impossible for Émile Durkheim (1858–1917) to either be an empiricist or to espouse democratic natural law theory, even in its form as nineteenth-century liberalism. The excesses of Jacobinism during the Revolution, the aggressive empire which succeeded it, the weakness combined with foreign rapacity that characterized the directory from 1795 to 1799, the restoration, the failure of the 'July days' of 1830, the vulgar, smug imitation of stability of the Second Empire and the capitalist, bourgeois villainies it condoned—all conspired to defeatism, a world-weariness that Max Weber was to articulate with regard to late nineteenth-century Germany. The degree of pessimism with regard to parliamentary solutions to social questions in France during the Third Republic, the Second Empire, and its successors is a condemnation of French politics and society rather than French social thought. Suffrage came early and completely to France, but parliament remained that expression of group or sectional interests it had always been in France, with its inevitable horse-trading, deals, and cynicism—the old *estates* re-embodied in other forms. Not so much a 'talking-shop' as a Bourse of class and material interests. In other words, the democratic ideal had either ceased to function, had never done so without the encouragement of the guillotine or by imposition, or had never consistently manifested itself in France, under the ancien régime or after its suspicious and recent provenance was swept away with so much else in 1815.

Instead, Durkheim confronted without a tradition of parliamentary action *on behalf of the disadvantaged* the full vigor of early, laissez-faire capitalism and industrialization. The only inheritance with which he was equipped for this confrontation was the tradition of French Positivism, itself optimistic and laissez-faire with regard to both social processes. Positivism, apart from being the first body or current of 'modern' social theory, was a strand of thought that straddled without discontinuity the whole of the revolutionary period, via Saint-Simon and Comte, and was therefore still of significance to Durkheim. He was also under the more direct influence of German social thinkers, though that does not necessarily imply the influence of Marx. Durkheim's theories may be characterized as a species of classicism in sociology, with their recognition of a living tradition and their concern as much with methodology as content; the basis of his search was for method rather than original ideas, and the fundamental concepts of his sociology are evidenced in his earliest works, with the exception of that 'revelation' as to the significance of some conception of the divine—of religious experience as much as theological belief—for society, which idea occupies the central work of his maturity, *The Elementary Forms of the Religious Life.*

The main tenets of the Positivism of Saint-Simon, and his disciple and sometime secretary Auguste Comte, can be briefly summarized, since recognition of and familiarity with them will occur in any examination of Durkheim's principal ideas. Their theories cluster around the intention to establish a science of society, and it may be claimed of both that they regarded the function of philosophy as little more than the examination and elucidation of the scope and methods of the sciences. For them, theological and feudal society in France had become modern scientific and Positivist society, and Positivism was to become the new faith of this society. Their belief in the beneficent and primary influence of the sciences upon society was entire. The laws of social organization, assuming that there were such proto-scientific laws to be uncovered, must be revealed by a scientific examination of empirical reality, that task to be undertaken by Saint-Simon's "priesthood of sociologists," after which the task of organizing society must be given to scientists and industrialists. The alacrity with which they embraced such a hierarchical society should be remarked, together with that impositional apportionment so recognizably descended from Plato's ideal state.

Comte, especially, regarded society from an evolutionary point of view, and his search was for a new, nonclerical and non-Catholic, publically accepted system of values which he considered he had discovered in the new philosophy of Positivism. Durkheim's search was for something very akin. The worship of humanity would replace the worship of God—which statement may simplify but does not distort Comte's final position. Again, it should be remarked that the likeness of Comte's outlook to that of the *philosophes* and even, to a degree, that of the Jacobins, indicates a tradition and continuity in French social thinking from Voltaire to Durkheim, especially a tradition of negativity in regard to clericalism and the Catholic church. The antagonism of materialism and then Positivism to established religion is a profoundly formative influence upon the election of objects of optimism. Society as it could be transformed, in essence, became the focus of that optimism in French thinking, as did human nature—though both must be 'freed' or remodeled, 'educated' and changed.

Durkheim accepted, crucially, Comte's theory of the division of labor, which was not that of Marx, whereby the increasing divisions of labor in modern society, the degree of "specialization" society required, Comte regarded as cementing society's members more closely together, promoting social interdependence and therefore harmony; Comte did, however, recognize that such relations had a negative aspect, allowing the possibility of an increase in social divisiveness. Durkheim, too, recognized this negative aspect of mutual interdependence in modern society's organization of labor, and it may be suggested that, in part at least, his theories are an attempt to reconcile the optimism of

Positivism with the doubts and pessimism it created in him and in almost every other social theorist of nineteenth-century Europe.

It is important to recognize *which* science influenced Comte, and Durkheim especially, as a paradigmatic model for their methodology *and* for their essential conception of the nature, and therefore the development, of society. That science is Darwinian evolutionary theory, nineteenth-century biology, empirical in its methods and, in part because of the degree of its impact upon the intellectual world of the last century, universal in its applicability. It was, of course, the science that no longer distinguished human nature from nature, and the profound influence of that coalescence cannot be overestimated. Human nature was confirmed as essentially 'natural', not distinctly created by God, history, or any other agency, and *therefore* at least a scientific method that was not solely analogous could be developed to deal with individual human nature and with that conglomeration of individuals called society. Social and political theorizing now had more than a model to imitate—they had a paradigm that included man in their sphere of inquiry; evolutionary theory is, in a fundamental sense, about *man* and his development.

Comte had presaged many of the applications of the new science, since his was an evolutionary theory of society which seemed to possess that necessarily huge time scale since he dealt, like Marx, with a handful of historical epochs as his 'units' of human development, which imitated the slow, millennial progress of evolution in the animal world. Durkheim, like Comte but with more scientific validity, supported by Darwin, developed the idea of the *organic* nature of society, with the implicit sense that societies 'behave' and 'develop'—*evolve*—and that, as Durkheim claimed, society's manifestations and elements can be examined as *facts* just as Darwin examined animals and plants. The organism, society, becomes *scientifically* more important than the individual 'cells' of which it is composed.

It is necessary to say here that evolutionary theories of society are often the most dangerous and debilitating as regards *political* theory. Evolution posits progress as a 'good' as well as a 'fact', not merely a law but a 'good' because natural selection and evolution have produced man from the original chemical soup—monkeys have been left behind and men have appeared, and their evolution has been, in part, the evolution of society. Therefore, evolutionary *progress* is an unquestioned assumption. Evolutionary theories of society also produce, together with this optimism, a sense of determinism, which in turn can create a pessimism as to social evolution. Change is slow and inevitable; the process of change is a mechanism which operates by its own rules and is driven by its own engine. The sphere of political thought and activity is reduced to a mere excrescence or a tinkering with an engine the power of which cannot be harnessed. Such theories of social change and progress are, therefore, the entire opposite of revolutionary theories like those of Marx and Locke, and this evolutionary view was adopted by Durkheim and held to throughout his writings. Society is assumed to function, develop, and change by forces other than those of a constitution, a parliament, the actions of political men, the suffrage of individual voters. Unlike Marx, however, in Comte and thus in Durkheim there is no sense of a "class that is not a class" that might affect society and change it, because such a conception tends toward revolutionary theory; sudden or dramatic change is eliminated from any evolutionary analysis. Indeed, the essential forces of development in a society are rendered so massive and epochal that the operations of government and any legislature have little or no meaning or influence.

Evolutionary analysis seeks to identify the most abiding, even static, elements in a society, since these must be of the *essence* of that organism. Thus, Comte and Saint-Simon distinguish only three kinds of society in history, each of them lasting for whole epochs of human history—theological, metaphysical, and scientific (Comte) and polytheism and slavery, theism and feudalism, and finally Positivism and industrialism (Saint-Simon). All of these may, in fact, be regarded as acceptable descriptions of stages of social evolution, but what they fail to do is to offer insight into the society experienced by its cellular members—individuals at any moment of history—during their rather short, sudden life-times; nor do they suggest that societies are vulnerable to dynamic change of any kind or to any degree. Our own century might suppose this somewhat misguided, given the profundity of change in Russia after 1917 or in Germany after 1945, even perhaps in Eastern Europe after 1989.

One further problem of evolutionary theories is that, in attempting to adapt the analogy of human and animal evolution as completely as possible to human social organizations, the attempt becomes one of creating a 'natural science' of society. As much as possible of Darwinian theory is made applicable to society—at which point the discussion has moved away from Comte and toward such contemporaries of Durkheim as Schäffle and other German social thinkers. It is in their work that Durkheim seems to discover the necessary sophistication of method to make a study of society entirely scientific, so that the principal element that emerges from his studies of contemporary German social theory is the idea of the "social fact." This may be characterized—and it was greatly expanded and made much more rigorous as a method by Durkheim—as the attempt to classify the prejudices, attitudes, beliefs, and conventions of a society as scientifically discussable and evaluable facts. In other words, *values* are to become the material of a science of society, its *facts,* and the basis of its 'empirical' method.

A diametrically opposed concept of the development of a society may easily be posited, if such a process can be discovered at all. It lies in the idea of tension between 'facts' (values) embraced by any society's members, even classes or sectional interests, which would be assumed to be in conflict or at least in a state of tension with each other. 'Groups' of values exhibited in political influence, style of living, wealth, et cetera, would, and perhaps should, oppose themselves to one another, out of which the conditions of society would deteriorate or improve through the pressure exerted by opposing value systems. The idea of progress through conflict or crisis of values might provide the necessary dynamic for any and all social progress. It is this other possibility which in evolutionary theory, as exemplified in the Positivists and in Durkheim, remains unconsidered. Durkheim identifies only those facts which contribute to the stasis and inevitability of society's condition. He erects *one* arrangement of facts (system or code of values), which may predominate but which could never achieve unqualified or unchallenged preeminence in any but a totalitarian society, since even in the most vigorous economically repressive society there is a lack of control exercised over every sphere of human expression and thought. He makes, in short, the erroneous assumption that the predominant or static facts are the *only* significant facts of that society.

III

In his earliest major work, *The Division of Labour* (1893), Durkheim distills many of his principal preoccupations for the first time. Further, he elucidates the crucial and abiding idea of anomie, and it is necessary to examine this idea before proceeding, since it is anomie that provides the fulcrum or point of balance for much of his theorizing, while also being a crucial identification of the nature of contemporary French society. It is the cause both of Durkheim's pessimism and of the possibility of optimism, since it is discussed in conjunction with the determination that contemporary society is an extended *transitional* period between the epochs identified by Comte. We have not yet arrived at Comte's third epoch; we are still traveling toward it and viewing it through a glass, darkly.

For its inventor, the term anomie signifies the relationship of the individual, and the society of which he or she is a member, to the social norms, to that body of beliefs and attitudes which Durkheim distinguishes as the conscience collective: the corpus of shared attitudes, outlook, prejudices, and beliefs which characterize and harmonize the society as a whole. It would be unkind, but not necessarily untrue, to characterize the conscience collective as the Penny-Guy figure representing Fawkes and his convictions in relation to that principle of consent to government, and therefore to society itself, of John Locke.

Anomie is that condition where the norms of the conscience collective are weakened, questioned, or otherwise fail to provide a harmony of attitude; or, in the individual case, where the members of a society can no longer relate to what norms there are; or again when society is bereft of any norms to which they can relate. In his own time, despite the Positivist claims that the third and modern epoch of society had already materialized (a century earlier in the case of Saint-Simon), Durkheim perceived the almost universal condition of anomie in the individual life and in the collectivity itself. The conscience collective of the second epoch, the fuedal–religious society, was universal and universally accepted Catholicism, but a much more secular age possessed no equivalent, collectively upheld body of intellectual norms binding it together. This was, naturally, a failing or weakness of modern society, rather than a 'fact' to be celebrated as suggesting intellectual diversity, freedom of thought, et cetera. The individual was estranged, in so many cases and ways, from the collectivity, and the collectivity itself was to be regarded as failing the individual by lacking a coherent and cohesive value system.

It may be supposed that anomie, in signifying dissociation and supplying the place in Durkheim's theories that Marx reserved for the idea of alienation, is not antithetical to Marx's theories, but that would be a misguided assumption. It is true that Durkheim regarded the modern division of labor as responsible for fragmenting social cohesion, and it is also true that he regarded human nature in a very Marxist light, without the balm of the conscience collective, as unrestrained ego, man motivated by self-interest; nevertheless, the present division of labor is a fact of modern society, it has epochally evolved and is therefore inevitable, indisputable, and unchangeable, except by evolution. Therefore, Durkheim responds to this problematic question with the theory of the transitional stages between epochs, when remnants of the old system and its conscience collective clash and rub against the emergent new. This period of crisis and uncertainty explains the existence of anomie. The third epoch has not yet fully arrived. We have the *forms* of modern society but not, as yet, its conscience collective, the necessary agent of cohesion and social harmony. It is in this sense, and only in this sense, that Durkheim's pessimism is alleviated and in which he employs what may be termed the future tense of social theory, which was so significant in any solution to capitalism posited by Marx.

Therefore, Durkheim is able to envisage a future when the division of labor will become a positive force in the sense that Comte envisaged it. Mutual interdependence will become recognized and practiced, alleviating or eradicating any form of exploitation or fragmentation in the social fabric, and a form of "guild socialism" will mediate between the individual and the state and begin to provide something of that sense of belonging that is the principal characteristic of a true and positive conscience collective. Durkheim looks forward to what he terms the "mechanical solidarity" of the second epoch being replaced by an "organic solidarity" in the modern age.

The irony of the idea of a transition from one epoch to another is that it extends the present both backward and forward in time, and thus produces, rather than a moment of crisis and tension in history, an explanation of a very stable, conventional, static society, that of the Second Empire and the Third Republic—a bourgeois, capitalist society confident and selfish in its appreciation of wealth and its vulgar demonstration, a society, indeed, that had *allowed* a second empire only decades after the ruin of the first. French society was excessively centralized in its forms of government, yet it regarded its legislature at worst as irrelevant and at best as identified with sectional interests. What persists in nineteenth-century French society is that aristocracy of money that Napoleon attempted to encourage with the Legion d'Honneur and his hereditary principle of office-by-wealth, together with the revolutionary alternative, in other words, the assumption that representative and legislative institutions were a bourgeois preserve, while the true opposition was *extra*parliamentary. Political life was bourgeois life; the political life of other groups and classes—and of other *ideas*—must perforce occur outside those representative institutions. Politics was, in a very real sense, a question of class in France, and this itself promoted a sense of *social politics*, the idea that politics provided no solution to the problems of society, since those problems were the creation of the group or class which controlled political life, much as was the case under the ancien régime. There had been upheaval and profound change in France since 1789, but Durkheim might well be forgiven for assuming that the age of transition was extending itself into the late nineteenth century, for in another sense little had changed. For Durkheim, it would have seemed that political solutions were inapplicable to the society he confronted. Perhaps he rejected political theory in favor of his own weary and rather vague species of mysticism because of the insistent parallels with pre-Revolutionary society, or perhaps he disregarded the Revolution in favor of the inevitability of evolutionary factors. Whatever the reason, it was possible for a pessimist—and in certain important senses Durkheim was a pessimist—to assume that even revolution changed nothing essential in a society, just as Marx concluded regarding the French Revolution and as Carlyle claimed in his infamous remark regarding "new masters" as the outcome of all revolutions.

It is therefore the organism, society itself, which will develop beyond the condition of transition and its associated anomie. It is beyond even radical change initiated by the members of a society to hurry or effect such a profound evolution. Yet evolution itself offers Durkheim the time scale necessary for a degree of cautious optimism, and his work after *The Division of Labour* is at least in one sense an attempt to identify what must be gradually, in the transitional period in which he lived, emerging as the new conscience collective. Meanwhile, anomie explains Durkheim's disappointment with late nineteenth-century French society, expresses his pessimism as well as his faltering allegiance in the face of the "facts" of his time to the optimism of Comte.

Where Balzac and later Zola mirrored their desperation, alleviated only by irony or rage, in their remarkable fictional documents, Durkheim attempted to reconcile the tawdriness of bourgeois-dominated political and social life under the Third Republic with the hopes of Positivism resting in the economic system and social model supposed to pertain to the late nineteenth century in France. In one sense, Durkheim never abandoned Comte. Indeed, he may be seen as attempting an even more traditional solution, that of the sacred or divine, to ameliorate the condition of contemporary society. However that may be, the earliest upsurges of a socialism that may in one school have owed much to Marx and in other branches almost nothing (just as in England Owenite socialism owed more to Wesley than ever it borrowed from Marx) had reduced the credibility of such a welcoming embrace for the capitalist economic system Comte offered, at least for industrial society organized on capitalist lines. It was no longer possible to reinvent Positivism as the basis of any science of society that purported to be judgmental as well as descriptively analytical by the time of Durkheim's major works.

Marx's search was an attempt to uncover the social essence of human nature; that of Durkheim should properly be characterized as the search for the true identity of society itself. Marx assumed that the goal of any society that purported to justice or goodness was the true freedom of human individuals, though his definition of freedom is not one that Locke would have understood or approved. For Marx, it is not a question of identification but the perennial problem of identity or personhood solved in an original manner. In Durkheim's case, however, freedom would appear to be a rather inessential social fact, if fact at all, since he deals with it so casually and briefly. It seems to have little or no importance either as part of the conscience collective or of the individual experience, whether in the second or current (third) social epoch. He does not even resort to some "state of Nature" philosophy to introduce it, something Locke did very subtly and others have attempted through a post-Marxist desperation, however the state of nature is disguised in ideas of the "minimal state" or distributive theories of social justice. The organic theory of society to which Durkheim adhered binds members of that society into a totally interdependent collectivity; cells in such an organism are not free, since their object is to exist as indivisible, contributary members of the life of the organism. Durkheim discounts such individualistic conceptions as freedom, liberty, equality, rights of property, and legislation, and he does so because they cannot be regarded as social facts, which one is tempted to suggest means they are not exhibited as social *values* in the contemporary as well as antecedent epochs of social development. Since they have been, from the time of the Stoics, more honored in the breach than in the observance, Durkheim is quite correct, as regards his strict methodology, in ignoring them. But then, what kind of social thinker can he be to do so?

What we have, in fact, in Durkheim's sociology, is a table of elements where the highest atomic numbers are given to the most general or universal social facts (values). These most general elements of the conscience collective (or its absence) are always the most static rather than dynamic, as has been observed. They are also the most conventional and 'unconscious', the most traditional and the most widely exhibited. Therefore, they are likely to owe little or nothing to the work of philosophers, other thinkers, or social critics; they are not likely to belong to the intelligentsia or to any radical elements in society. It is the *persistence* of ideas rather than their value or dynamism that elevates them to the level of the essential, admits them to the inner sanctum of the conscience collective. It is a value system that operates upon the principle of the lowest common denominator, the most traditional attitudes and modes of thinking, rather than one which answers the problems of society. Where Marx regarded all history to the present as "pre-history," it is possible to claim that for Durkheim the present was, or should be, entirely a part of history, its failings being those of a creature adrift from history. Indeed, there is little room in Durkheim's sociology for concepts such as the individual, government, even change, such is the combined mass and inertia of the most general and therefore most essential social facts. Marx postulated an eventual *minimal* society, truly free, whereas Durkheim envisages a *complete* society, one which embraces and thereby diminishes political society, Hegel's civil society, and the individual. While Marx posits the eventual decline and even disappearance of the state, the society that Durkheim envisages requires a State in the Hegelian sense, with its impositional order, collectivity, and harmony.

In Durkheim's view of society, there is only a social philosophy—no ethical theory or even political consensus, only a deterministically arrived-at view of a willing and fulfilling membership of society. A conscious unconsciousness with human beings playing the parts and displaying the qualities of indivisible, inseparable cells of the organism. Society is viewed neither as accidental nor as necessary or inevitable—merely as a *fact* to which there is no alternative and the homogeneity of which is of paramount importance. And yet it never seems to occur to Durkheim that dissent, conflict, disagreement, variety of intellectual outlook have any significant part to play in the dynamic of any society. There is, rather, an *inherent* organization in society, which does not require Durkheim to consider at any length the question of the positive organization of society through the organs of a state. It is the conscience collective of a society that gives it its organic coherence—all disruption is thus a matter of dissent from or ignorance of the conscience collective. Values, therefore (social facts, in Durkheim's view), may be regarded as 'valuable' so long as they are most widely shared and belong to that body of assumptions that constitutes the conscience collective. These common assumptions provide the ethical basis of society, while they may also be regarded as the 'docility' factor in any society, even the "opiate," to borrow a term.

Individuals, therefore, can re-acquire a pre-Cartesian coherence and lose anomie if they share in the conscience collective *within* a modern industrial society, so long as that society functions in what may be termed a Positivist and integrated manner, one both hierarchical and optimistic. As to the functioning of that society, one of its most important mechanisms is what Durkheim terms *guild socialism*.

This guild socialism seems at once modern and anachronistic, harking back quite deliberately to some idealized form of borough or town organization that often seems to owe more to *Die Meistersinger* than to the study of history, along the lines of medieval guilds with some—but only some—of the appurtenances and functions of a nineteenth-century trade union. A mediatory body such as a professional guild will interpose itself between men and their governors, the sociological priesthood, and their subordinate industrialists. Thus, unlike Marx where, whatever opinion one might hold of his collectivism and the promulgation of class attitudes and class values, there is a genuinely ethical view of others, Durkheim presents such a view only of society.

It is even possible to suggest that, at least by implication or omission, Durkheim regards political activity itself as a form of anomie, a dissension from society which results from the lack of a fully shared conscience collective or value system which satisfies those seeking redress and change. Put another way, a state exists where a conscience collective either does not exist or exists only in an unsatisfying form, in a period of transition. A society is genuinely governed by its evolved form, and by the conscience collective that has evolved as suitable to it, not by something called the state.

In Durkheim's work, there is little or no discussion of rights and liberties or, to that extent, of individualism which, giving rise to such discussion, is regarded as an expression of anomie. Ethics, that branch of philosophy closest to political theory, is descriptive of behavior and response in Durkheim only insofar as it forms part of the binding or cement of a society—that is, insofar as it has a social rather than individual purpose. The ethical system a society gives credence to is not intended as a means of judgment of either individual, social, or political activity, or of change by representing some ideal, only to act as a cohesive force.

Marx envisaged the final dissolution of all forms of the state into what may be termed its opposite, the non-state, where and when, at least, all individual men would be truly free. Opposing Hegel, he rejected all forms of the political state, while Durkheim seems simply to ignore them, a matter of omission rather than refutation, and this forms one of the principal weaknesses of his discussion of modern, complex, capitalist society. There is little or no consideration of the governance of society. In avoiding the giant shadow of Marx, Durkheim was at pains to avoid the only vigorous current of political theory in nineteenth-century France, that of Marxist-socialism. In attempting to reinvigorate the Positivist science of society of Comte and Saint-Simon, Durkheim virtually omitted discussion of the state. In seeking the harmony of the organism, he was obliged to remove from consideration any notion of political theory and political change. Political theory, after all, posits two distinct though related optimisms (or pessimisms, if one prefers)—that society requires change for the better and that society *can* be changed. There is little or no other point or purpose to political theory since Aristotle and Plato. The epochal optimism of evolutionary theory *and* its determinism are at odds with *all* political theory.

IV

For Durkheim, modern society lacks a satisfactory and satisfying conscience collective. Anomie is the condition of many, preventing them from fullest membership, even making 'individuals' of them. It is in his later work, the *Elementary Forms of the Religious Life* (1912) that Durkheim attempts to define the fundamental basis of a conscience collective, in his theory of "the sacred." It is through the discovery of a sacredness in modern society, he concludes, that modern man will defeat anomie.

Saint-Simon and Comte, as has been observed, anticipated a modern society, when fully emerged from its transitional chrysalis, the 'religion' of which would be science and the scientific interpretation of the world of experience and, together with a true science of society, a "priesthood of sociologists." It is to these antecedent (and one might have thought anachronistic) theories that Durkheim clings. Briefly, *belief* is required, that intensity of belief which may be described as religious, the objects of such response being regarded as sacred. Society is to provide the basis of what can only be termed a new metaphysic, and it is to this position that Durkheim journeys via his study of totemism among the aboriginal tribes of Australia. It may be suspected, however, that the persistence of organized religion and its power over individual experience was a factor of more than passing significance.

In essence, Durkheim's theories regarding totemism and the consequent significance of religious ritual as distinct from individual faith, the public expression of worship, veneration, and celebration are concerned to discover the cohesive forces binding primitive societies—those very forces lacking in a society that permits the growth of anomie. It is the apparently undiminished necessity in human society for a concept of the sacred and what may be termed social worship that provides much of the material from which an appropriate and modern conscience collective can be fashioned. What he propounds is the idea that, even with the departure or decline of faith in a scientific age, the framework of moral and social rules, its ethic, will survive and retain its importance. They require only a reinvigoration of acceptance to form new social norms. As he says of the "object of worship" in modern society:

> . . . it cannot be doubted that a society has all that is necessary to awaken in human minds the sensation of the divine, simply by the influence it exerts over them . . . A god is, in fact, first and foremost a being whom men think of as superior to themselves in certain ways and upon whom they believe they depend . . . Now, the modes of conduct to which society is strongly enough attached to impose them upon its members are, by that very fact, marked with a distinctive sign which evokes respect.

Durkheim is supposing that religion, in whichever of its historical manifestations, is the product of society, its invention, and therefore in a secular age we will come to believe in the real essence of religion, the society that invents it.

It is with statements such as the one above that Durkheim demonstrates his assumption not merely of the greater significance of society over its members but the idea of its detachment from them, its organic existence independent of its members. The culminative position that Durkheim arrives at is to regard the organism of society as in some manner sentient, self-perpetuating, 'alive'; and, at the very heart of society, its essence, is the conscience collective. Therefore, the vigor, cohesion, and dynamic of a society are those most general social facts that we remarked earlier. The 'truth' of a society is that it is really governed and given identity by the broadest and most persistent and least changing assumptions and beliefs—the deepest or most general conventions of thought and attitude. This remains true of societies whether or not such assumptions have any real significance or influence in individual lives. His analysis, too, leads to the unquestioned assumption that individuals have only, for the purposes of the science of society, a social identity, to the extent that society either fulfills them or fails them, but which is incapable of being changed by individuals in order that it satisfies, fulfills, is 'just' or 'good', et cetera. There is, ironically in a thinker who devised and encapsulated much of the methodology of modern sociology, a distinct paralysis of radical thought and action and a deep pessimism expressed in Durkheim's worship of society and its evolutionarily determined development.

As with Marx, Durkheim also assumes that all modern and industrial societies are identical and capable of identical analysis, as well as being capable of analysis by analogy with primitive paradigms such as aboriginal society. This reduction is a reductio ad absurdum.

To anticipate the examination of Max Weber's theories by way of example, it *has* to be assumed that Wilhelmine Germany, with its militarism, its bureaucracy, its nationalistic ideals and sense of historical destiny derived from Herder, Hegel, and hundreds more, distinguished itself essentially from other industrial societies in the nineteenth and early twentieth centuries. The elements of Germany's conscience collective during this period are remarkably and influentially different from those composing the fragmented conscience collective of France.

What we are reduced to, in Durkheim, is a biology of society, its *natural* science. The primacy of the most pervasive generalizations of the collectivity induces a misleading sense of scientific detachment and oversight, identifies society organically, and reduces the individual to little more than an ingestor and 'internalizer' of such social facts or norms, so that men become completely the creatures of their social history, and since pervasiveness of values is measured in time as well as the present, they are the prisoners or victims of the longest-lived assumptions, however derided or disregarded by 'modern' society. Durkheim preserves his detachment, too, in allowing little or no moral evaluation of society, an area where Marx was rarely, if ever, morally neutral. Society simply *is*, it has evolved, and judgments regarding its beauty or ugliness are of less importance than the elucidation of its attributes. Durkheim's real and lasting contribution, not to sociology but to the rise of collectivism in ideas of political society, lies perhaps in this elevation of custom, convention—the 'shared' values—to the status of discussable, indisputable, and irreparable *facts*.

The conclusion to be drawn, once the conscience collective has been identified, is that this spirit of sacredness in society becomes a form of ethical dictatorship, a totalitarianism of outlook which requires conformity, the reward for such coherence being the loss of anomie—happiness within the collective. Reminding ourselves of Hegel's elevation of the nation-state to the preeminence of the conscience collective, it should be remarked that Marx sought, persistently, to dignify and humanize the concept of the collectivity and its 'consciousness' out of a withering compassion for the victims of an economic system that was ethically unenlightened and unregulated, while also retaining the idea of some eventual freedom of and for the individual members of the collectivity. Real freedom for Hegel lay in a higher identity with the State, and in Durkheim exists the same kind of elevated identification with the conscience collective. Indeed, the parallel with Hegel can be extended to suggest that there is an identical sense of worship with regard to these two organisms, the state and the society. While Hegel's reaction was one of a German to the excesses of the Terror that succeeded the Revolution, Durkheim's thought is, strangely, the continuation of the Positivist tradition which remained remarkably untouched by the events of 1789 to 1795.

In Marx, a synthesis, albeit Arcadian, is reached in the "withering away of the state" and the consequent and complete freedom of every member of the "political economy" that is society in its real, skeletal form. Species-being will be recaptured and fulfilled; alienation will disappear. In Durkheim, however, there is no synthesis that follows examination. We are left where we were, with our evolved and evolving society organic and unalterable by our efforts, merely better informed of the conventions of our social existence, and happy and fulfilled if we have become accommodated to them or if they have themselves cohered. The concept of the sacred is Marx's revered, understood, and despised "opiate" in another form. And this sacredness is the property of the collectivity, not of its members, who are the worshipers at the shrine.

If we consider the perceived failure of the French Revolution in the eyes of most nineteenth-century European theorists, then it is possible to add to the conclusions already drawn the idea that one of the most damaging effects of the repudiation of revolution and its associated, though not inevitable, individualism was the resurgence of a concept of Hobbesian man, at the mercy of his egoistical "Wille," incapable of self-government or moral action. This seems, at first, less true of Durkheim than of Marx, but it is nevertheless implicit in his elevation of the collectivity to the condition of the sacred. Individualism—and the Enlightenment concept of grace by man rather than God—is so defunct as an *idea* or as the basis of ethical or social theory that it provides no degree of hesitation whatsoever to Durkheim's organic and collectivist theories.

Finally, it is the pressure of the methodology (its erroneous and analogous origins in Darwinian evolutionary theory, its seemingly 'scientific' detachment and procedures) that makes Durkheim important in any consideration of the rise of collectivist political theory. That, and the pervasive sense that the collectivity is 'sacred', is the sole repository of 'values', which reduces the individual to the role of social animal, parasitically attached to the social organism, a parasite whose best hope is to achieve the status of symbiosis with its host.

V

Any consideration of the principal theories of Max Weber (1846–1920), together with his methodology, cannot but help be tantalized by the apparent modernity and continuing 'relevance' of both the man and his contribution to the science of society. There is opposition to many of Marx's theories, particularly to those projections of the fate of capitalist society which history has confounded, and more especially those projections as the basis for political action. There is, too, a satisfying solidity to Weber's understanding of history, and the further appeal of ambiguity, complexity, and variation in the capacities he ascribes to sociology. Finally, there is the significance he attached to recent history and to contemporary society. Much of Weber's theoretical and methodological vocabulary has passed into the small change of sociological language, as with "charisma," or "status groups"; many of his concepts have had the most profound and terrible subsequent proofs in our century (his century, too, since his death did not occur until after the Great War). Proceeding directly from the Darwinianism of Durkheim, Weber's theories are unexpectedly, even absurdly, refreshing. In his theory of the development of capitalism in the modern world, to which we shall turn at the outset, he seems free both of dogma and determinism, of any sense of epochal or purposive history. After a ride through the tunnels of the Ghost Train of nineteenth-century political theory and social thought, might Weber not appear a fearful, white-knuckled but intact liberal, albeit a pessimistic one? This popular, enduring, endearing image of Weber is a convention of sociology textbooks. Could he, in all conscience, be described as just another collectivist, another heir to Hegelian thought? Surely not.

Weber's best-known and most influential work, *The Protestant Ethic and the Spirit of Capitalism* (1904–5), is perhaps the most readily convincing demonstration of those Weberian virtues mentioned above, as well as being his best chance of wriggling free of the octopod embrace of the collectivists—of the very 'science' he helped to found. However, in beginning with this work, it is necessary to begin with an idea—with Weber's concept of *rationalization,* since it permeates his theories, and indeed is for Weber the very essence of modern society, the principle upon which so many of its cultural, industrial, and governmental structures are based. By the idea of rationalization Weber intends to indicate the gradual organization on rational principles and procedures of modern society, together with the equally inexorable demystification of our apprehension of reality—the loss or abandonment of mysticism and ritual in the growth of an industrial society in all its modern complexity, all of which produces an inexorable necessity for a means of organizing and controlling that society, particularly by the invention and expansion of a bureaucracy. Weber does not intend that rationalization should, at least at this point, be regarded as an essence of modern society, a first principle to assist in the examination and evaluation of the present forms of capitalist collectivities. Rather, he is simply identifying a requirement of such a society, necessary to its rational, considered, and planned apprehension and management. Rationalization may mean, as indeed it does in Weber, secularization, but it means a great deal more than that. However, it is at the outset a process, a requirement imposed by society's complexity, the necessity that it be managed—whether efficiently or justly remains to be seen. When contrasted with the strange fruit of species-being and anomie, mere rationalization holds no terrors. It is an idea we can comprehend, and allow Weber, for the moment at least, to take our hands and lead us into a consideration of Calvinism and the "Protestant ethic."

To begin with, according to Weber, there is a manifest decline at the beginnings of capitalist, modern society in ritual and its cohering or organizational principle. Society, instead, becomes organized upon rational, secular principles. However, while Catholicism was unconcerned with control of its flock except in matters doctrinal, and Lutheranism, too, was traditional, Calvinism assisted in creating not only a pervasive religious awareness that entered man's secular and business lives (Hegel's and Marx's *civil society*), but it also created the idea of a "calling" together with the peculiar concept of the "Elect." It may seem that Weber is contradicting himself, since what he appears to be describing is an *increase* of religious awareness, but one has to remember that Calvinism was not universal like Catholicism (one of Weber's crucial arguments to support his thesis), nor was Calvinism magical or ritualistic. As a religion, it was intensely private doctrinally and in worship, and unfettering in the sense of civil society. In other words, it did not interpose magic and the spiritual between men and their apprehension of the rational world of appearances in which they performed their public lives. Calvinism, and other Protestant creeds not as traditional as Lutheranism in Germany, made religion more pervasive in one sense but also 'separated' it from the sensuous, material world. A duty was placed upon Calvinists of asceticism and preparation for the afterlife, while at the same time there was an irresistible pressure toward rational, hardworking daily life, whether as a sign of election or merely as the outward manifestation of sobriety of spirit Weber's critics differ. Whatever the exact interpretation of this ambiguously spiritual and yet rational religion, Weber asserted that Calvinism in northern Europe produced a cast of mind whereby the fruits of commerce—capital—were regarded as a convincing sign of the capitalist's election and the favor of the Almighty.

The significance of this general theory—and Weber's proof is extensive, even to considering the lack of capitalism in other parts of the world and eras of history—lies for us in the commitment Weber displays toward cultural, legal, and religious influences upon the development of society, rather than a holistic interpretation as in historical materialism. The legal basis of exchange and contract is another necessary ingredient in the feudal soup that is to become capitalist society, and its conjunction with Calvinism is both crucial and catalytic. As regards the individualizing effect of Calvinism, this is something that Weber does not consider but which would tend to support his general theory. Protestantism creates an individual relationship between man and his God and his salvation, and therefore the individual himself, without the intercession of virgins, angels, or priests, achieves his own marks of favor but, more importantly, requires such evidence, since his creed does not supply them in ritualistic or doctrinal forms.

The fact that Weber does not stress this individualism of belief and accountability, together with what we can only refer to as a resurgence of Hobbesian man in Weber, as in Marx, may make us pause. However, for the moment it suffices to summarize what Weber did state. He implicitly dismisses the Darwinian influences upon Durkheim by recognizing that not all capitalist societies are identical, nor did they evolve in identical ways. Rather, his is a theory of probabilities, a description of the combination of elements and circumstances required. Further, he evolves no theory of base-and-superstructure as Marx does to account for legal, political, cultural influences upon society. To express it bluntly, at first hearing many of Weber's ideas 'sound more like it' than species-being and the conscience collective do in discussing the emergence of a capitalist economy.

Out of the *Protestant Ethic* arise some of Weber's basic methodological concepts and implements, and we should now consider at least the most significant of these. And, to begin with, it should be stated clearly that nowhere does Weber assume the analogous nature of sociology and the physical or natural sciences. Indeed, he strenuously disproves it. There are no such sleights of hand as "social facts" when values are indicated, no slow, inexorable evolution of society, no epochal periods and the like. He disclaimed any capacity on the part of the science of society to discover universal laws of human behavior that would provide such an analogously scientific basis for the discipline. He also affirmed that sociology was incapable of elucidating any evolutionary progress in human societies, thereby rejecting the proudest claims of the French Positivists. Third, sociology should attempt to be "value-free," by which he meant that the discipline was incapable of either evaluating or providing any moral justification for any present or future state of affairs in human society. Thereby, he distances himself from Marx and his successors and from much of the tradition of German historical thought after Hegel. Finally, and most 'liberally', he claimed that sociology was incapable of developing any collective concepts, presumably such as the state or the conscience collective, unless they could be stated with equal validity in terms of individual action. If Weber is to extrapolate or generalize, therefore, it will be done from the firm, empirical standpoint of observation concerning individual human beings.

It would seem from the above summary that Weber's sociology owed a great deal to the quality of his mind and little to either current school of sociological inquiry, that founded by Marx and that inherited from the Positivists. The accompanying idea of *Verstehen* confirms this, since Weber means by the term an empathic understanding on the part of the social theorist with his subject. The scientific observer in the discipline must seek to understand the subjective motivations of individual social "actors," especially in historical circumstances where the observation is via secondary sources. He promulgates a deliberate attempt to *identify with* the object of study as a means of comprehension, to include motivation, subconscious outlook, subjectivity, political persuasion, cultural inheritance, et cetera, all as aspects necessary to sociological inquiry. All this is demonstrably unlike the methodology of any of the natural sciences and is perhaps Weber's most successful attempt to humanize his discipline.

What it also achieves, however, is a profound effect upon Weber's idea of causality, since the limitations he places upon the science of society reduce cause and effect to probability, from certainty, inevitability, and determinism. The *method* itself disallows system and systemizing. His theories ought, therefore, to be automatically rescued from determinism, the besetting sin of both Marx and Durkheim, but that, as will be seen, is not necessarily the case. Many of Weber's generalizations are, indeed, deterministic, in the guise of pessimism. What he uncovers is the increasing organization of society in one particular manner, and that *form* of society and social organization is *becoming* more and more determinist. It is to this pessimistic outlook that his theories finally succumb.

By excluding any capacity to postulate or operate predictively, Weber disqualifies himself and his method from any amelioration in the future (and therefore by means of present decision, will, and action) of 'the way things are', and from any means or hope of change in their gradual, inexorable progress 'from bad to worse'. This proscription of certitude regarding the future means, in fact, that Weber predicted only 'more of the same', since he assumed that the rationalized society was, if not evolving then certainly intensifying its *form*. In this he is assuming something akin to Marx's base-and-superstructure model, since the form of society is not, apparently, amenable to willed and legislated development. Capitalism requires and promotes this process of rationalization, and therefore the management of society by a group or class solely dedicated to such management becomes the essential 'fact' of such a society, its sole means of functioning as an organization of human beings, in short, its *essence*. Thus, the engine or dynamic of a capitalist society is in its manner of organization rather than its economic system, but each is as determinist and binding as the other, especially since Weber did not envisage the revolutionary option that Marx regarded as essential in changing capitalist society.

The flexibility of Weber's theories and their inability to become theories of political society, though they stand in the place of them, are perhaps most hamstrung by his ideal of a "value-free" discipline which alone may be regarded as a genuine sociology. Sociology, as opposed to political theory, may be regarded as having been founded by the Positivists and was not "value-free." It was, however, nonethical, deriving its values from evolutionary, epochal notions of history applied to the present (and Weber does avoid such historical evolution) and from a naive faith in the progress of science. It was a scientific materialism which disclosed the laws that operated upon the mechanism of society through history. Marx may be said to have created *ethical* sociology, but his values were determined by his understanding of history on the one hand and his view of capitalism on the other, and thus his ethical posture toward society is at once Arcadian, revolutionary, and of a piece with all perfectability theories of human nature, while at the same moment his view of human nature under capitalism may be called Hobbesian. Marx's ethic may therefore be regarded as systematic, a pattern of social change to produce human change. The ethical ideal of society is entirely absent under capitalism, and longed-for. To achieve it, *all* forms of society must disappear.

Weber's sociology, which one may suspect of attempting to be value-free as a rejection of the passionate, revolutionary pessimism of Marx, those often-cloudy sermons from the pulpit of historical materialism, has similarities with that of Durkheim with its pretensions to "fact" and scientific detachment. It may properly be regarded as nonethical, but nevertheless it does contain what might be termed an *ethical model,* since the underlying assumption of his analysis is that human nature within society is incapable of change and that society itself operates by means of forces beyond the control of human beings and their institutions. By his determinism also, Weber is presenting an *anti*-ethical rather than an ethic-free assessment of society. In doing so, he indicates the crucial distinction between theories of society and theories of *political* society.

It is not to the point that Weber may be indicating only the nonapplicability of the social theorist's values to the proper study of society because, despite the idea of empathic *Verstehen,* Weber extends his idea of a "value-free" discipline to the object of study itself. Society's values—those of any society—may be distinct, people may accept them, but the observer must not regard them as significant or essential, especially in his study of contemporary society, whose values he may well share. This dismissal or suppression of the observer's values, rather than merely the avoidance of polemic or partisanship, leads in Weber's analysis to a diminution of the importance of value systems within a society, the opposite of Durkheim's insistence on the pervasiveness and necessity of the conscience collective. Further, Weber's insistence invites a suspension of judgment on the values of any society or a determinist acceptance of them as a *fact* of a society. Value-free sociology as a method produces a static acceptance of socially shared values, if they are not to be judged and either applauded or refuted. The values of a society are characteristic and therefore 'right', an essential but not debatable aspect of the society under examination. The very idea of *rationalization* as the essential fact of modern society arises from the attempt to remain "value-free," since it is a process rather than a value, a mechanistic necessity to keep society functioning.

Determinism, however, and detachment are ethical stances, since they assume either that society is necessarily and unchangeably as it is or that change through judgment is not a function of theory, the sphere of ideas. And, to repeat, that is why sociology as Weber handed it down is disqualified from becoming or replicating political theory, however much it has usurped the position and eminence of such theorizing and however determinedly Marx confused the two. Sociology, from its beginnings, attempted to elucidate the *laws* governing a society rather than to consider the method of government (the justice) of a society. It is, in other words, a mechanistic approach masquerading as a scientific discipline by assuming that the *object of study* is analogous, even identical, to the objects of study in the various physical and biological sciences. Political theory has, since Plato and Aristotle, regard to the functions and governments and values of congregations of human beings. The founders of sociology, its methods and pretensions, concerned themselves with a science of society and with the closest degree of imitation of method and approach, and the assumption of the closest possible analogy. Science uncovered the laws of gravity, motion, light, sound, navigation, evolution. There were such laws to be similarly uncovered which caused society to function as it did and which would explain why it changed and why its 'atoms' behaved as they did. It is all but unnecessary to remark that the assumption that all societies, or at least all societies designated as of the same *type,* are identical in the 'laws' governing their behavior is one which scientific sociology cannot help but make.

Locke assumed no model of society, except the evident human model provided by the fact that societies or commonwealths were aggregations of individual human beings. There could be, therefore, no analogy with science, though Hobbes made himself the first sociologist by assuming that there was an analogy with at least one principle of science, that of motion. Locke further assumes that society may be what it will and may become unjust or 'bad' or unruly or anarchic—even 'capitalistic'—but that political society requires the function of government, a legal or contractual basis to mediate between individuals and to ensure that the disadvantages of social or communal existence are minimized. The *form* of society, therefore, is legislatable, subject to change.

However, the sociological founding fathers, and especially the pessimistic, determinist Weber, assumed the model of a sealed and functioning machine. Society existed and functioned in certain ways. It was not the creation of living men, only their context (or prison, Marx would have said), and therefore it either could not be tinkered with by the generation then living to their benefit or could be altered only by violent upheaval. The consensus may be regarded as being that it would slowly, by its own laws, evolve. Society has become regarded not merely as the object of scientific study but *scientific* itself, functioning like the material world by discoverable, unalterable scientific laws, at least as the nineteenth century viewed such laws. It may not be merely platitudinous to observe that in the age of the mechanical sciences and the growth of technology it was all too simple and superficial to regard society as another mechanism.

It must also be borne in mind that history, as it was understood in the nineteenth century, especially in Germany—whether as social history or as in the ideological or philosophical interpretation of history—added its undue weight and influence to a mechanistic view of society. Not only the perspective of known history but the idea of historical development both implicitly produce a view of the individual human life as fleeting and transitory, bestowing a vast inertia upon history, which bulldozes the present as it will. Social, industrial, and economic forces, persistent and historical, abiding and evolving for epochs, or at least eras, are not only more significant and potent but more real and therefore 'true' of societies than the efforts of congregated men and women to control society. There are, therefore, *scientific laws of society discoverable in history.*

One further point. Contract or natural law theories of society all compose themselves and draw their conclusions from a model of the *origins* of society, though this model has to be regarded as metaphorical. The assumption is of the free association of individuals for mutual advantage into a community. For sociology—and for the nineteenth century—society exists and has existed throughout history, disproving any point of origin or big bang to account for society's existence. Perhaps the natural law theorists had a more up-to-date science in mind than the social theorists of the last century. Natural law or contract theory is as 'real' as Genesis after Darwin or the rise of geology as a scientific study. Natural law theory, however, posits the necessity of legal (contractual) means of ensuring the greatest degree of equality of rights, liberties, and responsibilities for every member of this man-made and therefore artificial construct known as society. But these are not laws *of* society, rather laws imposed upon it. The natural law model is therefore inapplicable to a science determined to elucidate the *development* rather than the *origin* of society, especially any hypothetical model of any such origin. Thus, sociology became replete with *models* and bereft of *hypotheses*. Yet it is in hypotheses of society that the principle of change is enshrined, the possibility that the organization, form, and content of a society can be judged and altered in imitation of some ideal or hypothetical version of society. There never was any literal content to natural law theory's attempt to explain how society originated in prehistorical times, merely the construction of a metaphor which would allow a *just* model of a working, governed society to be created. Natural law theory offers the possibility of a political society rather than a mechanistic one— and the evolution of societies in history does, presumably, illustrate that political societies do change, if not always for the better—but even then the method of change is that of a political society, witness 1933 in Germany or 1917 in Russia—and that men can change society's operation, even its essential character. Natural law theory has always been, from the Stoics to Locke, an attempt to establish an *ideal* rather than a *model,* a means by man-made laws and systems to ameliorate the disadvantages of community—making community into a political society. Weber, in particular, but also both Durkheim and Comte, as well as Marx and Hegel, is concerned to regard society as a mechanism, an *end-in-itself* to paraphrase Kant, an integral aspect of the material world explicable in scientific terms. His inquiries may be value-free; they are not, however, archetype-free or model-free, and they are merely pessimistic as a result.

VI

Weber represents a succeeding generation to that of his great antagonist, Marx, and a sociology that has divested itself of the remnants of political theory that remain in Marxism. Marx's discussion of society was deliberately of the *"political* economy."

Weber's analysis, as suggested above, might be termed the analysis of *material* society by scientific method (as Marx believed himself to be doing—out of a sense of moral outrage). In his scientific method, however, he is as Hobbesian as Hobbes himself, obeying what Hobbes understood to be the Galilean (of Galileo Galilei rather than of the mystic of the Sea of Galilee) method of "resolution and composition," which creates the simplest principles or forces, almost by an act of imaginative projection, that might explain even the most complex of phenomena, which would then allow a logical process of compounding to achieve complex propositions or principles. In other words, the simplest and most general ideas are the basis of the 'scientific' method—it is this element of the Galilean method that Hobbes himself obeyed and which characterizes the sociology of both Durkheim and Weber. How, precisely, did Weber apply the method?

He begins with the adoption of very simple models or abstractions from the mass of social data at his disposal, which simple abstractions he terms "ideal-types," which has more to do with Idealism than with the perfect. *Ideal-types*, however, are to be regarded as firmly and irrevocably empirical, arising from evidence. His analysis of capitalism in the *Protestant Ethic* serves as an ample illustration of the method in action, since he abstracts certain elements of the situation which are then used, in more complex form, to explain why capitalism arose when and where and how it did in northwestern Europe. Since an ideal-type, to qualify for the function, is an abstract distillation of the principal features that are characteristic of the existing phenomenon under discussion, one might regard the basic method as essentialist rather than empirical. Thus, Calvinism, contract law, the collapse of feudalism, climate presumably, though it is not mentioned by Weber, and certain other social abstracts 'explain' modern capitalism in its historical appearance and development. It is legitimate to ask how value-free the selection and subsequent elevation of these abstracted social facts actually is, especially since Weber's abiding concern is with the social *order*—his ideal-types tend to be those which contribute to a stable, rationally organized society.

Hence the exaggerated importance of Calvinism which Weber has to supplement with an invention which he terms "salvation anxiety," his *real* explanation of the significance of Calvinist capitalism. The elect seek proofs that they are so elected to the number of the saints by acquiring worldly goods—God presumably allowing them to do so and not dashing the silver cup from their lips because he wishes to salve their anxieties regarding their eventual salvation. Therefore the ideal-type is the Calvinist who possesses salvation anxiety, not simply the thrifty, hardworking man who may be a Calvinist. But, did the elect, told they were such, have such doubts? This is hardly a social 'fact' capable of empirical proof. But Calvinism does provide a vision of a supremely rational and *ordered* community.

While this suggestion might imply a degree of accord with the tradition of natural law or contract theory, what intrigues Weber are models or precedents for his own society, that Second Reich that was the inspiration of Bismarck, much as he might resent it. It is *stable* and authoritarian societies that Weber employs for the process of abstracting ideal-types—all such exempla tend to be drawn from such societies; or their elevation to the role of ideal-types confirms the authoritarian homogeneity of society rather than any more 'liberal' conglomerations of human beings. It is the pursuit of understanding social order in its form of the ordering of society that leads Weber to the critical conceptions of "legitimacy" and "domination," which underlie his whole analysis of human nature in terms of simple principles (ideal-types). While Hobbes's abstractions and generalizations of human nature were merely malign, Weber's are concerned with ordered, predictable behavior, what he calls "social action," a term which includes any sort of human conduct which is "orientated to the past, present and future behavior of others." This means that, for Weber, a social relationship is established and exists wherever the actions of any person are consciously related to the actions of another, or within a reciprocity of action between two or more individuals. Weber distinguishes four inclusive types of social action—*purposively rational* conduct occurs where an individual consciously and rationally assesses the outcome of a course of action, weighing the various methods of proceeding and the various eventual outcomes of each method of proceeding; *value rational* action explains the pressure upon individual action of some overriding ideal which negates by its pressure all forms of rational calculation; *affective* action signifies any conduct carried out under the influence of any emotional state, and may be described as value action which is not 'excused' by the presence of some ideal or other profoundly motivating principle; finally, *traditional* action describes conduct carried out under the influence of convention or habit. Thus, we have what might be called a scientific catalog of human behavior, a classification that we have already seen hinted at in Durkheim, except that Weber always qualifies his categories with the dictum of probability rather than certainty.

Thus, Weber's *ideal-types* of human activity are reduced to four, and the categories are so inclusive that it would be difficult not to include almost any thought, intent, or action within at least one of them. What is significant, however, is the distributive weight of rationality among them. The majority of social actions belong to the second, third, and fourth categories, and in those individual reason, even the capacity of reflection, plays a much smaller role than does custom, emotion, fecklessness, and overriding ideals and passions. What is evolving in Weber's theories is a gravitational attraction toward those capacities deciding human activity which are representative of stability, the status quo, stasis. Conformity, acceptance, and rational indolence are preeminent in Weber's catalog of human activity, behind which lies some implicit suggestion of a "conscience collective," a habitual conformity among individuals and a passivity when confronted with the necessity of "social action." The pressure and mass of history allow such an interpretation. Things do not change radically or swiftly, we go on in the 'same old ways'. But categorizing human social action by means of four ideal-types of action is itself an ordering and categorizing which leads, simply and with apparent inevitability, to a categorization of the types of social order, the *forms* of society, which Weber distinguishes as various ideas of *authority* rather than consent (however Weber acquired the posture of a despairing liberal one begins to wonder!) or contract. What Weber is seeking is a solution to, or description of, what he calls *legitimate order*, by which he means that kind of order or *authority* in society which its members either require or accept (i.e., make legitimate by their acceptance). No society is stable unless its authority is legitimate, if society itself has authority without a concept of political society, which in natural law theory is no other than the ideal impartiality of a system of laws.

In other words, Weber is seeking to circumvent political theory by uncovering a social basis for government and authority. The problem with this is that as he characterizes human activity by means of four ideal-types, so he implicitly accepts the idea that authority is an inevitable consequence of society. It is not an arrangement that must produce consensus or agreement, a recognition of individuality-within-membership; rather, it is a fact of history and the present, complex, and unstable, requiring the imposition not of *legality* but of an *authority which is dignified by acceptance* ('legitimacy'). By considering material society rather than political society, Weber disallows himself the benefit of suffrage and change. Legitimacy replaces legality as authority replaces consent or contract. In his efforts to distinguish the limitations of sociology, he distinguishes what he considers the limits of society and of human nature, and that way lies madness, or at least authoritarianism.

As might be suspected, Weber regards bureaucracy as the legitimate order of modern society, with its increasing and inexorable *rationalization*. Bureaucracy transforms itself into what, again echoing Kant, we should call an "end-in-itself" rather than a means. All forms of authority seem to acquire this historical justification of becoming an end rather than a means, echoing what we concluded earlier regarding the *form* of society as its essence. It is, of course, a subversive form of *political* society or political theory that Weber concerns himself with, in the guise of sociology. Yet *the possible forms* of political society consist only of the authoritarian ideal-type. Bureaucracy, therefore, is the "rational" manifestation of authority appropriate to, and inevitable within, modern society. The indebtedness to Hegelian conceptions of the "rational State" should be clear. However, bureaucracy is only one of three ideal-types of authority (note that we passed from considering the ideal-types of human action to the ideal-types of *authority* rather than 'society'—the essentialism of rule and government), which others are *traditional* authority and *charismatic* authority (the familiarity of the term to us should not cause readers to jump the gun, recollecting that Weber was German). It is in his discussion of authority that Weber at last makes clear that it is political society he is indeed discussing, when he remarks in *Economy and Society* (1914) that "existence and order is continuously safeguarded within a given territorial area by the threat and application of physical force on the part of the administrative staff." He conflates the *existence* of society with its *order* (i.e., its manner of authority), of course, and assumes the inevitability of what we would term an authoritarian regime. He further states that "a political organization becomes a 'state' where it is able successfully to exercise a legitimate monopoly over the organized use of force within a given territory." (It sounds remarkably like the Prussian Reich on a bad day and very little like Switzerland—or even Britain at the time, let alone that loose confederation of 'States' across the Atlantic at the book's time of writing—though the book itself is a sprawling collection of essays written during the decade prior to the Great War.)

It *is* political society that Weber is concerned to analyze, therefore, but his assumptions are both *localized* (German and contemporary) and *nontraditional* (scientifically biased toward an analysis of the contemporary and eschewing the ethical or 'ideal'). In keeping with the above statements, it is clear that Weber regards every social relationship as, to some degree or other, a power relationship. If Weber's debt to Marx lies only in the negative, then it is possible and perhaps fruitful to guess at a much more positive inheritance derived from Hegel, at least in his adoption of the idea of *Volksgeist,* borrowed from Herder. It is something Weber deeply believed, and something which allowed, even drove him, to 'collaborate' with the authoritarianism of his country in his time, and has about it an 'illiberality' which is both salve and source of pessimism. The inexorable 'progress' of the German *Volksgeist* toward the Great War induces, perhaps, a sense of inevitability that colors the future as well as the present. It is from this and what precedes it that he derives his concept of *domination,* which is central to his social and political theories.

The seductive modernism in a century of collectivism is evident and convincing. The world-weariness these ideas imply, something Weber himself identified as a characteristic of modern society and the modern "soul," is supported by a grasp of recent history unequaled among social theorists and a methodology that seems fit to discuss the modern state. How *apt* an analysis for our century and its dominant nondemocratic societies, we may be deluded into concluding. How *correct* it all is—but only, perhaps, in relation to his own time and place, not as a methodology for a science of society. Weber never made his ideas conditional upon time and space, history and geography and, though he was intent upon determining the limitations of sociology, he allowed his analysis to extrapolate beyond the local and toward the universal. More than anything else, Weber infuses conceptual abstractions such as ideal-types, including authority, domination, and legitimacy, with a subjective attitude. This is indeed the narrow base for the scientific view of a mechanistic society.

Weber's Germany will be discussed below, but for the present we need to examine his categories of *legitimate domination*— domination rather than mere authority because Weber eventually and irrevocably conflates the two ideas. And in one of them, even if he does not predicate the future, he is not "value-free." There is an attempt, however disguised and haphazard, to achieve an equivalence to natural law theory, a description of political society in something like 'ideal' terms.

It might be concluded that Weber, in opposition to the position adopted by Durkheim, *is* discussing *political* as opposed to *civil* or *material* society, but, like Hobbes before him, he is concerned to examine it from the standpoint of civil society. He assumes what might be termed a Hegelian hierarchy of social organization, with the state at the apex, without, of course, Hegel's admiration of the state. Human social relationships are discussed in terms of the idea of *domination*, again like Hobbes, and these are exhibited in society, which in itself is proof that they are true individuals, while the state is the institution—the form of social organization—which orders or may even express that relationship toward the members of society. Therefore, individuals accept the authority of the state either because it mirrors their own social relationships, 'dominating' them, or because, as in Hobbes more than in Weber, only the state can suppress or control the naturally competitive and domineering proclivities of society's members.

This leaves Weber concerned to discuss the 'spirit' of the state rather than its form—the necessity of the state cannot be called into question because the state is an indisputable *fact* of modern society. Legality, the ideas of consent or contract essential to natural law theory, has become legitimacy—de facto rather than de jure. The consent of the people to be governed is conflated in Weber with their acceptance of authority. What we have is a model of the state rather than of political society; his model of the state, however, is limited to accepting the primacy of the contemporary and the local (Germany in the late nineteenth century), because he excludes the possibility of hypothesis and, unlike the thinkers of the French Enlightenment, the possibility of other 'national' models such as Britain or America. It is in this that his attempt at a value-free sociology displays its reality as determinism, and as Weber's failure to distinguish the state from political society.

Also, the model of the state, being limited by history, locality, and present circumstances, is constructed upon an *ideal-type* abstraction of human nature, especially of human activity in society; a *social abstraction* or an abstract from social behavior rather than a conception of *personhood*. Weber, like his discipline in the last century and much of this, assumes that human nature is conditional upon social, political, economic circumstances which may be indisputable, but theories of political society are not based on interpretations of human nature or the effects of society upon human nature but upon the idea of human *beings* in a social environment. The idea of individuals as equal *persons* preoccupies Locke, and preoccupies all democratic political theory, whether because of the advantage-disadvantage debate as to the form of social organization and justice—"justice as fairness" as it has been called—or because of the necessity to prevent the extrapolation of ideal-types, archetypes, or stereotypes of human nature which might lead to assumptions of control, of limitation of rights and liberties, even the introduction of impositional and coercive government: *moral* government. No political theory that pretends to justice can operate by stereotyping (i.e., without according to all members of a society the value of personhood, whatever their political or economic circumstances). The "objectification" of this lies in suffrage and equality before whatever laws have been adopted by the community. Personhood is not conditional and is therefore free of the kind of archetypalism of Weber's ideal-types and Hobbes's description of essential human nature as expressed in social activity—the "warre of everyone against everyone" which for Hobbes justifies and necessitates the "soveraign Power" and which for Weber, with his archetypes of domination, requires the final domination of society by the state. Sociology failed Weber as a means of discussing rather than merely describing political society, because the discipline and methodology he designed submitted political theory to the determination of history and the contemporary. But it would be an erroneous reading of Weber to assume that he does not promulgate political *theory* in his discussion of political *fact*, or present a model of the state, however poor the materials with which he allowed himself to work, the "iron cage" of the contemporary and the local, which neither Marx, Lenin, nor Hitler accepted as a limitation upon political theory and practice.

In his definition of the ideal-types of domination that occur in the *forms* of society (especially German society) he regards what he terms *legal domination* as the control and authority of a bureaucracy. The domination-authority of a bureaucracy is impersonal, and the manner of its authority has been established by means of purposive or value rationality. Its advance and importance in the modern world are in direct response to the division of labor. Weber asserts that "the larger the state, or the more it becomes a power state, the more unconditionally is this the case." It is the speed and decisiveness with which a capitalist economy requires decisions that encourages the growth of a bureaucracy, though this might not seem self-evident in the functioning of any 'real' bureaucracy. However, it is fair to observe that most current conventional wisdom regarding bureaucracies originates in Weber's perceptive analysis. He regards a bureaucracy as self-serving and, because it requires order and stability and the capacity to regulate social activity and to possess the machinery with which to so regulate, there is an inevitable tension between it and what can only be called democracy.

Traditional domination is, on the other hand, literally that form of domination with a 'history' or, as Weber terms it, with the admission by the subordinated of the "sanctity of age-old rules and powers." Patriarchalism and patrimonialism are classic types here, and the category of legitimate domination represented by traditional forms is virtually self-evident. In the third classification, however, Weber creates his infamous and prophetic idea of *charismatic domination.* Weber believes that this type of legitimate domination must break with the past to become the most revolutionary kind of domination. Its essence lies in subordination and loyalty to the "leader." It is based in the personality of the individual who possesses charismatic control of his followers, and its earliest historical precedent would be the tribal war leader. The sole basis of "legitimacy" for this type of domination is the recognition of the leader's authority. However, whenever charisma becomes "routinized," in Weber's inelegant term, its authority becomes that which belongs to the rationalistic legal domination of the bureaucracy.

It is necessary to observe here that Weber did, quite clearly, accept the necessity of such a leader if Germany were to become truly a world power, a power state to rival other power states, and to fulfill her national destiny, though there is no wild horse that should drag us to the conclusion that Weber would have accepted, let alone welcomed, the charismatic leader who eventually emerged in Germany. However, it is necessary to remark the nationalistic basis of Weber's sociology when it attempts to become political theory. He accepted, as wholly as Herder and Hegel, the idea of a "world-historical people," as Hegel termed the Germans, the idea of a national destiny, the assumption of the *necessity* that Germany become a power state. One should suspect the inevitability of such conclusions from Weber's social theories—or suspect the validity of the social theories if this is the point at which they coalesce, and they indeed do. His detestation of the kaiser, and the "charisma" of Bismarck, elected to a pantheon of German statesmanship and the rank of *man of destiny* alongside only the Great Elector and Frederick the Great, is plain in his writings, as is his belief in the rightness of the German side in the Great War. The necessity of a power state and its eventual destiny in a geopolitical sense is hardly "value-free" sociology— but it is the means whereby Weber develops a political theory from the strictures he placed upon the science. It also invalidates much of what Weber has to say regarding human nature and human social activity *in any universal sense*, rendering Weber a purely German, late-nineteenth-century social commentator, a pessimistic chronicler of his time and place.

Weber felt compelled to come to grips with his own time and place, but he did it as a sociological theorist attempting to establish the methodology and classifications of a *science* rather than as a commentator or politician, wherein lies the danger of adopting at least some of his ideas along with his methodology. Weber did not limit the application of his theories to his own society— his *ideal-types* are not conditional upon a type of society, except that it is "modern, capitalist society." (It still looks awfully like Wilhelmine Germany to an onlooker, however.)

In the same collection of theories-in-essay, *Economy and Society*, Weber deals with concepts of class, status, and party, and here, too, his influence upon succeeding generations of social theorists is clear. His theory of *class* may demonstrate a great deal of similarity to that of Marx, but Weber recognizes many sub-classes in a way that Marx does not, and he does not simplistically and utterly impugn any one class and idealize any other. *Status groups* are those groupings of individuals who follow similar patterns of life and who, more importantly, place restrictions upon the way in which others relate to them and upon possible membership in the group. He clearly regards status groups as having a greater significance throughout history than have classes, which he seems to view as a more modern phenomenon, probably one 'invented' by Marx. In terms of *party,* his pessimism gleams and his ideas seem ill thought-out and somewhat vague. In other words, it is permissible to state that his theory of *domination* is of far greater significance to Weber than any analysis of class or political party. Status groupings predominate and exist as something Weber tends to regard as a viable concept rather than some he can deal with dismissively. But then, status groups—though hardly part of a rationalized social organization—seem to offer something of the Arcadianism that affects Marx at his most dreamy. What status groups do, in society, is nothing less than induce passivity and a more or less complete identification with civil society, providing its order. Ignoring, as Weber does as a sociologist, personal motivation, he must regard social motivation as predominant, and therefore the most stable and rigidly hierarchical groupings, status groups with their similarities of lifestyle and outlook, offer a rationalization of society, in terms of its structure and stability, that is not an aspect of the state, as a bureaucracy must become. Weber, of course, in opposing an exploitative view of human beings in society, or even one of conditioning, returns to a concept of identification with society that Hegel propounded in a different way. Within self-imposed limitations, status groups are less oppressive and less modern than bureaucracies. Autocracy, social gradation, and the like ills of feudalism are, of course, incipient in status groups, but the sense of identity derived therefrom appears to be more important to

Weber—a rebuttal of modern society and also a defense of that kind of 'private life' that Hegel admitted at the level of civil society within a higher identification with the state. Weber's admiration, however qualified, for status groups rather than the classification of social identity by means of class or party, gives rise, perhaps, to the importance of the idea of social "role-playing" in modern sociology.

As regards political parties and politicians, as a kind of footnote to the above, Weber again seems traditionalist in his conception of the best "type" of political figure, reminding any English student of his work of Whig paternalism rather than of any sponsored or professional politician. One need only remark the unholy chaos and evident impotence of all German political parties at the time of Weber's observations to understand his exasperation. His return to some traditional, and probably fictitious, archetype, however, is another matter. Why Weber abandoned political solutions because of the base currency of contemporary German politics—both as a historian and social theorist—is inexplicable. Someone is required, in Weber's terms, who lives "for politics rather than off politics."

There can be little doubt from any reading of Weber that his model of domination and subordination for social behavior, the subordination willingly given, as in Hobbes, lies at the heart of his theories of modern society and its politics. His acceptance that even in the case of the SDP, the social democrats, the state would subsume the party rather than the party change the composition of the state indicates a total pessimism with regard to the political process—in his Germany, there was no such process. Yet, pursuing the empirical facts of his day relentlessly, Weber is confronted with the most radical party cooperating with the Wilhelmine state and the acknowledgment of a theory of naked power nakedly exercised, together with the supine acceptance of the people, as the only real political theory. True, he promulgated, rather like Hegel but without Hegel's optimism, some private areas of human experience where the rationalisms of modern society and the power state could not and probably would not intervene, unlike the totalitarian state. In rejecting Marx, he must also have rejected his famous dictum that "the purpose of philosophy is not to understand the world, but to change it." But such hypotheses require a perspective, and Weber was a social theorist of his present. To reintroduce Marx at this point leads one to elucidate some version of the "Good Life," as does Marx, and to remark that however much he is identified with the Platonic tradition, and whatever strictures one might place upon Plato's theories (and Professor Karl Popper's book, *The Open Society and Its Enemies*, deserves immortality upon that count), Platonic ideas of society fundamentally seek the 'just' society. Weber, however empirical his tradition and outlook, however scientific his approach, is bereft of hypothesis, marooned in the present, determinist as regards the future, if that future is at all imaginable.

VII

Weber's *present*, his contemporary Germany, had been late to industrialization but had nevertheless been triumphantly successful in instituting a full-blown capitalist economy with the assistance and supervision of the state to a degree that was unique in Europe. It also came late to empire, to its Second Reich. In Weber's own lifetime, it had possessed a leader of charisma, genius, and *states*manship, Prince Bismarck, its real imperial ruler. Further, it possessed a greedy and feckless middle class, untouched by Puritanism (in Weber's conception important, given his *Protestant Ethic*, in determining the rational morality of capitalism as well as its dynamic), and swayed by every breeze of fashion and materialism—children to capitalism's shiny new toys—a very small industrial proletariat and a feudal class system dominated by the Prussian *Junker* class, boneheaded, militaristic, embalmed in tradition, and landowners rather than entrepreneurs. It is from this evidence that Weber constructs his model of capitalist society, much as Marx did, and just as erroneously, since like Weber he disallows amelioration or progress. The Prussian bureaucracy was, of course, at the apex, 'running the show', and far more modern than the rest of German society. Indeed, it was Bismarck's chosen instrument of government, above the debased parliament, that contemptible nest of troublemakers and timeservers the *Reichstag* (and, in the case of the liberals and the SDP, ultimately the abode of the political coward).

Germany had become, by Weber's day, the strongest, most aggressive and militaristic nation in Europe, the complete and model *power state*. In abstracting the elements of an ideal-type of capitalist society from the German evidence, Weber retained the cultural, material, and military values of that society, *without comparative studies* except in Germany's own history, in his model. It was therefore inapplicable to other, related societies, to the future, and possessed no universal application whatsoever, far less than Marx's theories of class struggle, surplus value, and alienation. In Weber, the capitalist society becomes the bureaucratic, rationalized "power state." It is a remarkable analysis of early twentieth-century Germany, but it is little more than that.

To conclude, Weber's sociology is suspectly nationalistic and Hobbesian in its rigid classification, of an essentialist kind, of human motivation and activity, while his theory of political society is nonhypothetical, nonethical, and abstracted solely from his own contemporary, national circumstances. Two hundred years after Locke's *Two Treatises,* a German intellectual can despair of, and therefore discount, the political processes that spring from natural law theory and turn instead to dominative and impositional theories of political society and to the vague and irrational promise of a charismatic leader who will overturn the *rational State* that Weber had inherited intellectually from Hegel and Germany had inherited from Frederick the Great and Bismarck.

POSTSCRIPT

THE PRECEDING ESSAYS on conflicting and irreconcilable ideas of political society were intended, at the outset, to remark the tercentenary of the publication of John Locke's *Two Treatises of Government* and nothing more. However, it has been necessary, in order to demonstrate Locke's abiding radicalism—the cleaning of his portrait, as it were, of the grime and dubious revarnishing of successive generations of commentators—to remark the origins of modern social theory in the metaphysics of Hegel and the Positivism of eighteenth- and nineteenth-century French philosophers—in other words, in nonempirical spheres or modes of speculation. To do so, it has also been necessary to indicate that these sources explain the rise of ideological collectivism in the last century and our own. These ideologies, derived from metaphysical speculation upon human and nonhuman *reality* are responsible for supplanting the ideas of Locke and other empirical theorists in the century that divides Locke from Hegel. It has also been necessary to describe in some detail the intellectual inheritance of that most profound of influences in political and social theory after Hegel, Karl Marx.

Further, the essays are an attempt to indicate that essentialist theories of human nature and the 'world' such as metaphysics might be expected to promulgate, resulted in similarly essentialist theories of human community and political society, in which human individuals (or classes or masses) become *expressions* of social and economic forces. As a result, it has been necessary for the essays to demonstrate that a *theory of the individual* is essential to all just or 'liberal' political theories and systems, just as a lack of such a theory or concept of personhood leads inevitably to one or other form of collectivism, to the maximization of government, and to the assumption by government and the state of moral and ethical functions even beyond its centralization of power and its control of the economy and of the education, instruction, and management of the lives of the citizens of such a state. The logical extension of collectivism is the assumption that, through citizenship and/or nationality, human beings discover their identity. To apply a Kantian term, human beings in collective political systems become citizens in a more than phenomenal or empirical sense, they become citizens-as-noumena; their essential nature and reality is as citizens. Instead of the empirical assumption that membership is acquired by simple existence, we arrive at the noumenal condition of membership of the community, which is thus, though not solely, a state rather than a political society.

It is therefore the underlying contention of these essays (though this was not their point of departure) that there can be no political theory that may be termed democratic (and therefore no democracy in practice) without a recognition of the separate and distinct equivalence of human individuals, or without the (indivisibly) accompanying recognition that political society is an idea or system independent of all essentialist or metaphysical spheres of speculation and independent of the forces that operate in any human community. Democratic political theory recognizes (or must be made to recognize) that it is an artificial construct of law and government for the purpose of guaranteeing justice (at least, that is the ideal) to all individuals within the community.

The two separate and irreconcilable modes of political-social speculation that the essays identify and discuss, what I have termed the Platonic and natural law theory traditions, are clearly distinguishable, and their various encounters and crises one against the other resolve into one central difference—natural law theory assumes that, in the concept of political society (and especially in the *Two Treatises*) government can change society to the extent that it can be made more just and more equal in representation and before the law; it assumes that the artificial construct that is political society is not totally at the mercy of human, social, or economic groups or forces in a determinist manner or unchangeable except by upheaval in the face of history.

In 1990, Europe and much else of the world is witnessing perhaps the most profound crisis of opposition between the two traditions of political theory of which these essays treat, perhaps a crisis as great as that of 1789 and greater than those of 1776, 1848, and even 1917, and therefore it is necessary for this postscript to say at least something of the events that would appear to have overtaken it, and the century, at the beginning of its last decade.

II

Most of the work on these essays had been completed before the events of November and December 1989 in the German Democratic Republic, Czechoslovakia, and Romania and prior to the less dramatic but equally profound developments in Hungary and Poland. The relevance of Locke to the quasi-bulletin pace of change and uncertainty could not be more strikingly remarked. That the need to proselytize his political theories is incumbent upon all in the West who wish the reclamation of individuality and democracy in eastern Europe well is no longer in the slightest doubt. Immediate history bodes well and is the most vigorous refutation of the determinism of history and economic social forces—and even the force of impositional governments and ideologies—since 1789. The precedence of Locke over certain materialist theorists of the last and present century may not yet be assured but is less in doubt than at any time since 1848 and the publication of *The Communist Manifesto*.

Or so the conventional wisdom runs. Leninism (and its greater but less *practical* original, Marxism) has been pronounced a chimera, Locke's pale "image" of the substance of the political community. The collectivist states and even empires are retreating like a pollutant-foamed tide, down the beach of history (possibly even Matthew Arnold's *Dover Beach*). Which judgment is of the present, of course, and not the judgment of history—not yet, at least. What any student of current events in eastern Europe is therefore required to ask is the question as to whether socialism as a collectivist ideology, rather than as an alternative democratic experience, is a similar and similarly doomed chimera. (One might ask a further, and apparently unrelated, question regarding the sudden, and extremely confused, renewal of interest in the theories of Hegel in the U.S. State Department. If Hegel's deterministic theory of history is to be used to justify liberal democracy, in eastern Europe or anywhere else, then it is not only based upon a misunderstanding of *The Philosophy of Right* but is a sketch for a collectivist theory of the *democratic state*—which conjunction should be an impossibility, or at least a source of tension regarding ultimate sovereignty.)

The old specter of materialism, suppressed or concealed by the artifice of power in the collectivist states of Eastern Europe and the Soviet Union—is that, similarly, consigned to the dustbin of history? It has had a long, and not entirely dishonorable, history spanning almost three centuries in one or other of its manifestations, and it has become distinct, except in the minds of theorists, from the Leninist state. With the unbidden and ridiculous support of Hegelians in the democracy founded in 1776, it is possible that materialism, the "onlie true begetter" of metaphysical speculation *applied* to political theory (since materialism conflates and confuses *matter* with *essence* so that metaphysicians are able to pronounce upon governments, nations, and political communities with impunity, knowing that *essential* human nature is not distinct from its social manifestation in the phenomenal world) may have a longer life than the systems that have attempted to express and impose *dialectical* materialism. It would seem that Locke's insistence upon the separate, equivalent significance of every individual human being is perhaps more in need (or at another point of its perennial crisis) than ever. A renewed concept of the *person* is, perhaps, required in the legislatures and executives of the democracies; but in those of the crumbling, ideologically based collectivities beyond the crumbling Wall it must be *announced* as a new philosophy (i.e., the notion of sovereignty as it resides in the *community of individuals* rather than in one of the abstractions that have been supplemented for such a community since 1789—the nation, the state, the revolution, the cause, et cetera. It is interesting to note that the Declaration of the Rights of Man and Citizen of the first years of the French Revolution declares that "the source of all sovereignty resides essentially in the nation." The materialism inherent in the use of *essentially* and the identification of the community to be offered liberty, equality, and brotherhood with the *nation,* with a collectivity that *personates* them, is, to say the least, interesting. The distinction of each individual is something that materialism in any form has never admitted, and thus something that the currently existant human individuals of eastern Europe (to use an ugly phrase) have no experience of regarding themselves as being. They are and have been coached in the supposition that they are a collectivity rather than an agglomeration. And in such instances, it is possible to apply further and different collectivisms upon a receptive audience without actually dismissing materialism in favor of a theory of individuality.

Further, the emergent nationalism both within and without the Soviet Union is the awakening of old meat, suitably decayed, from the freezer of Leninist communism and Marxist materialism. Or perhaps, more kindly, it is the supplementation of a form of *identity* which is still collectivist but not Leninist. That is the problem with nationalism—that it, like materialism, refutes any theory of the individual and can in extremis impose a new or different collectivism upon what may well be struggling to become a political society. (The consequences of reuniting what is essentially Prussia with western Germany may already be seen in embryo and suspected in history. Yet it seems another form of Hegelianism which the U.S. State Department desires. I, like many, am ambiguous regarding the unification of Germany but unambiguous as regards the nationalism-collectivism which inspires many of the demands for it.) We may yet be faced in Europe with the continuity of nation-states along nineteenth-century lines (and that century is responsible for the ethnic groups that are misplaced by the boundaries of nation-states), even as we attempt some kind of denationalized, indeed *privatized*, Europe (though the kind of sovereignty that unelected Brussels seems to envisage is an altogether suspicious matter).

The empire that has steadily collapsed before our eyes every evening on television was not merely an empire of trade (as the nineteenth-century nation-states understood the concept of empire), or even one of imposed law and civilization (of however doubtful a provenance), but an empire unique in the history of the world, one of ideology impressed upon a collection of nations, states, democracies, and feudalisms. Further, that empire was impressed upon these disparate groupings and often time-warped quasi-entities by a feudal neighbor which required virtual enslavement in order to produce for itself an imitation of an Industrial Revolution that its richer, more advanced rivals had undergone and deeply suffered a century earlier. The empire presided over by Stalin after World War II was an expansion of that leader's previous policy of contained imprisonment, "socialism in one country," and indeed offered a life-support system to an economic polity that would not admit the gross error of its ideology. Developing or emergent nation-states were imposed upon by this monolith which announced that history was complete, had fulfilled its pattern. With its collapse, the ideology that had arrested their development as nation-states is disappearing, exposing the former colonies to their own past rather than to the future, encouraging them to attempt the continuity of *national* history while confronted by—and having to coexist with—not-unfriendly nations,

states, and one or two political societies that have hopefully fulfilled that period of their history and have other priorities at the
end of the twentieth century. The past, for eastern Europe, has
been forbidden for fifty years or longer. Who could blame them
now for rediscovering and enacting it, even though it would be
at the cost of the reinventing of collectivism and even materialism
in another of its manifestations, and further postpone, as did the
Stalinist empire and the Leninist ideology, the emergence of any
theory of the individual or at least its recapture from the more
distant past and from other countries?

Marxism-Leninism arrested history, even appropriated it, put
an end to it (which is why one should never believe any Hegelian
as to the beneficence of the "end of history"), offering completion
where Marx himself would have suggested a *beginning*. While
western Europe attempts a federal imperium of trade, regulations,
and money, eastern Europe and European Asia are becoming
attracted to the nationalisms that derive from the fragmentation
of an empire. To recognize matters in these terms is a part of
understanding how we have all traveled from there to here.

History has not happened, and does not happen, to all societies
and civilizations at the same moment, and perhaps that is the only
lesson of history worth learning. We, perhaps, should understand
that *history* is just another ideology and should be dispensed with
along with the other ideological luggage that has to be abandoned
as the ships of certain states set sail. Europe should not adopt new
ideologies (or new sovereignties if they depart from the Lockian
principle of the sovereignty of the community attempting to
become a political society), but perhaps be rid of them all, now
that the ideology that has held half the continent in its grasp for
fifty years is shown to be a mirage and a source of misery for
countless numbers of individuals. Perhaps we might try just to be
our *selves*, for the first time, ignoring psychology, which is another, subtler form of determinism, at least in its classic theorizing, and which tells us we have no selves to be concerned with
but are mere bundles of responses, experiences, neuroses, and
inheritances. We are, fundamentally, simply individuals who have

to rub along in the harness (as light as possible) of a political society, avoiding if we can membership of states and nations (where that is how we are asked to identify ourselves) and especially avoiding any sense of a national or international destiny, avoiding any and all collective identities.

It is necessary to remark also that what occurred in eastern Europe in the aftermath of 1945, and in Russia after 1917, was the substitution of the nation-economy for the nation-state. An economic ideology (or economic control and function as the levers of the state) became paramount, and it is this which remains battered though intact in eastern Europe. Because the betterment of the economy, presumably in market or capitalist terms, seems requisite to the continuance of democratic experiment, whatever interference or assistance is provided from the rich, mature capitalist economies of western Europe will not necessarily change the fundamental structure—or absence of structure—in the economies of eastern Europe. For, since history did not happen everywhere at the same time and pace, the nation-states of eastern Europe were also the least industrialized and most 'feudal' when their history ceased for half a century. Now that they are discovering their past, their economic future—which is the key to their ideological, even democratic, future—is paramount. Will they have to endure laissez-faire capitalism—the chain shops and hovels of the Midlands and Manchester that Engels so abhorred and which set Marx upon his course of enraged materialism—*before* they can arrive at the position of western Europe, where the economy *can* be moderated by society, in the sense that the engine is in the hands of the legislative and the executive *only* as regards the social and individual justice that an economic system, per se, cannot provide, from the first Factory Acts to industrial tribunals, as it were? In mid-Victorian England, as Engels and Marx so correctly identified, the legislative was the province of the controller of the forces of production, the landed capitalist. But what is often identified as the development of the economic system itself was *the development of the legislative* to cope with the force for injustice that the economy could be or become. A recaptured, though compromised, liberalism prevailed against the economic polity. Suffrage and succor both ameliorated, in the medium and especially the long term, the viciousness of unbridled, or at least unregulated, capitalism.

Whereas England, Germany, and other western European countries had economics that they had to attempt to make ethical and even just by the exercise of the powers of political society, eastern Europe now discovers itself without an economy and with the task of having to create one at least moderately capitalistic, in the wake of creating a political society. They must rid themselves of a *statist* view of economics just when they are ridding themselves of one form of the state (and may be embracing another, nationalism), while having to use the state to create an economy that actually functions capitalistically. The only lesson for eastern Europe is nineteenth-century Germany, and from that place and time the message is confused and possibly dangerous. Nationalism *can* make a capitalist economy, but it also makes a state, and an aggressive one at that. English liberalism was indicted by Marx for trailing after excesses of the political economy, as indeed was the case. But the tortoise did finally, and with reasonable success, overhaul the hare. In eastern Europe, and the Soviet Union *if* its *perestroika* survives and even burgeons, the tortoise must encourage the hare to run as fast and as far as it can, without letting the swifter, more aggressive animal beyond calling distance. And the mechanism of this process must be some form of state, one is sorry to recognize, rather than a democratic political society. That *liberal* states, if not political societies, emerge must be the hope of all interested observers. To misemploy, hopefully for the better, certain Hegelian turns of phrase, what must happen in eastern Europe is that the economy has to be *taken into* the idea of politics and the idea of politics has to become *aware of itself* not simply as a political economy but as a political society; an economy must, at once rather than in the course of fifty or a hundred years, become controllable for the purposes of justice and equivalence.

But if a political society cannot, without becoming a centralized state with all its rigors, create an economy, only done in history with the full panoply of states, then Marxist-Leninist collectivism may not yet be quite the chimera it is supposed to be. Further, Hegel's "end of history" may also not have arrived (if it ever could, since Hegel himself warned against announcing any arrival at the terminus of history, the future being impossible to predict). Only a state, in the past, has been able to muster and sustain the illiberality required to create a political economy, especially of the capitalist variety. Leninist states have failed, manifestly, to create a centralized, socialist economy that actually functions, makes, produces, or benefits. Post-Leninist states have a Herculean task ahead—a post-Leninist *political society* may find the task impossible.

INDEX